Buddhist Monasticism in East Asia

The area of Buddhist monasticism has long attracted the interest of Buddhist Studies scholars and historians, but the interpretation of the nature and function of monasteries across diverse cultures and vast historical periods remains a focus for debate. This book provides a multifaceted discussion of religious, social, cultural, artistic, and political functions of Buddhist monasteries in medieval China and Japan.

With contributions from leading scholars in the field, this volume explores the multiplicity of the institutions that make up "the Buddhist monastery." Drawing on new research and on previous studies hitherto not widely available in English, the chapters cover key issues such as the relationship between monastics and lay society, the meaning of monastic vows, how specific institutions functioned, and the differences between urban and regional monasteries. Collectively, the book demonstrates that medieval monasteries in East Asia were much more than merely residences for monks who, cut off from the dust and din of society and all its entrapments, collectively pursued an ideal cenobitic lifestyle.

Buddhist Monasticism in East Asia is a timely contribution to the ongoing attempts to understand a central facet of Buddhist religious practice, and will be a significant work for academics and students in the fields of Buddhist Studies, Asian Studies, and East Asian Religions.

James A. Benn is Associate Professor of Buddhism and East Asian Religions at McMaster University. He works on Buddhism and Taoism in Medieval China and is the author of *Burning for the Buddha: Self-Immolation in Chinese Buddhism* (2007).

Lori Meeks is Assistant Professor of Religion and East Asian Languages and Cultures at the University of Southern California. She has published extensively on the roles of women as consumers and practitioners of Buddhism in Japan during the Heian and Kamakura periods.

James Robson is Associate Professor of Chinese Buddhism at Harvard University. He studies Buddhism and Taoism in medieval China and is the author of *Power of Place: The Religious Landscape of the Southern Sacred Peak [Nanyue] in Medieval China* (2009).

Routledge Critical Studies in Buddhism
Edited by Stephen C. Berkwitz, Missouri State University, USA
Founding Editors: Charles S. Prebish, Utah State University, USA and Damien Keown, Goldsmith's College, London University, UK

Routledge Critical Studies in Buddhism is a comprehensive study of the Buddhist tradition. The series explores this complex and extensive tradition from a variety of perspectives, using a range of different methodologies. The series is diverse in its focus, including historical, philological, cultural, and sociological investigations into the manifold features and expressions of Buddhism worldwide. It also presents works of constructive and reflective analysis, including the role of Buddhist thought and scholarship in a contemporary, critical context and in the light of current social issues. The series is expansive and imaginative in scope, spanning more than two and a half millennia of Buddhist history. It is receptive to all research works that are of significance and interest to the broader field of Buddhist Studies.

Editorial Advisory Board:
James A. Benn, McMaster University, Canada; Jinhua Chen, The University of British Columbia, Canada; Rupert Gethin, University of Bristol, UK; Peter Harvey, University of Sunderland, UK; Sallie King, James Madison University, USA; Anne Klein, Rice University, USA; Ulrich Pagel, School of Oriental and African Studies, UK; John Powers, Australian National University; Juliane Schober, Arizona State University, USA; Donald Swearer, Harvard University, USA; Vesna A. Wallace, University of California-Santa Barbara, USA; Paul Williams, University of Bristol, UK

A Survey of Vinaya Literature
Charles S. Prebish

The Reflexive Nature of Awareness
A Tibetan Madhyamaka defence
Paul Williams

Altruism and Reality
Studies in the philosophy of the Bodhicaryavatara
Paul Williams

Buddhism and Human Rights
Edited by Damien Keown, Charles Prebish, Wayne Husted

Women in the Footsteps of the Buddha
Struggle for liberation in the Therigatha
Kathryn R. Blackstone

The Resonance of Emptiness
A Buddhist inspiration for contemporary psychotherapy
Gay Watson

American Buddhism
Methods and findings in recent
scholarship
*Edited by Duncan Ryuken Williams
and Christopher Queen*

Imaging Wisdom
Seeing and knowing in the art of
Indian Buddhism
Jacob N. Kinnard

Pain and its Ending
The Four Noble Truths in the
Theravada Buddhist canon
Carol S. Anderson

Emptiness Appraised
A critical study of Nagarjuna's
philosophy
David F. Burton

The Sound of Liberating Truth
Buddhist–Christian dialogues in honor
of Frederick J. Streng
*Edited by Sallie B. King and Paul O.
Ingram*

Buddhist Theology
Critical reflections by contemporary
Buddhist scholars
*Edited by Roger R. Jackson and John
J. Makransky*

The Glorious Deeds of Purna
A translation and study of the
Purnavadana
Joel Tatelman

Early Buddhism – A New Approach
The I of the beholder
Sue Hamilton

Contemporary Buddhist Ethics
Edited by Damien Keown

Innovative Buddhist Women
Swimming against the stream
Edited by Karma Lekshe Tsomo

Teaching Buddhism in the West
From the wheel to the web
*Edited by V.S. Hori, R.P. Hayes and
J.M. Shields*

Empty Vision
Metaphor and visionary imagery in
Mahayana Buddhism
David L. McMahan

**Self, Reality and Reason in Tibetan
Philosophy**
Tsongkhapa's quest for the Middle
Way
Thupten Jinpa

In Defense of Dharma
Just-war ideology in Buddhist Sri
Lanka
Tessa J. Bartholomeusz

Buddhist Phenomenology
A philosophical investigation of
Yogacara Buddhism and the Ch'eng
Wei-shih Lun
Dan Lusthaus

**Religious Motivation and the
Origins of Buddhism**
A social-psychological exploration of
the origins of a world religion
Torkel Brekke

**Developments in Australian
Buddhism**
Facets of the diamond
Michelle Spuler

Zen War Stories
Brian Victoria

The Buddhist Unconscious
The Alaya-vijñana in the context of
Indian Buddhist thought
William S. Waldron

Indian Buddhist Theories of Persons
Vasubandhu's refutation of the theory
of a self
James Duerlinger

Action Dharma
New studies in engaged Buddhism
*Edited by Christopher Queen,
Charles Prebish and Damien Keown*

**Tibetan and Zen Buddhism in
Britain**
Transplantation, development and
adaptation
David N. Kay

The Concept of the Buddha
Its evolution from early Buddhism to
the Trikaya theory
Guang Xing

**The Philosophy of Desire in the
Buddhist Pali Canon**
David Webster

**The Notion of *Ditthi* in Theravada
Buddhism**
The point of view
Paul Fuller

**The Buddhist Theory of Self-
Cognition**
Zhihua Yao

**Buddhist Studies from India to
America**
Essays in honor of Charles S. Prebish
Edited by Damien Keown

**Moral Theory in Santideva's
Siksasamuccaya**
Cultivating the fruits of virtue
Barbra R. Clayton

**Buddhist Thought and Applied
Psychological Research**
Transcending the boundaries
*Edited by D.K. Nauriyal, Michael S.
Drummond and Y.B. Lal*

**Buddhism, Conflict and Violence in
Modern Sri Lanka**
Edited by Mahinda Deegalle

Buddhism in Canada
Edited by Bruce Matthews

**Discourse and Ideology in Medieval
Japanese Buddhism**
*Edited by Richard K. Payne and Taigen
Dan Leighton*

**Theravāda Buddhism and the
British Encounter**
Religious, missionary and colonial
experience in nineteenth-century
Sri Lanka
Elizabeth Harris

Beyond Enlightenment
Buddhism, religion, modernity
Richard Cohen

Buddhism in the Public Sphere
Reorienting global interdependence
Peter D. Hershock

British Buddhism
Teachings, practice and development
Robert Bluck

**Buddhist Nuns in Taiwan and
Sri Lanka**
A critique of the feminist perspective
Wei-Yi Cheng

**New Buddhist Movements in
Thailand**
Towards an understanding of Wat Phra
Dhammakaya and Santi Asoke
Rory Mackenzie

Buddhism, Power and Political Order
Edited by Ian Harris

**Buddhist Rituals of Death and
Rebirth**
Contemporary Sri Lankan practice and
its origins
Rita Langer

Environmental Ethics in Buddhism
A virtues approach
Pragati Sahni

The Cultural Practices of Modern Chinese Buddhism
Attuning the Dharma
Francesca Tarocco

Mindfulness in Early Buddhism
New approaches through psychology and textual analysis of Pali, Chinese and Sanskrit sources
Tse-fu Kuan

Religion, Medicine and the Human Embryo in Tibet
Frances Garrett

Power, Wealth and Women in Mahāyāna Buddhism
The Gaṇḍavyūha-sūtra
Douglas Osto

Buddhist Manuscript Cultures
Knowledge, ritual and art
Edited by Stephen C. Berkwitz, Juliane Schober and Claudia Brown

Buddhist Monasticism in East Asia
Places of practice
Edited by James A. Benn, Lori Meeks and James Robson

The following titles are published in association with the *Oxford Centre for Buddhist Studies*

Oxford Centre for Buddhist Studies
a project of The Society for the Wider Understanding of the Buddhist Tradition

The *Oxford Centre for Buddhist Studies* conducts and promotes rigorous teaching and research into all forms of the Buddhist tradition.

Early Buddhist Metaphysics
The making of a philosophical tradition
Noa Ronkin

Mipham's Dialectics and the Debates on Emptiness
To be, not to be or neither
Karma Phuntsho

How Buddhism Began
The conditioned genesis of the early teachings
Richard F. Gombrich

Buddhist Meditation
An anthology of texts from the Pāli canon
Sarah Shaw

Remaking Buddhism for Medieval Nepal
The fifteenth-century reformation of Newar Buddhism
Will Tuladhar-Douglas

Metaphor and Literalism in Buddhism
The doctrinal history of nirvana
Soonil Hwang

The Biographies of Rechungpa
The evolution of a Tibetan hagiography
Peter Alan Roberts

The Origin of Buddhist Meditation
Alexander Wynne

Buddhist Monasticism in East Asia

Places of practice

**Edited by James A. Benn,
Lori Meeks, and James Robson**

LONDON AND NEW YORK

First published 2010 by Routledge
2 Park Square, Milton Park, Abingdon, Oxon OX14 4RN

Simultaneously published in the USA and Canada
by Routledge
270 Madison Ave, New York, NY 10016

Routledge is an imprint of the Taylor & Francis Group, an Informa business

This book has been published with the help of a grant from the Tzu Chi
Foundation, Canada

Typeset in Times New Roman by Swales & Willis Ltd, Exeter, Devon
Printed and bound in Great Britain by MPG Books Group

British Library Cataloguing in Publication Data
A catalogue record for this book is available from the British Library

Library of Congress Cataloging-in-Publication Data
Buddhist monasticism in East Asia: places of practice / edited by
James A. Benn, Lori Meeks, and James Robson.
p. cm.—(Routledge critical studies in Buddhism; 53)
Includes bibliographical references and index.
ISBN 978–0–415–48977–5 (hardback: alk. paper)
— ISBN 978–0–203–87571–1 (ebook) 1. Monasticism and
religious orders, Buddhist—China—History. 2. Monasticism and
religious orders, Buddhist—Japan—History. I. Benn, James A., 1964–
II. Meeks, Lori Rachelle, 1976– III. Robson, James, 1965 Dec. 1–
BQ6240.C6B83 2009
294.3'658095—dc22
2008055153

ISBN10: 0–415–48977–6 (hbk)
ISBN10: 0–203–87571–3 (ebk)

ISBN13: 978–0–415–48977–5 (hbk)
ISBN13: 978–0–203–87571–1 (ebk)

Contents

Illustrations		xi
Notes on contributors		xii
Acknowledgements		xiii

Introduction: "Neither too far, nor too near": The historical and
cultural contexts of Buddhist monasteries in medieval
China and Japan   1
JAMES ROBSON

1   Taking a meal at a lay supporter's residence: The evolution
of the practice in Chinese *Vinaya* commentaries   18
KOICHI SHINOHARA

2   Monastic spaces and sacred traces: Facets of Chinese
Buddhist monastic records   43
JAMES ROBSON

3   Pictorial program in the making of monastic space: From
Jing'aisi of Luoyang to Cave 217 at Dunhuang   65
EUGENE WANG

4   The monastery cat in cross-cultural perspective: Cat poems
of the Zen masters   107
T.H. BARRETT

5   The monastic institution in medieval Japan: The insider's view   125
WILLIAM BODIFORD

6   Vows for the masses: Eison and the popular expansion of
precept-conferral ceremonies in premodern Japan   148
LORI MEEKS

7   **Kōen and the "consecrated ordination" within Japanese
    Tendai**   178
    PAUL GRONER

    Bibliography   208
    Index   227

Illustrations

3.1 Transformation tableau based on the Lotus Sūtra. South wall, Mogao Cave 217. Early eighth century 98

3.2 Bottom section of the Lotus Sūtra tableau, Mogao Cave 217. South wall, Mogao Cave 217. Early eighth century 98

3.3 Left side of the Lotus Sūtra tableau, Mogao Cave 217. South wall, Mogao Cave 217. Early eighth century 99

3.4 Top section of the Lotus Sūtra tableau, Mogao Cave 217. South wall, Mogao Cave 217. Early eighth century 100

3.5 Right side of the Lotus Sūtra tableau, Mogao Cave 217. South wall, Mogao Cave 217. Early eighth century 101

3.6 Mt. Sumeru-centered cosmos moved by Vimalakīrti. Detail of transformation tableau based on the Vimalakīrti-nirdeśa-sūtra. North wall of Mogao Cave 335. End of seventh century 101

3.7 Mt. Sumeru on the robe of the Vairocana image. Detail of transformation tableau based on the Recompense Sūtra. Eighth century. British Museum. 102

3.8 View of the west-wall niche to the left; and north wall to the right showing the Transformation tableau based on the Visualization Sūtra. North wall. Mogao Cave 217. Early eighth century 103

3.9 Left side of the transformation tableau based on the Visualization Sūtra. North wall, Mogao Cave 217. Early eighth century 104

3.10 Tableau based on the Guanyin chapter of the Lotus Sūtra. East wall, Mogao Cave 217. Early eighth century 105

3.11 Śākyamuni ascends to Heaven of the Thirty-Three Celestials (Trāyastriṃśa) to preach for his mother Māyā. Painting on the ceiling of the west wall niche, Mogao Cave 217. Early eighth century 106

7.1 Kaikanjō gasshō 199

Contributors

T.H. Barrett, Professor of East Asian History, Study of Religions, School of Oriental and African Studies, University of London.

James A. Benn, Associate Professor, Religious Studies, McMaster University.

William Bodiford, Professor, Asian Languages and Cultures, University of California, Los Angeles.

Paul Groner, Professor, Religious Studies, University of Virginia.

Lori Meeks, Assistant Professor, Religious Studies, University of Southern California.

James Robson, Associate Professor, East Asian Languages and Civilisations, Harvard University.

Koichi Shinohara, Senior Lecturer, Religious Studies, Yale University.

Eugene Wang, Abby Aldrich Rockefeller Professor of Asian Art, History of Art and Architecture, Harvard University.

Acknowledgements

The origins of this collection of essays lie in a conference held at the University of British Columbia in 2003. The conference was organized by Professor Chen Jinhua, to whom we express our gratitude. The editors wish to acknowledge the kind assistance of the Tzu Chi Foundation Canada and its director Mr. Gary Ho. The Foundation generously funded the conference, and provided additional support towards the publication of this volume.

The editors would like to thank Steve Berkwitz, editor of the Critical Studies in Buddhism Series, as well as Dorothea Schaefter and Suzanne Richardson at Routledge.

The chapter by Lori Meeks first appeared in *Numen* 56.1 (2009) and appears here by kind permission of that journal and its publisher E.J. Brill.

Introduction

"Neither too far, nor too near": The historical and cultural contexts of Buddhist monasteries in medieval China and Japan

James Robson

Buddhist monasteries, with their sumptuous architecture, ornate furnishings, and striking natural settings, have always stuck out dramatically on the religious landscapes of Asia. Buddhist monasteries have constituted one of the most visible aspects of the Buddhist tradition, but until recently it has been rather rare to find explicit reflection on those fundamental elements of Buddhist practice.[1] While the term monastery appears on first glance to refer unproblematically to religious institutions that we all seem to have a general understanding of, it is worth noting how the topic of monasticism rarely enters into the discourse on religion in a neutral way, as the writings of Edward Gibbon and Max Weber attest.[2] Monasteries, as we shall see, have also been contested grounds within Buddhist studies, with much of that contestation centering on their nature and function across diverse cultures and vast historical periods. Therefore, any answer to the most basic question: "What is a Buddhist monastery?" will necessarily be as complex and multifarious as the diverse religious, historical and cultural contexts within which they have existed. Although the topic of Buddhist monasticism has long attracted the interests of Buddhist studies scholars and historians of religion, most representations of those entities have tended to be far more unified than their historical realities would suggest. The goal of this Introduction—and the collection of papers presented here—is not, therefore, to present a normative description of a singular entity called "the Buddhist monastery," and in the process try to house a variety of different institutional entities under a single roof. Rather, this volume aims to capture some sense of the multiplicity—both within and across traditions—of those institutions. The essays gathered here focus on facets of the religious, social, cultural, artistic and political functions of Buddhist monasteries in medieval China and Japan. It should therefore be stated clearly at the outset that this volume does not aim to constitute a comprehensive history of monasticism in Asia. There are no chapters on other forms of monasticism, such as Daoist monasticism, the role of nuns and nunneries is touched on only in passing here, and there is no treatment of Korean monasticism, Tibetan monasticism, or more contemporary forms of monasticism in East Asia.[3] Rather, what are presented here are selected topics of East Asian Buddhist monasticism. In this Introduction I do not intend to review all the recent, and not so recent, literature on Buddhist monasteries or to explore the full range of issues addressed by that literature here, since that project would require a separate monograph. Instead, I shall limit myself to a discussion of some key issues that lie in the background of—or provide some context to—the topics explored by the individual authors. If there is one thing that we can say for certain about Buddhist monasteries and monasticism it is that they warrant the sustained attention of scholars of Buddhist studies, since what goes on inside and outside of their imposing gates is of central concern to our understanding of Buddhism as it functioned as a living religious tradition.

It would be difficult to overstate the significance of monasticism within Buddhism, where entrance into the monastery was one of the defining character- istics of being a Buddhist practitioner. Indeed, it is a topic that some might argue has been distinctly understated given the central role that it has played throughout the historical development, and geographical spread, of the tradition. Studies of Christian monasticism have far out-paced studies of Buddhist monasticism, despite the claim that Buddhist monasticism is perhaps the oldest form of monasticism in the world.[4] It has also been argued that as a religious style monasticism is more cen- tral to the Buddhist tradition than it is generally understood to be for Christianity.[5] Indeed, monasticism is perceived to be such a central part of Buddhist self- definition that one of the final signs of the disappearance of the dharma is when monastic robes turn white—the color of lay robes. Some Buddhists have, how- ever, radically challenged the position of monasteries within the Buddhist tradition, serving as the exceptions that prove the rule. A Chan/Zen practitioner might, for example, ask: If a person already possesses inherent Buddha nature, what need is there to become a monk and pursue a path of spiritual cultivation within a monas- tery? Based on that perspective, the monastery is seen as merely a vestige of a dark view that required the individual to embark on a long path of self-cultivation, rather than just adopt a radically different self-perception. After the Tang Chan master Shitou Xiqian gave his assent to a verse by Layman Pang, for example, he followed with a question: "Will you put on black robes or will you continue wearing white?" Layman Pang responded by saying that "I want to do what I like" and so he did not shave his head, dye his clothing, or enter a monastery.[6] This account, which might be taken as evidence of the decline of the dharma, illustrates well the range of opinions within Buddhism about the necessity of putting on the robes of a monk and entering into a monastery.

The institutions that are commonly referred to under the general term "monastery" have been a fundamental component of many of the world's major religious traditions, including Buddhism, Christianity, Judaism, Islam, Hinduism, Daoism, and Jainism.[7] Some consideration of the general study of monasteries is therefore essential due to the ways perceptions of monasteries in other religious traditions have conditioned the ways that Buddhist monasteries have been conceptualized and imagined. Let us begin by considering the word "monastery" itself, since a host of intractable interpretive problems arise with that term. Etymologically, the word "monastery"—and all its cognates—derives from the Greek root *monos* meaning one or alone. It has become commonplace, therefore, to trace the origins of Christian monasticism to early cenobitic communities established in the Egyptian desert, where ascetic anchorites lived in cells, only coming together at prayer times. It is only much later, we are told, that those isolated entities developed into the more familiar monastic styles of the Benedictines, Carthusians, Franciscans, and Cistercians. One of the perduring characteristics found in descriptions of monasteries is the emphasis on their isolation from the daily workings of society. In addition to being marked by its position outside of society (or at least on its margins), monastic communities are also described as being marked off from society by other forms of distinction involving initiation rites, a specific program for living a disciplined life, distinctive clothing, bodily modifications (tonsure), symbolic articles, change of diet, and a special organization of time.

Yet, the word "monastery" is, even in its original Christian usage, imprecise and is a term that is rooted in ambiguity. In contrast to its etymological roots, monasteries essentially developed as places where religious "communities" gathered *together*. Scholars of medieval European monasticism have acknowledged this problem and noted that within studies on Christianity the term monasticism in its general usage "refers—somewhat paradoxically—to religious life within communities."[8] Others have argued that the aloneness of monasticism does not refer to a lack of a communal element, but rather that monks were single, in the sense of being unmarried and celibate, with a single-minded devotion to God.

Although the precise historical details remain unclear, the story that is often told about the origin of Buddhist monasticism is that a cenobitic Buddhist monastic community evolved out of a collection of wanderers (*parivrājaka*) who had set forth from the household (*pravrajyā*) and traveled without a fixed abode, except during the rainy season when they would take up temporary lodgings. Eventually, the temporary rainy season retreat began to extend into the dry season and the temporary retreat huts came to be replaced by elaborate shelters that were provided by wealthy patrons. Buddhism is thus marked by the way its postulants are said to "leave home," renounce "the world," join the family of the Buddha (*saṃgha*), and take up residence in a monastery, where the communal lives of the monks and nuns was governed by a set of detailed rules (*vinaya*) that pertained to issues of individual behavior, communal living, and liturgy. Monasteries were, according to this telling, the primary abodes for monks, the locus of their activities, and central to the functioning of Buddhism as an institution.

While the image of separation from society is played up in many descriptions of Buddhist monasteries, it is clear from other sources that early Buddhist monasteries were to be located "neither too far, nor too near" to urban settlements— neither entirely separated off from the world, nor entirely within the world. The *Cullavagga*, for example includes the story of the householder Anāthapindika who wanted to make an offering of a monastery to the Buddha, but according to the Buddha's wishes it had to meet certain specifications. When Anāthapindika went to Sāvatthī in search of a site he asked himself,

> Now where could the Lord stay that would be *neither too far from a village, nor too near*, suitable for coming and going, accessible to people whenever they want, not crowded by day, having little noise at night, little sound, without folks' breath, secluded from people, fitting for meditation?[9]

As is well known, it was Prince Jeta's grove that ultimately satisfied the Buddha's dual requirement of being neither too close nor too remote from society, and thus the formidable Jetavana vihāra was founded. In the *Visuddhimagga*, the fifth-century Sri Lankan monk Buddhaghosa also stipulates the importance of a place that satisfies five factors, of which I will only mention the first. "For this is said by the Blessed One 'And how has a lodging five factors, bhikkhus? Here bhikkhus, a lodging *is not too far, not too near*, and has a path for going and coming."[10] We will return to the important topic of proximity to and distance from society shortly, but suffice it to say here that although scholars of Buddhism have, like their counterparts in medieval Christian studies, generally found it unproblematic to employ the word monastery as a term of convenience for institutions that were communal in nature and clearly not rooted in aloneness, it has been rare for scholars to reflect on the adequacy of the term monastery—whose precise referent often remains unclear.

When Buddhist monasticism is discussed in general terms, it is often situated within a comparative context alongside Christian and Hindu forms of monasticism. A recent two-volume reference work on monasticism has, for example, an image of a Buddhist deity on the cover of one volume and an image of St. Bernard, Abbot of Clairvaux, on the cover of the other, while the cover of a book on the comparative study of Buddhist and Christian monasticism includes images of a medal-cross of St. Benedict and the Buddhist Wheel of Becoming.[11] While the ecumenical gesture implied by the inclusion of those images side by side, and the editor's acknowledgment of the importance of Buddhism to the general history of monasticism, is to be commended, certain questions naturally arise in regard to this alleged proximity. First, is the term monasticism a useful term outside of the Christian tradition that gave rise to its use? Does it make sense to unify the diverse range of Buddhist institutions that we find across different cultures and times under the single label of "monasticism"? If that question is answered in the affirmative, then other questions arise: Is there the danger that all specific uses of the term monasticism will necessarily be marked by such a range of equivocal meanings that it threatens the integrity of the term? Have depictions of Buddhist institutions suffered through the extension of this Christian term to a different religious milieu and overly colored those objects with the hue of the Christian lenses through which they have been viewed?[12] The interpretive problems raised by these questions are no doubt familiar to historians of religion, who have long brooded over the vexing issue of comparison. Despite much reflection on the enterprise of comparison, we are still haunted, as J.Z. Smith has suggested, by the problems opened up by Wittgenstein's pointed question: "How am I to apply what the one thing shows me to the case of two things?"[13] In order to adequately reflect on these issues, therefore, we must first understand how the term monasticism has evolved and what types of meanings have accrued to it in both the Christian and Buddhist contexts. Only then can we interrogate the ways that the one term—monasticism—has been applied to the two, and perhaps realize that our understanding of Buddhist monasteries is, like their ideal location, neither too close nor too far from the character of monasteries in other religious traditions.

That is to say, rather than merely revel in the comfort of resemblances, we also need to defamiliarize ourselves with the topic and take difference seriously.

Buddhist and Christian forms of monasticism have not always shared the comfortable proximity that they now enjoy on the covers of recent books. Following a brief flirtation with Buddhist monasticism by the Jesuits in China, Western images of Buddhist monasticism quickly became both distorted and disparaging. It is striking to note how in their initial interactions with the Chinese in the sixteenth century, Jesuit missionaries felt that the best way to represent themselves to the Chinese was as Buddhist monks, perhaps due to the formal resemblances between Jesuit religious institutions and practices and Chinese Buddhist institutions and practices.[14] Therefore, when the Jesuits chose "monastic Buddhism as the initial mode of enculturation" this appeared to be unproblematic for both parties. The Jesuits at first "imagined Buddhist monasticism to be a vehicle for becoming Chinese," since that guise was sure to not attract much attention or raise the suspicions of the Chinese. This experiment did not last long, however, and while Buddhist monasticism initially served a limited function, it was quickly renounced and ultimately denounced. In his discussion of the initial Western contacts with Tibet, Donald Lopez described well the ways that those expressions of Tibetan religion that appeared too similar to those found in Christianity were decried by missionaries as the product of "demonic plagiarism." The missionaries' task, Lopez explained, was to "transmit the word of that [Christian] particularity to those realms where it has not yet spread, to diffuse it from its unique point of origin . . . and to find them already there, suggests the workings of a power beyond history, which could only be seen as demonic."[15] The Jesuits in China may not have blamed their mistaken earlier impressions of Buddhist monasteries on the work of demons, but they did quickly demonize those religious institutions that they initially thought they knew better.

As the Jesuits came to their senses and abandoned the "indigent trappings of the Buddhist cloister" and eventually threw off their Buddhist monastic robes in favor of the "resplendent robes and headdress of the 'literati,'" so too did representations of Buddhist monasticism suffer a decline in the eyes of later European interpreters. The Jesuit Louis le Compte's skewed images of Chinese Buddhist monasteries, for example, were ultimately incorporated into a number of late seventeenth and early eighteenth century encyclopedias, such as *The Encyclopedia Britannica*.[16] The image that is presented in those reference works is typical of Victorian-era images of Buddhist monasticism as both morally suspect and home to a group of selfish, nonproductive, and often ignorant, idlers. According to some nineteenth-century scholars of Buddhism the problem stemmed from the nature of Buddhist monasticism itself, which, we are told, "was productive of evil tendencies and a selfish seclusion."[17] From the outset the Buddhist monastic ideal was taken to be a problem, and it was not looked upon kindly through the anti-Catholic lens of contemporary Victorian intellectuals. The pejorative representation of Buddhist monasticism by Western observers was, of course, nothing new, but was a distant echo of the types of critiques that Buddhist monasticism encountered early on in China, where Buddhist monks were belittled as being nothing more than mere parasites on society.

Significant new reflections on—and reinterpretations of—monasticism have steadily proliferated in recent years, but it has taken a generation of scholars to overcome the foundational early images that were painted of Buddhist monasticism. While Buddhist monasticism has fared somewhat better under the gaze of recent Western commentators, the newer—perhaps more benign—descriptions of those institutions may be as concealing as they are revealing. Under the increasing weight of contemporary scholarship there is less of an imperative to repeatedly decry the problematic impressions of Buddhist monasticism, but there is still unfinished work in detailing how perceptions of Buddhist monasticism in general have been conditioned by (mistaken) impressions about the evolution of Western monastic orders, and how interpretations of East Asian monasticism in particular have been conditioned by (again mistaken) interpretations of Indian monasticism, where canonical materials that present normative ideals are presented as reflections of historical realities.

Descriptions of monasteries as "worlds apart" that are inhabited solely by religious virtuosi, for example, have become increasingly suspect as adequate reflections of the socio-historical realities of monasteries throughout Buddhist history and across different cultures. Gregory Schopen has put a fine point on the issue:

> It is probably fair to say that, because of the way they have been studied, neither Indian Buddhist monasticism nor the Buddhist monastery in India has been allowed to have anything like a real history . . . Once it is allowed that, yes, both Buddhist monasticism and Buddhist monasteries had histories, that both developed and changed over time, then "early" Buddhist monasticisms—and we should probably begin to use the plural seriously here—and the "early" Buddhist monastery, become only one, and certainly not the only important object of investigation. We need no longer be implicitly or explicitly concerned primarily with the question of what Buddhist monasticisms originally were. We might be equally—and probably more fruitfully—concerned with what at given places and given points in time they had become. We might begin to meaningfully talk about "early" and "early medieval" and "medieval" and "late" Buddhist monasticisms and to study each of these in their own right and not, for example, as mere exemplifications of the decline and degeneration of some "early" and largely assumed single "ideal."[18]

These comments, directed at scholars of Indian Buddhist monasticism, are equally applicable to the history of the study of Buddhist monasticism in East Asia. Schopen's remarks highlight how considerations of monasticism have thus far been driven by what might be understood in terms of Gadamer's notion of "effective history." In trying to understand any historical phenomena we are necessarily influenced by the accrued history of the approach to those phenomena. That history, Gadamer argues, "determines in advance both what seems to us worth inquiring about and what will appear as an object of investigation, and we more or less forget half of what is really there—in fact—we miss the whole truth of the phenomena—when we take its immediate appearance as the whole truth."[19] The effective history of the study of monasticism that has provided the conditions for the present state of the field can be tracked along two lines: the tendency to hypostasize later images of Buddhist monasticism as reflective of an early pure state of Buddhist monasticism and the lingering effect of the Christian sense of monasticism that posits a clear separation between worldly society and the religious pursuits of monastics.

The negative images of Buddhist monasteries propagated up through the nineteenth century persisted into the modern period and are found expressed in the influential writings of Max Weber. Monasticism, including Buddhist monasticism, appears only episodically in Weber's writings, though it is clear that for him monasticism presented both challenges and opportunities.[20] Weber never fully or clearly conceptualized monasticism, as he did other religious institutions, and his image of the world-transcendent status of monasteries—where religious virtuosi push themselves into the rarified heights of religious self-perfection—was in noticeable tension with his imperative to note the ways in which monasteries functioned as rationalizing institutions. Salvation for the Buddhist practitioner, in Weber's reckoning, was

> an absolutely personal performance of the self-reliant individual. No one, and particularly no social community can help him. The specific asocial character of all genuine mysticism is here carried to its maximum. Actually, it appears even as a contradiction that the Buddha, who was quite aloof from forming a "church" or even a "parish" and who expressly rejected the possibility and pretension of being able to "lead" an order, has founded an order after all.[21]

Weber seems to have resolved this tension by portraying monasticism itself as a purely otherworldly entity in its earliest stages that only later devolved into landlordism, pandering to the laity, and participation in commercial functions. He summed up this viewpoint by saying that "the whole history of monasticism is in a certain sense the history of a continual struggle with the problem of the secularizing influence of wealth."[22] A similarly negative view of monasteries is found in Western scholarship on European monasticism, such as in the earlier work of Edward Gibbon, and those general views have infected portrayals of Buddhist monasticism. Indeed, one of the major thrusts of Gregory Schopen's recent work on Buddhist monasticism has been to show how Buddhist monks and monasteries have always been intertwined with economic concerns and it is, therefore, problematic to characterize an interest in money as a later sign of degeneration. Steven Kemper has also shown how in the Sinhalese Buddhist context wealth was not a problem, and in fact the truly detached homeless monk is the one treated with suspicion. Wealthy monks and monasteries are accorded social approval since wealth was deemed a visible sign of accumulated merit.[23] One of the problems with the devolutionary model of Buddhist monasteries is that they presuppose the identification of an ideal that has been deviated from. But, where does the interpreter stop in that return to an ever-retreating ideal point of origin? From one perspective, for example, Buddhist monasticism itself could be seen as a devolution from the earlier ideal to, as the *Khadgavisana-gatha* [Rhinoceros Horn Sūtra] says, "wander alone like the rhinoceros horn."[24] While it might be easy to dismiss Weber's views of Buddhist monasteries as merely based on early idealized images of Buddhist monasticism, one of the main questions that remains is how we are to analyze and portray both the "ideal" and the "real" aspects of monasteries.

The "ideal" image of early Buddhism that was deployed by Max Weber, Louis Dumont, and other early interpreters of Buddhism, as a gauge with which to measure all subsequent Buddhist developments is no longer tenable. Buddhist monasteries and monastics had at least two faces and neither one was entirely as detached from society as Louis Dumont's representation, which conflated Buddhist monks with other Indian renunciates, might have implied.[25] As Sukumar Dutt long ago noted, "monk-and-layman intercourse was a feature of Buddhist monastic life from the start."[26] Steven Collins has also underscored the point that a clear and distinct separation between the lay community and monastics would not only have been practically impossible, but would also have entailed a violation of vinaya proscriptions that say that the monk is forbidden to collect and cook his own food.[27] Thus, from the outset monasteries were structurally dependent on a relationship with the lay community, and the material support they received entailed obligations for them to come into contact with the laity to provide religious services to fulfill their side of the merit exchange relationship. Koichi Shinohara's chapter in this volume discusses these lay–monastic relationships through a careful study of the responsibility of monks to go out from the monastery and accept meals offered by the laity. Early Chinese Buddhist tales depict a world where lay supporters competed to place themselves in the rarified presence of the Buddha by offering a meal to him in order to aquire merit through the reception of a blessing. It was on these occasions that the lay world came into contact with the monastic world, where monks were obliged to partake of the meal, recite sūtras, and confer blessings. It was precisely due to the necessity of fostering monastic interaction with the laity that in the story related above the Buddha made sure that Anāthapindika did not establish the monastery too far from an urban area, but at a site accessible to them.

As contemporary scholarship on Buddhist monasticism has become increasingly colored by the theoretical and methodological concerns within Buddhist studies aimed at studying lived realities in "practice," a tension has emerged between a focus on the "ordinary" as opposed to the "extraordinary" aspects of Buddhism. The recent attention paid to monastic practices has resulted in evaluations of the day-to-day functioning of monasteries (cooking, cleaning, and management), the ritual and cultic practices of monastics (recitation of texts and propitiation of deities), as well as explications of monastic economies, land-holdings, and money-making business ventures.[28] While studies of both the mundane and supramandane aspects of monastic life have been well accepted by scholars of medieval European monasticism it has taken longer for those perspectives to take root among scholars of Asian monasticism. This may, in part, be due to a lingering preoccupation with romantic notions of "Eastern religious experience" that is allegedly fostered in the monastic environment.[29]

New methodological approaches aimed at understanding the full complexity of monastic institutions has been greeted with excitement by some, but deplored by others as being either of marginal concern or a minor element that merely reflects the devolution of monasteries away from some allegedly pure state—when those institutions were not yet polluted by economic activities. Those who pursue these new lines of inquiry are sometimes criticized for lowering their gaze too far, to the point of merely focusing on what has been called the "external trappings" of monasticism, rather than its true elevated purpose: the pursuit of enlightenment.[30] Those interested in the more rarified concerns of religious experience might acknowledge the social, economic, political, and sometimes magical dimensions of monasteries and monasticism, but they insist that sustained attention needs to remain focused on their soteriological function and the religious virtuosi that strive for the highest spiritual ideal through dedication to a cenobitic lifestyle.[31] That is to say, there is a general tendency to divide the study of monasticism into two rather different lines of inquiry. The first focuses on the religious practices of elite monastics. The second turns away from doctrine and the pursuits of the "spiritual aristocracy" and turns toward an acknowledgment of the complex motivations driving monks and nuns into monasteries, in addition to a detailed scrutiny of the intricate workings of monastic institutions that are seen to be deeply embedded in the worldly activities of society, sorcery, politics, and commerce.

In one recent articulation of this divide, Victor Sōgen Hori has written:

> Many—perhaps most—who wear the monk's robes do not seek enlightenment. But some few do. If you are a scholar, then the many monks who do not seek enlightenment are statistically representative of the monastery. If you are a practitioner, then the few monks who do seek enlightenment are representative of the true purpose of the monastery.[32]

This statement reflects generally held, but not often explicitly stated, sentiments about the fault line that runs between different interpretations of monastic practice. This fault line is not, of course, limited to East Asian Buddhism, but runs through interpretations of South and Southeast Asian Buddhism, as the writings of Melford Spiro attest. One of the main interpretive problems that scholars of Buddhism now face is the following: How we are to account for the real functioning of those institutions and at the same time capture perceptions of those sites as ideal settings that are somehow supposed to transcend the quotidian world that surrounds them? This tension has been articulated well by Stanley Tambiah:

> "The self-denials of the extreme ascetic may serve as models for the good life of the ordinary man," not so much models to be imitated, for lay life makes that impossible, but because as Durkheim perceived, "It is necessary that an elite put the end too high, if the crowd is not to put it too low."[33]

Tensions between a focus on the social, political, cultural, and economic realities of monasteries and a focus on the soteriological function of monasteries seem to come to the fore when modern scholars claim to be representative of the "true purpose" of a singular entity— "the Buddhist monastery." In the past, these approaches have been seen as inimical, but it is fair to say that there is a growing recognition that in order to account for the full diversity of monks and the monasteries that they inhabit, both the ordinary and the extraordinary need to be attended to. Robert Buswell has, for example, claimed that scholars need to do justice to the complex ways that Buddhist monasticism "weaves doctrine, praxis, and lifeway together into an intricate tapestry" and the ways that the "regimens of monastic life—indeed, the entire cultural context of Buddhist training—therefore interface directly doctrine and practice."[34] This is a worthwhile goal to strive for, but I suspect that not all aspects of practice and doctrine can ultimately be seen to be working in concert. Some aspects of monasticism will always remain outside the tapestry and irreducible to a doctrinal function. Nonetheless, those non-doctrinally oriented actions and tasks should not be set aside as ancillary concerns, but included within our inquiries as a part of a larger picture.[35] While these may seem like our modern problems and preoccupations, they do have some resonance with earlier representations of Buddhist monasteries.

If the pursuit of enlightenment is the primary goal of monasticism, then all other aspects of monasticism tend to be treated as impediments to practice. In the *Visuddhimagga*, for example, Buddhaghosa noted eighteen ways a monastery can be unfavorable to meditative practice. Those features include,

> largeness, newness, dilapidatedness, a nearby road, a pond, [edible] leaves, flowers, fruits, famousness, a nearby city, nearby timber trees, nearby arable fields, presence of incompatible persons, a nearby port of entry, nearness to the border countries, nearness to the frontier of a kingdom, unsuitability, lack of good friends.[36]

Or, to restate them in Paul Harrison's modern paraphrasing,

> too many administrative tasks, frequent distractions from students, constant official meetings, too much construction activity, too many people coming and going for their own purposes or wanting things from you (worse, he says, when the place is famous), and the need to deal with fractious or incompatible colleagues.[37]

It is precisely the topics and practices maligned by Buddhaghosa as detracting from meditation that some modern scholars yearn to account for in putting a human face back on Buddhist monks as inhabitants of complicated social environments and to fill out our picture of the practical functioning of the Buddhist monastery. Buddhaghosa's rich description of the potentially distracting features found in Buddhist monasteries reveals a very real concern for how some monastic institutions were in danger of becoming too deeply enmeshed in the complicated social worlds that they were situated within.

In order to gain a new vantage point into Japanese monasteries, William Bodiford urges scholars of Japanese Buddhism to turn their attention back to a number of medieval sources that include first-person accounts of institutional Buddhism. Those sources have largely been dismissed, or under-utilized, by modern scholars, but they provide an alternative view of medieval Japanese monasticism that helps illuminate important, yet largely occluded, aspects of monastic life. Those texts contain precious little about doctrinal developments, but they do describe a monastic world concerned with regular annual ceremonies, monasteries filled with miraculous icons, and a variety of people that do not all fit neatly into our traditional categories of "monks and nuns" or laity. The religious landscape of medieval Japanese monasteries that comes into view includes

> academic learning, rituals of ordination, initiation into doctrinal lineages, worship of gods and buddhas, participation in state sponsored ceremonies, advancement to ecclesiastical titles awarded by court, pilgrimages to famous temples, poetry, the performance of music, chanting scriptures, preaching, singing, fighting in armed conflicts and learning how to face death.

While Bodiford acknowledges the important contributions made recently in other mappings of the medieval religious landscape, such as the focus on "Kamakura New Buddhism" and the "Exoteric-Esoteric Establishment" models, he also notes how the new horizons opened up by those perspectives tend to leave us with a rather limited understanding of the role of "monasteries as settings for religious life and learning." Scholars wishing to arrive at a more robust picture of the ways that monasteries functioned in medieval Japan can no longer afford to ignore the insights provided by these first-person looks inside those monasteries, even if the historical picture is often rather distorted. If there is a common element to these accounts of monasteries it is that they were complex institutions that played diverse social and economic functions in addition to being meditation centers.

The conceptual frameworks that many scholars of Buddhism inhabit have presented difficulties in accounting for the ways Buddhist monasteries could operate in concert with social realities and social needs, and at the same time fulfill a more rarified soteriological function. In contemporary Japanese scholarship, for example, the medieval Tendai School is often held up as an example of a monolithic Buddhist institution that was enmeshed in society to the detriment of its religious function—an institution more interested in power and politics than precepts and practice. That is to say, Tendai monasteries were perceived to be Buddhist institutions that tipped the balance too far to the side of society. In Paul Groner's chapter, however, we are provided with a counter-example to those charges that nicely balances other views by examining the Kurodani lineage of Tendai through the lens of one key monk, Kōen (1262 or 1263–1317). While the Tendai tradition maintained an abstract interpretation of the precepts, rendering them irrelevant to most monks, the Kurodani lineage stressed the importance of adhering to the precepts. This stress on the importance of monastic discipline within the Kurodani lineage, which it grounds in the teachings of original enlightenment (*hongaku*), runs counter to traditional claims about those teachings that say that they ultimately lead to an increasing laxity in adherence to the precepts based on the fundamental position that people are enlightened just as they are and therefore need not practice. Through a study of Kōen and the Kurodani lineage's famous "consecrated ordination" (*kaikanjō*), Groner explores some of the ways that *hongaku* ideas were transferred to a ritual context. This type of doctrinal innovation, he suggests, was grounded not in textual precedent, but in the many dreams that are related in Kōen's biography. Kōen's authority was grounded in a close relationship to Saichō, the founder of the school, who appeared in his dreams and remained an important figure to be emulated. The Kurodani lineage sought to distinguish itself ritually from other Tendai lineages, and while the ritual of the "consecrated ordination" provided that distinction, it also raised the ante by conferring on its consecrated leaders the status of Buddhahood.

Many East Asian Buddhist monasteries were, it seems, home to a variety of individuals and not just a dedicated coterie of monks. Long ago Yan Gengwang demonstrated that Chinese monasteries, particularly those located on mountains, served as educational centers, where scholar officials took time out to retreat and pursue studies that included more than merely a Buddhist curriculum.[38] There is also evidence that Buddhist monasteries served as places of refuge for Daoists when the winds of political patronage shifted and therefore could in some cases serve as crucibles for the cross-fertilization of a variety of ideas and religious practices. Buddhist monasteries were, therefore, home to an astonishingly diverse array of people but, as Timothy Barrett argues, it was not only a diverse cast of human characters who played a role within Buddhist monastic life. Barrett highlights how the communal life upon which monasticism is based benefits not only monks and nuns, but also certain types of animals, especially cats. While cats lived in a symbiotic relationship with monastics, since they helped to keep the large stores of food rodent-free, they also seem to have taken on meanings not merely limited to their economic function. In his contribution, Barrett tracks the monastic cat as it appears in a wide range of sources from East Asian Buddhist poetry to the fascinating body of folklore collected by Minakata Kumagusu. Following the cat's presence around East Asia reveals early associations with tigers, their eventual domestication by the ninth century, and the ways that they have been used as potent images within Chan/Zen doctrinal tracts. One of the most famous Zen cats was, of course, the well-known one that was cut in half by Nanquan Puyuan (748–835). Yet, the symbolic meaning of cats was continually shifting. In the eighth-century *Lidai fabao ji*, for example, vinaya masters intent on the pursuit of profit and fame are described as cats stalking their prey. In other sources cats are described as being the reincarnated forms of lazy monks. Dōgen, for example, was explicitly told by his Chinese master to stay away from cats. Cats also served for some as positive symbols used to describe the concentration needed in Zen to attain awakening.

Just as Buddhist monasteries were filled with a variety of inhabitants that challenge us to refashion our images of what those institutions were like, it is also clear that the physical monastery itself came in a variety of shapes and sizes, and served a wide range of functions. One of the problems of trying to arrive at an adequate depiction of the function of Buddhist monasteries has been the tendency for scholars to throw diverse institutions under the single term "monastery." Scholars of Indian Buddhism have, for example, tended to use the term monastery for a wide variety of entities, including buildings of different sizes and functions—from simple caves and solitary cells, to much larger religious institutions. Rarely are distinctions made between a cluster of terms such as *vihāra, āvāsa, ārāma*, and *lena*. Indeed, the precise referents of all of these terms are still the focus of much discussion and debate. In an unusually honest assessment of our present ignorance on the topic, Gregory Schopen has remarked that "The term vihāra is—again conventionally—translated as 'monastery,' but even a quick reading of Buddhist monastic literature will show that the word is used to designate a large and wide range of types of dwelling places."[39] Similar problems are found in studies of Chinese and Japanese Buddhism, as the chapters in this volume demonstrate. James Robson's paper, for example, emphasizes that in studies on Chinese Buddhism the word "monastery" is used as a catch-all term for translating a variety of institutional arrangements found on the Chinese religious landscape. The referents for that term range from huge "officially established monasteries" (*guanli si* 官立寺) or "state monasteries," down through middle-range "private monasteries," to small-scale local institutions.[40] This type of evidence prompted Jacques Gernet to conclude that "one of the most obvious features of the imprint of religion on Chinese soil is the diversity: a salutary caution against the uniform and schematic view suggested by the official statistics concerning the numbers of monasteries and monks. The great monastery that permanently houses dozens of monks and the little village chapel or mountain hermitage inhabited by one or two have little in common."[41] Indeed, the term "monastery" referred to such a wide variety of entities that it later became difficult for the compilers of gazetteers to decide on an appropriate place for monasteries within those compilations.[42]

At the same time that palaces were being converted into monasteries and emperors and empresses were commissioning the construction of great Buddhist monasteries in China, monastic practices were also flowing outside of the monastic gates in Japan. Lori Meeks moves the discussion of Buddhist monasteries and monasticism beyond monastic institutions and monks and nuns to the ways that the laity sponsored ordination ceremonies. This shift in perspective problematizes the concept of "official ordination," since, in the evidence that Meeks discusses, "ordination" was not necessarily indicative of entrance into a monastery, but could be something that was done for a variety of complex reasons. In some cases lay ordinations were taken in order to create merit, or pursue worldly benefits, while in others they were the product of an attempt by court elites to be "fashionable patrons of Buddhism." Whatever their perceived powers were among the laity, it is clear that for Buddhist institutions—such as Eison's Esoteric Vinaya School—lay ordinations could serve as powerful economic and political tools that forged close ties between monastic and court elites.

There is much terrain left to cover in the study of both elite and local monastic institutions in order to gain new insights into the nature and function of Buddhist monasteries. Recent work on European monasteries has increasingly turned to considerations of the physical space of monasteries and how that space took on symbolic meanings.[43] By refocusing our attention on the physical space of

monasteries an important set of new questions arises regarding the symbolic layout of the monastery and the ritual context of both art and architecture. It might
be asked, for example, how Buddhist monasteries became imbued with religious
meaning? Eugene Wang posed the question in the following way: If early monastic
architecture in China shared many basic features with secular architecture—and
we know that many Buddhist monasteries were founded through the conversion
of aristocratic mansions—then what was it "that made the Buddha hall a distinctively symbolic space?" Clearly ritual performance could do its part, but here
Wang directs his gaze at the role played by wall paintings adorning the insides of
Buddhist monasteries. In order to carry out this research in the face of few surviving
examples, he draws effectively on the robust description by the ninth-century
historian and connoisseur Zhang Yanyuan of one site, the Jing'ai Monastery
in Luoyang. Zhang's account includes mention of both statues (primarily of
Maitreya) and wall paintings. It has been the interpretation of some of the wall
paintings, including the "Transformation [Tableau] of the Lotus Blossom and Heir
Apparent" and the juxtaposition of the "Sixteen Ways of Meditation" with the
"Transformation [Tableau] of King Yama," that have been particularly intractable
for modern scholars, due in part to Zhang's own incompetence in Buddhist iconography. In order to re-approach this problem of textual representation, Wang looks
to the pictorial programs that survive on the walls of Cave 217 at Dunhuang. The
wall paintings at Dunhuang serve as a key for understanding how Zhang erred in
his descriptions of the scene at the Jing'ai Monastery and at the same time provide
clues for understanding the contemporary political resonances of the paintings at
the Jing'ai Monastery under the reign of Empress Wu. Wang sees in all of this how
wall paintings served to negotiate between two key factors that shaped the character of the Buddhist monastery, namely its responsiveness to both the short-term
political climate and the long-term soteriological needs of the community.

Wall paintings, icons, and other forms of visual art served to fill the monastic
space with religious meaning, but it was not only the contents of Buddhist monasteries that have set them off as special sites. In his study of Buddhist monastic
codes, Gregory Schopen states that those codes are so full of descriptions of
monasteries that focus on their beauty, and the special nature of their settings that
it constitutes a cliché. Indeed, it was precisely the beauty of those sites, and their
ability to captivate "both the heart and eye" of the people, that generated further
giving to the monastery and ensured its long term-success.[44] John Kieschnick has
also noted that nowhere in Chinese Buddhist records "do we find praise of plain,
unadorned Buddhist images and inexpensive stupas, or descriptions of monasteries as simple, humble monastic dwellings."[45] The ideal Chinese monastery was
to be ornamented, spectacular, and resplendent (*huali*), and it was precisely the
focus on the aesthetic beauty of Buddhist monasteries that became the target of
the invectives issued by Buddhist critics. All of this splendor was not, however,
merely intended to dazzle the eye, but was conceived as the appropriate way
to manifest on earth the ideal domain of the Buddha's residence. Daoxuan, for
example, claimed that,

When the Buddha manifested a transformed [image on earth], it was done with a profound motive. Just as the form [of the transformed body] was different from the natural form, the dwelling [of the Buddha] was necessarily different from [those of] the profane world. Therefore a monastery and other living quarters were established [on earth] that were totally unlike ordinary human habitations, and images were created so strange as to stir the common heart to see the [Buddha truth]—so much so that when ordinary folk were made to hear of it, they would be shaken into knowing the words and the paths of the faith; when they were made to see, they would understand the form [of the monastery] and discern the extraordinary path [of deliverance].[46]

Buddhist monasteries, despite their earlier associations with aristocratic mansions, came to be clearly perceived as more than merely buildings housing sacred objects and the monastic community. James Robson's chapter explores how the site and the structure itself were perceived as sacred spaces by focusing on the representation of Chinese Buddhist monasteries in foundation legends, mountain monographs, travel records, inscriptions, and local gazetteers. Some of the under-represented characteristics of monasteries found in those sources include a focus on the siting of the monastery, the setting (natural landscape), the structure (architectural elements), and the history (eminent monks associated with the site, key political recognition) of those sites. There is evidence from the depictions of monasteries that the natural settings, both in terms of topography and its location under particular stellar formations, were an important aspect of the textual representations of those sites and added to the overall auspicious nature of the site. The accounts of a sacred site—or its sacred possessions—could therefore demonstrate that a monastery was both an efficacious place for a monk or nun to pursue their calling, and may have also had a profound effect on the future viability and economic success of the monastery, due to its ability to attract both pilgrims and patrons. Timothy Brook has noted a passage in a seventeenth-century gazetteer that says, "although monasteries are places where monks can withdraw from the world, it so happens that most of them are located in the most scenic spots in the country" and they did indeed attract the gentry who toured and held meetings in the monasteries at those special sites.[47]

The chapters gathered together in this volume are testament to the fact that monasteries in Asia have always been much more than merely residences for monks who, cut off from the dust and din of society and all its entrapments, collectively pursued an ideal cenobitic lifestyle. It would therefore be erroneous to think that all of the essays collected here add up to one synthetic (or normative) view of something that might be called East Asian monasticism. What has been offered are "perspectives" on different facets of monasticism, and those perspectives work towards complexity, the acknowledgement of diversity, and the need for temporal and geographic specificity in discussions about monasticism. The historical and cultural diversity represented in these chapters reflects different faces of Asian monasticism that have remained for the most part hidden behind the veil of traditional images of Buddhist monasteries. These and other aspects of those occluded histories call for further sustained attention by scholars of Buddhism and monasticism in general.

Notes

1 This is not to say, however, that there has been no work on the topic of Buddhist monasticism, but the focus of those, sometimes foundational, studies has tended to coalesce around topics of architecture and monastic regulations. See, among others (I will only refer to Western language books and articles, since the material in Chinese and Japanese is too voluminous to review here), Pichard and Lagirarde 2003, which focuses on the spatial layouts of monasteries, Dutt 1962, Pripp-Møller 1982, Welch 1967, Goossaert 2000. For solid general comments on pre-modern Chinese and Japanese monasteries see the entries on "Daiji (Inde)," "Daiji (Chine)," and "Daiji (Japon)" by Antonino Forte and Hubert Durt, in Demiéville and May 1929–1999: 679–711. On monastic institutions, rules, and function see, for example, McMullin 1984, Foulk, 1987 and 1993, Wijayaratna 1990, Brook 1993, Goodwin 1994, DeBlasi 1998, Adolphson 2000, Hur 2000, Blackburn 2001, Yifa 2002, and most recently the articles collected in Bodiford 2005a. For a more methodological engagement with the topic of monastic institutions see Brook 2005.
2 See Barnard 1990.
3 On Daoist monasticism see Yoshioka 1979, Kohn 2003, Herrou 2005, and Goossaert 2007. On nuns see, for instance, Tsai 1994, Arai 1999, Dobbins 2004, and Batchelor and Son'gyong Sunim 2006. On Korean Buddhist monasticism see Buswell 1992. On Tibetan monasticism see Dreyfus 2003, and the work cited therein. On contemporary Buddhist monasteries and monasticism in China and Japan see, among others, Welch 1967 and 1968, and Covell 2005.
4 See the comments cited below from Johnston 2000a: xi, and Thurman 1993: 121.
5 On these claims see Boisvert 2000: 960.
6 Sasaki et al. 1971: 46.
7 For general statements about the main features of monasticism see Weckman 2005, Lawrence 1984, and Burton 1994.
8 Burton 1994: ix.
9 *Cullavaga* VI. See Horner 1949–1966: 222. See also Wijayaratna 1990: 23–24.
10 Bhikkhu Nānamoli 1979: 125.
11 Johnston 2000b, and Henry and Swearer 1989.
12 These are similar questions to those posed by the editors of a volume on the cross-cultural study of the category of sainthood. See Kiekhefer and Bond 1988.
13 Smith 1982: 35.
14 The following account is based on Jensen 1997: 42–48.
15 Lopez 1998: 27–28.
16 Arnold 1988: 119–123.
17 Arnold 1988: 119.
18 Schopen 2004b: 1–2.
19 Gadamer 1995: 300–301.
20 See Bendix 1977: 315. See also Silber 1995.
21 Weber 1958: 213–214.
22 Weber 1993a: 174.
23 Kemper 1990: 152–169.
24 Salomon 1999: 35.
25 See "Appendix B: World Renunciation in Indian Religions," in Dumont 1980.
26 Dutt 1962: 26.
27 Collins 1988: 109. A similar point is made in Obeyesekere's critique of Weber's vision of Buddhism. See Obeyesekere 2002: 113–114.

28 Some of these approaches to the study of monasteries predated the more explicit turn towards an emphasis on "practice." Here we can mention the foundational early work of Jacques Gernet (1995). Interestingly, another early expression of an interest in Buddhist practice came not from within Buddhist studies itself, but is found in an interview with Michel Foucault during his visit to a Zen Temple in Japan. In that interview Foucault says, "I am very interested in Buddhist philosophy. But, this time, I didn't come for this. What interests me most, is life itself in a Zen temple, that is to say the practice of Zen, its exercises and its rules." See Carrette 1999: 110–114. His interest in Zen monastic practice was no doubt part of his larger project on exploring the mechanisms in place in monasteries—and later employed in hospitals, schools, and prisons—for instituting technologies of control and discipline in order to produce a rule governed body. See, for example, Foucault 1979.

29 On the problem of Buddhist monasticism and its relationship to experience see Sharf 1995.

30 On the tension between the focus on "external trappings" and internal religious training see Buswell 1992: 9.

31 The focus on the soteriological function of Buddhist monasteries is, for example, the general tenor of Thurman 1993. For an insightful critique of those who dismiss certain practices as merely Buddhist "accommodations" to society, see Blackburn 1998, which shows that the recitation of magical *paritta* texts was not an accommodation to the vulgar masses, but central to monastic textual practice and monastic education in Sri Lanka.

32 Hori 1996: 256.

33 Tambiah 1970: 148.

34 Buswell 1992: 9.

35 I take this to be one of the real contributions of Burton 1994.

36 Bhikkhu Nāṇamoli 1979: 122.

37 Harrison 2003: 12.

38 Yan 1992.

39 Schopen 2004c: 332.

40 Forte 1992. Mention should also be made here of Forte 1983 which deals with a variety of other types of monasteries, such as those founded by emperors and princes or for a mother, father, or spouse. See also Tsukamoto 1974 and Chikusa 1987: 1–28.

41 Gernet 1995: 3–4.

42 Brook 1993: 29 and 338.

43 See, for example, Cassidy-Welch 2001.

44 Schopen 2004d: 31.

45 Kieschnick 2003.

46 Daoxuan, *Zhong tianzhu sheweiguo qihuansi tujing* 中天竺舍衛國祇洹寺圖經 [Illustrated Scripture of Jetavana Vihara of Śrāvastī in Central India] T. 45.890a28-b2, translation here from Ho 1995: 18.

47 Brook 1993: 108.

1 Taking a meal at a lay supporter's residence

The evolution of the practice in Chinese *Vinaya* commentaries

Koichi Shinohara

Introduction

In the introductory chapter to this volume James Robson notes how in earlier studies Buddhist monasteries were often presented as communities of world-renouncing religious virtuosi who were forced to make compromises to secular power and wealth. More recent studies treat monastic institutions differently, preferring to see them as a diverse and dynamic community in which a wide range of legitimate concerns, some narrowly soteriological, but others more practical and this-worldly, co-existed and competed with each other. In this chapter I examine closely one particular practice in which lay supporters invite monks for a meal. Through this practice we are able to observe how closely monastic and lay concerns intersected. I further examine how this intersection affected the symbolic construction of Chinese Buddhist monasteries in the stories told about them. I show how the practice of lay devotees feeding the monks came to be understood in the light of a utopian vision of a supernatural monk who appears at such a meal in disguise. These accounts of visions ultimately gave rise to certain cultic practices.

The ceremonial meal at a lay supporter's residence was an important occasion when the community of monks and the lay community interacted with each other directly. In many scriptural passages, occasions when the Buddha accepted a formal invitation from lay persons and went to their residences with his disciples to take a meal are carefully noted.[1] Such a meal was an elaborate ceremony that followed a fixed and carefully laid-out protocol; each step of the meal appears to have been governed by complex rules. The invitation for the meal, for example, is made and accepted according to a set formula on the previous day; the Buddha and his disciples begin the procession to the residence when it is formally announced that the time for the meal has come; it is always the host himself or herself who serves the food; at the conclusion of the meal a blessing (or a spell, *zhouyuan* 咒願), often a familiar verse, is pronounced, and gifts (*dakṣiṇā*) are presented; the Buddha then gives a sermon, and the host is often said to have taken refuge in the Three Jewels and to have been given the Five Lay Precepts. In this chapter I begin with an examination of some of these scriptural passages that were translated into Chinese and then explore Chinese interpretations of the ritual of the ceremonial meal as we find them in the *vinaya* commentaries by Chinese monks and miracle stories that came to be associated with the ceremonial meal for the monks.

The influential *vinaya* commentary by Daoxuan 道宣 (596–667) devotes a chapter to the practice of taking a meal at the home of a lay supporter.[2] Daoxuan collected many scriptural passages, primarily from the *vinayas*, and organized them into systematic instructions, describing how the practice should be carried out step by step, from receiving the invitation to concluding the ceremony as the monks leave the host's residence. In the preface to this chapter, Daoxuan observes that food is offered in the various ceremonies of giving that provide the occasion for lay people to acquire merit. He thus appears to have viewed the ceremonial meal as an essential part of the relationship between the monastic community and its lay supporters.[3]

In Buddhist scriptures the meal taken at a lay supporter's residence often serves as a framework for an extended story about giving and merit making. Daoxuan's discussion is based on citations from scriptures, in this chapter largely from the *vinayas* of different schools translated into Chinese. Nevertheless Daoxuan adds new elements, some explicitly noted as distinctly Chinese. Merit making appears to be understood differently in his commentary and in the stories in the *āgamas* in Chinese translation presumably known to Daoxuan. In the discussion that follows I hope to place Daoxuan's chapter in a larger context and to reflect on the significance of these changes. My general hypothesis is that in the *āgama* stories the merit is seen to accrue from experiencing the extraordinary presence and power of the Buddha himself. In the *vinaya* passages Daoxuan collected, the human or ordinary monks who partake of the feast play a prominent role in assuring the merit making. By contrast Daoxuan's *vinaya* commentary, and a commentary by Daoshi 道世 (596?–683) closely affiliated with it, focused on the role of unrecognized or invisible supernatural guests who take part in the meal. Presumably, these visitors contributed greatly to the production of merit. I will begin first by reviewing two examples of the stories of this ceremony that are found in the *āgamas* preserved in Chinese translation (with parallel accounts in the *vinayas*).

Two stories of taking a meal in the lay supporter's residence in the *āgamas*

Ambapālī story

The story of Ambapālī's gift of a mango garden is typically told as the conclusion to the story of a meal that the Buddha and his disciples took at her residence.[4] The setting of the story is the Buddha's last journey. When the Buddha arrived at Vaiśālī, a prostitute named Ambapālī is said to have approached him and invited him to spend the night in her mango garden and to take a meal at her house the next morning. The Buddha accepted the invitation in silence and moved to the mango garden with his 1,250 disciples. In the *Chang ahan jing* 長阿含經 and other versions of the story a large part of the story is devoted to the exchange between Ambapālī and five hundred Licchavi princes.

After the Buddha accepted her invitation, on her way back to her house Ambapālī met five hundred people of the Licchavi clan of Vaiśālī, who had heard that the Buddha was in Ambapālī's garden and were rushing to get there. One of their carriages touched hers and was damaged. In the exchange that followed, Ambapālī told them that she was hurrying back to her house to prepare a meal for the Buddha. The Licchavis offered to pay her thousands of pieces of gold or even half of the wealth of their kingdom in exchange for the opportunity to serve a meal to the Buddha, but Ambapālī refused. When the Licchavis arrived at the garden, and invited the Buddha to a meal, the Buddha turned them down, saying that Ambapālī had invited him first.

The account of the meal itself is given on the basis of a well-established formula. Ambapālī is said to have spent the night making preparations for the meal. When the time of the meal came, the Buddha, surrounded by the 1,250 monks, all properly dressed and each holding a bowl, arrived and took a seat. Ambapālī presented a delicious meal both to the Buddha and the monks. After the meal the bowls and tables were removed, and Ambapālī took a golden pitcher in her hand and poured water for them to wash their hands.

The story of the donation of the mango garden follows. Ambapālī observed that her garden was the best among all gardens in Vaiśālī and then offered it to the Buddha. The Buddha told her to donate it to the Buddha and the Saṃgha of the Four Directions (14b17–20; ref. T. 22.856c7–13; 136a12–15); no one but the buddhas would be able to make use of it if it were given only to the Buddha. Having received the gift, the Buddha uttered some verses, promising daily increase in merit and good rebirths to those who make gifts of stūpas, gardens, bridges, juicy fruits in a desert, or buildings, and those who uphold the precepts (14b22–25; ref., 22. 856c14–18, where the verses are called "blessing," or *zhouyuan*).

Again a familiar account of the sermon given to conclude such a meal follows. Ambapālī took a seat in front of the Buddha, the Buddha preached to her about giving, the precepts, and rebirth in heaven. He explained to her the Noble Truths of suffering, the cause of suffering, cessation of suffering, and the Way of escaping from rebirth. Ambapālī took refuge in the Buddha, the Dharma and the Saṃgha, and as an *upāsikā* took the Five Precepts.[5]

In this story Ambapālī's dubious status is contrasted with the power and wealth of the Licchavis. Ambapālī is explicitly called a prostitute (*yinnü* 婬女), while references to the number and impressive appearance of the Licchavis occur repeatedly.[6] Their "jeweled carriages" (*baoche* 寶車), horses, clothes, banners, and attendants are carefully said to have been adorned with five colors in the *Chang ahan jing*; in the *Sifenlü* 四分律 and *Zengyi ahan jing* 增一阿含經 versions of the story, the description of the carriages and their appearance is even more elaborate (22.855c24–28; 2.596a20–27). When the Buddha saw the Licchavis approach in their carriages from a distance, he compared them to the gods in the Heaven of the Thirty-Three (1.13c23–24; 2.596b13–15; 22.956a14–17). When the Licchavis learned that Ambapālī had preempted them in extending an invitation to the Buddha, they offered thousands of pieces of gold or half of their wealth. Yet, Ambapālī refused and the Licchavis reviled her, saying that "this woman" had deprived them of the first opportunity to make merit (1.13c28; 2.596a29; ref. 1.14b7–8; 22.856a12–13). The story of Ambapālī explains the origin of the practice of honoring the first accepted invitation over later ones. At this level the story may then be read as one about lay patrons competing for an opportunity to make merit by having the Buddha and his monks at their residences.

The encounter with the Buddha is described in a similar way for Ambapālī and the Licchavis in the *Chang ahan jing* version of the story. When they came to greet the Buddha, the Buddha is said to have looked like the moon. [Ambapālī] saw the World-Honored-One from a distance. His face was handsome, endowed with extraordinary sense organs. Both primary and secondary marks [of the Buddha] were there, and [he looked radiant] like the moon among stars (13b22–23). As the Licchavis greeted the Buddha and sat on one side, the shining halo of the Tathāgata in his seat covered all the assembly, like the autumn moon or the sun in the clear sky shining brightly and alone. Then, one Brahman, called Bingyan 并 [既 / 食] (or Binqiyangtu 賓耆羊兔 in T. 22.856b3–4, Piṅgiya?), arose from his seat and uttered a set of verses.

> The kings of Magadha and Aṅga
> quickly secure beneficial gains.
> With his body wrapped in jewel-armor,
> the World Honored One appears in their land.
> His powers shake the Three Thousand Worlds.
> His name is prominent like the Himalaya mountain range.
> Like a lotus flower opening up,
> his fragrance is extremely subtle and pleasing,
> I now see the Buddha's halo,
> like the sun as it first comes up
> and like the moon traveling through empty space,
> no cloud or shadows anywhere.
> The Tathāgata is like this, throwing light over the world.
> Seen with the Tathāgata's wisdom,
> the darkness is illumined as if by a torch.
> He gives sentient beings clear eyes,
> removing decisively numerous doubts.
> . . .

(14a7–19)

The Buddha instructed the Licchavis on the five things that are "difficult to obtain": (1) the appearance of the Tathāgata in the world, (2) those who are capable of preaching the True Teaching of the Tathāgata, (3) those who are capable of believing in and understanding what the Tathāgata preaches, (4) those who can bring to completion what the Tathāgata preaches, and (5) those who having faced dangers and been rescued remember to return the debt (1.14a27–b3; ref., 22.836b19–25; 2.596b16–20; *Anguttara Nikaya*, III, 167, Woodward 1932: 127).

The metaphor of the moon and the sun and the instruction on the difficulties of encountering and receiving the Buddha's teaching in the story about the Licchavis explain in part why offering a meal to him and his monks produces such an extraordinary amount of merit. The Licchavis recognized how extraordinary an encounter with the Buddha is, but they could not gain merit from the rare event. For Ambapālī the meal culminated in the gift of the mango garden, and the Buddha promised her in the verses he uttered daily increase in merit and rebirth in a superior realm. In this story of Ambapālī, making merit by offering a meal to the Buddha and his monks is closely linked to the recognition of the extraordinary nature of the appearance of the Buddha.

Ambapālī's story briefly examined here suggests that lay donors competed with each other for the opportunity to offer a meal to the Buddha and his monks. In the story of Śrīgupta to be discussed below, however, a competition takes place between the Buddha and other teachers for lay patronage.

The story of Śrīgupta

In the story of the conversion of Śrīguputa the meal at a layman's house is presented as the setting for a competition over lay patronage. Again, the succeeding stages of the ceremonial meal are closely integrated into the plot of the story, and in the parallel versions of this story in the *vinayas* a part of the story appears to have been turned into an explanation of the origin of one important rite that forms a part of this ceremony. I will first summarize the story as it is told in the *Zengyi ahanjing*.[7]

The Buddha, accompanied by 1,250 monks, is said to have been staying at the Kalandaka bamboo garden in Rājagṛha; at that time a very wealthy elder called Śrīgupta is said to have been widely known as someone hostile to the Buddha's teaching who honored the followers of Nirgrantha Jñātaputra. Followers of non-Buddhist teachings said to each other, "Gautama [claims to] know everything, having the 'all knowing knowledge' (*yiqiezhi* 一切智, *sarvajñāna*). Consequently, we don't get donations, while he gets a lot. We must figure out a way of stopping him from getting donations" (2.773c27–29).

These non-Buddhist teachers came to Śrīgupta's residence. Having promised that he would be reborn in Brahma's heaven as a son of Brahma and would enjoy benefits accordingly, they told Śrīgupta to go to Gautama and, appealing to his compassion, asked him and his monks to come to his residence so that he could honor (*si* 祠) them there. They also instructed Śrīgupta to dig a large fire pit inside the house and to light a blazing fire and to put poison in all the food to be served to the Buddha and his monks.

[They explained,] "If *śramaṇa* Gautama has the all-knowing knowledge and knows everything in the past, the present and the future, he will not accept the invitation. If he lacks the all-knowing knowledge, he will accept, and with his disciples be burnt by the fire. Neither gods nor human beings will be harmed by the fire" (774a7–9).

The account of the invitation is thus framed as a challenge to claims of the Buddha's omniscience. Śrīgupta went to the Buddha, paid respect to him, and offered the invitation. The Buddha is said then to have known what was on Śrīgupta's mind and yet accepted the invitation in silence. On his way back Śrīgupta thought to himself, "I now understand clearly what the teachers of the Six Schools said. The *śramaṇa* does not know what I have in mind. He will certainly be burnt in the great fire."

Śrīgupta returned home and prepared two fire pits, one inside and the other outside of the gate, as well as the poisoned food. When poison was put in all the food, Śrīgupta came to the Buddha and said to him, following the established formula, "The appointed time for the meal has arrived." The Buddha put on his robe and picked up his bowl, and with many monks surrounding him in front and behind, he went to [Śrīgupta's] house. He told the monks, "You should not walk ahead of me, nor should you sit down before I sit. You should not eat before I eat."

People in Rājagṛha heard about the plot and cried aloud, fearing that the Tathāgata and the monks might be harmed. To those who came to the Buddha and begged him not to go to that elder's house, the Buddha said, "Do not be afraid. The Tathāghata will not be harmed by that man. Even if a fire in Jambudvīpa would reach up to Brahma's heaven, that fire still would not burn me" (774a29–b2).

Surrounded by monks, the Buddha then entered the city of Rājagṛha and came to Śrīgupta's house. The Buddha then repeated his instructions forbidding the monks to enter the elder's house ahead of him or to eat before he ate. When the Buddha raised his foot over the threshold, the fire pit spontaneously became a cool bathing pond; lotus flowers as large as a chariot's wheel with a stem made of seven jewels filled the pond. Śakra, Brahmā, the Four Heavenly Kings, *gandharvas, asuras, rakṣas* and ghosts saw the lotus flowers appear in the fire pit, and simultaneously praised the Buddha, saying that the Tathāgata was first among all superior beings.

At that time followers of non-Buddhist teachings were gathered in the elder's house. Lay Buddhist men and women (*upāsaka* and *upāsikā)* saw the Tathāgata's miraculous transformation, and were overjoyed. The followers of non-Buddhist teachings saw this miraculous transformation, and were distressed. Above in the sky many gods showered flowers over the Buddha's body. The Tathāgata floated up four inches above the ground and walked over to the elder's residence. At the place where the Tathāgata put his foot down a lotus flower as large as a chariot wheel appeared. Then the Tathāgata turned around and told the monks, "You should all step on these lotus flowers." Everyone (*śrāvakas*) accordingly walked over the lotus flowers and reached the elder's house (774b13–21).

The story continues, describing the Buddha's instruction on how the monks were to take their seats and eat. When the Buddha and the monks were seated, fragrant lotus flowers appeared under their seats. At this point, having seen these miracles (*bianhua* 變化), Śrīgupta confessed his faults to the Buddha. The Buddha accepted his repentance, telling him not to repeat these mistakes.[8]

A long passage on the poisoned food follows in the *Zengyi ahan jing* version of the story. When Śrīgupta confessed to the Buddha that the food he presented earlier was all poisoned and asked for a little time to have new food prepared, the Buddha told him that the Tathāgata and his disciples could not be harmed by others and instructed the elder to serve the food that had already been prepared.

Then the elder served the food to the Buddha with his own hands, as specified in other accounts of a ceremonial meal. The Buddha first recited a long verse; the Buddha, the Dharma, and the Saṃgha are said to destroy poisons completely; the world is said to be plagued by the three worldly poisons, such as greed and anger, but the Buddha is free of all poisons. Having uttered the verse, the Buddha then took the poisoned food. The Buddha had told the monks to wait until the Tathāgata ate before they ate. The elder then served the food to the monks, again with his own hands.[9]

When Śrīgupta saw the Tathāgata finish the meal, he removed the bowls and sat on a low seat in front of him. The Buddha preached a variety of profound doctrines to the elder and an assembly of 84,000. All took refuge in the Buddha, the Dharma, and the Saṃgha and received the Five Precepts.[10]

The story concludes, citing the *dakṣiṇā* verse that the Buddha uttered to conclude the ceremony.

> Among all forms of offering (*sisi* 祠祀), fire is the highest.
> In literature, verses of praise are the best.
> Among human beings, the king is the most honorable.
> For all streams, the ocean is the source.
> Among the stars, the moon is the brightest.
> Above, below, and in the four cardinal directions,
> Among everything that has a physical form
> in all heavens and worlds
> the Buddha is the supreme one.
> Those who seek merit
> Should make offerings to the three Buddhas.
>
> (775b21–28)

This long story, which began with an account of non-Buddhist teachers challenging the lay support received by the Buddha, concludes with verses that declare the incomparable superiority of the Buddha. This appears to have been a well-known verse and occurs in a number of passages in connection with different stories in the scriptures, but always in connection with a meal offered to the Buddha and his monks at a lay supporter's residence.[11] We might add here that while the story of Ambapālī highlights the remarkable appearance of the Buddha, it is the extraordinary knowledge of the Buddha that is emphasized in the Śrīgupta story. It is this omniscience that renders credibility to the Buddha's utterance of the blessing.

The story of Śrīgupta is not the only story in which the meal is set in the context of inter-sectarian religious rivalry. In two of the stories from the *Zengyi ahan jing*, the meal is preceded by a contest with a non-Buddhist teacher, either Nirgrantha Jñātaputra or Satyaka Nirgranthaputra. In the *Bieyi za ahan jing* 別譯雜阿含經 (Separately translated Saṃyuktāgama) story of Ugrataśarīra the Buddha persuades a Brahman who was about to sacrifice many animals that the ceremony meant as a gift that produces much merit in fact results in great sins. Instead he tells him that he should honor the "three fires," by honoring his parents, looking after his relatives, and giving to the merit-field of monks and Brahmans (T. 2.464b–465b; parallel in *Za ahan jing* 雜阿含經, T. 2.24b–25b). He is also told to remove the three evil fires of greed, ignorance, and anger. The animals were set free and the Buddha and his monks were fed. The verse as "blessing" (*zhouyuan*) appears to declare that the Buddha is even greater than the Brahmanical sacrifice ("fire"), even though sacrifice is acknowledged as the greatest among all forms of worship.[12]

Both the story of Ambapālī and Śrīgupta conclude with a verse, in some versions called "blessing" (*zhouyuan*, or "spell"). A blessing is mentioned in many other accounts of the meal offered by lay supporters, and appears to have been an important part of the ceremony. Having finished the meal that lay supporters have presented to the Buddha and his monks, the Buddha announces the effective production of merit in these verses. The verses took different forms in different contexts, as explained, for example, in some detail in a passage cited in Daoxuan's commentary to be discussed below. These verses also defined the nature of the merit that had been gained and perhaps were even meant to activate them. Further gifts (*dakṣiṇā*) are sometimes mentioned in this connection. As we saw in the emphasis on the brightness of the Buddha's appearance in the story of Ambapālī and in the verse pronounced at the end of the meal in the Śrīgupta story, the superiority of the Buddha is highlighted as if to guarantee the effectiveness of this form of merit making.

The chapter on invited meals in the *vinaya* commentaries of Daoxuan and Daoshi

In the chapter on "receiving the invitation for a meal at a lay supporter's residence" in their respective *vinaya* commentaries, Daoxuan (T. 40.135a–138a) and Daoshi (171b–173c) describe the ceremony in ten sections.[13] These ten categories follow the sequence of the ceremony itself. Thus, a complex discussion as to how the invitation is to be made and received (section 1) and how the monks should proceed to the residence as a group (section 2) is followed by an extended discussion as to how the Buddha images and the seat for the Holy Monk Piṇḍola Bhāradvāja are to be set up. Only after the seat for Piṇḍola is properly set up may the monks take seats according to their monastic ranks (sections 3 and 4). Both commentaries then note explicitly that while the instruction in the *vinayas* places the pronouncing of blessing (*zhouyuan*) after the meal, the practice in China based on Dao'an's 道安 (312–385) instruction was to carry out this rite before the meal. Incense is presented to the monks, scriptures are recited, and chanting takes place (section 5). The senior monk preaches according to the donor's wish and a proper verse appropriate to the occasion of the meal is recited (section 6). When food is served, the monks wait until everyone is served and the *samprāgata* (*denggong* 等供 or *sengba* 僧跋, indicating that the food was distributed equally) is pronounced (section 7). Even though the commentaries noted earlier in section 6 that the blessing was to be pronounced before the meal, the pronouncing of the verse of blessing is again mentioned as the meal is completed and the gifts are presented (*dakṣiṇā*), perhaps reflecting the practice described in many Indian scriptural sources (sections 8 and 9). The discussion of this ceremony concludes with a comment on how the monks should leave the residence and return to the monastery.

The core of this discussion in these thematic commentaries on the *Sifenlü* or *Dharmaguptaka vinaya* is primarily based on one extended passage in this *vinaya* and is expanded with quotations taken from another long passage in the *Mohesengqilü*, or *Mahāsaṃghika vinaya* (T. no. 1425). This account is then supplemented with a large number of other scriptural quotations.

Vinaya *passages on which the account of the ceremony in the commentaries are primarily based*

The instruction on taking a meal (shishangfa 食上法) *in the* Dharmagupta vinaya

Typically Daoshi's discussion of the various stages in the ceremony begins with a quotation from the *Dharmaguptaka vinaya*. Thus, sections 1, 2, 4, 5, and 6 first cite "this *vinaya*," taken from this source.[14] Though titled the "Discussion of the fundamentals of the vinaya" (*Pini taoyao* 毗尼討要), Daoshi's commentary is thus explicitly framed primarily as a commentary on the *Dharmagupta vinaya*.[15] In referring to the *Dharmaguptaka vinaya*, Daoxuan uses an abbreviation of its full title (as *Sifen*), not privileging it over other sources. Nevertheless, his discussion is also largely framed around this commentary; sections 2, 4, 5, 6, and 7 each open with a quotation from this *vinaya*.[16]

In a long passage on the topic of taking a meal at a layman's residence in the *Dharmagupta vinaya* the setting of the Buddha's instruction is given as follows: The Buddha was at Śrāvastī when a layman invited the community of monks for a meal the following day. An elaborate feast was prepared overnight and in the early morning the layman came to announce that it was time for the feast.

The monks accepted the invitation but they ate in a disorderly fashion. At any moment some were sitting down, some about to sit down, some had received food and others were about to receive it. Some had already eaten and some were about to eat. Some had already moved away from their seats and others were about to move. Some had already left the house and others were about to. The donor, not being able to tell who had received food and who had not, complained, "The disciples of Śākyamuni are shameless and do not know when to be satisfied. They say that they know the Correct Teaching, but they are disorderly in accepting the invitation for a meal from lay people . . ." Monks heard this, and those among them who knew when to be satisfied, practiced *dhūta*, took pleasure in studying precepts and knew shame, criticized those monks . . . The monks went to the Buddha and explained the situation. The Buddha reprimanded the monks and set down the proper procedure (*shishangfa*, or "the way of presenting a meal") (22.934c24–935a19).

The outline of this procedure corresponds closely with the presentations in the *vinaya* commentaries by Daoxuan and Daoshi. As is shown in the Appendix (see pages 35–37), in fact a large part of this passage from which I have just cited is quoted directly at the corresponding points in their accounts. Frequently, the quotations from this long *Dharmaguptaka vinaya* passage appear as the opening quotation in a new section in the commentaries.[17] My hypothesis is that the presentation of this ceremony in the commentaries by Daoxuan and Daoshi, or possibly an earlier version of it on which their commentaries were based, began first as a discussion of some key statements in the *shishangfa* passage in the *Dharmaguptaka vinaya*. Other passages from the same *vinaya* were added to this discussion.[18] Material from other *vinayas* and other types of scriptures was also collected and added around this basic structure of the ceremony.

The long passage from the Mahāsaṃghika vinaya

The *Mahāsaṃghika vinaya* contains another extended discussion of the origin of the Buddha's instruction on taking a meal at a lay supporter's residence, to which Daoxuan and Daoshi refer frequently. The setting of this instruction is again Śrāvastī. At the Jetavana monastery donors are said to have arranged a meal for the community of monks, but the most senior monk did not arrive and the meal became cold.

The donor said, "Have the monks gathered?" Answer: "Not yet." "Who has not come?" "The senior-most monk has not come." The donor became irritated and said, "I gave up work at the family business and came to prepare a meal for the monks, and yet the monks do not come." The senior monk then came, but not even blessing the meal, he ate quickly and clumsily and left. A younger monk asked, "Has the senior monk come?" Answer, "He came and left as soon as he ate." The younger monk became irritated and said, "The senior monk does not let people know when he comes nor when he goes." When the monks told the Buddha about this, the Buddha called Nanda (Ānanda?) and asked whether this was true. Receiving the answer that it was true, the Buddha gave the instruction (that follows) (22.499c29–500a8).

Daoxuan and Daoshi cite several passages from the long account of the instruction (see Appendix pages 37–38). This extended passage in the *Mahāsaṃghika vinaya* follows a broad outline very similar to the passage in the *Dharmaguptaka vinaya*: monks are instructed first how to receive the invitation and proceed to the house, and then how they should sit for the meal, have the food distributed equally, and eat together only after the *samprāgata* is uttered. The blessing is then to be given. But with the exception of quotation marked (ee) in the Appendix—that appears in section 8 of the commentaries—no citations from this long *Mahāsaṃghika vinaya* appear as the first citation in the respective sections of the commentaries in which they appear.[19] The original outline of the discussion, based on the *Dharmaguptaka vinaya* passages discussed above, appears thus to have been expanded at a second stage in the compilation with quotations from a parallel discussion in the *Mahāsaṃghika vinaya*.[20]

The evolving understanding of the ceremonial meal in the vinaya *commentaries*

The chapter on the ceremony of inviting monks for a meal at a lay supporter's residence in the Chinese commentaries by Daoxuan and Daoshi addresses the Chinese monastic community many centuries after the time of the Buddha's teaching career purportedly described in the scriptures.[21] Chinese commentators were aware of this distance in time and space and recognized departures from the scriptural model; the practice of pronouncing the blessing before the meal is said to be distinctly Chinese and to diverge from the scriptural account. I suspect, however, that these departures affected the meaning of the ceremony more fundamentally than the commentators may have realized.

Merit making is the central concern of this ceremony. In the stories framed around this ceremony in the *āgamas* and *vinayas*, it is the offering of food to the Buddha himself that produces merit. The extraordinary appearance and power of the Buddha are carefully noted. The monks who accompany the Buddha and take part in the meal play only a minor role. In the practical instructions for this ceremony in the *vinayas*, cited extensively by Chinese commentators as the basis of their discussion, the conduct of the monks at the ceremony is the focus of attention. But here, too, the Buddha is a powerful presence, setting down these rules. In the presentation in the Chinese *vinaya* commentaries, by contrast, the Buddha is only present as an image set up in the hall before the monks arrive. But even in the passage that describes setting up of the Buddha image, the emphasis quickly shifts from the Buddha image to the empty seat to be prepared for the supernatural monk (*shengseng*) Piṇḍola Bhāradvāja. The monks, hierarchically ranked according to their monastic standing, are headed by the Buddha present as an image, but more potently by the senior monk Piṇḍola Bhāradvāja, whose empty seat is where miraculous signs appear, announcing his participation and thus guaranteeing the effectiveness of the entire merit-making exercise.[22]

Feeding other supernatural beings, such as ghosts and gods residing in monastic buildings, is also emphasized in this Chinese *vinaya* commentary account of the ceremony.[23] The focus of the ceremony appears now to have shifted from the presence of the Buddha to the mysterious appearance of unexpected and invisible participants.

Setting up the seat of Piṇḍola

Both Daoxuan and Daoshi comment on the practice of setting up the Buddha image and the seat for the Holy Monk Piṇḍola Bhāradvāja at the host's residence (section 3).[24] They both note that Piṇḍola's seat must be set up before the senior monk and then that the other monks take their seats according to the monastic ranking (T. 40.136a1–2; XZJ 70.171d18). The discussion of Piṇḍola's seat appears as a part of the discussion of the seating of the monks. Next to the Buddha, represented by an image, Piṇḍola is given the highest rank among the monks; his seat must be set up before other lower-ranking monks take their seats.[25]

The Scripture on Inviting Piṇḍola (*Qing bintoulu fa* 請賓頭盧法, translated by Huijian 慧簡 in the second half of the fifth century, T. 32.784b–c) cited by Daoxuan and Daoshi, tells a story of a lay elder who often invited Piṇḍola and presented a large feast for the monks. The flowers that were placed under the mat kept wilting. After the third feast, an old monk appeared to the distressed host and told him that each time he was invited, he accepted the invitation, but when he arrived as an old man in shabby clothing the elder's servants beat him and chased him away. The elder realized that this old monk was Piṇḍola. Ever since then, when a feast is offered to the monks, the gate to the residence is kept open, and if Piṇḍola arrives to participate in the feast, the flowers are said not to wilt. This is the "sign" that Daoxuan and Daoshi mention in their summary of this scripture ("*youxiang* 有相" T. 40.135c26; XZJ 70.172a4).[26]

In the *Scripture on Inviting Piṇḍola*, Piṇḍola is said to have illegitimately demonstrated his supernatural powers to the Elder Jotika and for this reason was not allowed to enter *nirvāṇa*. He thus remains in this world, helping the Fourfold Assembly make merits (*zuo futian* 作福田) (32.784b7–8). By emphasizing the seat to be set up for Piṇḍola at the ceremonial meal for monks, Chinese *vinaya* commentators shifted the focus of the ceremony from an offering to the Buddha, whose extraordinary appearance and powers are highlighted in the *āgama* and *vinaya* stories reviewed above, to an offering to monks, headed by the supernatural monk Piṇḍola. As illustrated by the familiar story of Piṇḍola, merit is now produced by feeding monks as a merit field rather than by feeding the Buddha, who is distantly represented by an image set up at the beginning of the ceremony, but largely disregarded in the account of the concrete steps of the ceremony.

This unexpected reference to the Holy Monk Piṇḍola Bhāradvāja in the discussion of the meal offered to monks in a lay supporter's residence in Chinese *vinaya* commentaries points to the powerful influence of Dao'an and his followers. In section 6 of their respective commentaries, Daoshi and Daoxuan observe that the practice of uttering the blessing before the meal goes back to Dao'an. They state, "If one follows this, one will not depart from principle, *li* 理" (172c12–13; T. 40.136b15-16). This observation is based on a passage in the *Gaoseng zhuan* 高僧傳 biography of Dao'an (T. 50.353b17–23). Dao'an, commenting on various scriptures, is said to have been concerned that his view might not agree with principle (*li*). He consequently made a vow calling for a miraculous sign to confirm that what he wrote does not depart far from principle. This was followed by a dream, in which a strange foreign monk appeared and confirmed that his commentaries agreed with the principle of the Way (*daoli* 道理, 353b19–20). The monk said that not being able to enter *nirvāṇa* he was remaining in the Western Region. He proposed to collaborate with Dao'an in spreading the Teaching widely, and asked for a meal to be set out for him regularly. Later, when the *Sarvāstivāda vinaya* was brought to China, Dao'an's disciple Huiyuan 慧遠 (334–416) learned that the monk who had appeared in Dao'an's dream was none other than Piṇḍola Bhāradvāja. Consequently, Huiyuan is said to have set up a seat for Piṇḍola and fed him.[27]

Following this story, the *Gaoseng zhuan* biography mentions that Dao'an set down regulations for the monastic community, consisting of three categories.

No further record of these regulations is preserved and their contents cannot be determined in detail.[28]

Nevertheless, we may note that the title summarizing the first part of this instruction in the *Gaoseng zhuan* biography begins with the phrase "presenting incense" (*xingxiang* 行香). In the commentaries by Daoxuan and Daoshi the reference to Dao'an appears in the section called "Presenting incense and [uttering] blessings." Both Daoxuan and Daoshi explicitly mention as a distinctly Chinese practice the pronouncing of the blessing before the meal and attribute it to Dao'an. Daoxuan and Daoshi may have been referring to Dao'an's monastic regulations mentioned in the *Gaoseng zhuan*, and, though the *Gaoseng zhuan* passage does not mention uttering a blessing before the meal, this practice may have been a part of Dao'an's threefold regulations.

Pronouncing the blessing (zhouyuan) *before the meal*

In the stories of both Ambapālī and Śrīgupta reviewed above it is carefully noted that the Buddha, in return for the ceremonial meal, uttered verses of blessing. An exchange takes place at the ceremonial meal: a lay supporter offers the gift of the meal, while the monks in pronouncing the blessing confer merit on the donor. From the viewpoint of the lay supporter who offers the meal, then, the pronouncing of the blessing is a very important part of the ceremony.[29] Both Daoxuan and Daoshi note (in section 6 in both commentaries and repeated in section 7 in Daoxuan's commentary) that while the *Dharmaguptaka vinaya* specifies that the blessing or *zhouyuan* is uttered after the meal, the *Bianyi changzhezi jing* 辯意長者子經 places it before the meal and that the sequence adopted in China based on Dao'an's instruction agrees with the latter.[30]

Different verses are mentioned in the scriptures, as illustrated, for example, in our discussion of the stories of Ambapālī and Śrīgupta above. Daoxuan and Daoshi refer to passages in the *vinayas*. In the long *Dharmaguptaka vinaya* passage on "presenting a meal" (*shishang*) reviewed above, for example, it is stated that after the meal the senior monk is to utter a verse: "If the gift is made for the sake of certain benefits (*li* 利), these benefits will certainly be obtained; if the gift is made for the sake of happiness (*le* 樂), one will certainly secure this happiness (*kuaile* 快樂)" (935c14–15).[31]

The *Bianyi changzhezi jing*, translated by Fachang 法場 in the early sixth century, tells a story of two beggars who appeared at a feast offered by Bianyi (Pratibhānamati?). One came before the Buddha uttered the blessing (*zhouyuan*); the monks did not dare to give him food. The other appeared after the Buddha had uttered the blessing of *dakṣiṇā* and the monks all gave food to him. The first beggar left angry, cursing the monks, thinking that if he later became a king he would cut off their heads with the iron-covered wheels of a chariot. The second left feeling grateful, thinking that if he later became a king he would offer a feast to the Buddha and his disciples. After returning to the monastery the Buddha is said to have instructed that the blessing should be given before the meal is taken. Later, the grateful man became a king and the wheel of his chariot cut off the head of the one who left angry (T. 14.839b–840a).

This story of the two beggars in the *Bianyi changzhezi jing* may be read in connection with the story of Piṇḍola in the *Qing Bintoulu fa* story. Just as Piṇḍola, who appeared first as an old monk in shabby clothing was turned away, the first beggar in *Bianyi changzhezi jing* who appeared before the blessing was pronounced, was beaten and chased away. The second beggar, who arrived after the blessing was pronounced, was fed generously, and his wish as he left the meal resulted in his rebirth as a king and the benefits he brought to the community that had fed him. Just as Piṇḍola's later recognition led to the practice of keeping the door open for his return to the feast, the auspicious consequences of feeding an unexpected beggar are said to explain that new practice of pronouncing the blessing earlier in the course of the ceremony. The instruction in section 6 that the blessing should be pronounced before the meal may thus not be entirely unrelated to the instruction to set up a seat for Piṇḍola and keep the gate of the residence open in section 3. The purpose of these instructions would have been to welcome unexpected visitors, typically in the form of a supernatural being.

There is another dimension to this preoccupation with uninvited guests. In section 7, Daoxuan and Daoshi summarize the story of Āṭavaka in the *Mahānirvāṇa sūtra* (T. 12.703a) in connection with the practice of feeding ghosts (40.137a12–15; 173a2–5). After noting that the *Dharmaguptaka vinaya* mentions the shrine for ghosts (T. 22.874c26), a Chinese source (*zhuan* 傳 "tradition") is cited which speaks of the shrine for ghosts, the shrine for the god of the temple building, and the shrine for Piṇḍola, as places where food is offered (40.137a16–17).[32] These three activities, perhaps closely related to each other, appear to reflect an important concern in Chinese monasteries.

The discussion of the blessing pronounced early in the ceremony may suggest the presence and participation of other uninvited guests at the ceremony. Again, offering the meal to them must have been understood to produce merit, as does offering food to ghosts and other beings. As the Buddha receded into a distant past in a foreign land, the meal offered to monks at a lay supporter's residence became a liminal setting marked by the unexpected and often unforeseeable participation of supernatural beings. This shift is further reflected in the evolution of a new kind of miracle story that takes the setting of the ceremonial meal as its background.

Miracle stories in the Fayuan zhulin

The *Fayuan zhulin* 法苑珠林 (T. no. 2122, "Jade Forest in the Dharma Garden"), an encyclopedic anthology of scriptural passages and Chinese Buddhist miracle stories, was compiled at the Ximing monastery (Ximingsi 西明寺) where both Daoxuan and Daoshi were based, and though attributed to Daoshi, Daoxuan appears to have been closely involved in the collection of miracle stories preserved there.[33] A section on "accepting the invitation for a meal" (*shouqing* 受請) appears in the *Fayuan zhulin* (53.607b–617a) and the cult of the Holy Monk Piṇḍola Bhāradvāja occupies a prominent place in that discussion.

The subsection specifically on the topic of the Holy Monk begins with an introductory essay that traces briefly the history of this cult in China, mentioning early miracles and highlighting the Liang Emperor Wudi's 梁武帝 (r. 502–49) devotion to this cult. The Emperor is said to have been unwell, and all the cures he tried failed to have satisfactory effects. The emperor then made a vow and took refuge in the Holy Monk. A seven-day prayer session was arranged at the palace and food was offered to the Buddhas and holy beings. When the seven-day period was about to end, miraculous responses appeared. A powerful heavenly fragrance was perceived, overwhelming the fragrance of the incense burner. Traces of footsteps also filled the hall and the sound of the bells of a walking staff was heard outside the wall. When the seven-day session was over, the emperor's health was restored. Following the *Qing Bintoulu fa*, cited in full, the subsection concludes with a long comment that describes how the worship of Piṇḍola should be conducted (610b26–611a14). In this account of the ceremony the donor offers an invitation to all beings in the Ten Dharma Realms to come to his residence (53.610c1–3).

The section on Accepting the Invitation for a Meal in the *Fayuan zhulin* concludes with a small collection of miracle stories. In the first story excerpted from the *Mingxiang ji* 冥詳記 (Signs from the Unseen Realm), by Wang Yan 王琰 (b. ca. 454, fl. late fifth to early sixth century), He Chong 何充 (296–346), Minister of Works at Lu-Jiang 廬江 and a pious Buddhist, is said to have set up an empty seat in his dining hall.

At one large banquet, attended both by monks and lay people, a monk appeared. Dressed shabbily and behaving like a low-born person, this monk went up to the empty seat set up for Piṇḍola. He sat there silently without saying a word. Everyone in the hall was taken aback, saying that there must be some mistake. He Chong, too, was disturbed and showed his displeasure. The lowly monk took the mid-day meal at the high seat, and after the meal was finished he picked up the bowl and went out of the building. He then said to He Chong, "Your effort at Buddhist cultivation has been in vain," and threw the bowl high up in the sky and left. He Chong and others rushed out to look. The bowl shone brightly and disappeared. Everyone was filled with regret and carried out repentance over many days (616ab; Lu 1967: 577).

This is a story of a meal offered to the Buddhist community by an influential and powerful political figure. Though he is not explicitly named, the lowly monk must have been Piṇḍola. The congregation failed to recognize him even when he took the seat set up for Piṇḍola, until he finished the meal and threw the bowl, an object closely associated with this holy monk.[34]

This story is told against the background of the *Qing Bintoulu jing* story, where it is said that the Elder Jotika, having invited Piṇḍola to a feast, failed to recognize him because of his humble appearance. While in the story in the scripture Piṇḍola was eventually recognized, this Chinese miracle story ends with a failure. The failure proves the effectiveness of the ceremony. He Chong's effort to make merit by hosting a large feast has proved to be in vain, but nevertheless the appearance of Piṇḍola in this unexpected way testifies to the power of the ritual that brought him there to begin with. The original premise of the meritorious nature of offering a meal to monks at a layman's residence still powerfully animates this story, where the Buddha is not mentioned at all, and even the Holy Monk Piṇḍola Bhāradvāja is not explicitly named.

The subject of another story, taken from the *Gaoseng zhuan*, is a monk called Daolin 道琳 (447–519) (53.617a, taken from the *Gaoseng zhuan*, 50. 409a; Lu 1967: 578). This monk was staying at the Quanlin monastery (Quanlinsi 泉林寺) in Fuyang 富陽 District.

Ghosts used to live in the temple, but since Daolin moved there, they had disappeared. At one time, Daolin's disciple Huishao 慧詔 was hit by a collapsing roof which forced his head into his shoulders. When Daolin prayed for him, during the night Huishao saw two foreign monks who pulled his head out. In the morning he was back to normal. Thereupon, Daolin is said to have held a feast for the Holy Monk [Piṇḍola], spreading a new silk cloth on the floor (as instructed by the *Qing bintouluo fa* scripture, 32.784c10). When the feast was over, people saw traces of a human being [on the cloth], over three feet long. Everyone was impressed by this miraculous sign. From that time on people in this area set up a seat for the Holy Monk in each house and offered food to it.

Daolin, who chased the ghosts away from the temple building and caused two foreign monks to appear and perform the cure for his disciple, is said to have been well-versed in the *Nirvāṇa sūtra* and the *Lotus sūtra* and to have recited the *Vimalakīrti nirdeśa*, and it is this reference that explains why Huijiao 慧皎 (497–554) placed this biography in the section on "reciting scriptures." But the conclusion of the story suggests a different reading. Here Daolin is understood to have identified the "foreign monks" who appeared in the dream as the Holy Monk Piṇḍola; he thus offered a feast to him; everyone then recognized the miraculous sign on the white silk spread on the floor. The story of Daolin's magical powers is here turned into one about feasting the Holy Monk; the story is then used to explain the practice in Fuyang District of setting up a seat for Piṇḍola and feeding him at home. Here ideas about offering food to Buddhist monks are stretched awkwardly to provide a familiar context for what must have been a local story about strange foreign monks who appeared in a dream and performed a miraculous cure.

In another story found in a section in the *Fayuan zhulin* concerning "the dharma robe," the subject is a monk called Sengmiao 僧妙 (53.559b–560a).[35] He is said to have become a successful administrator and accumulated a great deal of wealth for the Longhua 龍華 monastery in Jiangling 江陵. Subsequently, a fire destroyed the monastery, and before he died in 464, Sengmiao instructed his disciple Fazong 法宗 to rebuild the lecture hall and the monastic dormitory. Fazong completed the lecture hall right away, but neglected to complete the construction of the dormitory.

In the first month of 467 Fazong is said to have become seriously ill. A monk called Daomeng 道猛 came to see Fazong. A few steps into the monastery quarters, he saw a monk, wearing a peach-colored garment and a yellow coat. As he walked, the monk shouted, "Fazong failed to honour the agreement! He has not built the dormitory and is wasting the funds!" Turning back and seeing Daomeng, the monk seemed embarrassed, covered his head and went into Fazong's room. Daomeng was a frequent visitor to the monastery, but had never seen this monk. He did not want to cause him trouble; he first talked to monk Fachao 法超 and described what he saw. Fachao was initially suspicious, and questioned him on the appearance and the voice of the strange monk. Daomeng gave a detailed answer, and Fachao said, "This monk is Fazong's teacher. It has been several years since he died" (53.559c12–19; 51.811a17–23).

In the evening of the same day a medium became possessed and ordered that Fazong be brought to him right away. When Fazong appeared, the medium reprimanded him gravely, again referring to the construction of the dormitory. The voice and the tone of the medium's speech are said to have been exactly those of Sengmiao. Fazong apologized profusely. In the exchange that followed Sengmiao explained that he had to present a complaint to an official but could not do so because he did not own a monastic *kaṣāya* robe. He requested Fazong to have one made for him. When Fazong asked how he could send the robe, Sengmiao told him to invite monks to a meal and present the robe as a *dakṣiṇā* gift. He would then get it.

Fazong feasted the monks and presented a robe as he was told. Daomeng was present at the meal and again saw Sengmiao outside, leaning against the door of the hall and listening to the recitation of scriptures. When the gifts were distributed, Daomeng saw that Sengmiao was already wearing the robe. Sengmiao came inside the hall; he was about to take his seat right next to Daomeng, when he asked him what his monastic standing (*la* 臘) was. When Daomeng mentioned the year he was ordained, Sengmiao replied that he was ordained only one month later and took the seat right behind him. Sengmiao listened to the scripture in the seat made for him and when the ceremony ended, he disappeared. When Daomeng and Sengmiao talked to each other, those around them heard only Daomeng speak. Initially Fazong's illness was grave, threatening his life. But after the exchange with the medium, he was cured. Yang Chan 羊闡, Governor of Lingling 零陵, was present at the ceremony and was converted; he subsequently carried out many meritorious deeds. The story concludes by noting that in the same year Yang Chan also sponsored a lecture at the monastery, offering a ceremonial meal and other gifts.

In this story the understanding of the ceremonial meal has evolved one step further. The meal is no longer presented primarily as an occasion for merit making, but rather as a liminal setting in which elaborate exchanges between the living and the dead take place. The theme of possession, of a previous abbot speaking through a medium, is superimposed on the story of the ceremonial meal. But we need to note that, even here in this complex story, certain distinctly Buddhist ideas about giving and merit making unexpectedly surface. John Strong translates a story from the Commentary on the *Dhammapada* in which King Bimbisāra is said to have offered first food and drink and then robes to his ancient relatives, who appeared as hungry ghosts. The idea of sending a robe to the deceased abbot through the mechanism of the ceremonial meal thus appears to have had deep roots in the Buddhist tradition.[36] The evolution of stories about supernatural visitors to the meal that I reviewed here may then not have been a uniquely Chinese development; the story also needs to be read as reflecting mainline Buddhist understandings of the ceremony.

Concluding comments

This brief exploration of the Buddhist monastic ceremony of inviting monks for a meal at a lay supporter's residence began with a consideration of stories in the *āgamas* translated into Chinese and moved to a discussion of passages in the *vinayas* of different schools preserved in Chinese translation and their Chinese commentaries. Finally, I discussed this issue in the context of miracle story collections in China. The investigation reveals first of all the remarkable consistency of the basic framework of the ceremony, which is often carefully described in our different types of stories. It also suggests that the understanding of the meaning of the ritual, or of its mechanism of merit making, underwent important changes, at least in emphasis. The evidence reviewed here further suggests that what appears on the surface to be a distinctively Chinese "miracle" story may in fact still be deeply rooted in widely shared Buddhist ideas. What is sometimes called "Sinification" was a complex series of multivalent developments.

To return to the general issues mentioned in the opening section of this chapter, this investigation suggests that as the practice of inviting monks for a meal in a layman's residence became a familiar *topos* in Chinese Buddhist miracle stories, the relationship between the monastic community and lay supporters was imagined more broadly to focus on the presence of visionary holy monks, such as Piṇḍola. As Chinese Buddhist leaders puzzled over the normative monastic rules that were laid out in detail in scriptural sources, they were also working out the relationship between salvation, represented by the advanced Arhat, and the need to provide opportunities for lay devotees to make merit. It is the traces of this complex process that we see in the evolution of narrative literature about monastic practice in China.

Appendix

Parallels Between Key Passages in the *Dharmaguptaka* and *Mahāsāṃghika Vinayas* and the Commentaries by Daoxuan and Daoshi

A. Dharmaguptaka vinaya *(T. 22. 934c–936a)*

(Passages are listed according to the order in which the quotation appears in the *Dharmaguptaka vinaya,* while highlighting the locations where they appear in the commentaries by Daoshi and Daoxuan.)

(a) The opening quotation in section 2 (Daoshi, 171d10–15; Daoxuan, 135c15–20): The Buddha first teaches that monks should wait for the invitation at the place where monks usually take food ("visible place where they take the smaller early morning meal [*xiaoshi* 小食] and the main meal before noon [*dashi* 大食]") and when the donor comes and tells them that the time has arrived they should proceed with the senior monk in front in the way elephants (or geese) travel. The monks are instructed to dress uniformly, exposing their right shoulder and taking off their leather sandals. Monks who have business to attend to may tell the senior monk and go ahead of time (935a19–28).

(b) The opening quotation in section 4 in Daoxuan's commentary (136a14–18; it appears as the second quotation in Daoshi's commentary, immediately following another quotation from the same *vinaya*, Daoshi, 172b2–5): When they arrive at the place where they are fed, they are to sit in an orderly manner one after another following the monastic hierarchy. Having sat down, the senior monks will look at the middle ranking and lower ranking monks so that they will sit properly and cover themselves well. If they are not covered properly, someone will snap his fingers to attract their attention or send a person to tell them. Having sat down, middle ranking monks will look at the senior and lower ranking monks in the same way. Lower ranking monks will do the same (935a28–b6).

(c) Another quotation in section 4 (Daoshi, 172b12–13 and Daoxuan, 136a26–27): The Buddha instructed that monks should not arrive late at the meal and make other monks get up to show respect. Monks may leave open seats for those who have not arrived (953b10–13).

(d) The opening quotation in section 5 (Daoshi, 172a7–8; Daoxuan, 136b10–11): If the donor gives the senior monk fruit, the monk asks whether it has been cleaned. If he receives the answer that it has not, he then has it cleaned (953b14–15).

(e) A quotation that appears in section 7 but not at the beginning of the section (Daoxuan, 137b2–4): Once the purity of the food is established, the senior monk asks to whom the food was offered, whether to the senior monk or to all the monks. If it is offered to the senior monk, he may take it as he wishes. If it is offered to the monks as a group, then it will be distributed equally among all monks. The same procedure is followed for other delicacies (953b15–19).

(f) Another quotation that appears at a yet later point in section 7 (Daoxuan, 137b22–23): If a monk cannot eat his food, the monk sitting next to him may ask for it. If a monk sitting next to him does not want it, the monk himself takes half of the food and gives it away (935b19–20).

(g) Still another quotation that appears in the middle of section 7 (Daoshi, 173a14–15; Daoxuan 137b6–7): Monks used to eat as soon as they received food. In response to criticisms, however, the Buddha instructed that they wait until everyone is served and *saṃprāgata* is pronounced before they begin eating (935b20–24).

(h) Another quotation that appears in section 7 immediately following the quotation (f) above (Daoxuan, 137b23–24): Monks used to scatter uneaten food all over on the ground. The Buddha instructed that discarded food should be gathered around their feet and taken away when the monks leave (935b28–c1).

(i) The second quotation in section 9 immediately following a brief gloss on the term *dakṣiṇā* cited from the *Mahīśāsaka vinaya* (Daoshi, 173b12–15; Daoxuan, 137c10–14; 16–17): After hearing the complaint that monks left silently after the meal without letting the donors know whether they the food was delicious and sufficient, while followers of non-Buddhist teachings all marvel at the gifts and praise the donors, the Buddha instructed the monks to preach a sermon that included a verse promising beneficial consequences of the gift. The Buddha also stipulated that the senior monk should speak these words. If the senior monk cannot, anyone who can should. At the time *dakṣiṇā* is spoken, only the senior monk and four attending monks should stay, the others may go (935c7–26).

(j) In the middle of section 6 in Daoxuan's commentary (136b27–c1) another part of the passage on blessing mentioned above is cited: If the donor wishes to hear a sermon on giving, the monk should praise giving. If he wishes to hear a sermon on the proper conduct of the donor, the monk should praise the proper conduct of the donor. If he wishes to hear a sermon on gods, he should praise the gods. If he wishes to hear about the past ancestors, the monk should praise the ancestors. For the sake of the donor, he should praise giving, the donor, the Buddha, the Dharma, and the Saṃgha (935c26–936a1).

B. Mahāsaṃghika vinaya *(T. 22.499c28–501c3)*

(aa) The third quotation in section 1 in Daoxuan's s commentary (135b2–7, in Daoshi's commentary the quotation appears at a later point in the same section, 171c6–10): When someone invites monks to a meal, the senior monk should not accept it right away. They should ask for the person's name and address. Because the invitation may be a joke on the monks, they should not immediately accept the invitation. If someone is acquainted with the man or woman, they can accept the invitation. Having accepted, they should not immediately go with the person. Early the next morning, monks should send a laborer, or a tenant, or a novice monk to make sure that everything is in order. Sometimes unexpected difficulties, such as a visit of a local government official, a flood, a fire, a theft, a birth of a new child, or a death occur, and the family cannot prepare the meal. In such cases monks prepare their own meal. The messenger asks the donor whether the meal is ready or not. If the donor asks who the messenger is or which meal he is talking about, then he realizes that the invitation was a fake. If there is food at the monastery, then an ordinary meal should be prepared there. If there is no food, then it should be declared that they have been duped, and each monk should go out and beg for food. If the donor says that the meal will be prepared for the honored guests properly, then the senior monk should be informed of the time of the meal (500a10–21).

(bb) As the second quotation in section 5, Daoshi, 172c8–10, Daoxuan, 136b11–13): The senior monk should make sure that both the monks who are looking after the sick and the sick monks are given food; the donor is to be persuaded not to begrudge the food for this and the food will be brought to them either before or after the ceremonial meal (500a29–b3).

(cc) Toward the end of section 6 in Daoshi's commentary (172d1–3; somewhere in the middle of the same section in Daoxuan's commentary, 136c1): "the senior monk should be informed beforehand for what purpose the meal is given, and bless the meal accordingly" (500b3–4).

(dd) As a part of a set of quotations on the same topic in the middle of section 7 (abbreviated in Daoshi, 173a14; Daoxuan, 137b7): "The senior monk should not eat the food as soon as it is given to him. He should wait until the food is served to all, pronounce the *samprāgata*, and then eat" (500b8–9).

(ee) As the first quotation in section 8 (Daoshi, 173b6–8, Daoxuan, 137c4–6): The senior monk should eat slowly. He should not eat quickly and then watch as younger monks scramble and fail to eat sufficiently. He should look over others as they eat. Do not finish quickly and leave before others. Wait until water is brought out. After the blessing is pronounced, monks leave (500b9–12).

(ff) Abbreviated in the middle of section 6 in Daoxuan, 136c7–15: Here the *Mahāsamghika vinaya* instructs not to use one set of verses as a blessing but to use a different set of verses on each of the different occasions, from benefiting the dead, through birth of a new child, completion of a new building, setting out of a traveling merchant, and taking of a wife, to when someone who has left the householder's life makes a gift. Having summarized this briefly in the corresponding section of his description, Daoxuan refers the reader for details to this passage in the *vinaya* (500b12–501c2).

Notes

1 Scriptures often note that the Buddha and his monks went into the city at the appropriate time to beg for food. For example, in the *Chang ahan jing*, T. 1.70a22; *Bieyi za ahan jing*, T. 2.380b3; 385b5–6; *Zengyi ahan jing*, T. 2.772a25. The practice is attributed to the Buddha's disciples in the *Mahāsamghika vinaya*, T. 22.233c3–4, 12–13; 21–22; 234a3–4; 12–13. The meal that the Buddha and his disciples are said to have taken at a lay supporter's residence may have evolved from this general practice, but is generally marked as a distinct ceremony. The account of such meals in the scriptural sources, though attributed to the Buddha, describes a monastic practice that may well have developed later. For a broader discussion of related practices in Dunhuang, see Hao 1998: 332–366. A brief reference to Daoxuan's discussion under consideration here appears on p. 356.

2 Daoxuan uses a rather unusual phrase *jiqing* 計請 ("arranging the invitation [for a meal]") in the heading of this section. The more familiar term referring to the practice he discusses in the chapter is *shouqing* ("accepting the invitation"). This term *shouqing* appears frequently in the Chinese translations of scriptures, particularly in the *āgamas* and the *vinayas*; the Buddha and sometimes his senior disciples accept an invitation from a lay person in silence.

3 In an important article on the reception of the bodhisattva precepts in China during the six dynasties period, Funayama Tōru (1995: 52–65) has emphasized the importance of *zhai* 齋 as the place of interaction between monks and laity and briefly traced its early evolution in China.

4 Different versions of the story are found in *Chang ahan jing* (*Youxing jing* 遊行經), T. 1.13b17–14c10; *Zengyi ahan jing*, T. 2.596a8–c14; *Dīghanikāya* (*Mahāparinibbāna suttanta*), ii, 95–98, [Rhys Davids 1899: I, 101–105]; *Wufenlü* 五分律, T. 22. 135b12–136a18; *Sifenlü*, T. 22.855c14–856c24; 1 *Mahāvagga*, VI, 30 (Horner 1949–1966: IV, 315–318. Some versions of the story lack the reference to the gift of the garden:

Fo panniyuan jing 佛般泥洹經, T. 1.163b27–164b24; *Panniyuan jing* 般泥洹經, T. 1.178c22–179b18; *Genben shuoyiqieyoubu pinaye zashi* 根本說一切有部毘奈耶雜事, T. 24.385c25–387a11. *Za ahan jing*, T. 2.174a2–b14 may also be a version of the same story.

5 In the *Sifenlü* the story of King Bimbisāra's gift of the bamboo garden (*Veluvana-kalandakanivāpa*) and the story of Anāthapiṇḍata's gift of the Jetavana are told in a very similar way to that of Ambapālī's gift of the mango garden (T. 22.936c; 941b). When King Bimbisāra and Anāthapiṇḍata offered the bamboo garden and the Jetavana to the Buddha, the Buddha is again said to have instructed them in virtually the same words to make the gift to the Buddha and the Saṃgha of the Four Directions. When the gift was made, the Buddha is then said to have uttered the same set of verses, promising a good rebirth.

6 In the *Zengyi ahan jing* version of the story the Buddha is said first to have warned his monks that a woman was coming and instructed them not to give rise to deluded thoughts (2.596a15). The Licchavis are said to have been decked out like kings.

7 *Zengyi ahan jing*, T. 2.773c–775b. Other versions are found in *Sarvāstivāda vinaya*, T. 23.464; *Mūlasarvāstivāda nidānamātṛka*, T. 24.444c–445c; Xuanzang 玄奘, *Datang xiyuji* 大唐西域記, T. 51.921a (Ji 1990: 722).

8 A story of King Ajātaśatru arriving at Śrīgupta's house on an elephant appears at this point in the *Zengyi ahan jing* version. The king had heard that the Tathāgata was about to be harmed by the large fire pit and poisoned food and was greatly distressed. But Prince Jīvaka assured him that the Buddha was not to be harmed, and told the king to go and observe the miracles. When the king entered Śrīgupta's house a large crowd gathered outside the gate. There the king saw the miracle of lotus flowers as large as a chariot's wheel and was delighted. When the king took a seat on one side of the Buddha, he is said to have observed the light coming out of the Buddha's mouth, and seeing the extraordinary color of the Buddha all over his body, was filled with uncontrollable joy. Again, as in the story of Ambapālī, the luminous appearance of the Buddha is noted carefully in this story of the meal offered to the Buddha.

9 The explanation of *denggong* (*saṃprāgatam*, described carefully by Yijing 義淨 [635–713], T. 54.209c) takes a prominent place in the versions of the story of Śrīgupta in the *Sarvāstivāda vinaya* (T. 23.464) and the *Mūlasarvāstivāda nidānamātṛka* (T. 24.444c–445c). In the *Sarvāstivāda vinaya* version this formula is called the spell (*zhouyuan*, 23.464c10–14) that the Buddha pronounces, in which the poison in the food is identified with the three poisons of desire, anger, and ignorance. The Buddha's teaching removes all these poisons. In the *Mūlasarvāstivāda nidānamātṛka* version Śrīgupta is a brother-in-law of Jyoṣtika, a pious Buddhist. Jyoṣtika first invited the heretical teacher Purāṇa [Kāśyapa] and his disciples. At Jyoṣtika's residence Purāṇa revealed his lack of omni-science. Then comes the story of Śrīgupta's invitation to the Buddha. Śrīgupta is first converted by the miracle of lotus flowers and his faith deepened when he saw how the Buddha removed the poison by having the *saṃprāgatam* pronounced.

10 In a carefully nuanced conclusion to this story of conversion, the Buddha reprimanded Śrīgupta when he said that he would no longer feast the followers of non-Buddhist teach-ers at his residence. Reminding him of the incalculable merits he would acquire by feed-ing these teachers, the Buddha instructed Śrīgupta only to declare himself to be a disciple of Śākyamuni when asked by students of non-Buddhist learnings (775b3–18).

11 In the *Zengyi ahan jing* the verse appears in the story of Sīvala as the conclusion of the meal at the residence of Elder Yueguang 月光 ("Moonlight") after the Buddha contradicted Nirgrantha Jñātaputra's prediction on the frightful consequences the new-born child was said to bring about (684a); at King Bimbisāra's palace (694c); in the meal Satyaka Nirgranthaputra is said to have arranged with the youths of Vaiśali (717a, ref., *Za ahan jing*, T. 2.37a; the parallel story of Saccaka in *Madhyama Nikāya* (MN) 35 lacks the verse in question). The verse also appears in the *Bieyi za ahan jing* story of meal presented by Brahman Ugrataśarīra (T. 2.465ab; ref., A. VII. 44 and T. 2.24b

where the verse does not appear). In the *Zhong ahan jing*, the verse appears to conclude the account of the meal Brahmāyu presented to the Buddha and his monks (T. 2.689c, ref., MN, 91: *Brahmāyu sutta*, again no verse). The Pāli version of the verse is found in Selasutta in *Sutta Nipāta* (*Mahāvagga*, 7: p. 111; parallel in *Vinaya Piṭaka*, I, 246) again as a verse uttered at conclusion of a meal. Notable parallels to these lines also appear in non-Buddhist sources: along with others similar to them in a more elaborate passage in the *Bhagavad gītā*, Chapter X. See also Jain *Sūtragṛtāṅga* (Jacobi 1884: 1, 287).

12 The fire pit that plays a central role in the story of Śrīgupta may also suggest a connection with Brahmanical sacrifice. The word *si* that appears in the request that the non-Buddhist teachers present to Śrīgupta, describing the invitation take a meal at his residence as a way of "honoring" them is used in the sense of offering Brahmanical sacrifice in the story of Ugrataśarīra (2.774a5 and 2.464b27).

13 Though the headings for each of these sections are given slightly differently in the two commentaries, both identify the ten stages of the ceremony as (1) extending and receiving the invitation, (2) traveling to the residence to which they are invited, (3) what needs to be done after monks arrive at the invited residence, (4) taking a seat and behaving properly as guests, (5) confirming the purity of food, (6) presenting incense and uttering blessing, (7) receiving food, (8) finishing eating, (9) gifts, and (10) leaving the residence (T. 40.135ab; XZJ 70.171b). The section on "receiving invitation" in the *Fayuan zhulin* (T. 53.607b–617a) is organized around nine sections: (1) introduction, (2) inviting monks, (3) the Holy Monk, (4) offering food (to other sentient beings), (5) time of the meal, (6) instruction on the proper way of taking the meal, (7) finishing the meal, (8) blessing, and (9) the merit of giving. A section on miracle stories is then appended. Though the content of some of these sections parallels closely what can be found in the *vinaya* commentaries, this work often cites passages from different sources.

14 In section 9 the brief passage from the *Mahīśāsaka vinaya* simply glosses the term *dakṣiṇā* and again a longer quotation from the *Dharmaguptaka vinaya* is introduced to explain the practice. Section 3 begins with a quotation from the *Sarvāstivāda vinaya*; section 7 and 8 with a quotation from the *Mahāsaṃghika vinaya*; and section 10 with a quotation from the *Mahīśāsaka vinaya*.

15 The *Song gaoseng zhuan* 宋高僧傳 biography of Daoshi mentions a work called "*Sifen taoyao* 四分討要," or "Essentials of the Four-part *vinaya* Discussed," in five fascicles (T. 50.726c28–9).

16 As in Daoshi's commentary, in section 9 a short gloss on the term *dakṣiṇā* from the *Mahīśāsaka vinaya* is followed by a longer quotation from the *Dharmaguptaka vinaya*.

17 Passages marked as a, b, and d in the Appendix below appear in sections 2, 4, and 5 in Daoxuan's commentary; quotations a and b in sections 2 and 4 in Daoshi's. The quotations in section 9 may have been presented as the opening quotation at an earlier stage of the evolution of this commentary.

18 For example, section 1 of Daoshi's commentary begins with a brief statement cited from a different part of the *Dharmaguptaka vinaya* that mentions separate or selective invitation as one of the two types of invitation (171b15; T. 22.790a19; ref., 657a20). This same discussion also appears in Daoxuan's commentary, but there it is placed somewhat later in the same section; Daoxuan begins the substantive part of his discussion in section 1 with a long quotation from the *Mahāsaṃghika vinaya* (135b2–7) as seen below.

19 In section 1 Daoxuan introduces a long quotation from the *Mahāsaṃghika vinaya* immediately following brief quotations introducing and glossing the title of the monastic office of *weina* or *karmadāna* (T. 40.135b). Daoxuan also quotes a long section from this passage in section 6 (passage ff).

20 A similar passage on the proper way of inviting monks appears in the *Wufenlü*, T. 22.179. One sentence is quoted from this passage in section 10 of the two commentaries (22.179b27 in 40.138a and 173c9).

21 Or perhaps more appropriately the situation of the monastic community centuries after the time of the Buddha is reflected in the *vinaya* passages cited in the commentaries.

22 A helpful summary of the sources on the cult of arhats in China is found in Sharf 2002: 312, n. 93. On the cult of arhats in the Theravāda tradition see Strong 1992: 236–252.

23 Gathering for a ceremonial meal for the purpose of feeding the hungry ghost is also mentioned in the *Mahāsaṃghika vinaya* (T. 22. 500a5). My suggestion is that this recognized theme in the discussion of the ceremony in Indian sources became more prominent in Chinese discussions and underwent further evolution.

24 Both Daoxuan and Daoshi mention the five-fascicle work attributed to the Liang emperor Wudi (T. 40.135c23–4; XZJ 70.172a2) without citing directly from it. Yuanzhao 元照 (1048–1111) notes in his secondary commentary on Daoxuan's *vinaya* commentary that this work by Emperor Wu was already lost by his time (*Sifenlü xingshichao zichiji* 四分律行事鈔資持記, T. 40.401a10). A brief account of the emperor's worship of Piṇḍola and the miracles that occurred in response is found in the *Fayuan zhulin*, T. 53.609c. This passage may have been based on the larger work attributed to Emperor Wudi.

25 Daoshi's discussion in the *vinaya* commentary is more extensive and this discussion appears to have been expanded in the corresponding section of the *Fayuan zhulin*, where the topic of setting up a seat for Piṇḍola is highlighted in a separate subsection called "The Holy Monk" (T. 53.609c–611a).

26 A story about Mahākāśyapa wearing coarse clothes and being refused admittance to a meal offered Anāthapiṇḍada is told in the *Mūlasarvāstivāda vinaya*. See Strong 1992: 67–68.

27 The story of Piṇḍola in the *Sarvāstivāda vinaya* is found in T. 23.268c–269a. In another passage Dao'an's biography tells the story of a strange foreign monk who came to the monastery and instructed Dao'an to bathe the Holy Monk (*shengseng* 神僧) (353c). Though the passage does not explicitly name the Holy Monk as well as the strange monk who appeared at Dao'an's monastery, both appear to represent Piṇḍola. The reference to Huiyuan and the arrival of the *Sarvāstivāda vinaya* suggests that Dao'an's association with Piṇḍola Bhāradvāja may have developed after Dao'an's death. A reference to Huiyuan's role in the translation of this *vinaya* appears in the *Gaoseng zhuan* biography of this monk (50.360a; ref., Zürcher 2007: 229 and 248; further details on the translation of this *vinaya*, p. 409, note 89). The translation began in 404. A later source, *Fozu lidai tongzai* 佛祖歷代通載, cites this passage from Dao'an's biography and notes that the practice of presenting offerings to Piṇḍola began with Dao'an (T. 49.524b7–8).

28 See Zürcher 2007: 188–189 and 389, n. 50 and Satō 1986: 42–52.

29 In the *Mūlasarvāstivāda vinaya* the story of Śrīgupta is preceded by one of the failed ceremonial meal offered by Jyotiṣka, the brother of Śrīgupta's wife, to the non-Buddhist teacher Purāṇa and his disciples. In the course of the meal Purāṇa's lack of omniscience is exposed, and this teacher favoured by Śrīgupta utters a verse that nullifies the merits that were to be made by the offering of this meal (T. 24.444a). By focusing on the deliberate act of uttering this verse, this story highlights the importance of the verse conferring merits that is pronounce after the meal under normal circumstances.

30 A blessing is also mentioned in the section on gifts (*dakṣiṇā*) offered at the conclusion of the meal (sections 8 and 9) in both their commentaries. Thus a degree of ambiguity remains in their commentaries.

31 In section 9 of his commentary (on *dakṣiṇā*) Daoshi cites the same verse, while in the corresponding passage Daoxuan mentions the verse without reproducing it (137c13). This verse also appears elsewhere in the *Dharmaguptaka vinaya* in the story of the meal the Buddha took after enlightenment (782a8–9). Having taken the food offered by two merchants in the bowl made out of the four bowls presented by the Four Heavenly Kings, the Buddha is said to have uttered the blessing (*zhouyuan*) in the form of this verse. The quotation from the *Dharmaguptaka vinaya* that appears at the beginning

of the discussion of the blessing in sections 6 in the commentaries by Daoxuan and Daoshi appears to have been taken from this same passage.

In section 6 of his commentary Daoxuan cites, as noted above, two other passages, one from the *Dharmagupta vinaya* and the other from the *Mahāsaṃghika vinaya*. These passages describe different verses of blessings to be given under specific circumstances.

32 Although the commentaries by Daoxuan and Daoshi present these passages as a part of the ceremony that takes place at a lay supporter's residence, the practices attributed to this Chinese source appear to have taken place at the monastery.

33 The contents of Daoxuan's miracle story collection *Ji shenzhou sanbao gantong lu* (T. 2106) parallel the corresponding part of the *Fayuan zhulin* miracle story collection.

34 The monk's statement to He Chong, "Your effort at Buddhist cultivation has been in vain," may be read as another instance of the negative blessing, similar to the one noted above that appears in the story of Jyotiṣka (note 28).

35 This story is attributed to "*Tang gaoseng zhuan* 唐高僧傳" (53.560a23), but does not appear in the *Xu gaoseng zhuan* 續高僧傳. A version of the story appears in *Shimen zijing lu* 釋門自鏡錄 by the Tang monk Huaixin 懷信, T. 51.811ab, where its source is given as *Mingxiang ji*.

36 Strong 2000: 79–80. Complex issues regarding transferring merit and sending gifts to deceased beings are discussed in Schmithausen 1986: 210–216.

2 Monastic spaces and sacred traces
Facets of Chinese Buddhist monastic records

James Robson

All sacred things must have their place ...

Lévi-Strauss, The Savage Mind 1966

Introduction: representing Chinese monasteries

Geomancy (*fengshui*) was another form of nonprofit divination carried on by men as eminent as the Venerable Hsü-yün [Xuyun]. On one occasion he told a group of monks who were planning to erect a temple on Chung-nan Shan: "To the North it faces the White Tiger and the Evening Star. There is no mountain behind it to lean on. It does not seem to me a good place." His view was confirmed when the temple failed.[1]

After relating this story, Holmes Welch proceeded to distance these concerns for the geomantic siting of a monastery from "real" Buddhism by interpreting them as heretical.[2] Some contemporary scholars might agree with Welch's modernist suspicion, but I would like to direct our suspicion in the other direction. Were Buddhist ideas about sacred space and the proper siting of Buddhist monasteries merely the result of superstitious "popular" beliefs infecting a rational Buddhist tradition, or have prescriptive ideas about what Buddhism *should be* interfered with our ability to perceive and represent Buddhism as it developed on the ground in medieval China? In order to resolve the tension set up by this opening passage and Welch's response, it is necessary to interrogate both the historical record for Buddhist concerns about the location of monasteries and the characterization of those concerns as inimical to Buddhism. Welch, to be sure, was not alone in downplaying or neglecting the importance of spatial issues in the study of monasteries. Indeed, his remarks are paradigmatic of the roads taken and not taken in the study of Chinese Buddhist monasteries. Therefore, this chapter—which resonates well with some of the issues raised in Eugene Wang's chapter—is focused on the characteristics and representations of Chinese Buddhist monasteries as sacred sites, rather than on the role of monasticism and the histories of monks, topics which are well represented in other chapters in this volume.

There are, of course, a variety of potential approaches to the study of monasteries, but one initial possibility is to proceed along two related axes: one that is concerned with the people and the regulation of their activities within the monastery; and one that deals with the site and the characteristics of the natural and built environment.[3] That is to say, there is as much a need for particular studies of monasteries as there is for the more general study of monasticism. While those two topics are not mutually exclusive, indeed the ultimate goal should be the convergence of these two lines of inquiry, they do not necessarily entail each other either. We need not enter into a long discussion of the potential relationships between those two enterprises here, though we can make the preliminary observation that these topics have generally been dominated by a focus on people over places.

Discussions of monasteries, for example, quickly depart from the actual monastery—the site or place itself—as attention turns quickly to its offices, regulations, and religious practices.[4] As important as those topics have been to forming (and reforming) our understanding of Chinese monastic institutions, we should ask the following questions: In what ways were monasteries perceived to be meaningful? How were they represented in contemporary sources? Although I focus my attention on how monasteries are depicted in local records, that is not to say that I intend to write a history of Chinese monasteries that is devoid of monks; it is merely to suggest that there is a different story about those monasteries that has yet to be adequately told.[5] Without giving away too much of that story at the outset, some of the underrepresented characteristics of monasteries found in contemporary local sources include a focus on the setting (natural landscape), the structure (architectural elements), the contents (relics, statuary, paintings, powerful deities), and the history (eminent monks associated with the site, key political recognition) of those sites. Before settling into a more detailed consideration of how Chinese Buddhist monastic records represented (and at times imagined) those sites, however, let me first set the context with some general remarks that will help to situate this study within the body of accumulated scholarship on Chinese monasteries.

Scholars of Chinese Buddhist history can attest that the walls of monasteries tended to be rather high, and the texts at our disposal rarely afford an unimpeded look inside their gates. Where does present scholarship on this topic now stand? Under the increasing weight of foundational studies on Chinese monastic institutions and monasticism it is now rare, except perhaps in general works where the influence of those studies has yet to be fully realized, to view Buddhist monasteries simply as sites where cenobites pursued the contemplative life.[6] It has been acknowledged for some time now—at least since the publication of Jacques Gernet's seminal study of the economic aspects of Buddhism in 1956 and the almost contemporary studies of Denis Twitchett and Yang Lien-sheng—that Chinese Buddhist monasteries, in addition to being places for traditional Buddhist contemplative practices, also served (like their European counterparts) as granaries, mills, treasuries, orphanages, pawnbrokers, land stewards, auction houses, and sites of marketplaces and community festivals.[7] Monasteries were, in other words, precisely where the linkage between the religious and the commercial was concretely realized.[8]

In addition to their economic roles, Buddhist monasteries were important centers for translation, scholasticism, and education.[9] By the Tang dynasty the Buddhist saṃgha was a well educated "secondary elite" and some Buddhist monasteries served as "community schools" that operated beneath the radar of the Confucian education system.[10] This research has been important for considering the role of Buddhist monasteries in Chinese society because it demonstrated that the doors to Chinese monasteries were open to aspiring elites who took up residence and were educated in a broad curriculum not limited to Buddhism, but also based on Confucian and secular texts. Buddhist monasteries became a conduit for students of humble social background to receive an "elite" education in preparation for the official examinations.[11] Recent research has shed much light on the complex internal workings of (primarily Chan) Buddhist monasteries in China through the detailed consideration of monastic regulations.[12] Based on this cumulative scholarship it is now clear that Chinese Buddhist monasteries were not monolithic entities or isolated institutions (despite the root meaning of the term monastery which means "alone"), but were securely plugged into a variety of economic, political, and social contexts.[13] After considering the broad range of material covered in these studies we are forced to return to the basic question that I sidestepped at the outset of this chapter: What precisely are we talking about when we use the term "monastery" in the Chinese Buddhist context? I think it is safe to say that it is often unclear what the referent actually is, despite the use of the term "monastery" as a general term for what is conceived to be the same type of entity.

If we begin our inquiries with the term "monastery" itself, then the first problem of interpretation is terminological. The word "monastery" is often used interchangeably with "temple" as catch-all terms for translating a variety of institutional arrangements found on the Chinese religious landscape.[14] Although the primary referent today is, of course, the term *si* 寺, it was not the only one used to refer to the residences of monks.[15] The term *si* is found in Buddhist texts from the third century, but surprisingly it is difficult to arrive at a succinct definition of that term from Chinese sources themselves and it is unclear when it began to be used as a common reference to monasteries. There has been much debate over the origin of the term *si*, which Maspero traced back to the almost homophonous term *ci* 祠, used to designate cultic centers. Others have traced it to a Chinese official term used for a government office *si* 司, and the Department of Foreign Relations (Honglu si 鴻臚寺), where the newly arriving foreign monks were housed.[16]

The most explicit definition of *si* that I am aware of comes from a Song dynasty commentator who cites a second-century lexical work. In the *Seng shilue* 僧史略 (Historical Digest of the Buddhist Order), Zanning 贊寧 (919–1001) says that according to the *Shiming* 釋名 (Explanation of Names),

> *si* 寺 originally designated the name of a government office (*si* 司). When monks coming from the West arrived [in China] they temporarily resided within government offices. In order to not forget their original connection to a government office, when they moved to separate institutions they continued to use the term *si* 寺 [to refer to their new residence]. This is the origin of the name used for Buddhist monasteries (*sengsi* 僧寺).[17]

Other terms used in the context of temples and monasteries, such as *dian* 殿, *tang* 堂, and *yuan* 院, also derived from terms used for administrative offices.[18] The initial connection between Buddhist monasteries and imperial administrative offices was retained in more than just name. Indeed, throughout later Chinese history, as Eugene Wang also notes in his chapter, it became common for officials or elites to donate their private palatial residences in order to have them converted into monasteries.[19] It is therefore not surprising that architectural historians have commented on how Chinese Buddhist monasteries were impacted by the secular tradition of palatial architecture and bear less resemblance to their Indian antecedents.[20]

The question of what constituted a Buddhist monastery attains a further level of complexity when different types of institutions are taken into account. Jacques Gernet noted that up until about the Sui dynasty all Buddhist establishments in China, regardless of size, were designated as monasteries.[21] The problem was not only one of scale, but also of type or function. We regularly encounter terms such as *sisha* 寺刹, *yuan* 院, *jingcha* 淨刹, *jingshe* 精舍, *fotang* 佛堂, *qielan* 伽藍, *guansi* 官寺, *lanruo* 蘭若, and the list could go on.[22] In writing about contemporary Chinese monasteries, Holmes Welch expressed a similar caution about subsuming all those various entities under the term monastery and noted that "a fact that should never be lost sight of in discussing Chinese Buddhism is that the character of monasteries varied."[23] While I do not intend to analyze and evaluate the similarities and differences between all these types of institutions, I merely raise the issue here to suggest that it may be time to start thinking about how we might adopt a more precise terminology in order to distinguish between these different entities and ultimately arrive at a better understanding of their function in the Chinese religious context.[24]

Some attention has already been focused on the difference between "public" and "private" monasteries or what John Jorgensen has referred to as "proletariat" and "elite" institutions.[25] "Private monasteries" tended to be small and were characterized by the fact that the abbacy was passed down within the teaching line of the ordination disciples of the abbot. "Public monasteries," on the other hand, tended to be huge bureaucratic institutions whose abbacies were open to all officially ordained clergy. T. Griffith Foulk has pointed out, however, that the "public"/ "private" distinction between monasteries did not begin until the Song dynasty, but that there may be a similar precedent that existed in the Tang with "large Buddhist monasteries that were registered with the government and smaller, privately maintained monasteries and chapels that escaped official notice."[26] Antonino Forte and Tsukamoto Zenryū studied the special status held by a category of "officially established monasteries" (*guanli si* 官立寺) or "State Monasteries."[27] Evidence of this type of diversity prompted Gernet to conclude that

one of the most obvious features of the imprint of religion on Chinese soil is the diversity: a salutary caution against the uniform and schematic view suggested by the official statistics concerning the numbers of monasteries and monks. The great monastery that permanently houses dozens of monks and the little village chapel or mountain hermitage inhabited by one or two have little in common.[28]

Given the nascent state of scholarship on the precise characteristics of Chinese Buddhist monasteries we would do well at this stage to defer making claims of a general nature in order to linger on particularities. Let us, therefore, set aside the elusive question of what a monastery was in the medieval Chinese context, since the term itself resists a unitary definition. Chinese Buddhist monasteries varied in size, character and function in different places and at different times.

My principal concern in this study of Chinese monasteries is with representations: both in primary sources and in secondary scholarship. Indeed, my initial thinking on this topic was spurred on while trying to account for the disjunctions between those two representations. In general studies of monasteries there has been a perduring tendency to discuss them as mere "containers" for the actions of a religious community.[29] The entries on "Monasticism" in various encyclopedias and reference works (such as the *Encyclopedia of Religion*) focus on monasteries only insofar as they were sites where contemplatives lived in isolation from the rest of society, studied, and participated in religious rites.[30] Nothing, however, is generally mentioned about the monasteries, their physical settings, or their particular institutional histories. This Aristotelian "container model" has been critiqued by philosophers of "place" and cultural geographers. Recently some scholars of medieval European monasticism have also begun to challenge the applicability of that model. The rationale for a critique of the "container model" is equally applicable to the study of Chinese monasteries, yet in both cases we should clarify a possible misunderstanding of what this critique implies. From a certain perspective monasteries can be considered as "containers" (of images, reliquaries, and stūpas), but that usage is rather different than what is implied in the critique discussed here.[31] The notion of "container" critiqued by historians of European monasteries referred explicitly to an excessive focus on the activities of religious actors living within monasteries to the exclusion of the monasteries themselves. Yet, when monasteries are perceived as housing sacred objects, often perceived to be the living presence of what they are a substitute for, then if they did function like containers we would have to acknowledge that they were nonetheless "special containers" that are worthy of study in their own right.[32] In either case, the focus returns to the setting and structure and not merely to the actions of the people inside.

One exciting area of research within the field of European monasticism, which exemplifies this shift in focus, is the study of particular monasteries and how they were established as sacred sites (both in material form as well as in textual representation).[33] That work has emphasized that monasteries were not just places for the gathering of the community, which was an influential Augustinian understanding that (at least in part) conditioned the approach to medieval materials.[34] Rather, monasteries were in themselves constituted as sacred spaces and foundation legends written about those sites served a "legitimating, glorifying—even sanctifying—[function] for the present."[35] Our field should at least be aware of those developments, if not for the very reason that we have already seen in the case of "relics" and "pilgrimage," for example, that useful insights can come out of a cross-fertilization between disciplines. One significant gap that remains in our understanding of Chinese Buddhist monasteries is also a precise consideration of the ways that monasteries are represented in historical texts as sanctified institutions or numinous sites.

The sacred nature of Chinese Buddhist monasteries

Shifting our gaze from prescriptive texts, monastic regulations, and official sources to sources such as monastic foundation legends, mountain monographs, travel records, inscriptions, and local gazetteers (sources that have until quite recently suffered scholarly neglect) reveals different facets of Chinese monasteries.[36] It would be desirable to survey a wide range of sources for different sites, but that would entail a larger project than is possible here. I will therefore initiate this discussion with a few general remarks about local historical records and then move to descriptions of some of the monasteries in those sources.

Chinese local history writing tends to maintain a balanced focus on "people" and "places."[37] Recent research on the advent of local history writing in China by Andrew Chittick discusses the changing meanings associated with the component parts of the binome *fengsu* 風俗. By the time Ying Shao 應劭 (ca. 140–ca. 206) wrote the *Fengsu tongyi* 風俗通義 (The Comprehensive Meaning of Customs) the term "feng" referred to "place," and "su" referred to "people."

> The idea of *fengsu* had by this time clearly been divided into two parts: *feng*, the local environment, the natural aura or *qi* of a place; and *su*, the customs and habits of the people who live there. The latter was human-centered, while the former was place-centered. In other words, customs were conceived of having two loci: person and places. In response to this conception, local history writing evolved two major organizational formats for dealing with narrative materials: biographies of individual men, and locality stories about particular places.[38]

Local histories sought to express a rich sense of local or regional culture, a "pride of place," and at the same time evince a keen interest in topomancy or geomancy (*fengshui* 風水). The result of that combination was a Chinese orientation to place that can be expressed with the term "geopiety," a term that was first used by J.K. Wright "to denote the sense of thoughtful piety aroused by human awareness of the natural world and geographical space."[39] That Buddhist monastic sites themselves were perceived as occupying efficacious terrains should not, however, be surprising to us given the traditional Chinese concern for the siting of buildings according to geomantic principles, whereby the fortunes of a site were thought to be dependent on how well the structure was adapted to local influences.[40] The unique nature of a locale, including the siting of buildings such as monasteries and pagodas, was determined in part by the morphology of the landscape and the nodes along which the *qi* of a place was perceived to flow or accumulate. In such places, Feuchtwang writes, "spirituality is more 'alert,' saturated, as it were, quickened . . . Everything in the landscape, down to the slightest hollow in the ground, is through its own particular disposition endowed with a particular, ever-renewed propensity one should rely on and exploit."[41] Wheatley has also commented that, "these local influences [*xingshi* 形勢], the dynamic powers of the *genius loci*, were modified from place to place by the morphology of terrain and from hour to hour by the dispositions and conjunctions of heavenly bodies."[42] Although there is little discussion of these factors in studies of pre-modern monasteries, we need to understand the Buddhists took those concerns seriously. The hesitant way that this topic has begun to enter into the discourse on Buddhist monasteries seems to stem from the fact that geomantic divination was seen to run counter to the Buddhist philosophical tradition. Welch, as we mentioned at the outset of this chapter, discussed Buddhist geomancy (however reluctantly) in a section dedicated to heretical practices, despite at the same time noting the importance of geomancy in the foundation and siting of modern Buddhist monasteries.[43] The location of a monastery was thought to have a direct connection not only to the individual practices of the monks, but also to the overall success or failure of the monastery. Although the explicit connection between topomancy and the siting of Buddhist monasteries in medieval China is an interesting topic awaiting further research, it is safe to say that the maintenance of a balanced focus on a concern for "place" and "people" reflected in native local histories is also characteristic of many Chinese Buddhist monastic records.[44] Rarely, however, is that dual focus reflected in scholarship on Chinese monasteries, which tends to tip the balance in favor of the latter over the former. What happens to our view of Chinese monasteries when that balance is restored?

Monastic records vary greatly in their style, content, and reason for composition. Certain monastic records, such as dedicatory inscriptions or encomiums written after renovations, overflow with hyperbolic praise for the glories of a particular monastery.[45] Commissioned works were no doubt related in part (and in some cases explicitly) to attempts to textually support the merit that accrues to the donor who financed the project, though there was some controversy over the role of merit.[46]

In other types of monastic records, however, the characteristics of the "place" figure in a rather different way. While the main contours of the differences between records for urban monasteries and those for rural or mountain monasteries await further study, it is safe to say that historical records for many monasteries begin with descriptions detailing the types of trees, plants, topography, and other noteworthy (or anomalous) natural features of the monastic setting.[47] Although there is a temptation to proceed quickly through that introductory material to get to data that is relevant to particular historical concerns, it is important to pause and take those passages seriously since they may tell us something relevant about how those monastic settings were perceived in medieval China.[48] Indeed, what is absent in those sources, namely details of religious practice, speaks loudly to what was considered important in the representation of monasteries. Timothy Brook has stated the case well for later monastic gazetteers, when he notes that "curiously perhaps, material pertaining to strictly religious matters is more the exception than the rule. These books attend to monasteries less as centers of religious practice than as cultural sites favored by devotees of Buddhism, landscape and local history."[49] Reflection on the material found in those sources suggests that in many cases the choice of an appropriate site involved more than just practical details, such as sufficient land and water. Some attention has already been given to this topic by those who have studied Chinese mountain monographs, which describe the settings where religious institutions were established, and I hope to contribute to that ongoing research by extending it to include a consideration of the setting and structure of Buddhist monasteries within those hallowed terrains. It should be noted, however, that Gregory Schopen has shown that this focus on the setting of a monastery is not something particular to China—as some might want to argue based on native theories of *fengshui*—but is also found with such regularity in Indian texts that it constitutes a cliché.[50]

Prior to narrowing our focus to specific local records, we may best begin this discussion with one important text that contains a collection of entries on different monasteries. Daoxuan's 道宣 (596–667) *Ji shenzhou sanbao gantong lu* 集神州三寶感通錄 (Collected Records of the [Mysterious] Stimuli and Responses Related to the Three Jewels in China) contains a separate section on "sacred monasteries" (*shengsi* 聖寺), which is placed alongside sections on "numinous images" (*lingxiang* 靈像), "supernatural monks" (*shenseng* 神僧) and "auspicious scriptures" (*ruijing* 瑞經).[51] In the section on sacred monasteries there is a pronounced focus on the landscape or setting of the monasteries. A common theme that runs throughout those records is that of an unsuspecting traveler who suddenly hears the sounds of temple bells, or sees a vision of light, and after some searching is finally able to perceive the esoteric qualities of the natural setting. Given the characteristics of Chinese local history discussed above, it is worth highlighting that, as the title of the text suggests, it is concerned with the miracles associated with the "three treasures" (*sanbao* 三寶), namely the Buddha (represented by relics and images), dharma (by scriptures), and saṃgha (by stories of supernatural temples and monks).[52] Or, to put it in other words, the primary topics are the Buddha, books, people and places. Many of the records in the *Ji shenzhou sanbao gantong lu* were carried over into a variety of other sources (such as the *Fayuan zhulin* 法苑珠林, *Gaoseng zhuan* 高僧傳, and other local records).[53] Raoul Birnbaum has noted, for instance, that the entry for a monastery at Wutai shan in that text was cited in the *Guang qingliang zhuan* 廣清涼傳 (Extended Record of Mount Clear and Cool [Wutai shan]).[54] Stories about "sacred monasteries" (*shengsi* 聖寺), therefore, circulated widely in conjunction with tales about wonder-working monks and miraculous images.

An example of a local record for one particular site that dedicates much of its space to the natural world is the encompassing *Record of the Collected Wonders of the Southern Marchmount* (Nanyue zongsheng ji 南嶽総勝集) [hereafter NYZSJ], a monograph on the religious history of Mt. Nanyue (also referred to as Hengshan 衡山), located in modern Hunan province, compiled by the Song dynasty writer Chen Tianfu 陳田夫 [*zi* Geng Sou 耕叟, *hao* Cang Yezi 蒼野子] (fl. mid-twelfth century) who wrote a Preface to the text that is dated 1163.[55] That text utilizes a variety of local records and inscriptions. Chen states that in compiling this work he roamed the peaks and valleys in order to collect the internal teachings (*neijiao* 內教), extant transcendent texts, and other old records. He also explicitly dedicated his work to detailing the history of the flourishing as well as decline of the Daoist abbeys and Buddhist monasteries on the mountain and is therefore a particularly rich resource on religious history.

The first *juan* of the NYZSJ is comprised of a short general history of the mountain, followed by entries on all the main peaks, the locations of the grotto-heaven (*dongtian* 洞天) and blissful realms (*fudi* 福地), lists of geographical features (rivers, creeks, springs, and cliffs), cultural relics (altars and stūpas), and textual references to ancient sages who came and attained the way at Nanyue. The second *juan* contains separate entries on all the Daoist abbeys (*guan* 觀), courts (*yuan* 院), palaces (*gong* 宮) and Buddhist monasteries (*si* 寺). There are entries for 14 abbeys, 5 courts, 7 palaces, and 63 monasteries. The second *juan* also contains a section on botanical information that includes lists of trees, plants, flowers, herbs, and other pharmacological information. The final *juan* contains biographical/hagiographical entries on approximately 45 eminent Nanyue hermits, Daoists, Buddhists, and other local cultic figures.

The records for the 63 monastic institutions at Nanyue are concerned with a variety of issues and themes that tend to be infrequently discussed in secondary scholarship on Chinese Buddhist monasteries. In addition to noting practical historical information on the date the monastery was founded and where it is located, some of the other main topics in those records include: the noteworthy natural qualities of sites (including notices of special trees, fruits, pure waters, and noteworthy topography), miracles associated with the monastery or its relics and images, the fact that some of the monasteries were founded on previously designated sacred sites (including the transformation of Daoist abbeys into Buddhist monasteries), and the connections of those sites to eminent monks and famous figures. What was also of particular interest to the chroniclers were the name changes and official types of recognition that the site received. Special attention was paid, for example, to noting the conferral of tablets of official sanction (*e* 額) for a monastery.[56] Although my concerns in this chapter are limited to issues about monasteries as sacred entities, these tablets highlight just how significant political power and sanction was to the long-term viability of those sites, a topic that deserves further study. The NYZSJ— like the genre of local records that it falls within—maintains a balanced focus on people and places, on the sanctity of the natural setting and the role of previous sages and eminent monks.

The entry for the Hengyue Monastery (Hengyue chansi 衡嶽禪寺) in the NYZSJ can be taken as a good example of how a monastic institution at Nanyue was represented in a textual record. The NYZSJ records that the Hengyue chansi was established in 503 by the Liang dynasty dhyāna master Huihai 慧海.[57] The name "Hengyue chansi" was not given to this site until the Song dynasty, however, and it was first known simply as Huihai's bodhimaṇḍa (Huihai zunzhe daochang 慧海尊者道場). The entry begins by noting the special natural qualities of the site, which has a noteworthy spring, tall and slender bamboo, a stone drum, and strange trees. The entry then shifts back to the eminent monks connected to the site. The Hengyue chansi was where the eccentric Tang Chan monk Mingzan 明瓚 (fl. eighth century) (otherwise known as Lancan 懶殘 [Lazy Leftovers] or Mr. Can 殘 [Mr. Leftovers]) lived. There was also, the NYZSJ relates, a stele entitled *A Stele Inscription for the*

Vinaya and Dhyāna Master Yuan (*Yuan luchanshi bei* 瑗律禪師碑), by Huangfu Shi 皇甫湜 (777–830) and a poem about this site by Han Yu 韓愈 (768–824) entitled "Spending the Night at the Hengyue Temple [Written on the] Gate Tower" (*Su hengyue si menlou si* 宿衡嶽寺門樓詩).[58]

Entries on the natural settings of monasteries in the NYZSJ emphasize what is *in* the site over, for example, the heights of the peaks. That is to say, these entries stress the fact that Nanyue is a potent site with rare and valuable herbs, plants, trees, pharmacopeia, and clear springs and other plants with magical qualities. While these attributes are also found in a variety of monastic records, it is perhaps due to an enduring modern rationalist perspective that those records have been mined primarily for what they say about the eminent monks and their histories, while the sacred nature of the monasteries themselves has tended to be disregarded. Not only have the sacred dimensions of monasteries been ignored by scholars of Chinese Buddhist monasteries, but monasteries have also rarely been discussed in the context of studies of Chinese sacred space.[59]

The emphasis on the sacred qualities of monastic sites is not limited to the records for Nanyue, but is found throughout inscriptions and local monastic records for other sites.[60] Consider the following passage from the Shaolin 少林 monastery stele on Songshan 嵩山:

> The Shaolin Monastery was founded by Xiaowen 孝文(r. 471–499) of the latter (Northern) Wei dynasty. Close to the Eastern Capital, on the western slopes of the Greater Chamber (Taishi 太室), the principle pneuma dwells at the centre of the six directions and the pure capital is the hub of the empire. The northern spur of Mount Hou 緱山 dovetails with the Heavenly Gate of Yuan 宛 and Luo 洛. The southern streams of the River Ying 穎水 connect with the misty marshes between [Mount] Jing 荊 and the [Yellow] River. Thus are laid out the sacred confines of the imperial domain, the blessed ground of Yangcheng 陽城.[61]

As Penelope Herbert's annotation to this passage astutely points out, there is a combined emphasis on the geomantic orientation of the monastery and the sacrality of the site, which stresses its proximity to what was perceived to be the central point of the Chinese world.[62] While the Shaolin Monastery stele is primarily concerned with a land grant controversy, it is also in large part an encomium of the natural setting itself. One passage, for example, states that "curious portents oft appeared among animals and plants and numinous responses frequently came forth from the monastic gardens."[63]

Similar concerns are also found in the *Luoyang qielan ji* 洛陽伽藍記 (Record of Buddhist Monasteries in Luoyang), where descriptions of various miracles and anomalies are found alongside notes on the presence of unusual natural objects, such as strange pomegranates and grapes, that grace the sites.[64] In the eloquent literary depictions of monasteries and nunneries we encounter passages such as the following for the Yongning si 永寧寺 and the Yaoguang Nunnery 瑤光寺. The entry for the former describes an enormous stūpa and the fine artisanship of a golden Buddha image and then proceeds to a description of the monastic setting:

The beauty of the cloisters was beyond description. Luxuriant cypress, juniper, and pine trees brushed the eaves of the building, while bamboo groves and aromatic plants lined the courtyards and stairways. [For this monastery] Chang Jing 常景 wrote an inscription that reads [in part]: Even the Grand Hall on Mt. Sumeru and the Palace of Purity in Tusita Heaven are no match for this.[65]

The entry for the latter proceeds from a description of the building to a passage that says, "there were rare trees and aromatic plants too numerous to be listed. Such trees and plants as evergreens, hollies, water lilies, and mallows were all here."[66] The mention of aromatic plants in these passages is significant since, as Piero Camporesi has noted

there can be no unspoiled place of pure joy, no Elysian fields and no Earthly Paradise without the bright floral architecture which brings sensuous pleasure and consolation to the nose and eyes. Paradise and the garden always fused into a single image in the dreams of both the East and the West. Herbs, flowers and trees have filled the fantasies and raptures of men who have interpreted their silent and discreet existences symbolically.[67]

The types of records found in the *Luoyang qielan ji* could be multiplied, but the main point of these descriptions seems to be to highlight the numinous quality of the monastic setting. One final example drawn from that text is even more to the point. The record for the Dajue Monastery 大覺寺 says:

The grounds were auspicious, sacred, and truly scenic. Therefore, Wen Tzu-sheng 溫子昇 wrote an inscription that says: "It faces the water and backs on the mountain." . . . The forest, ponds and "flying pavilions" are comparable with the Jingming 景明 [Monastery]. When the spring winds move the trees, the orchids unfurl their purple petals. When the autumn frost descends to the grass, the chrysanthemums send out yellow blossoms. Famous monks and virtuous masters would gather here in tranquil contemplation in order to eliminate disturbing illusions.[68]

The emphasis in this passage on the sacred purlieu of the Dajue Monastery in Luoyang, and the effect that such a setting could have on the religious pursuits of the Buddhist monks who gathered there, is a theme that (as will be seen below) resonates with other monastic records.[69]

While the numinous quality of a site is often marked with anomalous natural signs, such as those discussed in the previous records, the settings of Buddhist monasteries within the terrain of Mt. Nanyue (and elsewhere) were also perceived to resonate with particularly Buddhist characteristics. An entry for Lotus Peak (Lianhua feng 連華峰) in the NYZSJ, for instance, describes a monastery that was home to a community of *Lotus Sūtra* devotees that was perceived to be located within a topography that was itself in the shape of a lotus flower. That entry says that the Fangguang chongshou chansi 方廣嵩壽禪寺 is located below Lotus Peak.

Eight mountains and four waterways encircle it. The passage goes on to say that "the temple is within a lotus flower. The surrounding peaks are like the petals [of the lotus]." After commenting on the fitting Buddhist topography for the monastic community, the entry goes on to describe some of the magical properties of the site and notes that to the north are the origins of numinous cart tracks. The NYZSJ cites an unidentified text entitled the *Jiji* 迹記 which says,

> Previously Arhat(s) lived here. Ruts made by the carts of ghosts and spirits bringing provisions are [still found] on the road. The east looks to the Bajiao An 芭蕉菴 (Plantain Hut), and the site where the [Liu-]Song eminent monk Zong Bing 宗炳 (375–443) practiced. To the north is the Lingyuan Stūpa 靈源塔.[70]

This passage both emphasizes the numinous nature of the site, which has a special lotus topography, pure water, and the fact that the site was inhabited by spirits and arhats and was in possession of the relics of an eminent monk. The type of perception reflected here, whereby the landscape was read like a text and considered to have religious meanings encoded in its natural forms, is found in numerous Chinese Buddhist records, such as sites that are perceived to have an image of the Buddha's hand on a rock face, and, it is important to observe, is also characteristic of Daoist perceptions of the landscape.[71]

As important as representations of a diverse natural landscape were, by focusing just on the land we may unwittingly omit another fundamentally important way of denoting the sacred qualities of a site. While it makes good sense to begin discussions of a site with its main topographical features, that approach tends to run counter to how certain Chinese sources begin their descriptions. In an earlier attempt to counteract a tendency towards ahistorical and ungrounded approaches to the study of sacred geography, I wrote of the need for historians of religion to concentrate on what is on the ground under their feet.[72] In making that point I discussed an early Greek myth about Thales (c. 624–546 BCE) who, while contemplating the stars high above, fell into a well. Upon seeing this a Thracian slave woman laughed and then reprimanded Thales for having his head in the sky and not observing what was directly under his own feet. To the Greeks that story exhibited well the dilemma of theorists who lose their grounding. After spending more time reading other local sources it became clear that merely keeping to the ground might result in missing an important element of Chinese conceptions of sacred space. While I still hold to the important perspective that, as Michel de Certeau has put it so nicely, "history begins at ground level, with footsteps," it is equally important to ponder the skies above, even if this does mean falling into a few wells along the way.[73] The errors of my previous approach were impressed upon me when I opened the *Nanyue zhi* 南嶽誌 (Gazetteer of Nanyue) and in the first pages encountered a star map of the sky above Nanyue. When reading that source in conjunction with a variety of other material I realized that depictions of Nanyue often begin by situating the site in relation to key celestial features. The tendency to situate a site in relation to significant astronomical locations was not limited to the writings about Nanyue, but was in fact a feature common to texts describing Chinese geography.[74] Following the prefatory material in many gazetteers, for example, a section on "Astronomical Geography" (*xingye* 星野) or "Astronomical Divisions" (*xingdu* 星度) usually follows.[75]

The importance of locations on the ground in relation to the celestial sphere became more apparent as I studied the surviving fragments of a collection of biographies of eighteen eminent Buddhist monks from Nanyue entitled *The Biographies of the Eighteen Eminent Monks of Nanyue* (Nanyue shiba gaoseng zhuan 南嶽十八高僧傳).[76] Although the full text is no longer extant, the Preface to the work entitled *Preface to the Biographies of the Eighteen Eminent Monks of Hengyue* (Hengyue shiba gaoseng xu 衡嶽十八高僧傳序) [hereafter just Preface] by the important Tang scholar official Lu Cangyong 盧藏用 (656–713) has been transmitted down to the present.[77] In that Preface, after briefly introducing some of the eighteen eminent monks, there is a rather surprising change of tone. Lu refrains from expatiating on the virtues of each (or any) of the monks who comprise the list and instead focuses his literary flourishes on the beauty and numinous efficacy of the terrain at Nanyue that served as a setting for their practices in monasteries there. He writes: "Of the twenty-eight Lunar Mansions [in the sky] above, the brilliances of Yi (翼, Wings) and Zhen (軫, Chariot Cross-board) fly above [Hengshan].[78] . . . There are a myriad of resplendent pines with tree-tops reaching into the sky . . . The waters are azure and the cliffs are frosty white, nourishing pure clouds and mushrooms." Following this description of the natural beauty and the auspicious location of the place based on the correlates with the celestial sphere, Lu writes that it is precisely due to the magnificence of the site that special people are naturally drawn to it. Not only are they drawn to it, Lu tells us, but "those who live there will pick up its purity and have deep and peaceful spirits." Thus, Lu explicitly plays up the efficacy of the mountain site and the potential for the natural wonders of that place to rub off on those monks who practice in the monasteries there. It is no doubt due to the perceived influence the natural setting could have on a monk's practice that many of the entries on specific monasteries in the NYZSJ focus on the attributes of their surrounding natural environment. Wonderful trees, clear water, abundant herbs, strange stones, and a favorable position in relation to the celestial sphere above, could be as important to a monk's religious pursuits as a good master.

Based on the records for the monasteries discussed above, it is clear that the natural setting of a monastery was clearly more than just a backdrop, but could actually help to constitute its numinous qualities. Indeed, it was precisely that type of information about a site's special qualities that traveled widely and made emperors, writers, and potential patrons take note and encourage practitioners and pilgrims to travel there. One fine medieval example that explicitly discusses the way a Buddhist monk was drawn to a site based on its natural characteristics, and the promise it held for his personal religious development, is Huisi's well-known account of his decision to move to Nanyue, entitled *Nanyue da chanshi lishi yuanwen* 南嶽大禪師立誓願文 (Vow of the Great Dhyāna Master of Nanyue).[79] In that vow Huisi discusses his attraction to the numinous mushrooms and herbs at Nanyue that he hoped would allow him to complete an elixir that would preserve his body so that he would be around to meet Maitreya, who will eventually descend into this world to usher in the new period of the "correct dharma" *zhengfa* 正法.[80]

A more recent example of the allure a site's efficacious nature could have is found in Susan Naquin's discussion of the Tanzhe monastery 潭柘寺 near Beijing. She writes that

> the even greater attention given in the gazetteer to the sights of the temple and to the temple as a local sight suggests the considerable importance of this dimension to the monks as well as to their real or imagined patrons.[81]

Naquin further relates that

> written epitaphs of later generations of Tanzhe monks told stories of precocious piety, extraordinary visions and serene deaths, conjuring up other visions of concentrated holy power. Well-known monks from Peking and elsewhere acknowledged the temple's reputation by choosing it for their own final resting place . . . their stūpas at the site, as well as rooms associated with them, testified to this attractive power.[82]

It was not only the terrestrial and celestial locations or settings of Chinese monasteries that were marked off and perceived as sacred spaces, but there is evidence that at least some Buddhist structures themselves were consecrated as sacred objects.[83] A full consideration of this important (yet poorly studied) topic would ideally investigate possible Indian antecedents, such as how prior to their construction or inhabitation certain monasteries were ritually consecrated. When the seventh-century Chinese pilgrim Yijing 義淨 (635–713) traveled to India, for example, he noted five kinds of consecrated grounds, which included "ground consecrated by an individual's vow of building a monastery on the spot" and "ground chosen and consecrated with a sacred rite by Bhikshus."[84] Although further reflection on these concerns would lead us too far afield here there is, however, one particularly fascinating passage in the Shaolin Monastery stele related to the sacrality of a built structure that is worth mentioning:

> In the Taihe 太和 period (AD 477–499), [Emperor Xiaowen 孝文] ordered the authorities to place this monastery at [Buddhabhadra's] disposal and had offerings and vestments provided at public expense. The Master of the Law forthwith on the western terrace of the monastery constructed a Holy Relic Pagoda (*shelita* 舍利塔) and, behind the pagoda, constructed the Hall for Translating the Sutras (*fanjingtang* 翻經堂). Mixing the plaster with holy water and using a golden rope as a plumbline, putting heart and soul into their task, [the builders] worked night and day. The place for Prabhutaratna's complete bodily manifestation was achieved in less than a day and the sermons of the Tathagata's golden mouth were sheltered in the [building among] rolling clouds. . . Here [Buddha]bhadra, cutting off his mind from worldly things and enjoying the tranquility of his hermit existence, was moved to a full understanding and finally achieved enlightenment.[85]

This passage contains a number of important points worthy of further comment (including the enshrining of relics and the relationship of the fruits of the monk's practice to the site), but for the moment I want to highlight the detail that the plaster used for the walls was mixed with holy water and built into the site. Later, in a verse portion of the stele, this detail comes up again.

> A jade monastery here is established. A precious mountain bears it upon its peak. On the terrace of flowers, a bamboo grove, in the clear spring, holy water. Indeed, the true image of tranquility is lodged here in all its profundity . . . Our Master labored painstakingly, purifying the sanctified ground. He braced himself to build the chamber of images and concentrated all his efforts on constructing the sutra hall. The Vajradhātu (Realm of Wisdom) he delineated with a plumbline, and in his fragrant pepper plaster mixed holy water (*jiaotu shuixiang* 椒塗水香).[86]

This verse captures well the intertwining of the sacred natural site, images, the presence of the holy book, and the sanctification of the plaster used to build the structure itself.[87] All these elements contributed to enhance the sacred nature of the monastery, which was conceived of as the Realm of Wisdom (Vajradhātu). Other inscriptions which describe monastic architecture present those structures as "mimetic representations" of the Jetavana or the Pure Land.[88] Monasteries, it seems, could be conceived as idealized representations of Pure Lands as much as Pure Lands were represented in paintings through palatial monastic architecture.[89] In addition to being symbolic spaces drawing on the vocabulary of Pure Lands, Bernard Faure has also noted that by the late Tang "there developed a cosmic/human symbolism of the monastery, the main buildings of which were seen to correspond to the parts of the human body."[90]

Thus far I have concentrated on how the special qualities of the natural setting of monasteries figured importantly in the representations of those places. Although the siting of Buddhist monasteries based on features of the terrestrial and celestial locations were important, some monastic foundation legends focused less on the *genus loci* and instead infuse the site with other markers that set it off as a sacred site. The ways that Buddhists transformed the Chinese landscape into a Buddhist sacred landscape is a complicated history that has yet to be adequately told. Two of the many ways that special sites were identified as possible locations for monasteries were through extraordinary visions or dream divination.[91] One such account is found in a passage in the *Song gaoseng zhuan* 宋高僧傳 (Song Biographies of Eminent Monks) that relates the origins of the Xiangguo si 相國寺.[92] That monastery was reportedly built on a site located on the earth below where a strange celestial phenomenon was seen in the sky.[93] A famous example of dream divination determining the location of a new monastery is, of course, that of Fazhao 法照 (fl. eighth century). While still residing with Chengyuan 承遠 (713–803) at Nanyue, Fazhao had a vision of a not yet existing grand monastery at Wutai Shan, "but Fazhao took the visions to mean that he was charged to build it" and he moved from Nanyue to Wutai Shan.[94] As a result of Fazhao's effort to turn his dream vision into reality, the Bamboo Grove Monastery (Zhulin si 竹林寺) was founded. As Dan Stevenson's account of Fazhao's visionary dreams notes, this was not an isolated account and many other monasteries had similar foundation stories.[95] Further research on "record of origins" accounts of different monasteries would no doubt yield further examples.

A particular motif that appears regularly in monastic foundation legends and records is that of miracles associated with Buddhist images or relics.[96] The record for the foundation of the Jingyansi 浄嚴寺 (Pure Majesty Temple) in the NYZSJ, for example, states that,

> Of old in the Jingde period (1004) there was a monk who suddenly saw that from the ground there was a brightness ten or more feet high and when he excavated the ground, an image of the Buddha and seven worthies was found. Today the luster is still like new as it was in the past.[97]

In similar accounts found in other sources these kinds of auspicious events generally serve to mark the spot where a new monastery is founded. I will not elaborate on these accounts here since the relationship of miraculous images and Buddhist monasteries has been well studied by Koichi Shinohara.[98] Suffice it to say here that he concludes that,

> The tradition of Asoka images appears to have developed in the South, where these images served to enhance the prestige of temples, many of which had only been recently established in areas where Buddhist missionaries had arrived relatively recently. One function of the discovery and location stories would then have been to illustrate dramatically the importance of a new temple as the miraculously chosen home of a specially powerful image.[99]

Accounts of miracles associated with an image at a monastery not only entered into the collective memory about the site, but could, in short, put that site on the map.[100]

Earlier in this chapter I mentioned the possibilities and limitations of conceiving of monasteries as "containers." Yet, from a different perspective Buddhist monasteries could in fact be understood as containers, not just as houses for living monks, but in their roles as repositories for the living presences of the Buddha, various spirits and deities, and the relics of eminent monks. We know, for example, that the presence of shrines to local spirits (*tudi shen* 土地神), halls to protector deities of the monastery (*qielan shen* 伽藍神), the role of portrait halls, and the presence of mummies were taken seriously and the ritual protocol related to those entities was scripted into monastic codes.[101]

A closely related topic concerns miracle tales about relics housed in monasteries, which in effect turned them into large-scale reliquaries. The *Guang hongming ji* 廣弘明集 includes a fascinating text entitled *A Record of the Sympathetic Response to [the] Śarīra [Distributed to the Provinces]* (Sheli ganying ji 舍利感應) compiled by the Sui court chronicler Wang Shao 王邵 (fl. sixth century).[102] That record consists of a series of reports that were sent in from various monasteries that received relics during the Sui emperor's relic distribution campaign, and details the auspicious or miraculous events that accompanied the enshrinement of those relics.[103] Characteristic events that are mentioned include: auspicious rain, water flowing in previously dry rivers, five colored clouds appearing, and drastic changes in the weather.[104] These records of auspicious natural responses to the arrival of the relics were a significant omen that ensured that the emperor was pursuing the correct policies. For similar reasons, perhaps, emperors paid regular attention to—and actually solicited information on—auspicious occurrences from particular places and monasteries. Local officials were at times charged with surveying their jurisdictions and submitting memorials to the throne about cases of miracles in their respective locales. Once those tales became uprooted from a site and began to circulate, the impact on the site could be dramatic.[105]

Concluding thoughts

This chapter has attempted to reinstate the physical sites of "monasteries" into discussions about monasticism. By taking into account local monastic records, inscriptions, and gazetteers, different representations of Chinese Buddhist monasteries emerge. Although Buddhist monasteries served a variety of functions at different times and in different places, by reading the accounts of monasteries that are presented in those local sources we can begin to gain insight into what was at least thought to be important in representing those sites, even if the records are sometimes pious fictions.[106] One of the main elements found in those sources was a (sometimes quite detailed) treatment of the special qualities, or anomalous elements, of the natural setting, the connections with eminent monks who resided there, and accounts of miracles that were connected with the site and their sacred possessions. Those accounts could demonstrate that a monastery was an efficacious place for a monk or nun to pursue their calling and may have had profound effects on the future viability and economic success of monasteries, due to their ability to attract both pilgrims and patrons.[107] As visible as these resolutely anti-modernist themes are in local monastic records, they have remained topics that have largely been occluded from the ken of those who have studied Chinese Buddhist monasteries.

If Chinese Buddhists took the qualities of sites seriously and perceived certain sites as more efficacious than others, then it is understandable that there might have been an attempt to capitalize on the accrued sanctity associated with particular places. One striking, and yet rarely mentioned, aspect of the study of Chinese Buddhist monasteries that will be the focus of my future research is the evidence that Buddhists not only took the representation of place seriously, but also began to take over sacred sites and religious structures of other traditions and converted them into Buddhist monasteries. When we consider the evidence in local monastic records, it is clear that Buddhist monasteries were much more than just buildings, or "containers," where traditional Buddhist monastic practices took place. Buddhist monasteries were described as peaceful places separate from the concerns and stresses of urban life, as well as "enchanted gardens" full of wonders and miracles.[108]

Notes

1 Welch 1967: 122.
2 Welch 1967: 122.
3 As will be discussed below, this distinction between people and places is a key division found in Chinese local history itself from a very early period.
4 The tendency to focus on people, their actions and monastic offices etc. is not just limited to studies of Chinese Buddhism, but is also evident in the very limited work that has been done on Daoist monasteries and monasticism. See, for example, Kohn 2003.
5 An alternative story about the place of Buddhist monasteries in Chinese society has also begun to be told by Mark Halperin, John Kieschnick, and Timothy Brook. Their research deals with issues regarding elite and literati interaction with monasteries and with the material aspects of Chinese Buddhist monasteries in relation to the production of merit. My emphasis here, while very much in sympathy with their approaches, differs in that it focuses on the representation of the monastery itself and less on the social world that it was a part of. See Brook 1993; Halperin 1997 and 2006; Kieschnick 2003: 185–199.
6 Previous studies have tended to focus on one or another aspect of Chinese monasteries, but (for good reasons) wide-ranging treatments of the full complexity of those institutions are rare. A work by Zhang Gong (1997), however, traces the origin, historico-geographic spread, culture, and arts of Chinese Buddhist monasteries through a variety of official, canonical, and local sources.
7 There is an enormous amount of literature on these topics that it would be impractical to cite in full here, see, for example, Yang 1950, Twitchett 1956, 1970; and Gernet 1995.
8 Again, the literature here is vast, but see, for example, Niida 1961; Chikusa 1982; Michihata 1983; Tonami 1990; and Moroto 1990.
9 Yan 1992 and Zürcher 1989. There is, however, no single general treatment of Buddhist monastic scholasticism. For an illuminating discussion of Tibetan Buddhist scholasticism and its relation to religious practice see Dreyfus 2003 and the extensive bibliography that he has compiled on the subject. See also Cabezón 1998.
10 Zürcher 1989.
11 Zürcher 1989: 50.
12 Recent research by T. Griffith Foulk (1987, 1993, 1995) and a new study by Yifa (2002) on the operating code books for Chinese Buddhist monasteries have provided a much better sense of the complex internal workings of (primarily Chan) Buddhist monasteries in China.
13 For two recent treatments of the role of Buddhist monasteries in Chinese society see Brook 1993 and Naquin 2000.
14 See the useful discussion of terminology in Naquin 2000: 19–22.
15 Since most early monasteries included *stūpas*, the general term for monasteries was often a transliterated form, or abbreviated transliteration, of that Sanskrit word: such as *sudupo* 窣堵波, *fota* 佛塔, or *futu* 浮屠. See the discussion in Zhang 1997: 17–18.
16 Zürcher (2007: 38–39) discusses the dating of the term and the different theories of its origin proposed by Henri Maspero and Otani Seishin. There is also a useful note on the term "si" in Schafer 1962: 6.
17 *Sengshi lue* T. 54.236c19–22. The *Shiming* refers to an etymological work by Liu Xi 劉熙 (d.u.) that dates to the Later Han dynasty 後漢 (25–220). See the entry in *Dai kanwa jiten*, vol. 11: 411b–c; the entry on "Lei-shu" by Kenneth Dewoskin in Nienhauser 1986: 527, and the entry on the "Shih ming 釋名" by Roy Andrew Miller in Loewe 1993: 424–428.
18 Wu 1963: 39.
19 Examples for the conversion of palaces and elite residences into monasteries are found in a variety of Buddhist sources. See, as an example, the sheer number of cases mentioned in the *Sita ji* 寺塔記 (Record of Monasteries and Stūpas) T. 51.1022b22–1024a12.

An English translation of this text, which is merely a part of the longer ninth-century miscellany entitled *Youyang zazu* 酉陽雜俎 by Duan Chengshi 段成式, is available in Soper 1960.

20 Steinhardt 1998 and Wu 1963: 39.

21 Gernet 1995: 7.

22 See, for example, the list of cognate terms in Mochizuki 1958–1963: 1710. The complexity of this topic is also indicated by the comments on diversity and complexity of names in Zanning's *Sengshi lue*, see T. 54.236c13–237a16.

23 Welch 1967: 126.

24 This issue is not just a modern problem, but was faced by the compilers of gazetteers who struggled with how to classify monasteries. See the interesting discussion in Brook 1993: 29ff. For one attempt at distinguishing different types of Buddhist monasteries in the context of Kathmandu see Gellner 2001: 134–178.

25 Foulk 1993: 163ff and Jorgensen 2000: 284.

26 Foulk 1993: 164.

27 Forte 1992. Mention should also be made here of Forte 1983, which deals with a variety of other types of monasteries, such as those founded by emperors and princes or for a mother, father, or spouse. See also Tsukamoto 1974.

28 Gernet 2007: 3–4.

29 On Aristotle's "container" model of space see Casey 1993: xi.

30 The title of Johannes Pripp-Møller's foundational work (1982) is also quite telling: *Chinese Buddhist Monasteries: Their Plan and Its Function as a Setting for Buddhist Monastic Life*.

31 I would like to thank Koichi Shinohara for urging me to rethink the possible nuances of the "container" image.

32 See Blier 1987.

33 Markus 1998 and Remensnyder 1995. This is not just a topic of interest limited to that field. For a valuable collection of essays see Kedar and Werblowsky 1998.

34 Markus 1998: 140.

35 Remensnyder 1995: 3.

36 In addition to the story that I relate here, Meir Shahar has effectively demonstrated the potential for inscriptions to reveal Buddhist practices that tended to be edited out or left silent in traditional Buddhist histories, such as the role of monks in warfare. See Shahar 2000: 32–35.

37 Chittick 1997.

38 Chittick 1997: 15.

39 On the usage of the term "geopiety" among geographers see the entry on the topic in Johnston et al. 2000: 308–309. This term has been employed to good effect by Allan Grapard in his studies of Japanese sacred space. See, for example, Grapard 1994 and most recently his updated thoughts in Grapard 2003: 92. For a study of the development of Chinese ideas of topomancy or geomancy see Feuchtwang 1974.

40 See, for example, the chapter entitled "The City as Cosmo-Magical Symbol," in Wheatley 1971 and Feuchtwang 1974.

41 Jullien 1999: 92–94.

42 Wheatley 1971: 459.

43 Welch 1967: 122ff; and Pripp-Møller 1982: 3.

44 See also Shinohara 1999: 937–964.

45 These types of inscriptions have been studied in Halperin 1997.

46 Kieschnick 2003: 191.

47 See Birnbaum 1984.

48 For similar concerns regarding Daoist sites, which also focus on extraordinary people and strange natural elements see, for example, Verellen 1988.

49 Brook 2005: 178.

50 Schopen 2004d: 31.

51 *Ji shenzhou sanbao gantong lu* 集神州三寶感通錄, T. 52.423a26–426a18. This text, except for the section on monasteries, has been the focus of numerous studies by Koichi Shinohara (1991a, 1991b, 1998). For further comments on the three categories (*lingxiang, shengsi,* and *ruijing*) see Nishiwaki 2000: 262.

52 Shinohara 1991b: 74. For further comments on the character of this source and the meaning of the compound *gantong* see Birnbaum 1986: 135–137.

53 The relationship between the *Ji shenzhou sanbao gantong lu* and the *Fayuan zhulin* 法苑珠林 and other sources has been studied most extensively by Koichi Shinohara (see note 51 above).

54 The passage on Wutai shan is found in *Ji shenzhou sanbao gantong lu* T. 52.424c–425a and T. 51.1105a. See the translation and comments in Birnbaum 1986: 121.

55 Harvard-Yenching no. 606 in the Daoist canon and T. no. 2097. The fact that the NYZSJ survives under the same name in both the Buddhist and the Daoist canon is virtually unprecedented. I have studied this monograph in depth in Robson 2009. A brief summary of this text can also be found in Ono 1932–1936: vol. 8, 282d.

56 I adopt the phrase "tablet of official sanction" from Weinstein 1987: 50. On the imperial bestowal of name plaques see Foulk 1993: 164–165; Gernet 2007: 4; and especially the studies of Chikusa 1982: 83–94.

57 The following account of the Hengyue chansi is based on *Nanyue zongsheng ji,* T. 51.1070a.9ff.

58 T. 51.1070a15–16. A translation of that poem is found in Owen 1996: 485–486.

59 Two exceptions to this are Bernard Faure's work (1992) on the Shaolin si and Nanhua temple and the creation of their sacrality due to the possession of relics, and Susan Naquin's article (1998) on the Tanzhe monastery outside of Beijing, which deals with the site during the Ming and Qing period.

60 The most thoroughly studied sacred mountain in China is, of course, Wutai shan, which I will not discuss here. See, among others, Ono and Hibino 1942; Rhie 1977; Birnbaum 1983, 1986, 1989–1990; Gimello 1992; and Stevenson 1996.

61 Tonami 1990: 32.

62 Tonami 1990: 32. Shahar (2000: 21) has also pointed out the military significance of the location of the Shaolin estate.

63 Tonami 1990: 36.

64 See Wang 2000.

65 *Luoyang qielan ji,* T. 51.1000a17–20. Translation with some changes from Wang 1984: 16.

66 T. 51.1003a.15–17. Translation with some changes from Wang 1984: 48.

67 Camporesi 1994: 26. I would like to thank James Benn for urging me to consider the role of smells in representations of sacred space in his comments on the oral version of this chapter.

68 *Luoyang qielan ji,* T. 51:1017b19–27. See also Wang 1984: 203–204. I have emended the translation slightly to take into full account the meaning of the compound *shengao* 神皋. As Wang Yi-t'ung clarifies in note 256, this compound is attested in Zhang Heng's *fu* on the Western Capital in *Wenxuan* 文選 2.2b, where it clearly refers to "sacred areas of land." That interpretation is further adumbrated in Li Shan's commentary that says, "Gao means an area. It refers to a sacred area."

69 *Tiantai shan ji* 天台山記 [Record of Tiantai shan] by Xu Lingfu 徐靈府 [also known as Zhengjun 微君, or Mo Xizi 默希子], T. 51.1053a5ff. This record for the Waterfall Monastery [Pubu si 瀑布寺], for example, excerpts a passage written by Sun Xinggong 孫興公 about his visit to this site that says, "[I] crossed Numinous Stream [Lingxi 靈溪] and washed away all the vexations in my mind."

70 *Nanyue zongsheng ji,* T. 51.1061b. This passage is related to the entry for the Fangguang chongshou chansi 方廣嵩壽禪寺 later in the text that says that during the Tianjian reign period of the Liang dynasty [502–520] there was a monk named Xidun 希遁 who passed the summer [retreat] at Tiantai and encountered Master Huihai. Huihai

told him that he was to "establish a community at the Fangguang si at Nanyue." Dun then immediately went to Nanyue. He looked for the Fangguang [Temple] but was unable to find it. Later he came across a monastery called Fangguang, where the land was flat, numinous springs flowed and where ghosts and spirits transported provisions on carts drawn by golden oxen.

71 See, for example, the *Lushan ji* 廬山記 (Record of Lushan), T. 51.1031a for the reference to the Buddha's hand seen in the landscape.

72 James Robson 1995a.

73 de Certeau 1985: 129.

74 See for example the opening paragraphs of the *Tiantai shan ji* 天台山記 T. 51.1052a–b.

75 An interesting book worth comparative consideration on the relative role of the celestial sphere for siting monasteries is Heilbron 1999.

76 I study this text in detail in Robson forthcoming.

77 Text is found in *Quan Tangwen* vol. 5, *juan* 238, p. 3043. Lu Cangyong's biography is found in both the *Jiu tangshu* 舊唐書 (Old Standard History of the Tang, *juan* 94) and the *Xin Tangshu* 新唐書 (New Standard History of the Tang, *juan* 123).

78 The lunar mansions Yi (Wings) and Zhen (Chariot Cross-board) are appropriately part of those lunar mansions that comprise the Vermilion Bird (Zhuque 朱雀) or Southern Palace (Nangong 南宮) division of the sky. For more on Yi and Zhen see Ho Peng Yoke 2000: 117 and 133. On the symbolism between the Vermilion Bird and Nanyue see Robson 1995b: 233–234.

79 *Nanyue da chanshi lishi yuanwen* 南嶽大禪師立誓願文 (Vow of the Great Dhyāna Master of Nanyue), attributed to Huisi 慧思 (515–577), T. no. 1933. I discuss this topic in greater detail in Robson 2002: 397–405.

80 *Nanyue da chanshi lishi yuanwen* T. 46.791c11–17.

81 Naquin 1998: 194.

82 Naquin 1998: 187.

83 The following section should be balanced with the views of those who criticized Buddhist institutions for building monumental sites that were taken to be too extravagant. On those critiques see, for example, Halperin 1997: 140ff.

84 Takakusu 1896: 82–84.

85 *Shaolinsi bei* 少林寺碑 (Shaolin Monastery Inscription), composed by Pei Cui 裴漼 (665?–736), in *Jinshi cuibian*, 77. Trans. from Tonami 1990: 33.

86 *Shaolinsi bei*, 77. Trans. from Tonami 1990: 39–40. "Pepper plaster" refers to a concoction that was used on the walls of a room to impart a pleasant fragrance, see *Hanyu da cidian*, vol 4, 1101. David Knechtges (1982: 122–123) also points out that it can refer to the room within the palace where the empress lived. This interesting passage perhaps deserves comparison to the establishment of "perfumed chambers" [*gandhakuṭī*] in Indian Buddhist monasteries (in spite of the fact that the name given here is unprecedented as a Chinese translation or transliteration of *gandhakuṭī*) which John Strong (1977) has described as "a floral perfumed chamber in which the presence of the Buddha can be realized here and now." Whether or not there is a correspondence here is actually beside the point since the *gandhakuṭī* itself, even in its Chinese form, is an architectural element of the monastery that consecrates it as a sacred space and place for the Buddha (both then—as a residence, and now—for his image).

87 The focus on sacred architecture in medieval Europe has been profitably explored in Cassidy-Welch 2001. On the ritualized construction of Buddhist temples in the Japanese context, see Rambelli 2003.

88 See Halperin 1997: 391–392.

89 Steinhardt 1998: 50. Marsha Weidner also discusses how Buddhist monasteries borrowed from the highly symbolic visual culture of Han Chinese imperial planning and architecture, which was as Schafer has noted based on a "divine plan." See Weidner 2001: 119–120.

90 See Faure 1993: 162.
91 Birnbaum 1986: 119–120. Erik Zürcher, for example, has commented on the fact that origin of the Anle si 安樂寺 is traced to a dream vision that the monk Huishou 慧受 received (see Zürcher 2007: 150).
92 *Song gaoseng zhuan* T. 50.874b17–24.
93 See also Soper 1948: 20.
94 His move to Wutai Shan must have been in about 770. See Gimello 1992: 112 and 140, n. 69.
95 Stevenson 1996: 208. For the importance of dreams in the foundations of Buddhist monasteries in Japan see Bodiford 1999. For an interesting inscription on a monastery that shows the power of local spirits see Halperin 1997: 171.
96 In a related case, Koichi Shinohara (1992) has demonstrated the precise way that Guanding and other of Zhiyi's followers used reports about miracles around Zhiyi's grave to enhance the profile of that site.
97 *Nanyue zongsheng ji*, T. 51.1070a28. See also the discussion of other images in Zhang 1997: 662 ff; Soper 1959 (especially pp. 243–252), 1960; and the section on wall paintings in Buddhist monasteries in Acker 1954: 254–332.
98 Shinohara 1998.
99 Shinohara 1998: 163.
100 The role of images in contributing to the sacred architecture of a monastery has also been noted by Robert Sharf (2001: 2–3).
101 Foulk and Sharf 1993–1994: 179 and Pripp-Møller 1982: 48. See also the comments on setting up popular temples inside Buddhist monasteries in Hansen 1990: 58.
102 *Guang hongming ji*, T. 52.216bff. I have discussed this topic further in Robson 2004.
103 T. 52.216bff. For a detailed study of the Renshou relic campaign see Chen 2002: 45–80.
104 The story of the arrival of those relics at Nanyue the first year of the Sui (601) is recorded in the *Nanyue zongsheng ji* under the entry for the Gaocheng chansi 告成禪 寺, T. 51.1069c29–1070a8.
105 Faure and others have discussed why the emphasis on a monastery's sacred regalia was important, and detailed the dramatic effect that those holdings could have on the fortunes of a monastery and locale. See Faure 1992. Susan Naquin (1998) also addresses the way a monastery's reputation could be enhanced through stories about eminent monks and the possession of relics.
106 This is a similar approach that is suggested in Hertz 1983: 76.
107 Susan Naquin (1998) has written a valuable study that explores a series of questions about the Tanzhe monastery during the Ming and Qing: "What role did gods, holy people, history, and location play in the longevity of such a monastery? How did it establish and maintain a local reputation for sacred power?" In concluding her analysis, Naquin says that the monastery's success was due to the "interconnected dynamics of antiquity, sanctity, and scenery."
108 The image of the "enchanted garden" is derived from Weber 1993b: 270 and is discussed in the context of the relationship of Buddhist visions of space to that of local religions in Faure 1993: 167.

3 Pictorial program in the making of monastic space

From Jing'aisi of Luoyang to Cave 217 at Dunhuang

Eugene Wang

A paradox underlies the Buddhist monastery of medieval China. As a religious establishment, it amounts to "a closed space, an enclave of the cosmos within the surrounding chaos . . . a living organism, a utopia, a microcosm sufficient unto itself."[1] To this end, certain distinctive architectural features and signposts—in particular, the heavenward-aspiring pagoda—imbue the precinct with religious overtones to make the enclave nothing short of a monastery. There is hardly a Buddhist monastery without a pagoda. In Tang times, however, architectural style was not necessarily the primary feature that proclaimed a Buddhist monastery. Many Buddhist monasteries in the capital cities were converted from aristocratic mansions or a lay residence.[2] The monastic grandeur derived more from the sprawling spread of a cluster of compounds rather than from any specific architectural feature or design.[3] Indeed, a pagoda be added to the erstwhile residence as part of the conversion process.[4] By Tang times the pagoda gave way to the Buddha hall as the center of gravity in a Buddhist monastery.[5] There is, however, nothing distinctly Buddhist about the architectural design of the Buddha hall, for it shares basic features with secular architecture; its distinction stems more from its ceremonial character. Hence it was relatively easy to convert an aristocrat's house into a monastery. To press the architectural style of such a monastery for its religious character can therefore be misguided.

What is it then that made the Buddha hall a distinctly symbolic space? One readily thinks of the ceremonial practices held there, such as memorial services and sūtra lectures, heightened by such ritual procedures as incense-burning, drumbeating, chanting, and so forth. Just as important, if not more, were the statues and wall paintings that made the presence of the Buddhist deities more palpable and transported the devotee to other imaginary realms.

Unfortunately, few of the Tang-dynasty Buddhist monasteries in the metropolitan region have survived beyond some remaining lonesome pagodas. For the few monasteries that exist in far-flung or secluded places such as Mt. Wutai, the fragments of wall painting on the ceilings offer only glimpses of the full glories that once graced the walls of the Buddha halls. Dunhuang, with its interior-decorated cave shrines, is probably the only place that opens up a horizon onto the magnitude and dynamics of the pictorial imagination that once animated Tang-dynasty Buddhist monasteries. Still, one hesitates to equate caves with Buddha halls, and the northwest frontier with the capital cities.

Even at the level of textual description, what is available is limited. Ninth-century art historians and connoisseurs, such as Zhang Yanyuan 張彥遠 (ca. 815–?), Zhu Jingxuan 朱景玄 (fl. ninth century), and Duan Chengshi 段成式 (803?–863), catalogued and recorded the wall paintings adorning the walls of Buddhist monasteries. Their documentation, driven by their interest in great masters, anecdotal matters, and other preoccupations, resulted in cursory and sporadic note-takings. Rarely did they take care to lay out for us the entire pictorial program within a Buddha hall. It is our fortune, however, that they occasionally did. Zhang Yanyuan, for example, documented the full pictorial program in the Jing'ai Monastery 敬愛寺 in the city of Luoyang, the Eastern Capital.[6] However, Zhang's writing requires some informed and judicious processing before it can yield the kind of information we need. Before turning to that material, a brief history of the monastery is in order.

Monastery of Reverence and Love

In 656 CE, Wu Zetian (that is, Wu Zhao or Empress Wu) managed to have her own son Li Hong 李弘 installed as the heir apparent. The young boy had just recovered from an illness. To celebrate this occasion, Emperor Gaozong—with Wu operating at his side, no doubt—decreed the establishment of a Buddhist monastery called Ximingsi 西明寺 in the capital city Chang'an by converting the residence of a deceased prince in the Yankang 延康 Ward.[7] The next year, a counterpart of Ximingsi was established in Luoyang, named Jing'aisi, or Monastery of Reverence and Love.[8] It was renamed Foshoujisi 佛授記寺 in 691 and then changed back to its original name some time later, probably after Wu Zetian's death.[9] The name "Reverence and Love" explicitly registers Wu Zetian's intent to have her son pledge his filial allegiance to her.[10] Located in the Huairen 懷仁 Ward in the southeast side of the city, close to the Jianchun 建春 Gate,[11] the grand scale of the monastery was a source of marvel according to seventh-century accounts. The construction cost 200,000 in cash. "The splendor of its precincts, halls, sacred images, pennants and furnishings match the celestial order. The ingenuity of the workmanship equals the work of spirits and demons."[12] The picture is further enriched by the biographer of Xuanzang, Huili's 慧立 (615–?) description of the Ximingsi, its twin monastery in Chang'an, whose façade was "three hundred and fifty feet [wide]," and the monastic plan consisted of "ten courtyards and four thousand or so buildings."[13]

A number of events point to the eminence of the monastery. In 665, Wang Xuance 王玄策 (fl. 640–670), the distinguished Tang envoy to India, returned with Buddhist images acquired on his fourth trip to the Western Regions. He was appointed by the court to supervise the making of statues in the Jing'ai monastery based on the Indian models he obtained from his trips, which had gone into the imperial collection.[14] As a major national center of Buddhist scholarship under the imperial auspice, the monastery produced two major catalogues of the Buddhist canon.[15]

The extent to which the monastery was involved in Wu Zetian's revolution is striking. Around 685, the abbot of the monastery and two court-appointed monk-officers (*duweina*) of the monastery were inducted as *bhadantas* 大德 into the imperial chapel. In 690, monks from the monastery were among the "ten śramaṇas" who presented to Empress Wu the *Commentary on the Meaning of the Prophecy concerning the Divine Emperor in the Great Cloud Sūtra* 大雲經神皇授記義疏 (*Dayunjing shenghuang shouji yishu*),[16] a prelude to Wu's overthrow of the Tang dynasty. More telling is the watershed event of the translation of the notorious *Treasure Rain Sūtra* 寶雨經 (*Baoyu jing*) in 693, which proclaimed the reign over China by a female ruler. Heading the project was Wu's henchman Xue Huaiyi 薛懷義 (d. 693), a monk affiliated with the Great White Horse Monastery 大白馬 寺 (Dabaimasi) in the same city Luoyang. However, it is notable that the Jing'aisi was the venue chosen for the translation. The chief translator was Dharmaruci 達 摩流支, a monk from southern India, who changed his name to Bodhiruci 菩提 流支 by the order of Empress Wu. Twenty-nine collaborators, including monks, Indian Brahmans, and imperial court officials, participated in the project, serving as proof-readers and fulfilling other functions. Of the twenty monks involved in the project, seven of them were from the Jing'aisi, including the abbot Xinggan 行 感, and the *duweina* Degan 德感 and Zhijing 知靜. Among the monks participating in the project, seven of them were awarded the title of nobility, the Dynasty-Founding Duke 開國公 (*kaiguogong*). Three of them were monks from the Jing'ai Monastery.[17] It is no coincidence that Xue Huaiyi headed the expansion of the monastery and changed its name from the Jing'aisi (Monastery of Reverence and Love) to Foshoujisi (Monastery of the Buddha's Prophecy) in 691.[18]

The distinction enjoyed by the monastery under the Wu Zhou rule is obvious. In 695, the monk Yijing 義淨 (653–713) returned from his pilgrimage to India and arrived in Luoyang. He brought back close to four hundred Buddhist texts, a Buddhist statue, and three hundred grains of the Buddha's *śarīra*. Wu Zetian greeted Yijing outside of the Shangdong 上東 Gate, and decreed that the treasures from India should be deposited in the Foshouji Monastery (i.e., Jing'ai Monastery).[19]

Just as momentous was the massive translation of the *Avataṃsaka Sūtra*, which was started by the Khotanese monk Śikṣānanda 實叉難陀 (652–710) in 695 in the Dapiankong Monastery 大遍空寺 in the imperial palace of Luoyang; the project was continued by Fuli 復禮 (fl. 681–703) and Fazang 法藏 (643–712), the great Huayan master, and completed in 699 in the Foshouji monastery.[20] To celebrate the completion of the project, Wu Zetian ordered Fazang to lecture on the newly translated sūtra in the Foshouji Monastery (i.e., Jing'ai Monastery). When he reached the chapter on the "Cosmos," in his lecture "the ground of whole lecture hall and the monastery all trembled."[21] It comes as no surprise that the monastery, so favored by Wu Zetian, displayed a portrait of her.[22]

What happened to the Jing'ai Monastery after Wu Zetian's death in 705 is scarcely mentioned in historical texts and chronicles. The disappearance of the monastery from our standard sources, however, may not point to the immediate decline of the monastery in the post-Wu years. Two sets of historical circumstances must have placed the monastery in an interesting situation. First, the volatile period between 705 and 710 saw the rapid succession of the restoration of Tang by the Li clan and the subsequent wielding of power by Empress Wei 韋, Zhongzong's 中 宗 (r. 705–710) wife, who was closely allied with the Wu family through Wu Sansi

武三思, a bond strengthened by Princess Anle's 安樂 second marriage to a Wu family member.[23] This led to the revival of the adoration of Wu Zetian, a cult that was further intensified as Empress Wei, her daughter Princess Anle, and other female members of the royal family emulated Wu as an inspiring model of a powerful female ruler. The tide turned again with the violent end of the Zhongzong family in 710. Secondly, Princess Anle and other members of the imperial family and aristocracy also set the trend in lavishing money on building monasteries around this time. The wealthy families could be exempt from corvée by having their children ordained in the Buddhist order. This led to a massive wave of construction and renovation of Buddhist monasteries, which caused serious concern from court officials. They pleaded with the throne to curtail the excess of the monastery-building boom.[24] The question of how the Jing'ai Monastery fared in this context prompts speculation. The answer to this question lies in art historical sources: first, Zhang Yanyuan's documentation of the paintings in the Jing'ai Monastery, and then evidence from some other most unlikely places.

Zhang Yanyuan's account

Zhang Yanyuan offers a detailed account about the statues and wall paintings in the Jing'ai monastery.[25] As our concern is with the Buddha hall, we can focus on the relevant passage:

> Within the Buddha hall is a clay image of the Bodhisattva Maitreya under the Bodhi tree. It was modeled upon a Bodhisattva image that Wang Xuance had acquired in Western regions and brought back, which had been issued from the Palace in the second year of Linde 麟德 (665). [The craftsmen Zhang Shou 張壽 and Song Chao 宋朝 did the modeling; Wang Xuance directed the work; and Li An 李安 pasted on the gold (leaf).] In the easternmost intercolumnar space an image of Maitreya. [Modeled in clay by Zhang Zhicang 張知藏 who was the younger brother of Zhang Shou. It was finished by Chen Yongcheng.] In the westernmost intercolumnar space an image of Maitreya. [It was modeled in clay by Dou Hongguo 竇弘果. The haloes and emanations (*huasheng* 化生) etc. of the above mentioned three images were all carved by Liu Shuang 劉爽]. By the central door of the hall, a Divinity of the West. [Modeled by Dou Hongguo]. By the central door of the hall a Divinity of the East. [Modeled by Zhao Yunzhi 趙雲質. It is now called "the Sage Divinity."] In this whole hall the votive images (*gongde* 功德) are all equally fine. Ingenious craftsmen were chosen, and each of them gave free rein to his rarest thoughts (so that) all under Heaven praise the splendor and magnificence (of these works). . . . The wall-paintings on the east and west sides inside the great hall. [Liu Xingchen 劉行臣 limned them.] (There are also) a Vimalakīrti and a Vairocana. [Both were limned by Liu Xingchen, and finished in colors by Zhao Kan 趙龕. Aside from these, all the rest were made after the Shengli 聖歷 era (698–699) by Liu Maode 劉茂德 and Huangfu Jie 皇甫節, working in collaboration.] Further, a transformation [tableau] of the Lotus Blossom and Heir Apparent 法華太

子變 [Finished (in color) by Liu Maode. He was the son of (Liu) Xingchen.] On the west wall are a Buddha Assembly of the West 西方佛會 [Limned by Zhao Wuduan 趙武端], the Sixteen Ways of Visualization, and a Scene of King Yama 十六觀及閻羅王變 [These were limned by Liu Azu 劉阿祖].[26]

Zhang Yanyuan divides his attention by media, first noting statues and then wall paintings. The Maitreya statues in the Buddha Hall are a none too subtle reminder of Wu Zetian's self-identification with that deity, which makes perfect sense in view of Wu's patronage of the monastery.

More curious is the second part of the passage concerning the wall paintings. Zhang's report about the iconography on both walls has baffled modern scholars. To begin with, the "transformation [tableau] of the Lotus Blossom and Heir Apparent" does not quite make sense. In annotating Zhang's text, Ono Katsutoshi admits: "it is not clear what kind of composition this could have been."[27] Sharing Ono's perplexity, the art historian William Acker further speculates:

> . . . the only suggestions I can make are 1) that it might have been a loose way of referring to the story of the Prodigal Son in Ch. IV of the *Saddharmapuṇḍarīka-Sūtra*. Although the father in that story is not a king but a very wealthy and powerful man; 2) that it might refer to the two young princes Vimalagarbha and Vimalaneta of Ch. XXIV of the same sūtra, who convert their Brahmanical father to Buddhism by performing miracles, but both of them could scarcely have been Heirs Apparent; 3) that perhaps it refers to two works, a *fa-hua-bian* (*Saddharmapuṇḍarīka mandala*)—the familiar type with Śākyamuni and Prabhūtaratna sitting side by side in the stūpa—and a *tai-zi-bian* (lit. Crown Prince Mandala) which might conceivably refer to some painting showing scenes from Śākyamuni's early life as a prince.[28]

He is onto something in the first two suggestions but wide of the mark in the third, as will be demonstrated later. Further compounding the mystery is the juxtaposition on the eastern wall of a Vimalakīrti and an alleged Vairocana, an unlikely yoking together of two images entirely unrelated to each other in iconographic conventions of the time. Furthermore, one wonders, what does this hybrid, already odd in and of itself, have to do with the other monstrous hybrid, the "transformation [tableau] of the Lotus Blossom and Heir Apparent"?

The subjects on the west wall are just as perplexing. The conjoining of the "Buddha Assembly of the West" and the Sixteen Visualizations 十六觀 (*shiliu guan*) poses no problem, since the Tang-dynasty transformation tableaux based on the *Visualization Sūtra* typically place the vignettes of Lady Vaidehī's Sixteen Visualizations on the periphery of a central scene of rebirth in the Amitābha Pure Land.[29] What is odd is the yoking together of the Sixteen Ways of Meditation and the "transformation [tableau] of King Yama" according to Zhang Yanyuan's report, which baffled scholars. William Acker openly admits his perplexity:

> It may seem a little surprising to find Yama, King of Hell and Judge of the Dead, represented side by side with a paradise of Amitābha, since the *sūtras*

of that cult assure us that, even the lowest criminal, who believes in him and recites "Adoration to Amitābha (or Amitāyus)" ten times before he dies will immediately be reborn inside a closed lotus bud on one of the jeweled lakes of the Western Paradise, the only punishment being that the lotus bud (which opens at once in the case of the highest grade of the first class rebirth) remains closed for various lengths of time in the three grades of the third class rebirth, so that such souls are only dimly conscious of the glories around them until in due course the bud opens and they can sit on the open flower, see the Buddha and his attendants, etc., and then hear him preaching the Law. In any case then, a believer in Amitābha bypasses King Yama's court entirely. He can thus have no connection with Amitābha in religious thought except as the dread alternative.[30]

Similar perplexity is echoed in recent scholarship.[31] The problem is not to be attributed to our modern scholars' ignorance; rather, it may be that we place too much trust in Zhang Yanyuan's iconographic identification of the wall paintings to question the adequacy of his formulation. In fact, Acker has already sensed Zhang's apparent incompetence in Buddhist iconography.[32] What we need then is some evidence from actual early eighth-century wall paintings that show reasons why Zhang may have erred. Much to our gratitude, such pictorial evidence not only exists, its connection to the pictorial program in the Buddha hall of the Jing'ai Monastery runs surprisingly deeper than we expect.

Cave 217 at Dunhuang: family chapel of the Yin family

The extent to which the Dunhuang wall paintings vibrated to the political and cultural reverberations of the capital cities is striking. From the sixth century on, with the exception of the period under the Tibetan occupation (777–848), the design and stylistic qualities of the Dunhuang wall paintings rarely lose contact with the metropolitan region. In explaining compositions at Dunhuang, we need to take into account the larger context instead of treating them as isolated local products.

Cave 217 at Dunhuang is the family shrine of the Yin clan. From the seventh century on, the Yin family had emerged as one of the most prominent clans at Dunhuang.[33] Of particular interest to us is the pedigree started by Yin Chou 陰稠, who had four sons and eight grandsons. The latter include Yin Siyu 陰嗣玉 and Yin Siyuan 陰嗣瑗, whose portraits were among the donor images painted at the bottom of west wall of Cave 217. In 705, the Tang government established the Doulu Army 豆盧軍 in Shazhou 沙洲.[34] Some time after 708, Yin Siyuan became the Area Commander-in-Chief of the Doulu Army.[35] There is good evidence that Cave 217 was excavated some time after 708.[36] The donor images in Cave 217 include a host of women and ten men, filed respectively in a pecking order and rank of seniority from the center to the sides, with women to the left facing north and men to the right facing south. Most cartouches identifying the donor images are mangled. The following is a list of those cartouches.

1 [illegible]
2 [illegible]
3 [illegible]
4 . . . Deputy Guard, Right . . . Guard, on rotational duty at Liang Prefecture . . . general, Supernumerary, Supplementary [Official] . . . [bearer of] Crimson Fish Bag, Supreme Pillar of State.
5 . . . Standby Guard (*yiwei*) . . .
6 . . . Acting Left Guard . . . Acting left Guard, Yan Prefecture, Yan . . . chuan, Commandant . . .
7 [illegible]
8 [illegible]
9 . . . Baron . . . Glorification of Martiality Commandant, Acting Left Courageous Guard, Standby Vanguard, Lieutenant-Colonel (*langjiang* 郎將), Supernumerary (*yuanwai* 員外), Vice Director, Supplementary Supernumerary, [Bearer of] Purple Gold Fish Bag, Supreme Pillar of State [Yin] Siyuan.[37]
10 . . . rank, Viscount, Baron [Yin] Siyu.[38]

While the identity of the male donors preceding Yin Siyuan and Yin Siyu is unclear, their social eminence is not to be doubted. The three men whose accompanying cartouches can be partially read—the fourth, fifth, and sixth in line—all bear impressive titles of official appointment. Two of them were stationed in other prefectures (Liangzhou 涼州 and Yanzhou 延州). Out of the five partially identifiable donors, three of them carry the honorific title of "Supreme Pillar of State." We also know that Yin Sizhang 陰嗣彰, Yin Siyu's brother, was the Prefect of Guazhou 瓜州,[39] a neighboring prefecture of Shazhou where Dunhuang was located. There was hardly a more prominent family in early eighth-century Dunhuang than the Yin clan. It is not surprising that the pictorial program in the cave reflected the latest fashion in the capital city. It registers not only the aspirations of the local community of Dunhuang, but also the mood shifts in the metropolitan region.

The Yin family had a history of loyalty to Wu Zetian's government around 700 CE. In 690, Wu Zetian declared herself the Great Zhou Emperor. A man went to the court to present her with a "three-footed chicken," a rarity that would have qualified as an auspicious omen, only to be caught by the court officials as cheating: one of the chicken's feet was a fake! The opportunist got away with it, for the emperor forgave the fakery on the ground of the man's good intentions. The ingratiating man was not alone in his bird-watching; he had a counterpart in Dunhuang. In 692, Yin Sijian 陰嗣監 of the Yin family claimed to have spotted a "five-colored bird" in Dunhuang. The sighting went on the local official record of omen sightings.[40] Three years later, in response to the central government's call for the nation-wide construction of Great Cloud Monasteries as part of the campaign to legitimize Wu Zetian's rule, Yin Sijian's uncle Yin Zu 陰祖 headed the construction of the Great Cloud monastery at Dunhuang with its colossal 33-meter-high statue of Maitreya, Wu's iconic alter-ego, which has survived to this day in Cave 96. In 700 CE, another member of the Yin family dedicated a sūtra copy to Wu Zetian.[41]

A Tableau of "Lotus Blossom and Heir Apparent" 法華太子變 at Dunhuang

The murals in Cave 217 offer internal evidence. The cave is entered from the east side. On the south wall is a transformation tableau based on the *Lotus Sūtra* (Figure 3.1). The painting draws on various parts of the sūtra,[42] and its organization anticipates that its viewers will move in the clockwise direction. The starting point is at the bottom with an opposition between the Burning House and the "City of Nirvāṇa," shown as a walled enclosure with a four-gated stupa inside (Figure 3.2). Its textual cue comes from Chapter 14, "Peaceful Practice." The Buddha speaks of a parable involving a "wheel-turning sage king" who leads his troops against the evil forces. Upon victory, he presents his soldiers with awards, including a "City of Nirvāṇa." The chapter ends with the reader of the sūtra being promised a dream in which they will become the "king of a country/but casts aside palaces and attendants" to seek the Buddha's way and "enter nirvāṇa" in the end.

The motif of the king establishes a narrative thread that links various scenes derived from the sūtra. The scenes to the left of the City of Nirvāṇa are based on Chapter 19, "Benefits of the Teacher of the Law," which promises the sūtra disseminator a cosmic vision ("down as far as the Avīci hell and up to the Summit of Being"), the power to smell the scent of the "wheel-turning kings" and their followers, and the ability to predict whether or not a woman will be successful in conceiving and the prospect of her being "delivered safely of a healthy child." Inside the house next to the City of Nirvāṇa, the woman has just given birth to a child.

The narrative situation about the "king of a country" casting aside palaces and attendants to seek "the unsurpassed way" is continued, moving clockwise, by the scene of the King Wonderful Adornment (Chapter 27), who is converted to the Buddhist faith with the help of his wife and their two sons. The painting shows him clad in a yellow robe, paying homage to the Buddha in the central niche (Figure 3.3).

The king's two sons, Pure Eye and Pure Storehouse, are supernaturally gifted: one has mastered the "Lotus Samādhi 法華三昧 (*fahua sanmei*)" and the other "the samādhi of the escape from the evil realms of existence." Bending over a skeleton, which embodies "the evil realms of existence," the two sons practice their samādhi: Pure Storehouse exercises "the samādhi of the escape from the evil realms of existence" and makes it possible "for all living beings to escape from the evil realms." The sūtra also mentions the sons' supernatural feat of transformation, leaping up "into the air to the height of seven *tala* trees." The vignette here includes tall trees (Figure 3.3), not seen elsewhere in the painting.

Determined to enter the Buddhist order, the sons plead to their mother to allow them to "leave the household and become śramaṇas," since the encounters with the Buddhas are "as rare as is the *udumbara flower*." Accordingly, a luxuriant plant appears in the top middle scene, which is very likely the "udumbara flower" mentioned in the two sons' address.

The sons finally convert their father to the Buddhist faith, as shown in the right scene of the three Buddha-centered vignettes at the top. A noble couple, attended by retinue, venerates the Buddha who, flanked by the famous twin *sal* or *sāla* trees,[43] announces to the crowd that this King Wonderful Adornment shall be known as the "Sal Tree King." King Wonderful Adornment and his queen then present their necklaces of pearls to the Buddha. The couple then soars into the sky, cloud-borne with their attendants, and head toward a cloud-rimmed realm at the top (Figure 3.3).

The scene at the top, derived from Chapter 7, "Parable of Phantom City," continues the narrative of a royal family. Buddha Śākyamuni recalls his former life in which he was the youngest of the sixteen *princes* in the land of the Goodly City (Sambhava). Their father left the household and became the Buddha known as the Great Universal Wisdom Excellence. Upon hearing the news, the sixteen princes "all threw aside their rare objects" and joined the Buddha, as "their mothers, *weeping*, followed them" (Figure 3.4). Their grandfather, a wheel-turning sage king, with his ministers and subjects, follows the sons to venerate Buddha Great Universal Wisdom Excellence.

Following their trail, we see cloud-borne figures descend from the upper cloud-rimmed realm into the central niche where the Buddha preaches the *Lotus Sūtra* to the assembly at the Vulture Peak. The figures in monastic robes at the bottom rim of the niche—their stature ostensibly smaller than that of the bodhisattvas, and their heads unshaven—are presumably those princes. Joining the Bodhisattvas are a noble woman with her two maids on the left and a king on the right, who dons a distinct headpiece and a traditional Chinese court robe. As the only lay figure with a halo indicating his exalted status, he is likely the grandfather of these princes, the "wheel-turning sage king" mentioned in the text. By now the narrative involving the Wheel-Turning King runs full circle, harking back to the "City of Nirvāṇa" at bottom of the composition based on Chapter 14: "Again he will dream he is the king of a country/ but casts aside palaces and attendants . . . repairs to the place of practice . . . gains the wisdom of the Buddhas . . . And afterward he enters nirvāṇa."

The royal scenario continues to the right side of the composition (Figure 3.5). Just as Śākyamuni evokes the past in the Phantom City chapter, he also foresees the future, the time after he enters nirvāṇa. He is concerned that some of his disciples may harbor false notions of nirvāṇa and seek other vehicles than the one expounded in the *Lotus Sūtra*. To demonstrate this point, the Buddha tells the parable of the Phantom City, which is illustrated on the top right of the composition. As an embodiment of the false nirvāṇa, the Phantom City is opposed to the real "treasure trove," for which the painter used the parable of the Prodigal Son as the narrative frame. The royal scenario is thus continued.

The scene in the middle right illustrates the parable of the Prodigal Son told in Chapter 4, "Belief and Understanding," which concerns a king's son who abandons his father and runs away from the family. Reduced to a "lean and haggard" vagabond, he accidentally drifts into his father's house. The tramp has no idea that the dignitary in the house happens to be his father. The father knows all too well. He sends two secret messengers to coax his son into working for him, eventually rids his son of his lowly disposition, and declares the young man the heir to his throne and his riches.

The bottom scene illustrates the parable told by the Buddha in Chapter 16, "The Life Span." Here is yet another scenario involving a father–son relationship. A skilled physician leaves home to attend to business in a faraway land. In his absence, his sons drink poison and suffer the resulting pain. Upon returning, the father administers fine medicinal herbs to his sons who, as the poison takes a deep toll on them, refuse to take the medicine. The father then resorts to an expedient means. He goes off to another land and sends back a messenger with the announcement: "Your father is dead!" Grief-stricken and frightened by the thought of being orphaned, the children come to their senses and finally take the herbal medicine left by their father. They are thus cured. Hearing the good news, the father returns home.

The three parable scenes on the right of the composition combine to illustrate the Buddhist teaching about the three gradations of the path, or three vehicles, toward total enlightenment. All three are vehicles that deliver the sentient beings from the perils of the threefold world. But it is the *one* vehicle, the Buddha's way, *not three*, that is the ultimate goal one should seek, according to this composition.

This teaching is shown here with a pictorial economy. To the left of the physician scene is an open space where eight figures in monastic robes gather. The vignette is based on the Introductory Chapter of the sūtra concerning the "twenty thousand Buddhas" in the past with the same appellation of "Sun Moon Bright." The last one of these, before leaving family life, has eight princely sons. "When these *princes* heard that their *father had left* family life and had gained *anuttarāsamyaksambodi*, they all cast aside their *princely* positions and followed him by leaving family life. Conceiving a desire for the Great Vehicle, they constantly carried out brahma practice, and all became teachers of the law." The vignette here apparently illustrates this episode. The Buddha inside the three-bay hall is all radiance, thereby figuring the Sun Moon Bright or Sun Moon Lamplight 日月燈明佛 (*Riyue dengming fo*). The number of figures in *monastic robes* amounts to exactly *eight*, thereby representing eight princely sons leaving family life and entering the Buddhist order. The choice of this textual segment for illustration is felicitous, as it reiterates the father-son motif that recurs in the parables of the Prodigal Son and the physician.

The tableau here thus reconstitutes a pictorial scenario drawing on diverse textual blocks variously scattered in the sūtra. An intelligible agenda drives this assemblage. The composition is apparently skewed to highlight the storyline of a royal family. The sūtra contains parables of different royal families unrelated to one another; the painting reconstitutes them into one pictorial narrative which is essentially about the complex relationship between the parents and sons in a royal family. Overtones of tension and emotional attachment are both detectable.

While it is a stretch to map with precision the political circumstances of the Wu Zetian era onto the painting, we can nevertheless discern some embedded references here. For one thing, the reiteration of the Wheel-Turning King motif in the painting is striking. As Wu Zetian was hyped as the Wheel-Turning King, the phrase "Golden Wheel" quickly entered the vocabulary of the local gentry at Dunhuang. The memorial stele, erected in 698 by the Li family to commemorate the construction of Cave 332, speaks of "the thousand spokes of the Golden

Wheel rolling on, as the Great Zhou [ruler] steers the cosmos." The votive text also invokes the "Golden Wheel" and "Jade Tablet" in the same breath, thereby alluding to Wu Zetian's revised title, "Heavenly Tablet [Endowed] and Golden Wheel, Sagely Divine Emperor."[44] As the patron family behind the construction of Cave 332, the Li family's pledge of devotion to the Golden Wheel Sagely Emperor is reflected in the iconographic program of the wall painting inside the cave chapel.[45] More significant is the Yin family's attitude. In 700 CE, Yin Renxie 陰仁協 made a copy of the *Diamond Sūtra* and dedicated it to "the Golden Wheel, Sagely Divine Emperor," i.e., Wu Zetian.[46]

Some details in the Lotus tableau in Cave 217 are referentially pointed. The Buddha in the three-bay hall (Figure 3.5) is the only one ostensibly radiating other than the preaching Śākyamuni Buddha in the center, apparently to reinforce the identity of the image as that of "the *Sun Moon* Bright Thus Come One" 日月燈明 如來.[47] The highlighting of "the *Sun Moon* Bright" is heavily loaded. In 690, Wu Zetian adopted a new given name for herself. Its ideograph, Zhao 曌, consists of two radicals in the upper part: the "sun" 日 and the "moon" 月 that preside over the graph "space" 空 (*kong*; vast cosmic space) below. In 693, Wu Zetian's henchman Xue Huaiyi supervised the translation of the *Treasure Rain Sūtra* in the Jing'ai Monastery.[48] In the sūtra, the Buddha prophesies that the "son of heaven named Sun Moon Light 日月光 from the East" shall "the kingdom of Great China on the northeast part of the Jambudvīpa" and become a "Wheel-Turning King."[49] It is no surprise therefore that in the *Lotus Sūtra* tableau, the Sun Moon Bright Buddha is thus given such a prominence.

The gathering of the eight princes in front of the Sun Moon Bright Buddha thus becomes all the more suggestive. Emperor Gaozong, lest we forget, had a total of eight sons, four by Wu Zetian. The historical context further throws light on the significance of the neighboring scenes. Both the parables of the Prodigal Son and the physician are cautionary tales for wayward princes. Both tales portray a father attended by a shadow of death. The king in the Prodigal Son parable anticipates an imminent death: "Now the time of my death draws near."[50] The father in the physician tale says to his sons: "You should know that I am now old and worn out, and the time of my death has come." He departs, sending home the message: "Your father is dead." The sons are then "filled with great grief and consternation."[51] The high profile of princes in the *Lotus* tableau reminds us of the early Tang court politics in which one dominant motif is the friction between Wu Zetian and the princes, her own four sons, as rivaling contenders for the power and control of the throne.

Coping with princes remained one of the foremost concerns of the empress who found it necessary to reinforce and legitimize her political moves through ideological posturing. Nowhere is this more apparent than the extent to which the ethic of filial piety was manipulated to fit the circumstances. In 690, Wu Zetian, having taken over the throne and made herself the emperor, presided over the Bright Hall and had a minister lecture on the *Filial Piety Scripture* to the court. It was in the Shengli era (698–699) in particular that the issue of the heir apparent came to the fore. In 698, Wu Zetian's nephews, Wu Sansi and Wu Chengsi 武承嗣, jockeyed to have themselves installed as the heir apparent.[52] Upon much deliberation, and succumbing to old age and sickness, Wu Zetian restored her son Li Xian as the heir apparent.[53] The following year, concerned about the potential conflict between the heir apparent and the Wu clan after her death, Wu Zetian had them pledge harmony in the Bright Hall.[54]

The climate of filial piety continued even after Wu Zetian's death. The alliance between Empress Wei and the Wu clan quickly reversed the anti-Wu tide. In 706, Zhongzong conducted a ritual of pursuing the posthumous well-being 追福 (*zhuifu*) for his deceased mother Wu Zetian in the Buddhist monastery Shengshansi 聖善寺 in Luoyang.[55] The emperor also decreed the restoration of the Wu family ancestral temple.

The so-called "transformation [tableau] of Lotus Blossom and Heir Apparent" in the Buddha hall of the Jing'ai Monastery fell into this context. Two generations of painters—Liu Xingchen the father, and Liu Maode the son—were involved in the painting of this tableau, with the Shengli era (698–699) as the watershed moment. Before the Shengli era, it was the father's phase; after, the son took over. Moreover, the tableau was attributed to the hand of the son Liu Maode in the post-699 years.[56] The Lotus tableau in Cave 217 was painted some time after 708. The high profile of princes in relationship to the king or the Wheel-Turning King in the painting registers much with regard to the same political circumstances described above. Small wonder that the ninth-century viewer Zhang Yanyuan misnamed it as "transformation [tableau] of Lotus Blossom and Heir Apparent."

Moreover, the Dunhuang painting explains Zhang's mystifying report of the hybrid of "Vimalakīrti and Vairocana" on the east wall of the Jing'aisi hall. The center of the painting shows Śākyamuni preaching at the Vulture Peak. Behind the Buddha is the cosmic view of the top-heavy, mushroom-shaped Mt. Sumeru with its surrounding sea and Iron-Circling Mountains (Figure 3.1). A cosmic view of this kind would also appear in a standard Vimalakīrti tableau of around 700 which would show Vimalakīrti tossing the chiliocosm into a mustard seed. The chiliocosm being thus tossed is usually represented by a top-heavy mushroom-shaped Mt. Sumeru soaring out of an ocean ringed with mountains (Figure 3.6). The same cosmological image centered on Mt. Sumeru also appears on the robe of the Vairocana image (Figure 3.7). What Zhang saw in the Jing'ai Monastery was therefore neither a Vimalakīrti image nor a Vairocana image. Instead, it was more likely a *Lotus Sūtra* tableau like the one in Cave 217. The ostensible mushroom-shaped Mt. Sumeru must have first attracted his attention. Then the fact that this cosmological scene is emphatically circumscribed, as it appears in Cave 217, may have easily reminded Zhang of the similar image in the Vimalakīrti scene *and* a Vairocana scene. In so far as Vimalakīrti appears as a lay person just as the Wheel-Turning King in the Lotus tableau of Cave 217 does, it is easy to mistake the latter as the former. That may have led to Zhang's recognition of a Vimalakīrti scene. The prominent cosmological backdrop reminiscent of Vairocana may have led him to identify the main Buddha as a Vairocana. Then the vignettes involving the princes—the Prodigal Son, the King Adornment, etc.—account for the "transformation tableau of the Prince [from] the *Lotus [Sūtra]*." In short, what Zhang looked at may have simply been the *Lotus Sūtra* tableau that we see in Cave 217 (Figure 3.1).

Just as the *Lotus Sūtra* tableau on the one side wall faces the *Visualization Sūtra* tableau (i.e., The "Buddha Assembly of the West" *cum* "Sixteen Ways of Meditation") on its opposite wall in the Buddha Hall of the Jing'ai Monastery, so the same pictorial program appears in Cave 217 at Dunhuang.

The "Buddha Assembly of the West 西方佛會; Sixteen Ways of Meditation" 十六觀 in circumstantial context

On the north wall is a two-part transformation tableau (Figure 3.8). The central overlay shows the Amitayus Paradise based on the *Amitabha Sūtra*; the scenes on the surrounding underlay illustrate the tale of the "Enemy Before Birth" (*Weishengyuan*), based on the *Visualization of the Amitayus Buddha* (*Guan wuliangshou jing* 觀無量壽經) and its seventh-century commentary by Shandao 善導 (613–681).[57] The story concerns Ajātaśatru, Prince of Magadha, who, following an evil minister's exhortation, imprisons his king-father Bimbisāra with the intent to starve him to death. His mother, Queen Vaidehī, secretly visits her husband with her body smeared with buttered honey and parched flour so that he may have food. King Bimbisāra thus avoids starvation. The matter is leaked to Prince Ajātaśatru. In a rage, the prince carries a sword to the inner palace and wants to kill his mother. Two ministers talk him out of the attempt. As a compromise, the prince jails his mother in the inner palace as well. In utter misery, the queen prays for help from the World-honored One, i.e., the Buddha Śākyamuni. In response, the Buddha sends his two disciples, Pūrna and Maudgalyāyana, to her aid. Subsequently, Buddha himself descends to the royal palace, followed by two disciples, and teaches her Sixteen Ways of Visualizing the Land of Bliss.[58]

The way the Ajātaśatru tale is pictured in Cave 217 differs from the designs of other periods. We are hard pressed to explain why the walled city, which appears to be out of proportion in the narrative framework, should loom so unusually large here (Figure 3.9). Nowhere in the textual sources do we ever find the two arrays of armored soldiers in military formation under the command of the intimidating prince on horseback. The prince is supposed to carry a sword and burst into the inner palace to confront his parents, as he certainly appears in this way in the subsequent eighth-century compositions. So much fanfare is given to this martial scene and so much weight is invested in the architectural layout, one wonders about the circumstantial overtones of the design.

The scene decidedly recalls the successive palace coups between 705 and 713. In 706, Prince Li Chongjun 李重俊 (d. 707) was installed as the heir apparent.[59] He was rather incensed by the empress's adulterous alliance with Wu Sansi and their wielding of power in the interest of the Wu family in the post-Wu Zetian years. In 707, Li and a group of generals led 300 cavalry from the Forest of Plumes Army, an elite group of *mounted* archers of the imperial guards, to stage a surprise attack and palace purge. Having killed Wu Sansi and his son Wu Chongxun in their residences, the cavaliers led by the heir apparent broke into the Suzhang Gate with the intention of seizing Shangguan Wan'er 上官婉兒 (d. 713), another stalwart of the Wu clique serving as the spokesperson of the court. Taken by surprise, the emperor, empress,

Prince Anle, and Shangguan all scrambled onto the tower of the Dark Warrior Gate 宣武門 (*Xuanwumen*) north of the imperial palace. Shangguan sounded the alarm that the targets of the attack included herself, the *empress*, and ultimately, "us all." The emperor had the rest of the imperial guards man all the gateways in the imperial palace. Thus a stand-off ensued between the emperor's group on the gate-tower and the prince's cavalry on the ground. Confused by the unexpected grouping of the emperor, whom they had no intention to harm, with their intended target (i.e., Shangguan), the heir apparent and his allies began dithering. The emperor, however, was under the impression that he was facing a rebellion. He shouted promises of rewards to the prince-led cavaliers and it worked. The troops killed their commanders, sending the prince on a flight away from the capital city. He was killed by his followers on the way.[60]

It is hard not to see the Ajātaśatru tableau in Cave 217, painted shortly after 708, as a pictorial spin on the event. It was the first time that the palatial setting figured so prominently in the tableau. The military confrontation, absent in the textual narrative, is inflated out of proportion here to take the center stage. The gate-tower, so prominently featured on the north wall, may thus have an additional shade of relevance, since the Dark Warrior Gate of the imperial palace was located on—and symbolically associated with—the north. Moreover, the moral overtones of the narrative are consonant with the point of view of the emperor and the empress: here is a prince trying to imprison his parents. Of the series of palace coups that occurred between 705 and 713, it was the only instance in which the prince was cast as a villain in the immediate wake of the event. The scene of the horse-mounted prince shaded by a canopy in the tableau has all the trappings of the 707 event; it virtually disappeared in the subsequent Ajātaśatru tableaux. Thus, considering the pro-Wu climate in the years between 705 and 710, it is not surprising to see the entire pictorial program in the cave shrine echoing that perspective. Such a close echo of the political events in the capital cities further suggests that the design of the painting may have originated from the metropolitan center, such as the Jing'ai Monastery, given the latter's central role in both the political landscape and image-making arena.[61]

The parallel in pictorial program between the Jing'ai Monastery and Cave 217 goes beyond the two facing walls. As a Tang visitor entered the Buddha hall of the Jing'ai Monastery from the south, he would have been greeted by an array of three Maitreya statues, which held the pride of place in the iconographic program of the hall. Similarly, as one enters Cave 217 from the east, one faces the main niche on the west wall filled with clay statues, now badly damaged, representing a Buddha assembly. The ceiling of the niche features Maitreya's Tuṣita Heaven.[62] To the upper right is a seated Buddha preaching to eight figures—four monks and four lay people—symmetrically divided into two sides, with two lay women on the left and two lay men on the right. Below the preaching scene, presumably the same Buddha, holding a bowl, descends on a cloud to a walled city out of which emerges a woman who eagerly meets him (Figure 3.11).[63] The scene depicts Śākyamuni's conversion of his mother Māyā in heaven.[64] The mother/son reunion resolves the tension in the Ajātaśatru scenario.

As for how King Yama fits into this context, a different framework is involved.

Transformation tableaux and the "pursuit of posthumous well-being" 追福 (zhuifu)

The moral we can draw thus far is that the political circumstances and ideological climate of the time left an indelible mark on the design of transformation tableaux in Buddhist monasteries. However, we would substantially short-change ourselves if we are content with this finding, which, stated in general terms, is something of a commonplace by now. There is more to our case. In both the Buddha hall of the Jing'ai Monastery and Cave 217, the *Lotus Sūtra* tableau is placed on a side wall facing the *Visualization Sūtra* tableau on the opposite wall. The identical spatial distribution of the tableaux shared by two sanctuaries so distant from each other is by no means a coincidence. Each of the two tableaux evokes and opens up an imaginary horizon of its own; their convergence creates a special and distinct symbolic space that makes the Buddha hall and the cave chapel more than a mere physical setting. The question then is: What brings the two tableaux together to create a symbolic continuum?

The answer is not to be sought in the sūtras. Much of the scholarship on transformation tableaux is constrained by the misguided premise about the primacy of the sūtras, of which the transformation tableaux are deemed mere illustrations, something of secondary importance. We tend to compartmentalize these tableaux into unrelated boxes by way of the classification system of the sūtras. Confronted with a set of transformation tableaux laid out on different walls of a cave shrine, modern art historians are surprisingly timid and rigid in making connections among them, mainly because the subject matters of the sūtras, on which the tableaux are based, do not appear to have anything to do with one another. A proper understanding of the transformation tableaux in the medieval Chinese context requires a reckoning with their function. Transformation tableaux were mostly commissioned by monks or lay believers for the ritual purpose of "pursuit of posthumous well-being" (*zhuifu*) of the deceased family members or relatives.[65] The underlying conviction is that upon an individual's death, the outcome of his or her reincarnation is undetermined; the wandering soul may stumble in a state of limbo among the Six Paths of transmigration. It fell upon the living to "cultivate merits" on behalf of the dead. "If the father dies and falls among the hungry ghosts," as we read from the *Youposai jie jing* 優婆塞戒經 (*Upāsakaśīla sūtra*), "his son can be assured that, by performing the pursuit of the posthumous welfare, his father would be reborn in heaven."[66] The means of "pursuing the posthumous welfare" or "cultivating merits" include making Buddhist images and sūtra copies, building pagodas, repairing monasteries, ordaining monks, conducting ceremonial rituals (such as circumambulation), and so forth.[67] Transformation tableaux were often commissioned in this context.[68] As imaginary projections of the living, the tableaux map out the tortuous contours of the ways to paradise. Along the way, demons and spirits ought to be pacified, supernatural beings invoked as protective agents, purgatory anticipated but ultimately transcended, and paradises eventually gained. Such a soteriological agenda is the ultimate structure underlying the pictorial program of transformation tableaux.

In 706, Emperor Zhongzong observed the "pursuit of posthumous welfare" for his deceased mother, Wu Zetian, by renovating the Shengshan Monastery (Monastery of the Holy and Good [Mother]) in Luoyang and building a Pavilion of the Reward for [Maternal] Benevolence 報慈閣 (*Baocige*) inside the monastery,[69] which attained the status of a "dynastic monastery' of the Tang.[70] In view of the ostensible history of the affinity of the Jing'ai Monastery with the Wu Zetian regime, it is unlikely that the monastery was kept out of the ritual activity. Considering that the so-called "transformation [tableau of] the Lotus Blossom and Heir Apparent" in the Jing'ai Monastery was completed some time after 699, it may well be that the tableau was designed or revised in 706 to join Zhongzong's "pursuit of posthumous welfare" for Wu Zetian, an event that could hardly have been confined to the Shengshan Monastery alone. The conspicuous display of Wu Zetian's portrait and its excessive focus on Maitreya in the Jing'ai Monastery all point to its participation in the "pursuit of posthumous welfare" of the late empress. As the *Lotus Sūtra* tableau in Cave 217 was painted some time after 708, a product of the Zhongzong era, it has all the earmarks of a pictorial product born out of the same context. The high profile of the Wheel-Turning King in the *Lotus Sūtra* tableau reinforces this impression.

The patron family's agenda

That the design of the tableaux in the Jing'ai Monastery, which were rooted in the context of Zhongzong's "pursuit of the posthumous well-being" of Wu Zetian, reached Dunhuang does not necessarily mean that its original circumstantial purpose was preserved intact in the process of transmission. True, the Yin family was probably still pledging its allegiance to the central government. It is just as likely that the appeal of the design of transformation tableaux from the Eastern Capital may have primarily resided in its registering of the latest metropolitan fashion, and its general fulfillment of the ritual function of "pursuit of the posthumous welfare." The Yin family, therefore, may have had its own use for this function.

The relevance of the transformation tableaux to the local lay community mostly went beyond the political agenda attached to them. In 675, a lay woman at Dunhuang named Zhang 張 commissioned both a copy of the *Visualization Sūtra* and a *Guanyin Sūtra*, with the votive that the copy may

> benefit the myriad sagely deeds of the Heavenly Emperor [Gaozong] and Heavenly Empress [Wu Zetian] on high, and the forebears of the seven generations and the creatures of the Dharma world below, so that all shall transcend the gate of vexations, and arrive at the land of wonder and purity.[71]

While there is no limit to the ways in which local patrons may be attracted to the sūtra and its tableaux, one appeal the narrative situation of the *Visualization Sūtra* held for the lay community was the close bonding between the husband and wife (i.e. Bimbisāra and Vaidehī) in trying situations and the prospect of them both ascending to the Pure Land together in their next life.[72]

Such a soteriological agenda may underlie the entire iconographic program of the cave shrine sponsored by the Yin family. The votive inscription located in the center of the *Lotus Sūtra* tableau has unfortunately faded to the extent of unintelligibility. Only fragments of the text can be recognized:

> Thus it is heard . . . not gone without . . . Buddha says . . . recognized the body . . . Bodhi mind . . . venerable . . . body residing . . . the state of being that [one] aspires for. The mind [or heart] is turned toward [Mahāyāna] (*huixin*) all for the sake of . . . with human beings . . . recognized fortunately that it is not without the gate of arrival . . . feel the inconstancy of life and death; and know the [. . .] of the benevolent sage . . . if only . . . not . . . fire . . . coming . . . may . . . ground is . . . Buddha . . . in accordance . . . donate . . . horizon at the encounter . . . gone . . . forever . . . express the sorrow . . . [revived] . . . someone . . . acknowledge . . . recognize . . . disciple of Buddha.[73]

Some formulaic themes emerge out of the remaining legible fragments. The patrons of the pictorial program acknowledge the need to follow the Mahāyāna Buddhist teachings, such as devoting one's merits to the salvation of others. They come to recognize the transient nature of human existence within this world. Finally, a "sorrow" 恨 (*hen*) is expressed.

The local or family circumstances surrounding this project can only be vaguely surmised with the aid of some tenuous and slim corroborative evidence available to us. Five sūtra copies—dated between 679 and 708—commissioned by the Yin family members have survived[74]:

> 679 Yin Renxie, a copy of the *Diamond Sūtra*.
> 680 Yin Renxie, a copy of the *Diamond Sūtra*.
> 696 Yin Siyuan, a copy of the *Guanyin Sūtra*.[75]
> 700 Yin Renxie, a copy of the *Diamond Sūtra*.
> 708 Yin Siyuan, a copy of the *Diamond Sūtra*.[76]

Of these five, only two colophons indicate the purpose of the copy. Yin Renxie in the 696 copy makes it explicit that the aspiration for a higher official rank lies behind his appeal to the numinous efficacy the Buddhist deities may offer him.[77] It is remarkable how he steadfastly held on to the *Diamond Sūtra*. Yin Siyuan, his nephew, seems to be preoccupied by other things. Since he was one of the patrons of Cave 217, and because his copy of the *Diamond Sūtra* was completed in 708, shortly before the dedication of Cave 217, his copies are more relevant here.

The *Diamond Sūtra* remained one of the most popular scriptures in medieval China.[78] Its appeal to medieval lay believers resides not so much in its doctrinal teaching as in the miraculous efficacy associated with it. "For those who copy it," as an early-Tang popular tale goes, "its merits are boundless and incredible."[79] A year before Yin Siyuan made his copy of the sūtra, another illustrious patron named Xue Chonghui 薛崇徽, Magistrate of the Tonggu 同谷 District of Chen 陳 Prefecture (in modern Gansu), also made one copy of it to benefit the wandering spirit of his deceased grandson Xue Yingxiu 英秀.[80] The memorial context that occasioned the copying of the *Diamond Sūtra* alerts us to the possible parallel situation that may have prompted Yin Siyuan to copy the sūtra, a conjecture somewhat reinforced by the elegiac lamentation in the votive inscription in Cave 217: an awareness of the "inconstancy of life and death," and the expression of "sorrow." There are further ostensible points of contact between the *Diamond Sūtra*, which Yin Siyuan copied in 708, and the Cave 217 tableaux whose purpose is articulated in the votive inscription. Both are concerned with the body. "Terminating this Response Body," says a popular votive prefacing a number of copies of the *Diamond Sūtra* from Dunhuang, "all shall be reborn in the land of bliss."[81] Likewise, the character "body" 身 (*shen*) is a motif reiterated in the Cave 217 votive inscription. In all likelihood, the Yin family was having its own "pursuit of posthumous welfare" for one of its own members. In any case, this ritual function may have undergirded both the tableaux in the Jing'ai Monastery and in Cave 217.

The postmortem scenario and the "transformation [Tableau] of King Yama"

As the ritual function of the "pursuit of posthumous welfare" of the deceased shaped the transformation tableaux, it follows that the "correct" and faithful interpretation of the sūtra was of little concern to the painters. The sequential order of the chapters of the sūtra is completely disregarded. Some chapters are favored over others; some lines are seized upon and elaborated while large chunks of texts are left out. Rather than be constrained by the structure of the text, the medieval Chinese painters imposed on the text a spatial order of their own, a world picture they harbored, which already has its own internal topographic structure and spatial logic, a mental grid through which they plot the disparate scenes from the *Lotus Sūtra*.

When it comes to the postmortem scenario, the *Lotus Sūtra* comes up somewhat short. For the devotee, the *Lotus Sūtra* offers three afterlife prospects: the Tuṣita Heaven, the Amitabha Pure Land, and the Trayastrimśās.[82] It is not clear from the sūtra how the Trayastrimśās Heaven is situated in relation to the Tuṣita Heaven. Nor does the sūtra spell out what it is like between the point of one's death and these Buddhist paradises, or how the itinerary toward the destination is configured. The early eighth-century culture, preoccupied with Daoist realms and modes of existence, impinged a kind of Daoist sensibility on the painter and provided him with clues and solutions. With the richly textured mosaic of a postmortem scenario painted in the Daoist scriptures such as the *Salvation Scripture* 度人經 (*Durenjing*), he was able to fill in the gap left by the *Lotus Sūtra* in this regard.

The crossing-over from one religious tradition to another may fly in the face of our modern dogmatic taxonomy. In medieval China, however, it was less of a problem. Buddhist apocrypha and Daoist scriptures blatantly borrow from each other. Tableaux illustrating Buddhist and Daoist scriptures commonly appropriated images and references from each other. This excessive crossing-over alarmed the imperial court. An imperial decree of 705 noted "that the Daoist temples everywhere all paint Buddha images in an effort to convert the foreigners, whereas the

Buddhist monasteries also paint the image of the [Daoist] Mystic Prime."[83] For the eighth-century painter whose professional instinct it was to visualize situations out of a text—be it Buddhist or Daoist—he could not have cared less for dogma. Moreover, both texts in question—the *Lotus Sūtra* and the *Salvation Scripture*—contain such striking parallels that it required little effort on the part of the painter to conflate situations derived from them.[84] We also know that painters of the time were commissioned to paint transformation tableaux based on both Buddhist and Daoist scriptures. Wu Daozi 吳道子, the most celebrated painter of the eighth century, is said to have executed transformation tableaux based on Daoist scriptures. A votive inscription, which has survived on Mount Tai, dated 704, reads:

> In accordance with the decree, the following were made for the emperor [Wu Zetian]: a layout of ten images, including a stone Celestial Worthy, Supreme Thearch of Celestial Worthy, a composition of wall painting of thirteen images including the Celestial Worthy. Copied with veneration are the following: a *Benji* scripture and ten rolls of *Salvation Scripture*. Dedicated to the Sagely Throne with blessings.[85]

While the inscription does not specify on which of the two Daoist scriptures the painting was based, it is conceivable that such a tableau illustrating the *Salvation Scripture* circulated at the time, further evidenced by surviving cartouches accompanying the pictorial tableau based on the *Salvation Scripture*.[86] In light of this new climate, we can now look at the Cave 217 tableaux anew through the Daoist lens.

The left side of the Lotus tableau (Figure 3.3) shows four ascending cloud-borne figures, three of them headed toward the top cloud-rimmed sphere. One group faces directly the central niche without going along the upper-sphere route. These are scenes of "flight to transcendence" in the hierarchical ranking with different degrees of sanctity. A pecking order in this regard had gained currency by Ge Hong's 葛洪 (283–363) time: the first class soars into the sky to become the Heavenly Genii; the second class goes into the mountains to become the Earthly Genii; the third class "sloughs off the body after death and is designated Corpse-freed Genii."[87]

Much as this three-fold division was familiar to Tang authors,[88] an alternative four-fold scheme was also in currency in Tang times: (1) the flying transcendent, (2) the celestial transcendent, (3) the earthly transcendent, and (4) the delivery-from-corpse transcendent. Whether it is the three- or four-fold scheme, the basic idea is premised upon an opposition between heaven and earth. For those who soar into the sky in daylight, they are headed to the realm of transcendence with their body and spirit intact without being subjected to the inconvenience of bodily death. They consequently roam above the Three Realms, never having to worry about the vexing matters of birth, death, and worldly disasters. For those going through the "deliverance-from-corpse" process, they primarily remain earth-bound, roaming freely in the famous mountains with other-worldly grotto-heavens. After some cycles of transformation, they may eventually arrive in the celestial realms.[89] Li Shaowei 李少微, one of the Tang commentators on the *Salvation Scripture*, offers another four-fold scheme:

This scripture offers four ways of helping mortals arrive at salvation. The first is flight to heaven in daylight to achieve an instant salvation. The second is metamorphosis through the deliverance-from-corpse method to attain salvation. The third is death with an undecayed body which is soon revivified. The fourth is temporary demise of the intelligent spirit followed by its flight to the Southern Palace to receive purification.[90]

It is hard to determine exactly which theory is most relevant here for our purpose,[91] though the painting appears to match Li Shaowei's scheme closely. The King Adornment and his family represent the "ascent to heaven in daylight" before they are visited by death. Accordingly we see them headed directly toward the central niche without going through the detour of the flight to the top sphere as the other three groups do. Immediately above the scene of the King Adornment is the salvation by way of release-from-corpse. Then the top two flights represent the other two ways as outlined by Li. Whatever the case, it is clear that there is a differentiation between kinds of transcendental flight to heaven. The skeleton scene ostensibly visualizes the "Deliverance from Corpse," a typical Daoist scenario. According to Daoist tradition, one's spirit may be released from his body, like a cicada shedding its husk or a snake its skin, and disappearing into thin air.[92] While the majority of scriptures keep the spirit freed from the dead body earth-bound, in some cases, such corpse-released spirits deserve no better than the prospect of serving in the bureaucratic ranks of the netherworld.[93] The *Salvation Scripture*, however, is far more sanguine and generous with its postmortem prospects:

> When ordinary mortals receive and recite the scripture, they will extend their years and live long lives. At the end of their lives, they will achieve the way of *release from the corpse*. Their cloud-souls and bodily spirits will be obliterated for only an instant and will not pass through the earth-prisons, but will be immediately returned to the body so that they might roam the Grand Void.[94]

By affirming that "their cloud-souls and bodily spirits . . . will not pass through the earth-prisons," the *Salvation Scripture* tacitly acknowledges the better known theory of "release from corpse" that remain bound to the "earth-prison," a theory it makes a point of sabotaging. It offers an alternative prospect: one's cloud-soul may be joined with its body and "roam the Grand Void." Indeed, the Lotus tableau here depicts the cloud-soul heading toward the "Great Void," just as do the other ascending figures.

The next question is: What exactly is the celestial sphere at the top (Figure 3.4) supposed to be? In the *Lotus Sūtra* framework, it is the Summit of Being. However, nothing in the *Lotus Sūtra* prepares us for the kind of trappings we see in this sphere. Again, the *Salvation Scripture* sheds light on the matter. All the heaven-bound spirits are said to be headed toward the Southern Palace. Located immediately below the "Nine Palaces of the Great Purity,"[95] it is a very special domain in the Daoist cosmos, a primary way-station, or a "custom house" of sorts, where the spirits of the deceased get purified before they are cleared to move on to "ascend through the Golden Porte to roam and feast in the Jade Capitoline."[96] Here reside a host of deities in charge of life-and-death matters: Lord of Long Life, Deliverer of the Generations, Director of Equerry, the Lord of Life, Directors of Destinies, Director of Registers, and so forth. Here also are kept all the life-and-death registers of the mortal beings. Rebirth involves a change of records in the register that bears one's name: "'death' will be scratched out and 'life' written over it."[97] The hoard of secret writs and registers are revealed to the privileged visitor upon the latter's sworn confidentiality. The writs also include maps of sacred mountains or some inventory of nature spirits scattered around the cosmos who can be called upon for aid. Possessing these writs marks an attainment of transcendence and inures one against the menacing forces out there.[98]

This Daoist heaven informs the modeling of the Summit of Being in the *Lotus Sūtra* tableau here. The cloud-rimmed sphere is tantamount to the "Brahmā pneumas circling through the ten directions of space" described in the *Salvation Scripture*.[99] The central hall in the top celestial sphere has its front doors wide open, revealing a table placed on a couch, on which are placed five scrolls with alternating colored covers: the registers and writs, referred to in Daoist writing as "Five Tablets,"[100] or "Five Bolts of Silk."[101] According to the *Salvation Scripture*, the celestial deities associated not only serve as record-keepers of these vital registers, but they also go out to greet the prospective heaven-bound Daoist aspirant. The Perfected of the Southern Extremities, for instance, according to the medieval commentary on the *Salvation Scripture*, often checks the register of the names of the Daoist adepts. At the end of a "disastrous kalpa," he would dispatch a deity to greet those-to-be-saved "on a phoenix carriage,"[102] or on "carriages with cinnabar-red compartments, green shafts, feather canopies, and red-gem wheels, all formed of soaring clouds. ... Held aloft are blazons of nine colors and spirit banners of ten striations,"[103] or "a jasper carriage with a flying canopy and cinnabar shafts."[104] This helps to explain the cloud-borne chariot with two "spirit banners" in the Lotus tableau, which issues from the top sphere and descends to the left. The "spirit banners" flag special significance for this occasion. One Tang commentator of the *Salvation Scripture* glosses them as a symbol of "turn-around" pertaining to life-and-death matters.[105]

Within the Daoist framework, the sixteen tiny petal-shaped white dots on the ground acquire new overtones. In the *Lotus Sūtra*, Śākyamuni describes a distant past when, in his former life, sixteen princes—Śākyamuni being the youngest of them—all followed their father's example by leaving the household and becoming followers of the Buddha. To illustrate the remoteness of that past, Śākyamuni resorts to an analogy. Suppose, he says, someone took all the earth particles of the entire cosmos, ground them into ink power, and dropped one grain, the size of a speck of dust, at a time until he dropped them all. One particle of dusk represents one *kalpa*. One can then imagine how far away that past era is. The crux here is the phrase "earth particles," which, as it appears in Kumārajīva's translation, is rendered as "*dizhong*" 地種 (earth seeds) in Chinese.[106] The word "seed" 種 (*zhong*) is loaded. According to the *Salvation Scripture*, the sphere above the Three Worlds is known as the Heaven of Seed People 種民. These are the people whose deeds of virtue and good work have been duly tracked by the watchful eye of the celestial spirit luminaries. They are thus slated to be the "elect of Daoist eschatology," unharmed by the cataclysm of the end of time and favored to "form the germ of the new populace at the beginning of a fresh age."[107] Moreover, it is the realm that ensures its inhabitants a freedom from the worries of lapsing into the cycles of birth, death, and Three Disasters.

The composition seems to imbue Śākyamuni, or the World Honored One 世尊, of the *Lotus Sūtra* with the overtones of the Celestial Worthy 天尊 of the *Salvation Scripture*. Both gather an assembly of attendants from "ten directions" of the cosmos. The Celestial Worthy's "universal announcement," made in a hushed solemnity of a Judgment Day, has a soteriological overtone for a tableau in service of "pursuit of posthumous welfare." It reaches the "illimitable spirit lands" of the entire cosmos:

> Above we have released the primogenitors, together with their seed and descendants for millions of kalpas. Forthwith withdraw their ledgers of transgressions and eradicate the roots of evil within them. Do not shackle or detain them; do not compel them to join the ghostly hordes. The talismanic command of Primordial Commencement ensures that they be immediately transferred above. The Cold Pool of the Northern Metropolis, with its cohorts to guard their forms and cloudsouls, controls all demons to ensure their ascent, transferring their documents of salvation to the Southern Palace, where the cloudsouls of the deceased are refined and, through transcendent mutation, become human; where the body is vivified and receives salvation, to endure for kalpa after kalpa. With the turning of kalpa cycles, they will enjoy a longevity equal to that of heaven, forever free of the three kinds of servitude, the five sufferings, and the eight difficulties. Skimming beyond the Three Realms, they will roam unhindered in Upper Clarity.[108]

This scene is of paramount importance since it officially declares the spirit of the deceased eligible for ascension to celestial transcendence. In doing so, it maps out the structure of the cosmos in which the death-to-rebirth transformation takes place. It reaches "the illimitable spirit lands of the Three Realms, down to the Bureau of Spring-Bend and Luofeng 羅酆 of the *Northern Metropolis*, addressed to the Three Offices, the Nine Agencies, and the Twelve River Sources" (Ibid.). Its topographic significance ought not to be lost on us. Here is a spatial interplay between the *south* and *north*, between the "Southern Palace" and the "Northern Metropolis." The Southern Palace is where one's soul gets refined in preparation for a further flight to transcendence in the Jade Purity. The Northern Metropolis is the locale of "six celestial palaces of Fengdu" 酆都, which provides a numinous sanctity for the souls of those who have not transcended but registered deeds of virtues in their lives.[109]

This south/north bipolar opposition alerts us to the way transformation tableaux are assigned to the walls of different directions within the same cave shrine. In Cave 217, what first catches our attention is the felicitous location of the pictorial scenario of the souls' ascent to the Southern Palace on the south wall (Figure 3.1). This is no coincidence. If we hold on to our assumption that the entire cave shrine constitutes a coherent imaginary space, the logic underlying the tableau on the south wall—a pictorial universe ordered on a cue of a Daoist imagination—extends to the north wall (Figure 3.8) just as well. To return to the Daoist spatial opposition between Southern Palace and Northern Metropolis, we now see why the walled city and military parade receive such a visual prominence in the composition on the north wall. The latter apparently complies with the scheme of the imaginary cosmos depicted in the *Salvation Scripture.*

The Celestial Worthy makes an announcement to the bureaucracies of the spiritual world that they should release the primogenitors of the follower of the *Salvation Scripture* and their descendants, withdraw their ledgers of transgressions, eradicate the roots of evil within them, and spare them the misery of joining the ghostly hordes. The announcement reaches "the illimitable spirit lands of the Three Realms, down to the Bureau of Spring-Bend and Luofeng of the Northern Metropolis."[110] Luofeng is a mountain located in the north, "the abode of ghosts and spirits of heaven and earth," under the charge of Northern Thearch, the Great Demon King. It has six palaces divided according to the scheme of Three Primes (Heaven, Earth, Water) or Three Offices. Each Office in turn consists of Three Agencies, thus totaling Nine Agencies. Spring-Bend and Northern Metropolis are bureaus in this numinous realm,[111] cold, watery, nocturnal, and apparitional, inhabited by the souls and spirits, particularly of one's forebears of distant past, or those who have failed to make it to the transcendence. Here the documents and registers of the life-and-death matters are kept.

It is fitting that the Northern Metropolis should become the shadow setting for the Ajātaśatru tableau on the northern wall (Figure 3.8) and explains the latter's oddities. Its northern orientation is significant. The metropolitan setting and the hierarchical division into different offices and agencies conjure up the image of the walled cities and architectural structures. The Ajātaśatru narrative, steeped in sins and transgressions, comes into an easy association with the Northern Metropolis, where "ledgers of transgressions" are kept and the sinful or yet-to-be-released souls dwell. As the Northern Metropolis is a ghostly domain, order is often kept by way of the military might of the celestial generals. The thearchs and demon kings here lead a formidable force:

> Their flying processions are attended by drumming. They have overall command of the demon soldiers. With banners, streamers, drums, and insignia, they roam on tours of inspection throughout the Grand Void. They proclaim themselves "resplendent," . . . To safeguard the transferal of souls to the Southern Palace, the Northern Metropolis is to be "strictly regulated," lest the ghosts get out of hand: . . . The Three Offices and the Palace of Northern Feng thoroughly oversee the demon armies, so that they may not hide away.[112]

The word picture matches the scene of military exercise outside the city gate (Figure 3.9). Not that the painting illustrates these lines; but it is the sort of topography the early eighth-century painters would harbor when it came to depicting a postmortem numinous realm.

Testifying to the existence of this imaginary topography are the imaginary scenarios in stories, hagiographies, biographies of medieval monks, nuns, and lay people gathered by Tang monks in special collections dedicated to the *Lotus Sūtra*, such as the *Tales of the Lotus Sūtra*.[113] What is striking about these tales is how tangentially these narrated events are related to the topography of the sūtra world. Just as striking is their insistent reiteration of certain imaginary set scenarios cursorily mentioned or simply absent in the sūtra, such as the death scene of the devotee, how he is greeted by the *Amitābha Buddha* and his entourage in the air,[114] or how he suffers a sudden death, and, having been captured by the King Yama's emissaries, sleepwalks through the oneiric landscape of the bureau of the *King Yama's* hell and gets away on the ground of his life-time recitation of the *Lotus Sūtra*.[115] King Yama's emissaries are often portrayed on *horseback* blocking the escape way; the netherworld ruled by the King Yama into which the hapless protagonist stumbles is almost invariably set in a *walled city* consisting of interconnected compounds.[116] Moreover, some of the dream journeys to the numinous world oscillate between hell and paradise. A seventh-century man named Yu Lintong 虞林通, for instance, allegedly died of sickness. He was taken by six "netherworld officers" 冥官 to the gate of a great city. There, however, he encountered the Medicine King who, on the basis of Lin's previous merit of sūtra-learning, taught him a *gāthā* which would enable him to turn a hell into a lotus pond. He then met King Yama who released him upon learning Lin's ability to turn "Eighteen Hells into lotus ponds."[117] It offers us a refreshing way of attending to the *Visualization Sūtra* tableau on the north wall in which the infernal scene is so close to the lotus pond of Amitābha's Pure Land.

From these scenarios, we can piece together a mental topography of sort, which is aptly laid out in the *Visualization Sūtra* tableau on the north wall of Cave 217 (Figure 3.8). Small wonder that the walled city is given such a visual prominence (Figure 3.9). Prince Ajātaśatru on horseback enacts the role of the King Yama's emissaries on horseback. Now we are better equipped to deal with Zhang Yanyuan's mystifying yoking of the Western Assembly, Sixteen Visualizations, and the so-called "transformation [tableau] of King Yama." With his mind filled with similar scenarios derived from the journey-to-the-netherworld tales, he apparently took Prince Ajātaśatru as King Yama's emissary or Yama himself, and consequently identified the scene as a "Transformation [tableau] of King Yama." His iconographic blunder would have, in fact, gratified the early eighth-century painter, for it was precisely the sort of effect the painter wanted to produce: namely, to use the Prince Ajātaśatru story as a narrative frame, and the city as the setting, to enact the infernal scenario of sin and its ultimate redemption in the netherworld ruled by King Yama.

It is repeatedly asserted in the *Salvation Scripture* that souls of the deceased individuals, particularly those of the forebears, would depart the Northern Metropolis. Their "register of transgression" would be tallied, and their record re-adjusted. It is consequently easy to see how the programming of the transformation tableaux on north and south walls of Cave 217 was premised on the medieval Chinese notions of postmortem situation, and not closely in line with the Buddhist doctrinal teaching.[118] To the north wall is aptly assigned the Ajātaśatru story with its military trappings and palatial setting (Figure 3.9) befitting the imaginary Northern Metropolis, and the Amitayus Paradise, with its association with water (hence *yin*) and Nine Classes of Rebirth, a hierarchical structure commensurate with the Nine Ranks through which the transcendent-to-be is expected to go through and graduate.[119] To the south wall is assigned the *Lotus Sūtra* Tableau (Figure 3.1), with its evocation of the Southern Palace (Figure 3.4) heralding the celestial beyond. In the overall scheme, the entire cave shrine spells out the imaginary cosmos traversed by the soul of the deceased. The east wall marks the boundary between this and the other numinous world, a boundary signified by the Many Treasure stupa on the upper right of the actual gateway. It features scenes, based the Guanyin chapter of the *Lotus Sūtra*, of various perilous situations that the wondering soul may run into, and the ubiquitous manifestations of Guanyin who safeguards against these perils (Figure 3.10). The tableaux on both the north and south walls define moments of transformation. The spatial drama culminates in the niche of the west wall. There, painted on the ceiling is a cloud-rimmed Buddha land, the Tusita Heaven, as discussed earlier, where Śākyamuni Buddha converts his mother Māyā in heaven (Figure 3.11).[120] This scene within the overall pictorial program carries layers of "suggestive aptness":[121] Māyā resides in heaven, which is the destiny for the soul's journey. That goes without saying. Moreover, Māyā is also known as "Great Purity" 大清 (*daqing*),[122] a term unmistakably resonant with the Daoist "Great Purity" 太清 (*taiqing*). Furthermore, the dynamics of the narrative situation involving a mother/son relationship thematically echoes some parallel situations on the south and north walls. In the *Lotus Sūtra* tableau (Figure 3.1), the vignette of King Adornment's tale involving the bonding between the queen and her two sons is shown in prominence; in the Ajātaśatru narrative painted on the north wall, the wrenching tension between Lady Vaidehī and her son Prince Ajātaśatru (Figure 3.8) is all too self-apparent. At the soteriological level, the conversion scene on the ceiling of the west-wall niche picks up where the north wall leaves off. Lady Vaidehī's practice of Sixteen Ways of Meditation on the afterlife culminates in both the vision of the Amitayus Pure Land and the city-gate scene on the ceiling of the west-wall niche, where Māyā, Śākyamuni's mother, emerges (Figure 3.11), as a visual denouement of the north-wall scenario. At another level, the visual echo here caps an emotional line of force that has been building up on the neighboring walls. The mother/son reunion symbolically resolves the tension seen in the Ajātaśatru scenario.

The parallel between the Buddha hall of the Jing'ai Monastery and Cave 217 at Dunhuang is certainly striking. According to Zhang's record, only the east and west walls featured transformation tableaux. It makes perfect sense considering that the Buddha hall mostly faces south.[123] Stepping into the hall, one would face the Maitreya statues. On one's right (east) and left (west) would be respectively the *Lotus Sūtra* tableau (east) and the Visualization tableau (west). In the case of the Cave 217 at Dunhuang, since the cliff into which caves were excavated faces east, so the south and north become side walls flanking the viewer as he enters the shrine from the east and faces the main niche on the west wall. Despite the difference in physical orientations between the Dunhuang cave and the metropolitan Buddha hall, one essential relationship remains constant: the close symbiotic spatial relationship between the two tableaux facing each other. Such an interlocking relationship links the respective worlds of the tableaux on the two facing walls, thereby mapping out a "virtual" spatial continuum in which the movement by souls or spirits is envisioned.

Ritual space of the Buddha hall and cave shrine

Much as the pictorial program in both the Jing'ai Monastery and Cave 217 may have been occasioned by a specific event and some circumstantial contingencies, such as the "pursuit of the posthumous well-being" of the deceased, their overall function transcends specific circumstances and caters to a variety of occasions, as evidenced by the dizzying variety of ritual texts that have survived in Dunhuang manuscripts.[124] These included rituals performed on the occasion of the founding of a cave shrine, a monastery, a tableau, lamp-lighting, dissemination of sūtras, the dedication of merit to others (*huixiang*), making a procession banner, prayer against disasters, famine, flood, grave illness, funerals, national days of burning incense, wishing for a male progeny, women having difficulty during pregnancy, prayer for a relative's journey, death of the family-owned horse or cows, and so forth.[125] Considering the number of annual ritual abstinences (*zhai* 齋) and observations in medieval China, one gets a sense of the frequency of ritual occasions; some of them must have involved the use of the shrine. A medieval classification neatly encompasses the variety of votives into ten categories:

1 Eulogy of Buddha's virtue: Birth at the Royal Palace; Departure from Home; Wheel-Turning; Great Extinction.
2 Celebration of the Imperial Order: the prosperity and stability of state; appearance of auspicious omens; subjugation of the barbarians of the four quarters; harvest of five crops.
3 Ordering the Official Present.
4 Posted at the frontiers: civilian; military.
5 Votive of gratitude: monks, nuns, Daoist priest, priestess.
6 Prayer for travel: corvée—east, west, south, north; expedition—east, west, south, north.
7 Mourning the spirit of the deceased: monks, nun, Dharma master, *vinaya* master, dhyāna master, layman, parents, man, woman, girl.
8 Declaring patronage for merit [of giving]: making of images on silk, finished weaving; stone sculpture; polychrome painting; wood sculpture; gold and bronze; making of banner; sūtra-copying; construction of Buddha halls.
9 Prayer and expressing gratitude: praying for rain; thankful expression at rainfall; thankful expression at snow; first month of newborn baby; birthday; dismissal of school; . . . hook-hiding game; closure of lecture; Three Growth Months (i.e., 1st, 5th, 9th months of the Chinese calendar); peace; fraternity; survival of disaster; concern about corvée labor; ordinance; expressing thankfulness in moving in to a new house.
10 Prayer for animals: release of living creatures; praying for life; death of horse; death of ox; death of camel; death of ram; death of dog; death of pig.[126]

The list comprises an inventory of the concerns and activities encompassed by the medieval Chinese universe and provides a sense of order that begins with the Buddha's power and imperial prosperity and ends with the well-being of human and animal lives. In spite of the diversity of the enumerated items, the prayer text more or less follows some common patterns. Not surprisingly, the ultimate goal is to obtain peace and prosperity. The question is how to obtain them. Many of these aspirations were premised upon the vision of a spiritualized cosmos teeming with deities of all kinds. Spirits defined space and time. Both heaven and earth were identified with their celestial gods and chthonic spirits. Mountains and rivers all had their representative deities. The past made its presence felt through the ancestral spirits; the future was already taken up by such Buddhist deities as Maitreya. This imaginary universe was much more densely populated than our modern counterpart mainly because the temporal and spatial allocations were not kept as far apart as our modern scheme of things would have them. They jostled together and made equal claims on the medieval consciousness.

This medieval premise about the spiritualized cosmos had an immediate bearing on the way people attributed causes, and came up with solutions, to their problems. A family member's sickness may be attributed to the workings of an errant spirit of an ancestor of the *past* who may have died an unnatural death and was wreaking havoc in the *present*. To cure the disease was essentially to find ways of having the listless spirit ushered to a paradise in the *future*. The most effective way would be to identify the exact grievances. Yet the spirits were elusive and circumstances of the remote past so faded, there was no way for the living to discern the exact causes. The best they could do was to cast their net wide in order to cover the possibilities. Not knowing which spirit was wreaking havoc, they prayed for all the spirits of past and wished them all to ascend to heaven.[127] Unable to intervene in the scheme of things in the numinous realm, they had to rely on the supernatural powers of the bureaucratized spirit world, whether it was the Buddha, bodhisattvas, King Yama, or Daoist gods. The rituals of the Buddhist lay community in this regard were not fundamentally different from Daoist or popular religious practices: typically, they involved setting aside a symbolic space that was often evocative of the cosmological order. One primary procedure was to invite the spirits of all quarters of the universe to "descend" and take their proper places in this sanctified setting or enclosure. In order to make this happen, it was essential that the setting itself be fitted with features of identification, such as images and tablets and so forth, so that the deities may indeed take their proper places. This visitation from on high and the human contact with the supernatural were expected to lead to a good outcome.

Another important factor was the prosperity and stability of imperial order. War and disturbances would predictably affect and impact the lives of local communities. It is therefore understandable that, following the eulogy of the Buddha's virtues in the prayer manual (P2940), the second most important agenda is to pray for the well-being of the imperial state.

The design of the Buddhist cave shrine in many ways answered those ritual needs. The cosmological composition of the *Lotus Sūtra* tableau, for instance, mapped out the cosmos so that all the spatial and temporal segments (locales of past deeds, destinies of future, etc.) came into full view, so that the spirits of family members, whether newly deceased or ancestral, were shown an optimum itinerary in the numinous realm. The motifs of royal figures and their family dramas can serve as a pictorial counterpart to the prayer for the maintenance of imperial order. One votive text from Dunhuang is practically a sustained effort at "name-dropping."[128]

The name-dropping here is actually a way of mapping out time and space, so we actually end up with a well-coordinated cosmos. Moreover, the topographic grid of this cosmos is none other than the *Lotus Sūtra*: "Before countless kalpa is the Great Universal Wisdom Excellence 大通智勝 (Datong zhisheng) and the Sixteen Princes; after numerous kalpa are Śākyamuni and five hundred disciples." It is precisely this temporal scheme articulated in Chapter 7, "the Parable of the Phantom City," of the *Lotus Sūtra*. If we were to visualize this cosmos, we find it easy to map this textual cosmos onto the *Lotus Sūtra* tableau. At top is the Summit of Being, the cloud-rimmed celestial setting for the Great Universal Wisdom Excellence and his Sixteen Princes, a realm of distant past (whose distance is measured by the grain of dust they drop as they go along) narrated by Śākyamuni in the present. The same above-below spatial structure serves another mapping in the votive text: "the dragon palace of the heaven above with its five vehicles of mysterious tomes, and the Vulture Peak in the human world, with its twelve sūtras." The supplicant of the votive text also invites the "Son of Heaven of Sun and Moon" (*riyue tianzi* 日月天子); we see how this prayer is served by the radiant Buddha Sun Moon Bright next to the central niche.

As the supplicant is done with the high, he turns to the deities on the lower scale of this spiritual hierarchy and bureaucracy, especially the chthonic forces. The votive text goes on to enumerate all the deities, heavenly kings, chthonic gods, demon kings, the Wheel-Turning king, mountain spirits, guards of hells, to "descend" to the bodhimanda. Of special interest to us is that this remaining list of spirits includes

> *King Yama*, man-eating raksas, demon-king of epidemics, great spirit of Five Paths, god of Mount Tai administration, life-inspector, keeper of the registers of life, five Yama kings and eight petty kings, . . . report-commissioner and record-inspector, Judge of Right and Wrong, Good and Bad Boys, . . . and other miscellaneous demons and spirits.

Again, the supplicant is operating within the temporal-spatial framework as defined by Cave 217. Correspondingly, we turn to the north wall tableau where Prince Ajātaśatru's palatial setting, reminiscent of King Yama (and was often recognized as such, as Zhang Yanyuan did), provides a pictorial locus for the prayer in this regard in the votive text.

It is apparent that the iconographic program in a Buddha hall or a cave shrine maps out a highly spiritualized space. As a symbolic way-station, it puts the patron family in touch with spiritual beings of the past and future, above and below. The original design, upon which the Dunhuang composition is based, issuing from the metropolitan center may also bear the imprint of contemporary circumstances, such as imperial politics, palatial intrigues, propaganda, etc. Such an agenda does not, however, prevent the composition from serving the ritual needs of local lay communities, as prayer for the stability of imperial order is integral to the overall wish for a harmonious cosmos. It is remarkable how many factors go into the making of this imaginary space in a monastic or shrine space. It is just as striking how it both answered the immediate circumstantial occasions and served a variety of long-term purposes. Hence the enduring need for pictures and images to make the Buddha hall of a Buddhist monastery what it is: an overpopulated space where the pantheon of spirits and deities may visit and take their proper places, a way station for the earthlings to get in touch with the other world.

Notes

1 Faure 1996: 194–195.
2 The practice began with members of the imperial family or the imperial consorts' clan who donated their houses 舍宅 (*shezhai*) to serve as monasteries. It started around the fourth century (see Falin 法林, *Bianzhen lun* 辯正論, T. 52.502c), and grew into a fashion in the Sui and Tang periods. The local gentry and commoners also followed suit. See Zhang 1997: 186–204.
3 See Zhang 1997: 167–171.
4 Such is the case of Jianfusi 薦福寺 in Chang'an, see Ono 1989: vol. 1, 3–4.
5 One indication of this shift is the trend of placing pagoda(s), hitherto occupying the center of the Buddhist monastery, away from the central axis to make room for the Buddha hall.
6 *Lidai minghua ji*, 3.71–73. Acker 1954: 306–354. Antonino Forte (1983, esp. 700–703) has noted its importance.
7 *Tang Huiyao* [*THY*] 48.990. Huili 慧立 and Yancong 彥琮, *Da Tang Daci'ensi Sanzang fashi zhuan* 大唐大慈恩寺三藏法師傳, T. 50.275bc. Xu 1985: 4.109; Yang 1999: 126–127. The site of the monastery was partially excavated in 1985, yielding the foundation of the Buddha hall, corridors and other sections. See Ma 1987.
8 *Fayuan zhulin*, T. 52.1027. *THY*, 48.993.
9 Ibid. *Jiu Tang Shu* [*JTS*] 183.4741.
10 Forte 1983: 701.
11 Li Jianchao 1996: 261.
12 *Fayuan zhulin*, T. 52.1027c.
13 *Da Tang Daci'ensi Sanzang fashi zhuan*, T. 50.275b–c.
14 *Lidai minghua ji*, 71. Forte 1983: 701. For Wang Xuance's domestic and foreign itinerary, see Sun 1994: 23.
15 The first is *Da Tang Dongjing Dajing'aisi yiqie jinglun mulu* 大唐東京大敬愛寺一切經論目錄, compiled by Jingtai 靜泰 at imperial command in 664 and 665. See T. 55.180–218. The other is the *Da Zhou kanding zhongjing mulu* 大周刊定眾經目錄, compiled by Mingquan 明佺 by imperial decree in 695. See T. 55.372–476. The latter also survives in fragments in Dunhuang manuscripts, S11962 and S5943. Other Dunhuang manuscripts make references to it, e.g., P3986 and P3869, included in Fang 1997.
16 Forte 1983: 702. Fragments of this text are also in S2658, and S6502.
17 To the end of chapter 2 of *Foshuo baoyu jing* 佛說寶雨經 is attached a list of the participants of the translation project. See T. 16.292a–b. A similar colophon also appears on the copy of the sūtra in Shōsōin of Todai-ji in Japan. Fragments of this sūtra are in S7418, S2278, and Li 26, 31 at Beijing Library. S2278 contains the list of participants of the translation. The event is also mentioned in *Kaiyuan shijiao lu* 開元釋教錄, T. 55.570a.

18 *THY* 48.993; *JTS* 183.4741. Forte (1983: 702) notes the significance of this change.
19 *Song Gaoseng zhuan*, T. 50.710b.
20 *Song Gaoseng zhuan*, T. 50.718c. Śikśānanda also based himself at the Foshouji Monastery while translating *Wenshu shouji* 文殊授記 (Mañjuśrī's prophecy) and other sūtras. Ibid., 719a. For a thorough and definitive study of Fazang, see Chen 2007. At the time I was writing the present essay, I did not have the benefit of consulting Chen's monumental work. Chen's insights into Fazang may have superseded what I have to say regarding Fazang.
21 *Song Gaoseng zhuan*, T. 50.732b. Tang Yongtong (1982: 168) considers the completion of the translation of the sūtra to have taken place in the Foshouji Monastery.
22 *Lidai minghua ji*, 3.73.
23 Prince Anle was first married to Wu Chongxun 武崇訓; following his death, she was remarried to Wu Yanxiu 武延秀, *Zizhi tongjian* 209.6628.
24 See the impassioned memorials presented to the throne in 710, *THY*, 48.996–98.
25 Zhang makes a mistake in noting that "Jing'ai-si was founded by the Emperor Zhongzong for Gaozong and Empress Wu." As Pelliot (1923) and Forte (1983: 701) point out, Zhang must have confused the posthumous titles of Xiaojing Emperor 孝敬皇帝 (Li Hong 李弘) and Xiaohe Emperor 孝和皇帝 (Li Xian 李顯, i.e, Emperor Zhongzong 中宗).
26 *Lidai minghua ji* 3.71–72, translation based on Acker 1954: vol. 1, 306–318, with modifications.
27 Cited from Acker 1954: vol. 1, 316.
28 Acker 1954: vol. 1, 316. Yu Jianhua, in his annotation of Zhang's text simply identifies the painting as referring to Chapter 27, "Former Affairs of King Wonderful Adornment," of the *Lotus Sūtra. Lidai minghua ji*, 72, n. 6. In making this claim, Yu basically concurs with Acker's second suggestion.
29 For studies on the tableaux, see Waley 1931: 60–61; Warner 1938; Nakamura 1979–1981; Sun 1990; Wu 1992.
30 Acker 1954: 318, n. 2. The iconography on this wall is also discussed in Teiser 1988: 444–445.
31 After glossing the phrase "the transformation of King Yama," Cheng Zai (1999: 274–275, n. 11) allows: "It is not clear from which sūtra is derived the 'transformation [tableau] of King Yama' mentioned here."
32 Acker (1954: 314, n. 1) notes that Zhang even failed to identify Mañjuśrī and Samantabhadra on their characteristic mounts, describing instead that "The bodhisattva on the west side is riding a lion and the one on the east side rides an elephant." Acker concludes that Zhang "was almost certainly not very conversant with Buddhist iconography and its terminology," and that he "had little or no interest in iconography."
33 The Dunhuang manuscript (P2625), written between 709 and 733, states that "since the Sui and Tang dynasties, the Yin in particularly has been a distinguished family." P2625; Zheng 1989: 110. See He 1986: 204 on the date of the manuscript. Based on the colophon of the copy of the *Diamond Sūtra* made by Yin Siyuan in 708, who had not yet acquired the title of the Area Commander-in-chief of the Doulu Army, one may deduce that the manuscript P2625, which bears this title, must date after 708.
34 *THY* 78. 1690. He 1986: 203.
35 P2625; Zheng 1989: 111.
36 When Yin Siyuan made a copy of the *Diamond Sūtra* in 708, he did not yet bear the title of the Supreme Pillar of State as he did when his portrait was painted in Cave 217. This indicates that the wall paintings in Cave 217 were executed after 708.
37 Also transcribed as [Yin] Siqiong 嗣瓊, Dunhuang Yanjiuyuan 1986: 100.
38 Dunhuang Yanjiuyuan 1986: 100.
39 Wan 1986: 185.
40 P2005. *Shazhou tujing* 沙洲圖經.

41 It was a copy of the *Diamond Sūtra* dedicated to "the Golden Wheel, Sagely Divine Emperor," i.e., Wu Zetian. S87. *CKSSS*, 248.

42 Points of contention among existing exegeses (*ZSDM*, 3; *ZBQD*, 6:6–9; *DSQ*, 7:62–69) invariably pertain to the identification of specific scenes. Questions concerning the organizing principle governing the entire composition have never been raised.

43 Śākyamuni entered nirvāna in a grove of sal trees on the outskirts of Kuśinagara. The twin sal trees appear only once in the present tableau. The *Lotus Sūtra* also mentions it only once: in the context of the King Wonderful Adornment.

44 Jiang 1985: 268; Su 1996: 265.

45 A new motif, never seen before, is added to the Vimalakīrti tableau on the north wall. It shows the celestial realm of a wheel-turning king called Precious Canopy. Just as significant, one of this wheel-turning king's sons is named Lunar Canopy. *Vimalakīrtinirdeśa*, 130–34; *DSQ*, 7:196–197. The addition of this episode was apparently a way of glorifying the allusion to the wheel-turning king, hence, to Wu Zetian.

46 It survives in S87. *CKSSS*, 248.

47 T. 9.3c; *LS*, 1.14.

48 The date is indicated by the colophon. T. 16.292.

49 T. 16.284b.

50 T. 9.17c. *LS*, 4.88.

51 T. 9.43a. *LS*, 16.228.

52 *ZZTJ* 206.6526.

53 *JTS* 6.127; 7.135. *ZZTJ* 206.6534. *Xin Tang Shu* is inconsistent regarding the date of the restoration of Li Xian as the heir apparent. The biography of Wu Zetian dates the event to the 1st year of Shengli (698), *XTS* 4.99; the biography of Li Xian dates it to the 2nd year of Shengli (699), with the explanation that Wu "had grown old and sick." *XTS* 4.106.

54 *ZZTJ* 206.6540.

55 *THY* 48.993. *ZZTJ* 208.6617.

56 *Lidai minghua ji*, 72. Acker 1954: 316.

57 For studies of the tableau, see note 34.

58 *Guan Wuliangshoufo jing* 觀無量壽佛經, T. 12.340–346. See also Waley 1931: 60–61.

59 *ZZTJ* 208.

60 *ZZTJ* 208.6611.

61 Of the Tang monasteries in Luoyang, the Jing'ai and Shengshan enjoy the highest reputation: "Shengshan and Jing'ai both have ancient paintings." *Taiping guangji* 212.1623, citing the *Lushi zazhi* 盧氏雜誌. Kang Pian 康駢, a ninth-century author, also notes the paintings in the Jing'ai Monastery in the Eastern Capital: "the paintings are marvelous and exquisite, all of a divine order." See *Jutan lu* 劇談錄 (895), in *Tang Wudai biji xiaoshuo daguan*, 2:1488. Kang made a mistake of rendering Jing'ai 敬愛 as Aijing 愛敬.

62 Several factors support this iconographic identification. First, the Buddha assembly is set against trees with blooming flowers, which suggest the "Dragon Flower Trees," the standard backdrop for Maitreya Buddha assembly. Second, some cloud-borne figures are seen in ascent and others in descent, thereby signaling the well-known "Maitreya's ascent" 彌勒上生 (*mile shangsheng*) and "Maitreya's descent" 彌勒下生 (*mile xiasheng*).

63 Dunhuang scholars commonly identify the scene as an episode from Śākyamuni Buddha's life story: After Śākyamuni attains enlightenment, he returns to Kapilavastu, his birthplace. There he meets his aunt Prajāpatī, who brought him up after his mother Māyā had died seven days after giving birth to him. Upon his return, Prajāpatī pleads to be ordained into the Buddhist order. See *ZSDM*, 3:231. This arbitrary identification

is questionable, for it makes an isolated case and completely disregards the role the scene plays in the overall pictorial program of the cave shrine.

64 *Fo suo xing zan* 佛所行讚, T. 4.3039c; *Fo ben xing jing* 佛本行經, T. 4.88–89.

65 In fact, a number of Buddhist monasteries were founded for reasons of pursuing the posthumous well-being of the deceased relatives. See Forte 1983: 683, 685, 688.

66 *Fayuan zhulin*, T. 53.753c.

67 T. 53.754c.

68 *Duyizhi* 獨異志, in *Tang Wudai biji xiaoshuo daguan*, 931.

69 *THY*, 48.993.

70 Antonino Forte (1988: 219–225) discussed the importance of the monastery and its surrounding circumstances.

71 S1515; *CKSSS*, 221.

72 Thus a colophon on a copy of the *Visualization Sūtra* states that the copy was commissioned because a man named Hu Sijie and his wife were both ill. S4631.

73 Dunhuang Yanjiuyuan 1986: 100–101.

74 Liu Youyun Collection, Manuscript *san* no. 655, *CKSSS*, 232; Beijing University Library, no. 698, *CKSSS*, 233; S217, *CKSSS*, 246; S87, *CKSSS*, 248; Beijing Library, *Lü*, no. 2, *CKSSS*, 270.

75 Ikeda is uncertain about the last character following the name Yin Si-[?]. Zheng Binglin identifies it as Yin Siyuan. See *CKSSS*, 246; Zheng 1989: 247, n. 16.

76 Dunhuang manuscript at Beijing Library, *Lü* 2. *CKSSS*, 270.

77 *CKSSS*, 248.

78 Two thousand or so surviving copies of the sūtra from Dunhuang—with 60 of them dated, spanning the period between the sixth and the eighth centuries—testify to its popularity. *DDC*, 682.

79 P2094; T85.

80 Dunhuang manuscript at Shanghai Library, No. 026. *Dunhuang yanjiu* no. 2 (1986), 96; *CKSSS*, 268.

81 S5699. Hao 1996: 68.

82 T. 9.54c; T. 9.61c. *LS*, 23.287; 28.322.

83 Zhongzong, "Jin *Huahujing* chi" 禁化胡經敕, in *QTW* 17.141.

84 I have discussed this in Wang 2005.

85 Cited from Rao 1993: 517.

86 A surviving piece of seventh-century calligraphy from the hands of prominent officials of Taizong's court presents a summary of the *Salvation Scripture* designed to accompany pictorial representations of its contents. See Naba 1962, Barrett 1996: 81–82.

87 Ware 1967: 47.

88 Meng Anpai 孟安排 quotes it in *Daojiao yishu* 道教義樞, *DZ* 24:811a.

89 Li Fengmao 1996: 33–92.

90 *DZ* 2:196c.

91 All these scenarios are possible. If the painting subscribes to the four-fold scheme, then the scene of King Adornment illustrates the "Flying Transcendent" idea. If it actually assumes the three-fold scheme, then the top three clouds are to be counted.

92 On "Deliverance from Corpse," see Robinet 1979: 57–66; Miyakawa 1983: 439–457; Li Fengmao 1996: 77–90; Campany 2002: 52–60.

93 Xiao 1989: 274, 281.

94 *DZ* 1:2c; Bokenkamp 1997: 411–412.

95 *DZ* 2:196a.

96 *DZ* 1:2. translation from Bokenkamp 1997: 411. *DZ* 2:196a.

97 *DZ* 1:2; translation from Bokenkamp 1997: 412.

98 See, for instance, *Hainei shizhou ji* 海內十洲記, in *Han Wei Liuchao biji xiaoshuo daguan*: 71.

99 Ibid. The Sanskrit-colored term *dafan* 大梵 (Brahmā) makes the appropriation from the Daoist cosmos all the more smooth.

100 *DZ* 1:4; Bokenkamp 1997: 422.
101 Zhen Luan 甄鸞 (ca. 535–ca. 566), *Xiao Dao lun* 笑道論, T. 52.146. Translation based on Kohn 1995: 74.
102 *DZ* 2:205.
103 *DZ* 1:3; translation from Bokenkamp 1997: 417.
104 *Tianguan santu* 天關三途 (Three Ways to Go Beyond the Heavenly Pass), cited from Robinet 1993: 258. The *Renniaoshan jing tu* 人鳥山經圖 also mentions that, for those who attain transcendence, the "Celestial Thearch would send a cloud carriage with feather canopy to greet him . . . thereby ascending to heaven." *YJQQ* 80.505.
105 Cheng Xuanying's 成玄英 commentary in *DZ* 2:207a.
106 T. 9.22a.
107 Bokenkamp 1997: 157, 297, 346.
108 *DZ* 1:3c; translation from Bokenkamp 1997: 418.
109 Bokenkamp 1997: 193.
110 *DZ* 1:3c; translation from Bokenkamp 1997: 418.
111 This is the opinion held by Yan Dong 嚴東 of Northern Qi who considers the right one of the tripartite Low (Water) Office to be the Northern Metropolis (or Luofeng Metropolis), and the Spring-Bend to be one of the latter's agencies. The Tang commentator Xue Youqi 薛幽棲, however, regards the Northern Metropolis as the capital atop Mount Luofeng. *DZ* 2:209.
112 *DZ* 1:4; trans. from Bokenkamp 1997: 420–421.
113 These tales are gathered in Huixiang 惠祥, *Hongzan Fahua zhuan* 弘讚法華傳 and Sengxiang 僧祥, *Fahua zhuanji* 法華傳記, in T. 51.12–48; T. 51.48–97. Some of them are translated into English by Daniel Stevenson (1995).
114 See, for instance, *Fahua zhuanji*, T. 51.55–62.
115 This sort of "return-from-death narrative" has attracted quite some scholarly attention. See Gjertson 1989; Campany 1995; Teiser 1988.
116 See, for instance, the tale of Fayan, in *Fayuan zhulin*, T. 53.640b–641a. The story is told in a slightly different version by Huixiang, in *Hongzan fahua zhuan*, T. 51.42a, translated by Stevenson 1995: 445–446.
117 *Fahua zhuanji*, T. 51.75bc.
118 In characterizing medieval Chinese notions of postmortem survivals, Liebenthal (1952: 337) resorts to the phrase "Buddhist Folklore," by which he means "all that material which is not included in Buddhist theory."
119 See Bokenkamp 1990: 126.
120 See *Fo suo xing zan* 佛所行讚, T. 4.309c; *Fo ben xing jing* 佛本行經, T. 4.88–89.
121 This formulation comes up in Meyer Schapiro's (1945) discussion of the symbolic significance of Saint Joseph making mousetraps.
122 Eitel 1976: 86. If the scene indeed depicts Śākyamuni's return to Kapilavastu, its resonance is just as suggestive: for Kapilavastu is also rendered "City of the Immortals" 仙城 (*xiancheng*) in Chinese. Soothill and Hodous 1977: 166a.
123 A large number of Buddhist monasteries in the metropolitan region were converted from lay persons' residences which normally have their building facing south.
124 See Hao 1996: 68–69.
125 Hao Chunwen (1996: 69) has compiled a list of 74 different types of fasting texts (*zhaiwen* 齋文), which he still considers incomplete.
126 P2940. *Dunhuang yuanwen ji*: 67.
127 Nickerson 1994.
128 S5957, S3875, S5456; *Dunhuang yuanwen ji*, 416–417. For a complete translation of the text, see Wang 2005.

Figure 3.1 Transformation tableau based on the Lotus Sūtra. South wall, Mogao Cave 217. Early eighth century.

Figure 3.2 Bottom section of the Lotus Sūtra tableau, Mogao Cave 217. South wall, Mogao Cave 217. Early eighth century.

Figure 3.3 Left side of the Lotus Sūtra tableau, Mogao Cave 217. South wall, Mogao Cave 217. Early eighth century.

Figure 3.4 Top section of the Lotus Sūtra tableau, Mogao Cave 217. South wall, Mogao
Cave 217. Early eighth century.

Figure 3.5 Right side of the Lotus Sūtra tableau, Mogao Cave 217. South wall, Mogao Cave 217. Early eighth century.

Figure 3.6 Mt. Sumeru-centered cosmos moved by Vimalakīrti. Detail of transformation tableau based on the Vimalakīrti-nirdeśa-sūtra. North wall of Mogao Cave 335, Dunhuang. End of seventh century.

Figure 3.7 Mt. Sumeru on the robe of the Vairocana image. Detail of transformation tableau based on the Recompense Sūtra. Eighth century. British Museum.

Figure 3.8 View of the west-wall niche to the left; and north wall to the right showing the transformation tableau based on the Visualization Sūtra. Mogao Cave 217. Early eighth century.

Figure 3.9 Left side of the transformation tableau based on the Visualization Sūtra. North wall, Mogao Cave 217. Early eighth century.

Figure 3.10 Tableau based on the Guanyin chapter of the Lotus Sūtra. East wall, Mogao
Cave 217. Early eighth century.

Figure 3.11 Śākyamuni ascends to Heaven of the Thirty-Three Celestials (Trāyastriṃśa) to preach for his mother Māyā. Painting on the ceiling of the west wall niche, Mogao Cave 217. Early eighth century.

4 The monastery cat in cross-cultural perspective
Cat poems of the Zen masters

T.H. Barrett

If we are to integrate the study of Buddhism into higher education in the English language, not as an exotic extra but as a field of study on a par with any other area of humanistic inquiry, then there is much to be said for allowing due prominence to the study of Buddhist monasticism. For monastic institutions within Buddhism, just as within Christianity, have more than played their part in the preservation of learning. Were anyone interested to do so, it would be quite possible in this regard to compare, for example, the medieval monastery in Britain with Zen monasteries in Japan at the same time, though a full study would inevitably be somewhat lengthy.[1] Western academics, at any rate, whilst generally not evincing much enthusiasm for the celibate life, still tend to feel some form of atavistic respect for monastic communities, at least if they are familiar with universities of the older sort, where, as Gibbon for example noted with his derogatory remark about the "monks of Oxford," muffled echoes of the medieval past still reverberate through court and quadrangle.

I am not too familiar with the seat of learning criticized by Gibbon, but the University of Cambridge, which I know better, is still close enough to its own past to demonstrate features that allow us some insight into what it must have been like to live in a closed community devoted to the spiritual and scholarly life. Thus a remarkable pictorial volume, evidently designed for the tourist trade, *Cambridge Cats,* turns out to be almost entirely devoted to cats associated with specific colleges, where as often as not they seem to make the entire college, rather than the premises of one individual, their homes. The text also reveals that this is a tradition going back by some centuries at least, for it is asserted that the current Pembroke cat, Thomasina, is named after the Pembroke poet Thomas Gray (1716–1771), who allegedly celebrated a predecessor in his *Ode on a Favourite Cat, Drowned in a Tub of Goldfish;* it further asserts that Sir Thomas Adams, an early professor of Arabic, dedicated a translation of Aristotle to the same cat, though since Sir Thomas became professor in 1632, I suspect that there has been some confusion here with William Adams, a Master of Pembroke, whose dates are 1706–1789.[2]

Trivial this publication may seem, but at least it should serve as a reminder that the communal life upon which monasticism is based often benefits not only monks and nuns but certain animals too: in rougher times, no doubt, guard dogs, and, even today, cats prepared to earn their keep by protecting communal food supplies from the attention of rodents. Or is their function purely economic? Today, of course, college cats would seem to be little different from the pets to be found in many other Cambridge homes, but one may still imagine from farming communities around the world that a much looser relationship between man and animal might originally have obtained, with semi-feral cats living in a form of symbiosis with the community that involved keeping their distance to a far greater extent than their descendants have usually chosen to do, surviving mainly off the rodents attracted by communal stores and being granted in return a certain degree of toleration.[3] In medieval Western Europe, as recent historical research has tended to suggest, Christian suspicions concerning witchcraft and the cat probably discouraged many from pursuing any closer contact.[4]

And what of the Japanese medieval monastic cat? So far, it seems, no one has seen fit to ask, or even to assemble for the tourist trade of today a *Monastery Cats of Kyoto*, or the like. Yet if we collect the surviving materials, particularly from poetry, a picture emerges that illuminates to some extent not simply the status of the Zen monastery cat but also various broader aspects of the cultural situation of the monastery in medieval times. It is with this purpose in mind that the following remarks have been put together. But, before homing in on this topic, we must start by taking a broader view, for the Zen master's cat, at least as a cultural and literary construction, certainly has a history, whatever we may say of Zen.

In order to trace that history, moreover, we must look, as with Zen itself, to the continent of Asia before turning to developments in Japan itself. It is clear from references in Heian period (794–1185) literature that cats actually established themselves in Japan before Zen was able to gain acceptance, which only happened in the Kamakura period (1185–1333). A considerable portion of the *Tale of Genji*, for example, hinges on the consequences of a kitten's actions, and here not for the first time in Japanese literature we find humans sharing their thoughts with cats in speech, suggesting that the aristocracy of the country at least took a more than purely economic view of the cat's role in their company, though perhaps we cannot generalize from the life of the aristocracy to assume that cats were widely kept as pets throughout the land.[5] The *Tale of Genji*, moreover, makes particular reference to "Chinese cats," suggesting that in matters feline the Central Kingdom was seen as leading the way just as much as it did at this point in matters of Buddhist belief.[6] In order to establish the history of the monastic cat, then, we must look to China and even to India before we are able to understand how things stood in the medieval Zen monastery.

In fact, despite what has been said about cats and monasteries, there would seem to be no particular doctrinal reason in Buddhism for cats to have any special status. Those Buddhist sources which may be taken as reflecting the common perception of cats in India through their adaptation of folk tales to religious purposes would seem simply to reflect, as do similar tales in Europe, the perception of the cat as sly and hypocritical.[7] Minakata Kumagusu 南方熊楠 (1867–1941), who was inspired by the Dick Whittington story to publish a wide-ranging essay on cat lore, located in two Buddhist texts translated during the early phases of Chinese Buddhism the belief that greedy people will become reincarnated as cats, something that carries over into later texts written in China.[8] He does, however, point to a passage in the

Vinaya of the Mūlasarvāstivādins suggesting that cats are lazy monks reincarnated, which suggests a slightly more relaxed view.[9] In China itself it is hard to find any early mentions of the cat at all, and it would seem that it was only with the advent of Buddhism that the animal started to be noticed, even if there is no direct evidence that it only arrived in China through trade with India.

It is not possible to be entirely sure, either, when cats started to be accepted as domestic pets in China. A dictionary of the sixth century defines the cat in beguiling terms: "Like a tiger but smaller; people raise them and cause them to catch rats," but even this leaves some room for doubt.[10] By the early eighth century, however, it is clear that experiments had been carried out in turning both kittens and puppies into vegetarians, suggesting perhaps an upbringing in Buddhist monasteries, for we read in a medical work of the period cited by H.T. Huang that "feeding [polished] paddy or glutinous rice to young cats and dogs will so bend their legs that they will not be able to walk."[11] Madeleine Spring has studied some interesting late Tang discussions of the advisability or otherwise of feline domestication.[12] Perhaps the best evidence that cats eventually became not just economic adjuncts to humans but fully accepted as harmless pets, suitable as family companions, is a poem on children's play by Lu Deyan 路德延, a *jinshi* 進士 graduate of 898, which mentions a cat being tugged along on a string, evidently by a child, though this may be later in date than some of the Heian evidence already mentioned.[13] By the ninth century, in any case, cats had clearly joined dogs as the domestic animals kept in the greatest numbers amongst the populace: a somewhat unpleasant street person of Chang'an 長安 at this time, who is said to have survived by eating domestic cats and dogs, is credited with having accounted for a sum total of four hundred and sixty animals, though we are not told by our horrified Buddhist source, a miracle story of divine retribution, in what proportions the two species made up that number.[14]

It is equally obvious by the end of the ninth century that cats and dogs were accounted the most everyday of sights in Zen (or rather, Chan) monasteries as well, for Xuansha Shibei 玄沙師備 (835–908) mentions them in this role in one of his dialogues, along with "the green mountain in front of your face."[15] The cat had already, of course, made its appearance in the Zen tradition some time before this. The *Lidai fabao ji* 曆代法寶記, a work of the late 770s, which describes Vinaya masters of the day as being as intent on the pursuit of fame and profit as a cat stalking its prey, introduces to the tradition a metaphor later used to describe the concentration needed in Zen to gain enlightenment.[16] But as the one mention of a cat that was to have the greatest impact within the longer term within the Zen tradition as it spreads from China to Japan one cannot ignore the alarming case of Puyuan 普願 of Nanquan 南泉 (748–835) and his encounter with a cat over which two groups of monks were disputing their claims to ownership. The *locus classicus* for this incident in the form in which it is most familiar to Western students of Zen is probably the 1228 collection known as the *Wumenguan* 無門關, or "Gateless Barrier," which was translated several times in the mid-twentieth century.[17] This begins: "Monk Nanquan, since the East and West Halls were disputing over a cat, picked it up and asked the monks to say something to save its life, or it would be chopped in half. There was no reply, so he chopped it in half." His best student, Zhaozhou

Congshen 趙州從諗 (778–897), arrived later and on being told what had happened, put his sandals on his head and walked out, which actions, Puyuan declared, would have saved the cat.

Famous though this story may be, the earliest source bearing on it suggests that at the very least it has been refined over time, though this text, a compilation of 952, does at least attest to a strong interest in cats on the part of Puyuan, who is said to have described cats and oxen as "knowing reality," and to have been saved from a tiger which his rescuer treated as a cat.[18] This Zen master's apparent interest in animal life as a whole has been the topic of careful study by Okimoto Katsumi 沖本克己, who is particularly suspicious of the textual foundations of the story just quoted. He notes, for example, that there are stories about chopping earthworms and snakes in half—still not good deeds by normal Buddhist standards, but more understandable—which may have provided the original inspiration for the cat story.[19] Whatever the truth of the matter, the story could not have gained currency if cats had not been commonly kept in Buddhist monasteries, not simply for economic reasons (though it has been suggested that a single cat can save up to 250 tonnes of grain from contamination per annum) but as objects of affection on the part of their human fellow-residents.[20]

For the purposes of documenting the status of cats in medieval Japanese Zen monasteries, however, it is perhaps fortunate that the tradition had another *locus classicus* mentioning the cat to look back to, and to serve as a model for cultural emulation. This is a cat poem, or rather in essence a poverty poem mentioning a cat, that is part of the poetic corpus going under the name Hanshan 寒山, "Cold Mountain." The problems associated with the origins of this corpus are many, and I do not wish to discuss them in detail here, especially since my views are contained in an essay included in a volume of lively translations from Hanshan by the late Peter Hobson.[21] Suffice it to say that I accept E.G. Pulleyblank's conclusion based on his study of rhyme schemes that the corpus must derive from at least two separate hands working in different historical periods and I also accept that Hanshan (to follow, notwithstanding this awkward fact, a convenient designation for the corpus) was not himself a "Zen poet." But he did certainly come to be represented as a Zen poet by the late eighth century, when the corpus seems to have achieved its current state, and his influence on later Zen poets was immense. At the very least, Hanshan's cat poem did legitimate the writing of further poems about cats.

And if, as its rhyme scheme suggests, it derives from an early part of the corpus, which may go back to the seventh century, it may even be the first cat poem in China, though there is another longer seventh-century work by a court poet about a cat and a parrot that should otherwise claim that honour.[22] It is certainly not as old as a trio of cat poems (or rather, dead bird poems) in the *Greek Anthology,* which go back to the sixth century.[23] It may, however, be the first cat poem by a religious figure, unless Hanshan is later than the unknown eighth-century Irish monk who wrote the well-known verse on his cat, Pangur Ban, in the margin of a manuscript, not long before an interlinear drawing of a cat and a rat was inserted in the *Book of Kells*.[24] All translations offered here aim neither at achieving any literary standard nor at providing an accurate prose equivalent, but simply at giving enough sense of an original poem to allow discussion of the relevant content; otherwise, my chief aim has been to keep to something of their concision.

昔時可可貧，　In the past, tolerable poverty;
今朝最貧凍。　Today, I'm utterly poor and cold.
作事不諧和，　Everything I do goes wrong,
觸途成恡傯。　Everywhere I go there's trouble,
行泥屢腳屈，　Breaking my legs in the mud,
坐社頻腹痛。　Starving at the village feast.
失卻斑貓兒，　And since I lost that brindled cat
老鼠圍飯甕。　The rats besiege my food supplies.[25]

Again, though there is much that could be said about the spread of Hanshan's influence to Japan, for present purposes it is worth noting that Hanshan and his companion Shide 拾得 are very frequently mentioned in medieval Japanese Zen literature, and that the poems of Hanshan were popular enough to be reprinted by monks of the Gozan 五山 monasteries, the "Five Mountains" of the Rinzai 臨濟 school that dominated that literature. Indeed, this reprint of 1325 from what was evidently a Chinese edition of the Song period is allegedly the oldest reprinting of a Chinese poetry collection in the country.[26] We should not discount, either, the indirect influence of Hanshan mediated via later Chinese Zen poets, and perhaps Koreans as well, since Korean Zen, too, shows evidence of cat poetry.[27] David Pollack also reminds us that Chinese secular poetry of the Song period "seems to abound in eulogies to cats," and this too may well have influenced Gozan poets who were in direct contact with China or Chinese travellers.[28] In the rival Sōtō 曹洞 tradition, however, it may perhaps turn out that cats were less important, though I have not tried to confirm this supposition. The Japanese founder of the school, Dōgen 道元 (1200–1253), was at any rate firmly told by his Chinese teacher, Rujing 如浄 (1163–1228), that "Abbots and others at many temples nowadays keep cats, but this is truly not permissible, the conduct of the unenlightened."[29]

If, however, we look at the two major collections of Gozan literature that have been compiled to date, we do find about a dozen poems about cats—depending on whether you count warnings to rats about cats, and poems by Chinese monks exiled to Japan. This is not a very high total out of a complete corpus of a dozen volumes, each running to more than a thousand pages, and it may well be eclipsed by the aggregate of Gozan poetry about smaller creatures, though no single invertebrate seems to dominate their concerns. Doubtless, too, it is no more than the modern Western interest in pets that has caused about half of these poems to appear in English translation already.[30] This is in fact all the more impressive a total when we take into account the argument that Japanese literature in Chinese has been unduly neglected by Japanologists.[31] But while the cat poetry of the Zen masters does not exactly provide us with a wealth of material to study, it does raise some intriguing questions, of which the most obvious and well-known—a question that, moreover, I venture to take up only because it does not require a detailed knowledge of medieval Japan in order to address it—is that of the relationship between the Gozan poets and Chinese culture.

As enthusiasts for the introduction of Chinese culture to their own land the monks of the Gozan exceeded even Korean Confucians and Western Maoists in the depth of their devotion to China, since frequently theirs was a passion not even quenched by the reality of having to study there for years at a stretch. But we should remember that Japan at this time was represented on Buddhist world-maps then in circulation as being on the very periphery of Buddhist civilization, if not right off the map altogether, so that studying China, and particularly studying in China, quite literally represented getting oneself on the map.[32] To some of our monk poets stories of the heroic pilgrims who had made the dangerous further journey to India from China or Korea half a millennium and more earlier served as a standing reproach to their own inadequacies: "What sort of men are we, so warm and well-fed?" asks Mugan Soō 夢巌祖應 (?—1374), on reading of their spirit of self-sacrifice.[33] For Japanese culture as a whole, despite the stirrings of independence from the continent that have been detected in some religious developments of the Kamakura age, had already been long accustomed to accepting the continent, especially China, as a yardstick against which to measure itself.[34] The material culture of the Gozan monasteries seems therefore to have incorporated a wealth of art objects exported from China to Japan.[35] A recent study of the calligraphy of Zhongfeng Mingben 中峰明本 (1262–1323) shows this particularly well through its almost total dependence on writings in the autograph of this master preserved in Japan to this day, in several cases because they were first sent there by Mingben in response to requests from Japanese monks or laymen.[36]

Another Chinese monkish calligrapher of a somewhat earlier generation whose work was also transmitted to Japan by Japanese students was Xutang Zhiyu 虚堂智遇 (1185–1269).[37] As I point out in my essay, he was also an admirer of Hanshan, though I notice too that I accidentally imply there (Barrett 2003: 133) that Zhiyu ended his days in Japan, which he did not. But, most significantly for present purposes, he was also a cat poet.

求貓子	Asking for a cat
堂上新生虎面狸,	In the hall there's a newborn tiger-faced thing—
千金許我不應移。	I'd give anything to have it, but they won't budge.
家寒故是無偷鼠,	Yet I'm so poor no thieving rats come near:
要見翻身上樹時。	I just want to watch it rolling over, climbing trees.

Unlike Hanshan's poem, where the old tabby cat obviously had a certain utilitarian role, even if we suspect that the hermit also misses its company, Zhiyu's quatrain constitutes quite explicitly a rejection of the economic argument for cats.[38] But though we have suggested that cats were not especially privileged in the Buddhist tradition, it has been pointed out that Indian Buddhist monasteries clearly extended their compassion, especially at meal times, to animal companions—the Buddha himself, after all, had spent time as an animal in a number of reincarnations, and though animals were all placed in the spiritual hierarchy below humans, their capacity for improvement over karmic time was recognized, even if Zen masters of the sterner sort found them a distraction.[39] So a non-economic approach to cats would not have seemed amiss. And not surprisingly, in view of Zhiyu's standing in Japan, this poem seems to have been in the thoughts of several Japanese Zen masters when they came to write about cats.

Most obvious is the case of Seiin Shunshō 西胤俊承 (1358–1422), whose own poem "Asking for Kittens" has been translated by David Pollack—in fact, since his translation "kittens" derives from the content of the poem, the titles are identical.[40] But it is also possible to find verbal echoes from the body of the Zhiyu poem elsewhere. Here is a piece by Ryūsen Ryōzei 龍泉令澤, son of an emperor, who died in 1365.[41]

> The cat has had its praise from age to age,
> Its style not always second to the tyger's.[42]
> Rolling over, climbing trees, its faculties at full stretch –
> And, when all is said and done, still my rogue!

And compare also this, by Kampō Shidon 乾峰士曇 (1285–1361), evidently about a successful rat catcher at rest, though since it is in the "Paintings" section of his works, it may not be taken from life, so adding a degree of piquancy to the last line:

> To preserve life, you kill all,
> And, all killed, have great compassion.[43]
> On the roof under the hill you lie –
> I just want to see you rolling over.[44]

Shidon was evidently an avid reader of Zhiyu's writings, for this poem is one of a pair, the second of which reads:

> Tiger-faced little rogue:
> Knows reality, doesn't care.
> The rat's gone down the cow's horn –
> We'll have to await the outcome.

Here the third line is a direct quotation of a saying of Zhiyu concerning the state of one who has been trapped in everyday reality, unable to reach enlightenment.[45] But, as is readily apparent, the second line also contains an allusion to Puyuan's estimation of cats and oxen. Just how much of an education in the Zen tradition and in Chinese literature in general was expected in their readership by Gozan authors is, however, most aptly illustrated by another poem by Ryūsen Ryōzei, which discusses the important question for Zen masters as to whether they could justify keeping cats when it was in their nature to commit murder on smaller animals. By a stylish use of ellipsis, however, no victim is named in the quatrain, nor is the specifically carnivorous nature of the cat explicitly mentioned at all. It is up to the reader to recall a phrase from the ancient philosopher Zhuangzi, aptly recycled in a verse by Hanshan, to the effect that the famous steed Blossom Red (Hualiu 驊騮) was less well suited to catching mice than a lame cat—though in view of what has been said concerning the murky beginnings of the domestic cat in China, it is worth noting that the original animal indicated by Zhuangzi in the comparison may have been what the Japanese call a *tanuki* 狸.[46] The message, however, is clear enough: we must all fulfil our destinies and do what comes best to us, and catching little animals is what a cat excels at.[47]

> Cat
> Head straight, eyes ahead, every faculty engaged—
> But were Blossom Red to lose its speed, it would look a dolt.
> Master and monks' iron bowls are not the best of vessels.
> I don't know who it is provides the meal.[48]

In other words, these apparently trivial observations of monastic life were not completely spontaneous portraits, documentary snapshots of scenes in monastery gardens, but were written very much within a self-conscious literary tradition. Though I have not explored any further than the particular objects of my own investigation, this fondness for silent allusions may well be there throughout Gozan poetry as a whole, to an extent that earlier translators were perhaps not always able to detect, lacking the dictionaries and concordances that we now have for Zen studies. It turns out, for example, according to the three-volume dictionary of Zen compiled by Komazawa University, that a mention in a poem by Gidō Shūshin 義堂周信 (1325–1388), on a painting of a kitten lying by its mother, to its "blood-oath spirit" actually reflects yet another reference to an allusion first used by Zhiyu, pairing the apparent moral behaviour of cats with that ascribed to tigers, though one I have not managed to locate.[49] Since Shūshin in a second, paired cat poem suggests using the picture of the cat to keep mice at bay, we may even start to doubt that our Zen masters met any real cats at all.

> All night long a crowd of rats, swarming like bees;
> They've gnawed the precious books by my bedside.
> I frivolously hang up my new painting on the wall,
> And all is quiet –no need to chase them out.[50]

Some evidence against this completely gloomy conclusion may, however, be found in a verse by Banri Shūkyū 萬里集九 (1428–1502).[51]

> He mostly sheathes his claws, no need to scratch,
> Under the peonies, asleep, averse to fights.
> But soon it's dark beneath the springtime breeze:
> You rats are many, but you won't survive.

Now it must be admitted right away that a painting of cats and peonies did inspire another of his poems, though evidently a painting with a slightly different content.

So that the peony should have no disordered flowers
The mother cat does not sleep, all through the afternoon.
You butterflies so lightly clad – in whose dream are you?
It's fine to fly together, but don't touch those teeth! [52]

And there even survives in Taiwan a medieval Chinese painting of a cat and peonies of a type that may possibly have inspired the poem just quoted.[53] But whatever the immediate occasion for writing the first poem, it can only have been written by someone familiar with a real domestic cat, since sheathed claws are a detail unlikely to be picked up either from paintings or from brief encounters with semi-feral cats on the monastery outskirts. We can, I believe, feel reassured that it was not just cats brought from China by elderly Chinese masters exiled to Japan that really did end up as full-time residents in Japanese monasteries.[54] Equally, however, we must accept that cats were viewed in those monasteries very much in the light of Chinese ideas about their significance. And here there is one major anomaly by comparison with the Japanese situation that needs to be addressed, one that will already have become clear through the materials I have cited so far.

For right from the start any occurrence of a cat in Chinese or Gozan sources tends as often as not to be accompanied, as in the passage attributed to Zhiyu that I have just mentioned, by some sort of cross-reference to a tiger: "like a tiger but smaller"; treating a tiger as a cat; "tiger-faced thing," "its style not always second to the tyger's"; tiger-faced little rogue" are the instances I have already mentioned. One of the many Chinese poems written in reaction to Puyuan's cat chopping is even apparently gratuitously invaded by the comparison, and speaks of that master "seizing the head of the tiger, while Zhaozhou Congshen got the tail."[55] In a sense there is nothing unusual in this, since until relatively recently in historical terms tigers were much more common than was comfortable in China, and doubtless many Chinese had an opportunity to observe the comparison. For obvious reasons connected to the history of imperialism, the English-speaking world tends to think of the tiger primarily as an Indian animal, ignoring its widespread distribution throughout China, but it is quite clear that the tiger held on for quite awhile against the encroachments of civilization that have now made it a rarity. As late as the seventeenth century, for example, we find the intrepid traveller Xu Xiake 徐霞客 (1586–1641) troubled by rumours of tigers on the road ahead only ten miles from present-day Ningbo, hardly one of the wilder parts of China.[56] Tiger attacks actually increase in the next couple of centuries, though this has been interpreted as marking man's elimination of their natural habitat, and so a prelude to their extinction.[57] In the early 1930s the great sportsman Arthur de C. Sowerby (1885–1954), while noting the more restricted range of the beast in his own day, was presented for example with photographic evidence of the survival of tigers in southwest Shansi, and accepted an account of their presence between Nanjing and Shanghai, though most Westerners in search of a good tiger shoot found the Amoy region their most rewarding territory.[58] Even in 1936 the New Territories of Hong Kong witnessed a tiger panic.[59]

So it is not surprising that the tiger should feature in religious contexts dating back much further than the first appearance of the cat. Tiger cults as such do not concern us, for they are generally associated not with "higher" forms of religion but with regional or "barbarian" forms of worship.[60] But it is worth noting that in pre-Buddhist China tigers were also known as attendants of the immortal Pengzu 彭祖.[61] To this day the great Daoist figure Zhang Daoling 張道陵 is depicted with a tiger.[62] In this tradition, however, at least in the late sixth century, the tame tiger is compared not to a cat, but to a dog.[63] Eventually Chinese Buddhist figures, too, were given tiger companions: Charles E. Hammond, in his study of the weretiger, a particular Chinese concern, remarks with reference to early Buddhist hagiographical writing that "If the biographies of Buddhist monks are to be believed, many monks raised tigers as a matter of course."[64] His research brings out a certain ambivalence in the relationship, perhaps due to the underlying notion that shamans could transform into tigers, though he does also point to the orthodox Buddhist belief that monks should use the dharma to subdue or even convert tigers. This belief came to be symbolized eventually in the mysterious arhat-figure, unknown in Indian tradition, termed the "tiger-tamer," Fuhu 伏虎. In discussing this figure, Victor Mair has pointed to ninth- and tenth-century manuscripts depicting holy travellers accompanied by tigers found at Dunhuang.[65] Though Fuhu does not seem to have been particularly popular in medieval Japan, he is certainly mentioned in Gozan poetry.[66]

But at about the same time, though apparently independently, the Zen tradition also acquired a tiger-keeper, the monk Fenggan 豐干. This individual is first attested in the preface to the poems of Hanshan, which to judge from references to it must also have been written by the tenth century, if not before. Fenggan is supposed to have been a monkish friend of Hanshan who worked in some monastery kitchens; one day he is alleged to have amazed his fellow-monks by riding a tiger into his place of work.[67] Amongst the monks of the Gozan he is a figure almost as well known as Hanshan, and like him seems to have been the subject of both poetry and painting. A particular innovation in the latter medium, first attested by a poem in praise of a painting by Dōgen's teacher Rujing, was a type of composition featuring Hanshan, Shide, Fenggan and the tiger all snoozing together in a heap. Gozan artists in turn produced their own versions of this scene, so that we now possess both Chinese and Japanese variations on the theme.[68]

Now the tiger, it would seem, plays something of the same role in religious thought in East Asia that the lion plays in Europe. You may know, for example, that there is a Chinese, tiger-related version of the story of Androcles and the lion, though one which has a somewhat ironic twist to it. We find it related by the famous Tang period poet and statesman Liu Yuxi 劉禹錫 (772–842), who was asked to provide a job for a relative of someone to whom he was himself somewhat indebted for his own position.

There was once [said Liu] an old lady who encountered a tiger which lifted up its foot, and she saw that it had a thorn in it, which she plucked out. The tiger ran off gratefully, and from time to time repaid her by tossing her fresh game. One day, it tossed her a dead man, and her fellow-villagers detained her as a murderess. The old lady then climbed the wall and said to the tiger "I'm certainly grateful, but please, sir, no more dead men!"[69]

In Christian circles the parallel story, which would seem to date back to a real incident during the reign of Caligula, first assumed a religious dimension in the apocryphal *Acts of Paul and Thecla,* where its presence in the text is first alluded to in the third century.[70] Here Saint Paul meets up in the circus with a lion whom he has already baptized rather than saved from lameness—and the Christian lion knows better than to reward him with dead men, though a lion rewarding its benefactor with its prey is mentioned by Pliny.[71] It is not gratitude that motivates the lion in Christian thought, but its recognition of the superiority of holy men, to whose aid they or other animals frequently come in early Christian literature. In Jerome's biography of Paul, for instance, lions help to dig a grave to bury the saint.[72] Symbolically, moreover, the submissive lion has been interpreted as representing the control of sexuality.[73] How much of this has any relevance for the tiger as companion I cannot say, though as I have observed elsewhere the notion of the animal helper, whatever its significance, is quite prominent in Asian religion.[74] Even so, research on the meaning of the cat in ancient Egypt does present an interesting picture of the cat taking the place of the lion in religion in much the same way as the cat takes the place of the tiger in East Asia: we find for example the case of goddesses with both awesome lion and more friendly cat manifestations.[75] Might it not be therefore that the cat functions in the Zen monastery as a miniature tiger substitute, or rather "hand-reared tiger," to use what seems to have been the Japanese expression?[76] For as surely as there are no snakes in Ireland, there are no tigers in Japan and in all matters tiger-related, medieval Japanese, at least, were completely and unequivocally obliged to depend on China. Given, too, Japanese feelings about their peripheral position, there are some grounds for believing that, rather than congratulate themselves on this absence, Japanese monks somewhat regretted their lack of opportunity to live life on the heroic scale.[77]

We have, however, already noted the presence of tiger paintings in Japan, and one of the Gozan poets, Ōsen Keisan 横川景三 (1429–1493), does actually react to a picture on a fan of two tigers amongst some bamboo by imagining them as his companions.[78] Indeed, Japanese pictures of tigers among bamboos survive, at least from a slightly later period, but they can only have been painted on the basis of Chinese originals.[79] Even in the late eighteenth century, when live tigers were occasionally imported from China into Japan, most artists either had to copy Chinese work or rely on their imagination, with the result that one painter, Nagasawa Rosetsu 長澤蘆雪 (1754–1799), who created a famous tiger image in 1787, "seems to have converted into huge size and power the playful ferocity of a domestic kitten," to quote a modern verdict on his work.[80] As it happens, one of our monastic Gozan cat poems is precisely about this entire problem, a short verse written by the great historian and scholar of things Chinese, Kokan Shiren 虎関師錬 (1278–1345), as part of a series on animals, including tigers and mice.[81]

The cat
Making friends with the wild fox, the cat is a true rogue,
Seeing the breeze stir the grass, it's off into the undergrowth.
Though it bears a certain likeness, it's not the real thing:
When I can't paint a tiger, my mistake is that my model's too remote.[82]

The last line of the poem was evidently written for readers with a fair degree of sinological education, for the more common Chinese proverb is "When you can't paint a tiger right, it may end up looking like a dog."[83] But does this lack of tigers explain the attention paid to cats by medieval Japanese Zen masters? Did they wish to walk with tigers, but in their absence found solace in the company of cats, whom they could imagine as very much bigger than they were? It is surely preferable to believe that this explains the situation, than to suspect that these men had a secret hankering for domesticity, in preference to walking on the wild side. For we should not imagine for a moment that the world they lived in consisted solely of cats sleeping quietly under well-cultivated peonies, even if this was perhaps a more common sight in the civilized urban gardens of the Song. Kampō Shidon, for instance, wrote not only cat poems but also a funerary lament for a former guard dog, which says that "Over the many years he was kept as 'dragon guarding the household'/ Not the hint of a bandit ever troubled the gate."[84] In an age marked by constant warfare and disruption other monasteries were doubtless not so lucky.[85] That is not to deny, of course, that the Zen tradition showed a strong interest in the ordinary and everyday, and cats were, with dogs, as we have seen, the quintessential everyday animals.[86] But surely it is precisely the simultaneous presence of cosy domesticity with the spontaneity of a wild animal, the tiger's untroubled killer instinct dressed up in a pet's clothing, which made cats unusually intriguing to Zen masters, with their studied appreciation of immediacy. If the law of the jungle operated in human society, too, in Ashikaga Japan, then the lessons to be learned from cats were that much more valuable.

All this, of course, can only be speculation, since as I have attempted to demonstrate, the handful of poems I have submitted in evidence are not themselves unpremeditated reactions to cats, but complex poetic statements that can doubtless be read in a number of different ways, and perhaps especially so by those familiar with the Zen way of life. Though we have been criss-crossing cultural boundaries quite a bit already, mainly from China to Japan but also with the odd excursion to ancient and medieval Europe and North Africa, it may now be time to look at the broader picture of animals and monastery dwellers in a completely cross-cultural perspective. Of course any such perspective cannot prove anything, either: things that may be so in one culture just are not so in others, and that is precisely why trying to understand separate cultural patterns like man–animal relations on their own account is so important. But modern Western research on the significance of pet ownership does bring out some interesting possibilities that may be relevant to medieval Japan.

Thus while some have sought to interpret pet ownership solely in terms of the human need for dominance, a considerable body of research suggests that there are much broader physical and psychological health advantages to keeping pets.[87] Could there have been a call for such therapeutic presences in the cloisters of medieval Japan? We know that monastic pets were kept in medieval Britain, for William of Wykeham (1324–1404) was obliged to warn the nuns of Romsey Abbey that they were thereby bringing their immortal souls into peril, a spiritual disincentive to what was evidently a widespread practice even more cogent than that offered somewhat earlier by Rujing to Dōgen.[88] At first it may seem strange that the cloistered life should apparently warrant such stress-reducing measures. But if we think back to the way in which I introduced monastic communities of East and West, as centres for the spread of learning, then it is possible to point to a problem common to all such institutions. For just as British and other West European monasteries were islands of Latinity in a no doubt somewhat threatening sea of vernacular culture, so the Gozan monasteries were islands of contemporary Chinese learning in the equally stormy waters of medieval Japanese life.[89] It has, of course, always been important to monasteries both of East and West to maintain good relations with their benefactors, and with all capable of extending their protection and patronage to such vulnerable communities, whoever they were.[90] But like all institutions of higher education, even today, they no doubt experienced a degree of cultural tension with their immediate surroundings, and not just with the would-be bandits, but also (to adopt again a piece of Oxbridge terminology), with the whole Town beyond the identifying uniform of the Gown. Indeed, according to David Pollack, this tension surfaces quite clearly in some of the lines by Mugan Soō on meetings with the peasant tenants of his monastery.[91]

So if today academics often find that their work goes more smoothly thanks to the presence of some four-legged friend, be it a loyal dog or a congenial cat—or even some other form of animal life, such as a mute, finny presence swimming with dependable regularity in its own miniature watery world—perhaps, as I suggested at the outset in the case of the Cambridge college cats in particular, this is a widespread tradition passed on down from the days of monastic learning in East and West. And if we are to establish the study of Eastern traditions of religious learning within the Western academy, as I also proposed at the outset, then I hope that the notion that the great masters who resided in medieval Zen communities faced some of the same human problems as we do, and found like us some of the best solutions to involve calling on the companionship of another species, will bring them all just that little bit closer culturally than might at first sight seem to be the case.

Or is this all that our sources can tell us? Before a final recapitulation and conclusion, let us return to the place where we began, for a story told to me of Cambridge college life. There lived in the recent past in a certain college a brilliant scholar devoted to the criticism of texts who kept a cat as a companion in his rooms. Unfortunately, his college was one that was riven with dissension, and even more unfortunately the fact that keeping pet cats in college was a practice not allowed by college statutes became the pretext for complaints from a rival faction. The master of the college supported him, but was voted down by the majority of the fellows. The master then resigned, and cat and don decamped to another college where regulations were less severe. All hostilities then appeared to have died down, and the new master therefore concluded that the entire episode had been a bit silly, and invited the exiles back. This proved a sad miscalculation, for exactly the same thing happened again, and yet another master was voted out. Exhausted, however, by their quarrels, both sides now agreed to look for a compromise candidate, and duly elected a scholar of such unworldly and obscure interests that he was deemed incapable of generating further strife. And so it was: my informant, a former school friend who acted as student representative under this new regime, told me with some bemusement of the—shall we say—Daoist approach to governance that then prevailed. On his retirement, however, the compromise master was enabled through his unexpected elevation to public eminence to found a research institution in his field that stands to this day. And in his study in this building during his long years of retirement there hung a prominent photograph of one of his chief academic collaborators, holding in his arms a very handsome cat.

Now the cat in the picture had no special meaning, except as a clue to another story. In the same way the cats in Zen poetry allow us to reconstruct only the most slender of feline histories, but they do serve as suggestions to us of some important stories that we might otherwise overlook. Thus several essays in this volume, and several other earlier volumes besides, remind us of the complex history of the Buddhist monastery as an institution in society. A patient and insightful reading of the sources is beginning to allow us to recover dimensions of Buddhist institutional life in India in a way that has been neglected for too long.[92] For China, at least for the time and place covered by the Dunhuang manuscripts, a rather vivid picture of the monastery in local society has been pieced together on the basis of a longer tradition of research.[93] But as we are just beginning to achieve something in these areas, research elsewhere is moving on to consider not simply socio-economic history, but environmental history besides, in a way that as yet the history of religion in Asia has so far ignored almost completely. Even so the cat does serve to remind us that Buddhist monasteries formed part of a larger ecological history—a history, for instance, of land reclamation or forest preservation.[94] As part of a network of communications, too, Buddhist monasteries served not only as habitations for humans, but for other life forms whose effects could be very important for human society. A pioneer of this approach in the West has pointed out for example that the spread of cats in Europe seems to connect with the spread of black rats, the prime bearers of plague infection—perhaps this correlation may help explain the association between cats and witchcraft noted above.[95] In the case of East Asia, we simply do not know yet if this correlation applied or not, but the notion of using cats as an indicator of the spread of rats may be worth exploring.

If, however, the story of the cat as part of the total ecology of the monastery remains unwritten, when it comes to human culture we are on much more familiar ground. The Buddhist saṃgha was without a doubt first founded to serve a soteriological function, as James Robson's introductory analysis makes clear from the outset, but in this role one of its most basic functions was to transmit the dharma, originally through collective memorization and recitation—another important area of recent research.[96] Over the centuries, however, the monastic community developed a prominent role in the preservation and dissemination of Buddhist culture in a much broader sense. In the course of Buddhist history this culture could be carried far from its point of origin in time and space, just as tales of the people of Israel still preserved a meaning in Irish monasteries a long way from Palestine in the West. Thus any community of monastics in medieval Japan preserved—sometimes in a complex mixture of textual and oral forms—a wealth of stories going back through continental East Asia to South Asia a millennium or more earlier.[97] The Gozan monks, as we have seen, are particularly associated with a further wave of cultural importation. But whether new or old, the culture of the monastery served—in whatever local society it was located—to open up cultural horizons, and to give access to a world far wider than any local culture could ever do. This aspect of Buddhism is evidenced quite graphically in Japan by the circulation of the world maps already mentioned, depicting the Five Indias at a time when no Japanese ever travelled thither—and when, lacking experience of tigers, Zen masters found cats more than "good to think with" as representatives of that wider world.[98] Domestic our Zen poets may sometimes appear to be, but they are never parochial.

And, finally, when we look at the Zen cat neither as an element in an ecological nor a symbolic system but simply as a human companion, we are brought up against yet another phenomenon that James Robson likewise stresses in his introductory remarks: that the single term "monastery" covers a very wide diversity of institutions. If we were to consult normative texts on monastic life in East Asia, we might conclude that cats were entirely absent, for as we have seen the sacred texts determining the parameters of that life left no room for them, and one might add that great interpreters of the regulations from Daoxuan (596–667) on to Rujing consistently reaffirm that point.[99] Yet just as some Cambridge colleges seem to have been more flexible than others in the matter of admitting cats as companions, so our poems testify to a flexibility on the part of some but not necessarily all monasteries that we might otherwise have overlooked. A cross-cultural perspective on the Zen master's cat may not be central to the study of Buddhist monasticism, but it does give us an angle on the world of the Buddhist monastery that affords some views not otherwise easily obtainable—and no doubt more than the three views chosen here to conclude these tentative remarks. The monastery cat certainly deserves its place in the historical record, just as much as the college cat, and concerning both there still surely remain many other tales that are worth the telling, even if here and now we come to an ending.

Notes

1 For a summary of British monasteries as centres of scholarship, see Burton 1994: 187–209. For an institutional overview of the main centres of Zen scholarship, see Collcutt 1981, and for contemporary institutional ideals in the distinct Sōtō tradition, Ichimura 1993. One significant difference in Japan is the presence of printing in the Zen monasteries, for which see Kornicki 1998: 119–125.
2 Jedrej 1994: 72.
3 Note the remarks on "barn cats" versus "village cats" in Engels 1999: 11–12.

4 For a recent summary of research on the fate of the cat in medieval Western Christianity, see Engels 1999: 152–162.
5 See Seidensticker 1981: 582–583, 589–590, 614, 626: I am grateful to Tom Harper for pointing this out to me. Imamura 1986: 254–260, provides some additional references in Heian sources.
6 "Chinese cats [*karaneko* 唐貓 in the original] are different"—Seidensticker 1981: 589.
7 Grey 2000: 45, 106–107, provides the main references, which in some versions substitute other animals for the cat.
8 Minakata 1971. His references are to texts now in the Taishō Canon edition vol. 17, specifically to passages on pp. 447c and 521a. These are earlier translations than those discussed in Barrett 1998: 22–23.
9 Minakata 1971: 103; *Genben shuoyiqie youbu pinaiye* 根本說一切有部毘奈耶 (*Mūlasarvāstivādavinaya vibhaṅga*), T. 23.880a–b.
10 Barrett 1998: 19, and 36 n. 74.
11 Huang 2000: 581.
12 Spring 1993: 53–63.
13 Imamura 1986: 134.
14 *Youyang zazu*, 202, translated in Reed 2001: 115–116.
15 See App 1997: 346, reproducing the text of p.364b16–17 of the *Zoku Zōkyō* edition of the collection *Gu Zunsu yulu* 古尊宿語錄.
16 See App 1996: 310, reproducing the text of this work found at T. 51.194b24-26. For this metaphor in later texts, see Barrett 1998: 21.
17 See App 1994: 118, reproducing the text of *Wumenguan* 無門關 T. 48.294c12–22. For early translations of this source into English and German, see Miura and Sasaki 1966: 343–344.
18 Barrett 1998: 15.
19 Okimoto 1997: 394–421.
20 The estimate is that of Engels 1999: 17.
21 See Barrett 2003: 115–147.
22 See Imamura 1986: 124–125, for a discussion of this work.
23 See Engels 1999: 148–50.
24 For Pangur Ban, see Engels 1999: 138; I am indebted to Professor Jan N. Bremmer of the University of Groningen for sending me a card illustrating the detail concerned from folio 48r of the *Book of Kells*.
25 *Quan Tang shi* 806, p. 9083.
26 This according to Ōtani daigaku toshokan 1961: 74–75.
27 Okimoto 1997: 413–14, quotes one example from a compilation by Hyesim 慧諶 (1178–1234), which I have not had to hand.
28 Pollack 1985: 156.
29 Cf. Kodera 1980: 121, 231.
30 See principally Pollack 1985: 136–137, and also Ury 1992: 73, for a further example.
31 Note Wixted 1998: 23–31, a very useful survey of the state of the field.
32 Ayusawa 1953: 123–127.
33 The text cited may be found in *Gozan Bungaku Zenshū* [*GBZS*] vol. 3, p. 817, below. Cf. Pollack 1985: 157–158 for biographical details on this poet.
34 This theme is well treated in Pollack 1986, of which the first five chapters are very relevant to the poems considered here.
35 Note Collcutt 1981: 79–80.
36 Lauer 2002.
37 Lauer 2002: 30, Miura and Sasaki 1966: 206–207, 361–362.
38 Text in *Xutang heshangu yulu* 虛堂和尚語錄 7, T. 47.1035a. For the significance of Zhiyu's poetry in China and Japan, see Parker 1999: 29, which refers to some of the secondary literature on the subject in Japanese.

39 This participation of animals in the Indian monastic community has been particularly
    noted by John S. Strong in his research into the animal phase of the career of another
    Buddhist figure: see Strong 1992: 51.
40 Pollack 1985: 137, and biographical section, 162–163: for the original text, see *GBZS*,
    vol. 1, p. 810.
41 Biography in Pollack 1985: 162, text in *GBZS*, vol. 2, p. 579.
42 The author uses a somewhat recondite synonym for "tiger": cf. *Wenxuan*, p. 5.9a.
43 Perhaps a hint of the folk view of the cat as hypocrite, which still survives in Chinese
    proverbs: see e.g. *Xiehouyu cidian*, 234.
44 Text in *Gozan bungaku shinshū* [*GBSS*], p. 645.
45 *Xutang heshang yulu* 4, T. 47.1017a15.
46 Barrett 1998: 16–17, 25–26. "Blossom Red" is the translation of this equine name in
    Graham 1960: 63; compare, however, Graham 1981: 147.
47 For this hidden allusion, see Henricks 1990: 13, 88.
48 Text in *GBZS* vol. 1, 612.
49 Ury 1992: 73, and *Zengaku daijiten* 1978: 1000d.
50 *GBZS*, vol. 2, p. 473. We should perhaps note that for all his frivolity the poet, to judge
    by his other writings, was well aware of issues concerned with reality and illusion: see
    Parker 1999, chapter 5.
51 Biography in Pollack 1985: 145–146; text in *GZSS*, vol. 6, p. 711.
52 For this second poem, see *GZSS*, vol. 6, p. 771: note the allusion to a famous saying of
    Zhuangzi 莊子 in the third line, one that, as far as I am aware, was not used by Hanshan.
53 Cahill 1980: 231.
54 For a Chinese Zen master's cat exiled to Japan, see the two poems translated by Pollack
    1985: 136.
55 See Jingfu, comp., *Zongmen niangu zongji* 9, p.308c, in edition of *Zoku Zōkyō* 2A-20:
    I have been unable to identify the author, one Wu Shengyu; the compilation dates to
    1664.
56 Strassberg 1994: 320.
57 Marks 1998 shows how information on tiger attacks can be put to good historical use.
58 Sowerby 1933.
59 Alec-Tweedie 1936: 193.
60 Note the Han example given in Sterckx 2002: 62.
61 Sterckx 2002: 152.
62 Sowerby 1933: 94.
63 See the biography of the Taoist priestess Xiao Lianzhen, translated in Bumbacher 2000:
    295.
64 See Hammond 1992–1993: 245. These phenomena had earlier attracted the attention of
    Minakata Kumagusu (1994) see pp. 22–23, 71–72.
65 Mair 1986: 29–42.
66 See *GBSS*, vol. 5, 879.
67 See Wu 1957: 413, 415.
68 Brinker 1987: 76–82.
69 This tale comes from the *Liushi jiahua*, a collection of jottings about Liu Yuxi 劉禹
    錫 (722–842) that I do not have to hand. Note, however, the approving comment on
    the story by the iconoclastic Li Zhi 李贄 (1527–1602) in his excerpts on "Friends and
    Teachers": *Chutan ji* 17, p. 282.
70 See Adamik 1996: 71.
71 Adamik 1996: 68.
72 Adamik 1996: 73.
73 Adamik 1996: 65, 67.
74 Barrett 1998: 2–3.
75 See te Velde 1982: 128, 135–137. My thanks once again to Jan Bremmer for providing
    me with a copy of this article.

76　Minakata 1994: 9.

77　Thus even much later, in the seventeenth century, Kumazawa Banzan 熊沢蕃山 (1619–1691) is obliged to defend Japan's failure to follow China in using oxen in sacrifice by arguing that Japan was just "a small country": see McMullen 1999: 207.

78　Text in *GBSS* vol. 1, p. 245.

79　See Watson 1981: 14–15, dating to 1631.

80　Watson 1981: 57–58. Apparently at least one classical Western artist seems to have got into trouble by using a cat as the model for a depiction of a leopard: see Engels 1999: 175.

81　Kokan Shiren 虎関師錬 (1278–1346) and China is the topic of the fourth chapter of Pollack 1986. For his work as a historian, see Bielefeldt 1997: 295–317.

82　*GBZS,* vol. 1, p. 154.

83　See Wen 1989: 363–364.

84　*GBSS,* Supplement 1, p. 630. Cf. *GBZS* vol. 1, p. 640 for another lament, though I have not searched systematically for these.

85　Cf. Collcutt 1981: 165, which gives some revealing excerpts from monastic regulations.

86　For a discussion of this aspect of the tradition, see Prince 2002: 49–73.

87　Serpell 1996, chapter 6, and note also the arguments against Yi-fu Tuan, p. 52.

88　Serpell 1996: 159.

89　Parker 1999 provides a compelling though of course far from comprehensive picture in English of just how "Chinese" the culture of the Gozan monks became; for one aspect of sinology that he does not cover, see Ng 2000: 6–10.

90　On the British situation, see Burton 1994, chapter 10; on the Gozan, see Collcutt 1981: 57–78, 84–89, 98–102. It has recently been suggested, however, that in China cultural tensions between contemporary Chan monasteries and the imperial bureaucracy were less than one might imagine: see DeBlasi 1998.

91　Pollack 1985: 158.

92　I have in mind Schopen 2004a.

93　A revealing contribution to this field is Trombert 1995.

94　Note on the latter score Elvin 2004: 78–80, for one example.

95　The correlation is remarked in passing by McCormick 2003: 21; my own gloss on this is just a guess.

96　For a statement on oral tradition that has formed the starting point for much recent research, see Norman 1997: 41–57.

97　Insight into this legacy may be found for example in works such as Mills 1970, where stories going back to India and China turn up in what is largely a collection of Japanese stories.

98　Besides the article by Ayusawa mentioned above, the Buddhist influence on conceptions of the world in East Asia is also explored concise in Harley and Woodward 1994: 173–175, 371–376.

99　Daoxuan, *Liangdu qingzhong yi* 量度輕重儀, 2, T. 45.845b26. Keeping cats was in fact a problem for lay Buddhists as well as the clergy, so Buddhist ethics and the cat could easily form the topic of another study: see Martine Batchelor 2004: 76 (where "breeds" signifies "raises"); Shih Heng-ching 1994: 82.

5 The monastic institution in medieval Japan

The insider's view

William M. Bodiford

The transition from the court-centered society of Heian Period (ca. 794–1221) Japan to the more tumultuous warrior administrations of the Kamakura Period (ca. 1185–1333) witnessed the unprecedented production of numerous first-person accounts of institutional Buddhism and its role in society. Despite having different formats, these works share a perceived need to provide a changing society with a comprehensive explanation of the key features of Japanese monasticism and their genealogical bases. Written both by laymen and by Buddhist monks, they provide us with a heretofore neglected perspective on the mainstream Buddhist monasteries. With only a few exceptions, previous scholars have examined these first-person accounts merely as raw databases to be mined for names and events, to be cited or dismissed according to modern standards of historical accuracy. In this chapter I propose a different approach to these sources. I wish to suggest ways that these insider accounts can be examined on their own terms as first-hand ethnographies of a world long lost, ethnographies which reveal the categories of knowledge, ceremonies, lifestyle, modes of learning, and religious concerns of Japanese monks and nuns. I hope that data from these accounts can contribute toward a historiography of medieval Japanese Buddhism that charts a middle way between (and thereby avoids some of the pitfalls of) the "Kamakura New Buddhism" and the "Exoteric-Esoteric Establishment" models of medieval Japanese Buddhist history.

These two historiographical models each have their own unique strengths, but they share a common weakness. They ignore important aspects of monastic Buddhism in medieval Japan. Scholarship on so-called Kamakura New Buddhism generally approaches religious life in terms of doctrinal and textual issues, especially those related to the emergence and growth of the Pure Land, Nichiren, and Zen movements that eventually became the dominant sectarian denominations of modern Japan. It emphasizes points of disagreement and divergence within these movements and between them and the main monastic institutions from which they broke away. Therefore it usually ignores the common religious landscape, beliefs, and practices common to broad cross-sections of society during the medieval period. The Exoteric-Esoteric Establishment (*kenmitsu taisei* 顕密体制) model proposed by Kuroda Toshio 黒田俊雄 (1926–1993) focuses more closely on the mainstream medieval monastic institutions and their relationships to the aristocracy and warrior families in government. Kuroda's approach reminds us of the economic, political, geographic, and military power of Buddhist monasteries.[1] In spite of the importance of these topics for our understanding of medieval society, this approach tends to overlook the roles of monasteries as settings for religious life and learning.[2]

It is to this topic, monastic institutions as settings for religious life, learning, and ceremony, that I wish to draw our attention. For, while medieval Japanese Buddhist monasteries played an indispensable role in the exercise of all forms of social power, they also constituted a religious landscape that reveals as much about medieval religion as about social structures. By way of illustrating my approach, I will briefly examine a few of the religious themes found in the following seven texts: *The Three Jewels with Illustrations* (984), *Overview of Monastic Life* (1193), *Sand and Pebbles* (1283), *Miscellaneous Discussions* (1305), *Leaves Gathered from Stormy Streams* (1348), *Genkō Era Account of Buddhism* (1322), and *Chronicle of Gods and Sovereigns* (1339). All of these texts are well-known. English translations already exist for several of them. Nonetheless, in spite of the wealth of information they contain and their ready accessibility, they remain underutilized. Examined together these texts (and others like them) provide us contemporaneous overviews of monastic ceremonies, institutions, social distinctions among the clergy, monastic learning, and routine daily activities. This kind of overview of the religious landscape as it would have appeared to or been perceived by the authors of these works too rarely appears in published accounts of medieval Japanese Buddhism.

Limitations

First-person accounts naturally suffer from many limitations. Their authors inevitably tend to be men, members of the ruling elite, educated in Chinese modes of discourse and, therefore, uninterested in or even unaware of the possibility of other points of view. They generally write only about people, places, and events located near the court and urban centers. They can reveal little direct knowledge of the lives of women and commoners, or of regional customs. As pious insiders, they tend to obfuscate what Allan Grapard calls the "economics of ritual power" that reinforce the status quo.[3] Frequently they exhibit biases and sectarian prejudices. They cannot be relied on for historical accuracy, even when supposedly reporting events witnessed first-hand. We cannot always detect when they exaggerate the importance of minor matters or ignore truly significant ones, but we know for certain that such distortions occur.

The eminent scholar-monk Gyōnen 凝然 (1240–1321), for example, wrote *Jōdo hōmon genrushō* 浄土法門源流章, a detailed account of the new Pure Land movement founded by Hōnen 法然 (1133–1212; a.k.a. Genkū 源空). Gyōnen describes each of Hōnen's major disciples, but fails to mention Shinran 親鸞 (1173–1263)— the person now regarded not only as Hōnen's most important disciple but also as the founder of modern Japan's predominant denominational orientation. Obviously, Gyōnen lacked our historical perspective. It is precisely this kind of alternative to our own hindsight that interests me.

Tamenori's *Three Jewels*

The *Three Jewels with Illustrations* (*Sanbōe* 三寶繪, 984) by the nobleman Minamoto Tamenori 源爲憲 (d. 1011) presents one of our earliest surviving accounts of the annual cycle of major Buddhist ceremonies performed in Japan (see Appendix 1, on p. 141). From his description of some thirty-one annual events, we can learn that the most important monasteries were sponsored by high aristocrats or members of the royal family and founded by monks famous for their learning, their accomplishments, and the many miracles that accompanied their lives. Similarly, each of the yearly rituals can boast ancient pedigrees, scriptural justifications, and numerous examples of miraculous benefits. While lay people do not necessarily participate in the events described by Tamenori, he occasionally indicates that they can gain the most merit by practicing Buddhist rituals at the same time as they are being performed at major temples and palaces. For example, if women observe the eight restraints (*hassai kai* 八齋戒) during the eighth day of the second and eighth moons when nuns perform the Ānanda Rites of Repentance (*Anan senbō* 阿難懺法), then their prayers will be answered.[4] The springtime ordination of new monks constitutes prayers for abundant harvests.[5] Likewise, the best time to give robes to a temple is during the twelfth moon, when the court presents offerings of robes to all the major monasteries.[6] From these kinds of examples we can begin to detect something of the ways in which Buddhists configured the passage of time so as to assign cultural value to daily activities. Perhaps we can even gauge somewhat the relative prominence of the various monasteries near the capital. Mount Hiei 比叡山—the headquarters for Tendai—occupied a preeminent position. At least seven of the thirty-one Buddhist events described by Tamenori occur there. The other events were scattered about at a wide variety of locations near the capital. Three of them occur within the royal court. Seven more are located at the major temples near the former capital town of Nara: two at Kōfukuji 興福寺 (Yamashinadera 山階寺), two at Yakushiji 藥師寺, and one each at Daianji 大安寺 and at Tōdaiji 東大寺.

Eisai's *Overview of Monastic Life*

The *Overview of Monastic Life* (*Shukke taikō* 出家大綱, 1193) by the Buddhist monk Eisai 榮西 (1141–1215) presents a concise list of prescriptive exhortations concerning robes, meals, and deportment. Eisai laments widespread acceptance in Japan of monastic norms that he regards as non-Buddhist. From the content of Eisai's complaints, we know that during cold winter months Japanese monastics would wear the same clothes as lay people to provide extra warmth. They frequently ate meals after the noon hour and drank alcohol. Many of them had acquired religious identities and religious titles simply by self-declaration or by adopting the appearance of a religious practitioner. The adoption of these titles did not require that they undergo a Buddhist initiation ceremony, become affiliated to a Buddhist institution, or receive any Buddhist training. In other words, distinctions between secular or religious status could be based on social conventions, not on government regulations or on Buddhist ceremonial procedures.

Mujū's stories

The Buddhist essayist Mujū Dōgyō 無住道曉 (Ichien 一圓; 1226–1312) wrote—
or collected and retold—more than 280 didactic stories in two compilations: *Sand
and Pebbles* (*Shasekishū* 砂石集, 1283; about 160 stories) and *Miscellaneous
Discussions* (*Zōdanshū* 雜談集, 1305; about 67 stories). In many respects Mujū's
stories are typical of Buddhist edifying tales found across Asia. Just as in other
examples of this genre, Mujū describes the mysterious results of karma from previous lives, the dangers of moral transgressions, the rewards of piety and acts of worship, and the miracles worked by buddhas and bodhisattvas. Many of the stories,
however, focus on topics of particular concern to Buddhists of Mujū's own time and
place: medieval Japan. Mujū repeatedly emphasizes the equivalence of Sanskrit
dhāraṇī and Japanese-language verse (*waka* 和歌), devoting at least thirteen stories to this notion. Likewise the local gods (*jinmyō* 神明) frequently appear in
dreams and oracles as the voice of the buddhas, whose teachings they promote and
protect. The unity of buddhas and gods is the main subject of at least nine stories.
The failure of Japanese monks to observe monastic vows is another reoccurring
theme (six stories), as is the importance of facing death with the correct spiritual
composure (five stories). Although we cannot assume that Mujū's stories meet
even journalistic standards of reporting, they nonetheless allow us to see the human
faces of medieval Japanese Buddhists and to detect something of their activities,
opinions, follies, and spiritual values. Just as important, his reporting allows us to
see the growing importance of Buddhism outside the central provinces. Since Mujū
did not live in the capital, he seems uninterested in its annual cycle of ceremonies
(mentioning only the Eight Lectures Assembly, *Hakkō'e* 八講會, by name). The
range of monasteries he mentions also differs. Most often he simply says "a certain
mountain temple" (*aru yamadera* ある山寺; 35 times). The Shingon mountain
monastery on Mount Kōya 高野山 (in modern Wakayama Prefecture) is named
most often (31 times), followed by various monasteries of Nara (31 times), the two
main Tendai monastic complexes at Mount Hiei and Onjōji 園城寺 (a.k.a. Miidera
三井寺; 23 times), three of the new Zen monasteries (17 times), and Kiyomizudera
清水寺 in Kyoto (11 times).[7]

Kōshū's *Leaves from Stormy Streams*

The fourth example, *Leaves Gathered from Stormy Streams* (*Keiran shūyōshū* 溪
嵐拾葉集, 1348), consists of excerpts from treatises, brief notes, and secret initiations (*hiketsu* 秘訣) compiled by a Tendai monk on Mount Hiei named Kōshū
光宗 (1276–1350) over the course of his education. Even though most of his collection was lost, 113 fascicles (out of 300 total) of notes along with a detailed table
of contents for the entire work still remain. Taken together, Kōshū's notes and
table of contents provide an unparalleled, detailed overview of his academic training during a 36-year period (from 1313 to 1348). Kōshū names 85 teachers from
whom he received initiations in more than fifteen separate subjects. He learned
the following (T. 74.505–507):

	Subject	Learned from # teachers
1	tantric (*shingon* 眞言) traditions	33 teachers
2	Tendai 天台 traditions	24 teachers
3	Zen 禪 meditation traditions	12 teachers
4	Sanskrit (*shittan* 悉曇) traditions (i.e., writing *dhāraṇī* in Siddham letters)	6 teachers
5	secular literature (*zokusho* 俗書)	5 teachers
6	Abhidharma (Kusha 倶舎) traditions	4 teachers
7	poetical (*kadō* 歌道) traditions	"
8	military strategy (*hyōhō* 兵法)	"
9	Yogācāra (Hossō 法相) traditions	3 teachers
10	Pure Land (*jōdo* 浄土) traditions	"
11	mathematical (*sanjutsu* 算術) traditions	"
12	medical (*ihō* 醫方) traditions	"
13	arts and crafts (*jutsuhō* 術法)	"
14	Kegon 華嚴 traditions	2 teachers
15	Sanron 三論 traditions	"

This long list of fifteen subjects, each with multiple teachers, testifies to the broad range of learning available to elite monks on Mount Hiei. It encompassed not just Buddhism, but also secular subjects such as artistic crafts, medical arts, mathematics, and military affairs—all of which Kōshū learned from other monks. It should alert us to the medieval marriage of Buddhism to all aspects of Japanese life.

Not apparent from the above enumeration of subjects are two of the most important characteristics of Kōshū's compilation. First, the Tendai traditions he studied consisted largely of initiations into the secret Buddhist significance of the gods of Japan. These initiations reveal the formative development of what subsequently came to be known as "Shintō" or, more precisely in this case, Sannō Shintō 山王 神道. Kōshū (T. 76.503b) refers to these initiations as consecrations that invoke the powers of the buddhas who "soften their radiance and meld with dust to benefit the kingdom" (*wakō dōjin riyaku kokudo kanjō* 和光同塵利益國土灌頂). These rituals aimed to transform the land of Japan into a sacred realm where buddhas became localized as the tutelary gods of the ruling houses (*kuge* 公家). Thus, Buddhist practices can never be purely soteriological, but always involve local places (identified as localized gods) and the elites (identified as descendants of the gods) who rule over the people living in those places. Second, in spite of the fact that Kōshū cites large numbers of Buddhist scriptures and uses transliterated Sanskrit and complex Chinese Buddhist terminology, his notes exhibit almost no interest in Buddhist doctrines. That is, if one understands "doctrine" as entailing some kind of systematic presentation of teachings, ideals, philosophy, or terminology, then it cannot be found.

Rather than presenting doctrines themselves, Kōshū's notes simply cite doctrinal points to substantiate and legitimate his real concern, which is ceremonial lore. This lore, recorded in documents called chronicles (*ki* 記), concerns ritual expertise, historical precedents, royal power, local places, secret relationships, and gossip.

The teaching of ritual lore already had a long history among the court aristocrats. Members of certain familial lineages, known as ceremonial houses (*yūsokuke* 有職家), specialized in knowing the precedents, established practices, and customary forms of behavior that were believed essential to assure proper control of the realm. By Kōshū's day every one of the ruling houses—not just those of court officials (*kanke* 官家), but also clerical houses (*shakke* 釋家), shrine houses (*shake* 社家),[8] and warrior houses (*buke* 武家)[9]—had begun to compile their own collections of established procedures (*kojitsu* 故實) that would allow them to lay claim to their own unique spheres of professional expertise. Kōshū's notes, therefore, reveal the range of expert lore that allowed the monks of Mount Hiei to claim control over the gods of the land, the divine rights of rulership, and the security of the realm.

This medieval Buddhist lore rested on a logic of resemblances, consisting primarily of linguistic and performative (i.e., ritual) homologies. Linguistic resemblances developed out of an education that stressed the acquisition of literacy in at least three mediums: *siddhaṃ* glyphs used for Sanskrit *dhāraṇī*, pictorial glyphs used for Chinese, and syllabic glyphs used for Japanese. All three of these mediums could be converted phonetically into one another and could be translated from one language into equivalent vocabulary from either or both of the other two languages. The resulting vocabulary could be interpreted semantically according to either the rules of Chinese grammar or the very different word-order of Japanese grammar (*jikunshaku* 字訓釋). Moreover, Chinese glyphs could be given new resemblances simply by breaking them apart into their component elements (*jizōshaku* 字象釋), each of which could be recognized as separate glyphs in their own right, or by interpreting them as homophones for other words (*tenshōshaku* 轉聲釋). In this way, every single word became pregnant with limitless significance.

To cite a couple of well-known examples, Kōshū states that the name of the mountain god, Sannō 山王, who protects Mount Hiei actually signifies the perfect integration of unity (i.e., the horizontal line of 山 and the vertical line of 王) and trinity (i.e., the triple vertical lines of 山 and triple horizontal lines of 王) so that it is none other than a revelation of the highest Tendai teachings of one mind viewing three truths (*isshin sankan* 一心三觀; T. 76.510a–b) and each instant of thought encompassing three thousand realms (*ichinen sanzen* 一念三千; T. 76.514a–b). Similarly, Kōshū reveals that the name of the Japanese kingdom, Dai Nippon koku 大日本國, actually signified Mahāvairocana's homeland (*Dainichi honkoku* 大日本國; T. 76.511a), the original dwelling of the great sun buddha.

Performative resemblances resulted from the application of these linguistic transformations to ceremonial rituals so that every gesture (*mudrā*), implement, and offering became a substitute for something else of greater value.[10] Thus, Kōshū notes that a single-pronged *vajra* is none other than the main island of Japan (T. 76.519a) while a branch of the evergreen *sakaki* 榊 tree is the timeless *prātimokṣa* (*haradaimokusha* 波羅提木叉; T. 76.516b), and so forth. The resulting resemblances consisted not simply of so-called Shintō-Buddhist combinations, but encompassed all human endeavors—Daoist, Confucian, military, mathematical, poetical, and so forth—and refracted them through a multifaceted Buddhist prism that tied each element to all the others. For this reason, it is a mistake to examine the medieval logic of homologies only in terms of the relative equivalencies of buddhas and gods.

Kokan Shiren's perspective

The most fully realized attempt to provide an insider's perspective on mainstream monastic Buddhism can be found in the *Genkō Era Account of Buddhism* (*Genkō shakusho* 元亨釋書, 1322; hereafter cited as "*Shakusho*") by Kokan Shiren 虎關 師鍊 (1278–1346). Shiren was an elite monk who served as abbot of Nanzenji 南禪 寺 and Tōfukuji 東福寺—two top-tier Five Mountain (*gozan* 五山) Zen monasteries in Kyoto—and authored numerous works written in Chinese, including Japan's first dictionary of Chinese poetics, the *Shūbun inryaku* 聚文韻略 (20 fascicles, 1306) and a textbook on writing Chinese prose and poetry, the *Zengi gemon shū* 禪 儀外文集 (two fascicles, 1341)—both of which exerted a major influence on the genre we now know as Five Mountain literature (*gozan bungaku* 五山文學). His *Shakusho* is famous as Japan's earliest large (30 fascicles) and comprehensive (444 entries) hagiography of eminent monks.

Although famous, today the *Shakusho* is largely ignored. It might be cited when no other sources can be found, but it suffers a poor reputation for historical accuracy. Modern scholars frequently dismiss it as a work of sectarian scholarship designed to place the Zen 禪 lineage at the center of Japanese Buddhism.[11] The work begins, for example, with Zen, which implies that Japanese Buddhism also begins with Zen. Its very first biography is of Bodhidharma—the legendary Indian monk who supposedly introduced the Chan (Zen) lineage to China. Shiren's account, however, concerns neither China nor India. It locates Bodhidharma in Japan. According to the *Shakusho* (fasc. 1, K 31.27), Bodhidharma arrived in China in 520, returned to India nine years later, and then came to Japan in 613. Shiren's uncritical inclusion of this kind of fantasy causes modern historians to breathe a sigh of relief whenever they can find another source to cite instead. Among comprehensive Japanese Buddhist hagiographies, the one titled *Biographies of Eminent Monks of Our Kingdom* (*Honchō kōsōden* 本朝高僧傳, 1702; 75 fasc.) by Mangen Shiban 卍元師蛮 (1625–1710) enjoys far more prestige for its historiographical accuracy and even-handedness.

With its flawed reputation, it is not too surprising that—as far as I can detect—only two studies of the *Shakusho* have appeared in English. In 1970 it was the subject of an unpublished doctoral dissertation by the late Marian Ury. She provided a partial translation (consisting of the major biographies) along with an introduction that focuses on the *Shakusho*'s literary relationship to Chinese models and to Japanese popular literature (e.g., *setsuwa bungaku* 説話文學). More recently Carl Bielefeldt has published an essay in which he examines *Shakusho*'s "sectarian uses of history" as part of his on-going research on the formation of sectarian identities in medieval Japanese Buddhism.[12] Neither of these studies examines the *Shakusho* for what it might reveal in general about the practice of Buddhist monasticism in Shiren's time. That is a subject about which Shiren's *Shakusho* actually reveals a great deal.

Although scholars most frequently cite (and criticize) its hagiographies, Shiren modeled his work as much on Chinese dynastic histories (see Appendix 3, on p. 145) as on previous Chinese hagiographical (i.e., *gaoseng zhuan* 高僧傳) collections.[13] Shiren titled his text (see fasc. 30; K 31.447 and 448) with the word *sho* 書 (of *Shakusho*; Chinese *shu*) to explicitly indicate that it is a comprehensive history (*zenshi* 全史) just like Chinese dynastic histories such as the *Hanshu* 漢書 (78), *Jinshu* 晉書 (644), and *Tangshu* 唐書 (1060).[14] The word *Shaku* 釋 (of *Shakusho*) refers, of course, to the Buddha Śākyamuni and to the monks and nuns who are his (spiritual) descendants. Shiren argues (fasc. 30; K 31.448) that because the buddha's body and the land are indivisible (*shindo funi* 身土不二) and since the labels "Han," "Jin," and "Tang" were as much family names (*shō* 姓) as dynastic designations, therefore Japanese Buddhism should be described according to the format of a dynastic history. Moreover, for Shiren a comprehensive dynastic history must include not just biographies (*den* 傳, Chinese *zhuan*), but also a chronological table (*hyō* 表, Chinese *biao*) as well as topical treatises (*shi* 志, Chinese *zhi*). Accordingly the *Shakusho* includes all three.

Shiren was not the first Buddhist historian to adopt the format of a dynastic history. The same section titles of biographies, tables, and treatises also were used in the *Unified Record of the Buddha and Ancestors* (*Fozu tongji* 佛祖統紀, 1269) by the Chinese Tiantai monk Zhipan 志盤 (see Appendix 3, on p. 145). Zhipan goes even further than Shiren since he also uses the section titles of basic records (*benji* 本紀) and of hereditary houses (*shijia* 世家). Zhipan's use of section titles from dynastic histories, however, was completely different from that of Shiren. Zhipan's record focuses on the Tiantai lineage alone. Regardless of their titles, practically all the sections—basic records, hereditary houses, biographies, and the various treatises—consist of biographies of Tiantai patriarchs and their disciples. Zhipan did not reproduce the different types of content normally associated with each distinctive section title, and he made no attempt in his topical treatises to identify or describe the overall features of Chinese monastic life. In Shiren's *Shakusho*, in contrast, the topical treatises are exactly that: they provide an insider's perspective on the main topics concerning Buddhist monasticism in Japan.

Before discussing Shiren's topical treatises, though, let me point out another difference between him and Zhipan. While Zhipan focuses just on members of his own lineage (i.e., Tiantai), Shiren's hagiographies actually represent all manner of Japanese Buddhists regardless of lineage or doctrinal affiliation (see Appendix 4, on p. 146).[15] In spite of the prominence afforded to certain Zen patriarchs such as Bodhidharma (the first biography), Eisai and Enni Ben'en 圓爾辯圓 (1202–1280)—who receive one fascicle apiece—Shiren mentions very few Zen monks. Of the monks whose names are associated with specific temples, the temples mentioned most often are the two main Tendai monasteries of Mount Hiei and Onjōji 園城寺 (located near the base of Mount Hiei). The other temples frequently mentioned to identify monks consist almost entirely of those associated with the Buddhism of the former southern capital of Nara or with the Shingon lineage. The fact that the monks described by Shiren primarily represent rival (non-Zen) institutions tells us that, in his own mind at least, Shiren tried to draft a comprehensive and nonsectarian account.[16] Shiren's rejection of the kind of partisanship displayed by Zhipan helps explain why Shiren never acknowledged the existence of Zhipan's work.[17]

Shiren's collected biographies display a few more noteworthy characteristics. First, he adopted the same tenfold division of bibliographies as found in previous Chinese hagiographical collections, but he rearranged and re-titled many of the sections (see Appendix 2, on p. 144). Since the Japanese rely on Chinese translations of the scriptures, he replaced the category of "translators" (*yakkyō* 譯經) with "transmitters of wisdom" (*denchi* 傳智). He replaced the category of "vinaya exegetes" (*myōritsu* 明律) with "*śīla* exegetes" to reflect the Japanese preference for Buddhist morality as an abstract ideal rather than as concrete discipline. He eliminated the category of "defenders of the dharma" (*gohō* 護法) altogether because (he explains) in Japan there were no anti-Buddhist rulers from whom the dharma needed defending (fasc. 30, K 31.448). Second, he self-consciously identified each of the ten categories with one of the ten bodhisattva perfections (*pāramitā*) so that every hagiography depicts Mahāyāna Buddhists who cultivate the bodhisattva path. Shiren, like many authors of his period, asserted that Japan (unlike either India or China) was populated entirely by followers of the Mahāyāna (*jundai mushō* 純大無小). No one followed the inferior vehicle (*hīnayāna*) and in Japan (unlike either India or China) there exist no other religions (*mu idō* 無異道).[18] In other words, Shiren asserts that in Japan the scholars of Confucian learning, the practitioners of Daoist longevity techniques, the celebrants at shrines to local gods as well as the god themselves all were Buddhists who practiced Buddhism. Shintō did not yet exist apart from Buddhism.

The third notable feature of his hagiographical collection reflects this assertion: All beings in Japan practice Mahāyāna Buddhism. As indicated by Shiren's tenth category concerning the perfection of vows (*praṇidhāna*), "all beings" includes not just the usual eminent monks (*kōsō* 高僧) or virtuous patriarchs (*kotoku* 古德), but also: kings and ministers (*ōshin* 王臣), aristocrats and commoners (*shisho* 士庶), nuns and women (*ni'nyo* 尼女), local gods and wizards (*jinsen* 神仙), and apparitions (*ryōkei* 靈怪). These categories represent Shiren's sociological taxonomy of Japanese Buddhists. The lack of any clear distinction between the members of the clergy and lay people is especially noteworthy. We have already seen in Eisai's *Overview of Monastic Life* that rigid distinctions between secular or religious status did not exist. This lack of distinction reflects the Mahāyāna precepts used for clerical ordinations on Mount Hiei, which also can be bestowed on lay people without affecting their lay status.

Who are mainstream Buddhists?

This section on the biographies of lay people and spirits contains 107 entries, making it the second largest category among Shiren's collected biographies. The largest section, which concerns miracle workers (those who cultivate the perfection of vigor, *vīrya*) contains 117 biographies. Together they constitute nearly half of the hagiographies included in the *Shakusho*. In other words, Shiren saw miracle workers, the pious lay people who support them, and supernatural spirits as the mainstream Buddhists. He argues (fasc. 30, K 31.452) that Buddhist wisdom is valuable precisely because it generates supernatural events that benefit the realm. He criticizes Chinese Confucian scholars, such as Ouyang Xiu 歐陽脩 (1007–1072), for their failure to appreciate the supernatural and to mention it in their records.[19]

Shiren provides individual entries for only five gods. Naturally, he begins with Tenshō *daijin* 天照大神, the god enshrined at Ise whose worship signifies legitimate succession to the throne.[20] Tenshō is none other than Vairocana (Birushana 毘盧遮那), the great buddha of the sun (Dainichi). Hakusan *myōjin* 白山明神, the god enshrined on the White Mountain (Mount Hakusan 白山) who is worshiped throughout northern Japan, actually is Izanagi 伊奘諾 (i.e., the father of Tenshō), a bodhisattva of marvelous wisdom (*myōri bosatsu* 妙理菩薩). Niu *myōjin* 丹生明神, the god that protects Mount Koya, insures the spread of esoteric (tantric) Buddhism throughout Japan. Shinra *myōjin* 新羅明神, a god that came from Korea, protects the Tendai monastery Onjōji—which competes against Mount Hiei as the second branch of Japanese Tendai. Kitano *tenjin* 北野天神, the deified minister Sugawara Michizane 管原道眞 (845–903) who is worshiped as god of thunder and lightning, works to control the unruly demons who otherwise cause disasters and hardships. Surprisingly, Shiren does not provide entries for perhaps the three most important gods: Hachiman 八幡 (Yahata, who protects Tōdaiji) Sannō (who protects Mount Hiei), and Zaō 藏王 (who protects Mount Kinpusen 金峰山). He might have regarded separate entries for these deities as redundant, since all three of them figure prominently in the *Shakusho* (Sannō is mentioned 30 times, Hachiman 27 times, and Zaō 13 times).[21] Shiren's subsection on apparitions reminds us of the importance of dreams and oracles in Japanese Buddhism. Shiren argues that fervent faith results in visions of the buddhas, revelations via dreams, and reports from the afterlife. Religious dreams figure prominently in all literature from premodern Japan.

Shiren's overview of monastic Buddhism

The least studied portion of the *Shakusho* are Shiren's topical treatises. They cover the following ten areas: (1) learning (*gakushu* 學修), (2) ordinations (*doju* 度受), (3) doctrinal lineages (*shoshū* 諸宗), (4) ceremonies (*egi* 會儀), (5) ecclesiastical titles (*fūshoku* 封職), (6) monasteries and icons (*jizō* 寺像), (7) aural arts (*ongei* 音藝), (8) strange phenomena (*shūi* 拾異), (9) avoiding strife (*chussō* 黜爭), and (10) Shiren's explanation of the *Shakusho*'s organization (*josetsu* 序説). If the *Shakusho*'s collected biographies constitute Japan's earliest comprehensive hagiography, then its treatises are the earliest attempt at a systematic description of mainstream monastic Buddhism. Unfortunately, all of the treatises are too short and Shiren's explanations too terse to satisfy the curiosity of modern scholars. He fails to describe any one of his topics in detail. His intent is historical, rather than ethnographical. For that very reason, however, the details that he does provide must be given due consideration. Shiren would not have included them unless they were (to his eyes, at least) especially significant. I will briefly summarize them below.

Learning

In this section, Shiren explains that learning consists of the standard Buddhist category of threefold learning (*sangaku* 三學; i.e., morality, mental cultivation, and wisdom). All of these ultimately derive from letters (*monji* 文字; i.e., literacy), but encompass all forms of cultivation from chanting words of dharma (*hokku* 法句; *dharmapada*) to practicing austerities (*zuda* 頭陀; *dhuta*). Monks on Mount Hiei gain fame for their chronicles (*chūki* 注記; i.e., compilations of lore), while the monks of Nara become renowned for participating (*tokugō* 得業) in lecture ceremonies. This last statement tells us that Kōshū's *Leaves Gathered from Stormy Streams* (*Keiran shūyōshū*) is representative of the type of learning pursued in Tendai and that the three lecture ceremonies (the Yuima'e 維摩會 at Kōfukuji, the Misai'e 御齋會 at the court, and the Saishō'e 最勝會 at Yakushiji) described in Tamenori's *Three Jewels* (*Sanbōe*) remained central events for the monks for the Nara schools.

Ordinations

This section constitutes one of the *Shakusho*'s longer treatises, reflecting the complicated and controversial nature of this topic in Japan. (a) First, Shiren identifies Japan's two separate ordination systems, the one based on the Chinese Vinaya school introduced by Ganjin (Jianzhen 鑑眞, 688–763) and the Mahāyāna method established by Saichō 最澄 (767–822), the monk responsible for winning Mount Hiei's independence from the Buddhist monasteries of Nara. (b) Second, the vinaya ordinations distinguish between the fourfold saṃgha of monks, nuns, laymen, and lay women, while Mahāyāna ordinations can apply equally to everyone. (c) Third, there exist only three ordination platforms in Japan. The one in Nara (at Tōdaiji) and the one in western Japan (at Kanzeonji 觀世音寺) both conduct ordinations according to the vinaya, while the one on Mount Hiei conducts Mahāyāna ordinations.[22] The Tendai monastery Onjōji had been granted court permission to erect another Mahāyāna ordination platform, but armed opposition from Mount Hiei had prevented it from ever being built. (d) Fourth, there exist both universal (*tsū* 通) precepts and distinct (*betsu* 別) ones. Shiren's explanation of this distinction differs from our usual understanding of these terms.[23] According to Shiren, the precepts conveyed either via the vinaya ordinations or the Mahāyāna ordinations are universal. The esoteric precepts (*sanmaya kai* 三摩耶戒) and Zen precepts (*zenkai* 禪戒) are distinct because they can be conveyed only to someone who is initiated, respectively, either into an esoteric lineage or into a Zen lineage.

Doctrinal Lineages or Schools (shū 宗)

This section also is lengthy and complicated. Shiren lived at a time when surveys of doctrinal lineages (*shoshū tsūsetsu* 諸宗通説) had begun to emerge as a new genre of Japanese Buddhist literature.[24] At this point, I want to turn to the author of one of those surveys who presents basically the same information as Shiren, but who organizes it in a way that I find more interesting.

That author is Kitabatake Chikafusa 北畠親房 (1293–1354), a man who is remembered today primarily as a supporter of the failed restoration of Godaigo 後醍醐 (1288–1339) and the author of a genealogical history of the royal family, the *Chronicle of Gods and Sovereigns* (*Jinnō shōtōki* 神皇正統記, 1339). Not so well-known today is the fact that Kitabatake had been ordained as a Buddhist monk in 1329 and actually was quite knowledgeable about Buddhism.[25] For Kitabatake—and for Shiren—a religion exists in practice only if its rituals and lore are handed down within a master–disciple lineage. Without a living lineage, it is just an abstract theory. It is on the basis of this criterion that Kitabatake and Shiren asserted that no followers of inferior (*hīnayāna*) schools of Buddhism exist in Japan. Japanese studied inferior doctrines (i.e., Abhidharma), but formed no master–disciple lineages based on them.[26]

Kitabatake recognizes seven doctrinal lineages in Japan, several of which can be subdivided into multiple branches (*Jinnō shōtōki*, pp. 110–116). Kitabatake calls the first one "Shingon" 眞言 (True Words), by which he means esoteric or tantric lineages. This school consists of three separate branches: Tōji 東寺 temple in Kyoto (i.e., the lineage now known as Shingon) and the two rival Tendai monasteries of Mount Hiei and Onjōji. Next, according to Kitabatake, there are four Mahāyāna schools: (1) the Tendai school (divided into the two rival branches of Mount Hiei and Onjōji), (2) the Kegon 華嚴 (Chinese Huayan) school located at Tōdaiji monastery in Nara, (3) the Sanron 三論 (Three Treatise) school also located at Tōdaiji, and (4) the Hossō 法相 (Yogācāra) school located at Kōfukuji monastery in Nara.[27] Of the aforementioned monasteries, Mount Hiei is responsible for the rituals that guard the emperor's life (*tenshi honmyō* 天子本命) while both Mount Hiei and Onjōji represent mixed exoteric-esoteric (*kenmitsu* 顯密) teachings.[28] Next is the Vinaya (Ritsu 律) school, which also is divided into two branches: the Saidaiji 西大寺 monastery (established by Eison 叡尊, 1201–1290) near Nara and the Sennyūji 泉涌寺 temple (established by Shunjō 俊芿, 1166–1227) in Kyoto. Finally, there is the Zen or Buddha-Mind (*busshin* 佛心) school, which also is divided into two branches: the Kenninji 建仁寺 and Tōfukuji 東福寺 monasteries in Kyoto. Kitabatake was completely unaware of distinctions between other divisions within Zen, such as the Five Mountain (*gozan* 五山); i.e., urban) and Forest (*rinka* 林下) lineages (of medieval times) or Sōtō 曹洞 and Rinzai 臨濟 (the two main Zen denominations of modern Japan). Kitabatake concludes his survey by saying that all seven of these doctrinal lineages are promoted by bodhisattvas and protected by the local gods. Neither Kitabatake nor Shiren acknowledged the existence of the new Buddhist movements that have dominated modern scholarship on this period: the Pure Land school (Jōdoshū 浄土宗) founded by Hōnen and the Lotus school (Hokkeshū 法華宗) founded by Nichiren 日蓮 (1223–1283).[29]

Ceremonies

Shiren briefly surveys the history of Buddhist ceremonies, which he describes as occasions when lay donors sponsor meals for members of the clergy. He primarily mentions events sponsored by the ruling courts—first of Chinese dynasties and then of Japan—but without providing any indication of which ceremonies are most important or performed regularly.[30]

Ecclesiastical titles

Shiren is concerned primarily with titles awarded by the court. He begins by noting that originally in China there existed only three titles: elder (*jōza* 上座), temple supervisor (*jishu* 寺主), and group leader (*ina* 維那). The titles *upādhyāya* (*oshō* 和尚; master), *acārya* (*ajari* 阿闍梨; instructor), national teacher (*kokushi* 國師), treatise master (*ronshi* 論師), tripiṭaka master (*sanzō* 三藏), and venerable (*sonja* 尊者) all came from the western regions (i.e., Central Asia and India). Later, the Chinese court added the offices of saṃgha chancellor (*sōshō* 僧正), saṃgha dean (*sōtō* 僧統), saṃgha registrar (*sōroku* 僧録) as well as the titles of national teacher (*kokushi* 國師), great teacher (*daishi* 大師), and meditation teacher (*zenji* 禪師). In addition, they initiated the practice of honoring eminent monks with posthumous titles (a subject that Shiren discusses at length). In Japan the court adopted all of these and added saṃgha provost (*sōzu* 僧都) as well as the court post known as the ten meditation teachers (*jūzenji* 十禪師). Finally, each ecclesiastical title corresponds to one of the court ranks that are awarded to members of aristocracy. Shiren does not mention the title of disciplinarian (*risshi* 律師).[31]

Monasteries and icons

This treatise is one of the longest in the *Shakusho*. After discussing the legendary origins of the buddha image in India, Shiren describes thirty famous temples and monasteries in Japan. These are the places where pious monks, nuns, and lay people would travel on pilgrimage. He explains who founded them, what icons they house, and what miracles are associated with them. He includes most of the prominent monasteries that figure in the hagiographies of monks (see Appendix 4, on p. 146), but not all of them. (Out of this list, he includes Mount Hiei, Onjōji, Kōfukuji, Tōdaiji, Gangōji 元興寺, Daianji 大安寺, and Zenrinji 禪林寺 a.k.a. Taimadera 當麻寺, but omits Mount Kōya, Daigoji 醍醐寺, Ninnaji 仁和寺, Tōfukuji 東福寺, and Yakushiji.) Shiren adds: (a) temples associated with the legendary origins of Buddhism in Japan, such as Mukuharadera 向原寺 (supposedly founded 552 to house a buddha image from Paekche), Shitennōji 四天王寺 (supposedly founded in 587 by Shōtoku *taishi* 聖德太子, 574–622, Chōhōji 頂法寺, which houses a buddha image once worshiped by Shōtoku); (b) monasteries that are famous for their miraculous origins, such as Inudera 犬寺 (which enshrines images of two magical dogs), Sufukuji 崇福寺, Saidaiji 西大寺, Tōshōdaiji 唐招提寺 (the monastery founded by Ganjin) and Kaimanji 蟹満寺; as well as (c) temples and monasteries that are famous for their gods and buddhas. This latter group includes two temples mentioned for the local gods they enshrine: Jinganji 神願寺 (a temple on Mount Hiei which enshrines the god Hiyoshi *daijin* 比吉大神, a.k.a. Sannō) and Jingoji 神護寺 (which enshrines the god Hachiman *daijin* 八幡大神).

Most of them are mentioned specifically for their buddha images. Temples housing famous images of Avalokiteśvara (Kannon 觀音) include: Hasedera 長谷寺, Ishiyamadera 石山寺, Kokawadera 粉河寺, Kuramadera 鞍馬寺, Seisuiji 清水寺 (a.k.a. Kiyomizudera), Kannōji 感應寺, Sannōin 山王院 (on Mount Hiei), Kachiodera 勝尾寺, and Enkyōji 圓教寺. Other famous icons include the Maitreya (Miroku 彌勒) at the nunnery on Mount Katsuragi 葛木山 and the Bhaiṣajyaguru (Yakushi 藥師) at Teidenji 鵜田寺. Clearly, for Shiren the practice of Buddhism could not survive without the worship of images. Finally, he mentions Jōkanji 貞觀寺 temple as being famous for its festivals of dance and music.

Aural arts

Shiren explains that sound is the primary medium for propagating the truth. He focuses on four types of aural communication: sūtra cantors (*kyōshi* 經師) who chant the scripture, hymns (*shōmyō* 聲明 or *bonbai* 梵唄) which are sung during ceremonies, sermonists (*shōdō* 唱導) who preach the dharma, and chanting the names of the buddhas (*nenbutsu* 念佛). He does not discuss music or the musical instruments used in Buddhist ceremonies.

Strange phenomena

This treatise is easily the longest one in the *Shakusho*. It consists of edifying tales of karmic rewards and retributions similar to other Japanese Buddhist literature.

Avoiding strife

The content of this treatise is less optimistic than indicated by its title. It actually recounts the origins of hostilities between the rival Tendai branches of Mount Hiei and Onjōji. Shiren laments how both sides have resorted to armed troops to settle their conflicts.

Conclusion

The works discussed above present us with an insider's perspective on the monastic institution in medieval Japan. It is a perspective that I believe deserves more attention. From this perspective, these monastic institutions are organized around annual ceremonies, populated with miraculous icons, and home to all kinds of people (monks, non-monks, nuns, and those in between) who strive to master rituals and secret lore for the purpose of obtaining dreams and oracles, acquiring political favors, and eliciting the blessings of gods and buddhas. In these endeavors they take pride in their evaluation of themselves as being the most devout Buddhists and most faithful adherents to Mahāyāna path. That path entails academic learning, rituals of ordination, initiation into doctrinal lineages, worship of gods and buddhas, participation in state-sponsored ceremonies, advancement to ecclesiastical titles awarded by the court, pilgrimages to famous temples, poetry, the performance of music, chanting scriptures, preaching, singing, fighting in armed conflicts, and learning how to face death.

While this list does not include all aspects of mainstream monastic practice, it does depict a religious landscape that medieval Buddhists themselves probably would recognize. If we wish to understand how monasteries functioned in medieval Japan, then—in addition to whatever other interpretive approaches we employ— we must become familiar with the features of this landscape. If we want our students to understand the roles of monasteries in medieval society, then it behooves us to include this perspective among those that we present in the courses we teach, in our lectures, and in our publications.

Appendix 1

Annual ceremonies of Japan according to the *Three Jewels with Illustrations* (*Sanbōe* 三寶繪, 984) by Minamoto Tamenori 源爲憲 (d. 1011)

Month	Ritual	Location	Notes
1　*1*	New Year's (*shushō'e* 修正會)	all temples	on 1st day: visit temples, practice abstinence, make offerings to order of monks and nuns (saṃgha)
2	Royal Banquet (*misai'e* 御齋會)	Daigokuden 大極殿 (part of the Inner Palace)	on 8th–14th days: second of the three major ceremonies (*san'e* 三會); court sponsors chanting of and debates on the *Golden Radiance Sūtra* (*Kongōmyō saishōō kyō* 金光明最勝王經), Śrīmahādevī repentance (*Kichijō keka* 吉祥悔過), and vegetarian banquet
3	Lotus Repentance (*Hokke senbō* 法華懺法)	Mt. Hiei 比叡山	on 1st day (of 1st, 4th, 7th, & 10th months): performance of half-walking half-sitting samādhi (*hangyō hanza zanmai* 半行半坐三昧) based on *Contemplation of Samantabhadra Sūtra* (*Kan Fugen bosatsu kyō* 觀普賢菩薩經)
4	Bath (*unshitsu* 温室)	all temples	on 14th and 29th of each month: members of the order bathe in preparation for their fortnightly assemblies (*fusatsu* 布薩)
5	Fortnightly Assembly (*fusatsu* 布薩)	all temples	on the 15th and 30th of each month: members of the order recite the bodhisattva precepts as listed in *Brahmā Net Sūtra* (*Bonmō kyō* 梵網經)
2　*1*	Second Moon (*shuni'e* 修二會)	all temples	on 1st–7th days: cutting silk flower petals, burning incense, decorating altars, etc. (the second moon ceremonies at Tōdaiji 東大寺 in Nara are the most famous)
2	Ānanda Repentance	Saiin 西院 (Junnain 淳和院) near Kyoto	on 8th day (of 2nd & 8th months), nuns should perform repentance

Month		Ritual	Location	Notes
		(*Anan senbō* 阿難懺法)		ceremonies and lay women should observe eight restraints (*hassai kai* 八齋戒) to repay debt of gratitude to Ānanda for his help in founding the order of nuns
	3	Buddha's Nirvāṇa (*nehan'e* 涅槃會)	Yamashinadera 山階寺 (Kōfukuji 興福寺) in Nara	on 15th day: The Buddha's Nirvāṇa is commemorated at all temples, but the ceremonies at Yamashinadera (Kōfukuji) are famous for their music (Kōfukuji is associated with the Fujiwara family)
	4	Stone Stūpas (*sekitō* 石塔)	all locations	erect stone stūpas in the spring time, especially performed by (and for) children
3	1	Dharma Transmission (*denbō'e* 傳法會)	Sūfukuji 崇福寺 in Shiga 志賀	ceremonies actually revolve around worship of the bodhisattva Maitreya (*Miroku'e* 彌勒會), the founder of the Hossō lineage (Sūfukuji is associated with the Tachibana family)
	2	*Golden Radiance Sūtra* (Saishō'e 最勝會)	Yakushiji 藥師寺 in Nara	third of the three major ceremonies (*san'e*); chanting of and debates on the *Golden Radiance Sūtra*
	3	*Lotus Sūtra* (*Hokke'e* 法華會)	Takaodera 高雄寺 (Jingoji 神護寺) in Kyoto	chanting and lectures on the *Lotus Sūtra* (*Hokke kyō* 法華經)
	4	*Flower Garland Sūtra* (*Kegon'e* 華嚴會)	Hokkeji 法華寺 in Nara	nuns make doll images of Sudhana and his meetings with more than 50 teachers, then they make offerings to them (origin of doll festival?)
	5	Promotion of Learning (*gangaku'e* 勸學會)	Sakamoto 坂本 at the base of Mt. Hiei	on 14th day: monks and laymen gather together to lecture on the scriptures and to compose Chinese poems on Buddhist themes
	6	Ten Thousand Lanterns (*bandō'e* 萬燈會)	Yakushiji in Nara	lighting ten thousand lanterns at Yakushiji, each lantern symbolizes the light (i.e., wisdom) of an individual buddha
4	1	Relics (*shari'e* 舍利會)	Mt. Hiei	worship of relics that were brought back from China by Ennin 圓仁 (794–864); offerings to these relics will engender rebirth in heaven
	2	*Great Perfect Wisdom Sūtra* (*Daihannya'e* 大般若會)	Daianji 大安寺 in Nara	when *Great Perfection of Wisdom Sūtra* (*Daihannya kyō* 大般若經) is chanted all the dragons come to worship it, the dharma rain they bring anoints all the poisonous dragons and frees them from their suffering
	3	Buddha's birthday	Seiryōden 清涼殿	on 8th day: the Buddha's birthday is celebrated at all temples, but the

Month	Ritual	Location	Notes
	(*kanbutsu'e* 灌佛會)	(part of the Inner Palace)	ceremonial washing of the newborn buddha at the sovereign's residence (Seiryōden) inside the court is the most important one
4	Ordination (*jukai* 受戒) at the same time	Mt. Hiei	bodhisattva ordinations for monks; prayers for abundant harvest also given
5 1	Lay Ordinations (*bosatsu kai* 菩薩戒)	Hasedera 長谷寺 near Nara	bodhisattva precepts for lay people
2	Rice Donations (*semai* 施米)	all temples	each year the court donates 300 bushels of rice to temples where monks observe the summer monastic retreat
6	Thousand Flowers (*senge'e* 千華會)	Tōdaiji 東大寺 in Nara	flower offering to Vairocana Buddha
7 1	Mañjuśri (*Monju'e* 文殊會)	all temples	whoever hears Mañjuśri's name will be freed from the sufferings of twelve million lifetimes
2	Ghost Festival (*urabon* 盂蘭盆)	all temples	rituals for feeding hungry ghosts and confession rites on last day of summer retreat
8 1	Ceaseless Contemplation (*fudan nenbutsu* 不斷念佛)	Mt. Hiei	on 11th–17th days: Seven-days of Constant Walking Samādhi (*jōgyō zanmai* 常行三昧) of the Buddha during which monks contemplate, circumambulate, and chant the name of Amitābha Buddha in an effort to eliminate sins
2	Releasing Living Beings (*hōjō'e* 放生會)	Iwashimizu Hachimangū Gokokuji 石清水八幡宮護國寺 near Kyoto	liberating animals in the presence of the great bodhisattva (*dai bosatsu* 大菩薩) Hachiman 八幡 (Yahata) brings long life
9	Initiation Rites (*kanjō* 灌頂)	Mt. Hiei	initiation rites (*abhiṣeka*) into Diamond and Womb maṇḍala conducted on alternate years
10	Vimalakīrti Sūtra (*Yuima'e* 維摩會)	Yamashinadera (Kōfukuji) in Nara	first of the three major ceremonies (*san'e*); monks who lead these ceremonies earn title of lecturer (*kōshi* 講師)
11 1	Eight Lectures (*hakkō'e* 八講會)	Kumano 熊野 in Kii Province	series of eight lectures on the *Lotus Sūtra* conducted at Buddhist temples attached to two Kumano shrines (Kumano ryōsho 熊野兩所): the New Shrine (Shingū 新宮) houses dual deities, mother (called Musubi 結, i.e., Bhaiṣajyaguru) and daughter (called

Month	Ritual	Location	Notes
			Hayatama 早玉, i.e., Avalokiteśvara); the old shrine houses Shōjo 證誠 (also called original deity, *mototsukami* 本神); lectures performed to eliminate sins of local hunters who kill living beings
2	Autumn Moon (*shimotsuki'e* 霜月會)	Mt. Hiei	memorial service for Tendai patriarch Zhiyi 智顗 (538–597); monks conduct ten lectures on the *Lotus Sūtra* (*Hokke jikkō* 法華十講) and make offerings in memory of all Tendai patriarchs
12	Buddha Names (*butsumyō* 佛名)	Seiryōden (part of the Inner Palace)	chant names of 3,000 buddhas; afterwards the court gives offerings of robes to protect monks from cold winter

Appendix 2

Categories of biographies used in Chinese and Japanese accounts of eminent monks

	Gaoseng zhuan 高僧傳 *by Huijiao* 慧皎 *(497–554)*	*Xu* 續 *& Song* 宋 *gaoseng zhuan by Daoxuan* 道宣 *(596–667) and by Zanning* 贊寧 *(919–1002)*	*Genkō shakusho* 元亨釋書 *by Shiren* 師鍊 *(1278–1346)*	*Note: 10 bodhisattva perfections (pāramitā) (nos. 7–10 are aspects of no. 6)*
1	譯經 translators	譯經 translators	傳智 transmitters	智 (10) knowledge (*jñāna*)
2	義解 meaning	義解 meaning	慧解 wisdom	慧 (6) wisdom (*prajñā*)
3	神異 thaumaturges	習禪 meditators	浄禪 pure meditators	定 (5) meditation (*dhyāna*)
4	習禪 meditators	明律 vinaya exegetes	感進 thaumaturges	進 (4) effort (*vīrya*)
5	明律 vinaya exegetes	護法 protectors	忍行 self-immolators	忍 (3) tolerance (*kṣānti*)
6	亡身 self-immolators	感通 thaumaturges	明戒 śīla exegetes	戒 (2) morality (*śīla*)
7	誦經 cantors	遺身 self-immolators	壇興 fund raisers	施 (1) giving (*dāna*)
8	興福 promoters of works of merit	讀誦 cantors	方應 wanderers (incl. hijiri & yamabushi)	方便 (7) liberative technique (*upāya*)
9	經師 hymnodists	興福 promoters of merit	力遊 travelers abroad	力 (9) powers (*bala*)
10	唱導 sermonists	雜科聲德 (combines Huijiao's nos. 9 and 10)	願雜 accomplishing vows (incl. lay people & local gods)	願 (8) vows (*praṇidhāna*)

Appendix 3

Categories used in Chinese dynastic histories and in two Buddhist histories

Chinese dynastic histories	*Fozu tongji* 佛祖統紀 (1269)	*Genkō shakusho* 元亨釋書 (1322)
本紀 *Basic Records* significant court (official) actions arranged by reigns	本紀 *Basic Records* 釋佛本紀 Śākyamuni's career 祖紀 careers of Tiantai 天台 ancestors in both India and China	列傳 *Collected Biographies* 1 傳智 transmitters of wisdom 2 慧解 wisdom exegetes 3 浄禪 pure meditators 4 感進 thaumaturges & cantors 5 忍行 self-immolators 6 明戒 śīla exegetes 7 壇興 fund raisers 8 方應 wanderers 9 力遊 travelers abroad 10 願雜 accomplishers of vows 古德 virtuous patriarchs 王臣 kings & ministers 士庶 aristocrats & commoners 尼女 nuns & women 神仙 gods & wizards 靈怪 apparitions
表 *Tables* chronological table of significant events during each year of the dynasty genealogical tables		
志 *Topical Treatises* 天文志 astronomy 律曆志 calendar 食貨志 financial administration 刑法志 penal law 河渠志 rivers & canals (etc.)	世家 *Hereditary Houses* biographies of Chinese disciples in each generation of Tiantai patriarchs 列傳 *Collected Biographies* biographies of other Tiantai monks	
世家 *Hereditary Houses* accounts of aristocratic families	表 *Tables* 歷代傳教表 transmission of Tiantai doctrines during each reign 佛祖世繫表 genealogical chart of disciples of each Tiantai patriarch	表 *Tables* 資治表 chronological table of significant Buddhist events during each reign year from 540 to 1221
列傳 *Collected Biographies* accounts of eminent individuals		
— usually accompanied by: 贊 evaluations 論 critical comments	志 *Topical Treatises* 山家教典志 Tiantai texts 浄土立教志 Pure Land biographies 諸宗立教志 non-Tiantai lineages 達摩禪宗 Chan biographies 賢首宗 Huayan biographies 慈恩宗 Yogācāra biographies 南山律宗 Vinaya biographies 三世出興志 3,000 buddhas 世界名體志 cosmological schemes 法門光顯志 icons & worship	志 *Topical Treatises* 1 學修 learning 2 度受 ordinations 3 諸宗 doctrinal lineages 4 會儀 ceremonies 5 封職 ecclesiastical titles 6 寺像 monasteries & icons 7 音藝 aural arts 8 拾異 strange phenomena 9 黜爭 avoiding strife

法運通塞志 chronological table of how Tiantai overcame obstacles	10　序説 rationale for this compilation
名文光教志 eulogies & proclamations praising Tiantai	Appendixes 略例 abbreviations
歴代會要志 chronological list of imperial edicts regarding worship	智通論 wisdom & miracles

Appendix 4

Names of temples associated with the hagiography of three or more monks in *Genkō shakusho*

Temple	Main Affiliation	Number of Hagiographies	Times Mentioned Overall
Mt. Hiei 比叡山	Tendai	48	156
Onjōji 園城寺	Tendai	15	54
Kōfukuji 興福寺	Nara	13	107
Mt. Koya 高野山	Shingon	7	45
Tōdaiji 東大寺	Nara	6	126
Daigoji 醍醐寺	Nara	6	21
Gangōji 元興寺	Nara	4	43
Ninnaji 仁和寺	Shingon	4	50
Tōfukuji 東福寺	Zen	4	19
Daianji 大安寺	Nara	3	49
Zenrinji 禪林寺	Nara	3	16
Yakushiji 藥師寺	Nara	3	38

Appendix 5

Distribution of biographies by category in *Genkō shakusho*

傳	*Biographical Categories*	*(subtotals)*
1	傳智 Transmitters of knowledge	10
2	慧解 Wisdom exegetes	85
3	浄禪 Pure practice & meditation	23
4	感進 Vigorous miracle workers	117
5	忍行 Patience in austerities	14
6	明戒 Śīla exegetes	10
7	壇興 Fund raisers	19
8	方應 Wanderers who promote Buddhism	9
9	力遊 Energetic travelers (across the ocean)	29
10	願雜 Accomplishers of vows (subsections & subtotals)	
	古德 Virtuous patriarchs	8
	王臣 Kings & ministers	27
	士庶 Aristocrats & commoners	15
	尼女 Nuns & women	15
	神仙 Gods & wizards	13
	靈怪 Apparitions	19
		107
志	Categories of topical treatises	
8	拾異 Unusual phenomena	21
Total:		444

Notes

1 Adolphson 2000.
2 Regarding the study of religion in medieval Japan, see Bodiford 2006.
3 Grapard 2000.
4 *Sanbōe*, 158.
5 *Sanbōe*, 188.
6 *Sanbōe*, 222–224.
7 I calculated the number of times institutions are named by searching the digital version of the Nihon Koten Bungaku Taikei 日本古典文學大系 edition available on-line (http://www.nijl.ac.jp/index.html). A more precise breakdown would be: mountain temple (35 times), Mount Kōya (31 times) Nara monasteries (Tōdaiji 東大寺 12 times; Yakushiji 藥師寺 9 times; Daigoji 醍醐寺 6 times; and Kōfukuji 興福寺 4 times), Tendai monasteries (Miidera 12 times; Hie 日吉 6 times; Tōtō 東塔 2 times; Hiei 比叡, Saitō 西塔, and Yokawa 横川 1 time each), Kiyomizudera 11 times, and Zen monasteries (Kenninji 建仁寺 8 times, Jufukuji 壽福寺 5 times, and Tōfukuji 東福寺 4 times).
8 See Hagiwara 1962.
9 See Hurst 1997: 226–231.
10 See Hatta 1991.
11 See, for example, Yanagida 1972: 443.
12 Bielefeldt 1997.
13 Shiren expressly acknowledges (fasc. 30; K 31.447) relying on three Chinese hagiographical collections, which he refers to the Liang 梁 (i.e., T. no. 2059), the Tang 唐 (i.e., T. no. 2060), and the Song 宋 (i.e., T. no. 2061). Of course, these collections already had adopted many of the literary conventions of dynastic histories (see Wright 1990).
14 The *Hanshu* is a historical account of the Han Dynasty covering the years from 206 BCE to 24 CE; the *Jinshu* is a historical account of the Jin Dynasty covering the years 265–419; and the *Tangshu* is a historical account of the Tang Dynasty covering the years 618–907.
15 Appendix 4 is based on counting the names of temples that appear as part of the designation of the monks whose hagiographies are listed in the *Shakusho*'s table of contents and by computer searches of the electronic edition of the *Shakusho* published by the International Research Institute for Zen Buddhism (see *Genkō shakusho* 元亨釋書. 1322. By Kokan Shiren 虎關師錬 (1278–1346). 30 fascicles. (1) K vol. 31. (2) *Electronic Text of the Genkoo Shakusho by Kokan Shiren*).
16 Bielefeldt (1997: 315) suggests that Shiren's combination of a few prominent Zen hagiographies amidst more numerous ones devoted to non-Zen monks presents a different kind of sectarian construct that places Zen at the center of a new Japanese Buddhism order which transcends the old sectarian divisions of Nara versus Tendai. The net result is that Shiren attempts to provide Zen with a something akin to an "ecumenical hegemony."
17 Ury 1970: 170–171, n. 1.
18 Shiren writes (fasc. 30, K 31.448–449) that in India followers of the inferior vehicle always outnumbered followers of Mahāyāna and there also existed 95 varieties of Brahmanism. In China, Mahāyāna is more popular than Hīnyāna, but China is plagued by non-Buddhist religions such as Confucianism and Daoism. Thus, only Japan enjoys pure Mahāyāna. These kind of sentiments are common in the literature of this period. In the *Keiran shūyōshū* (fasc. 100, T. 76.835c), for example, Kōshū explains that Japanese have perfect, pure and mature Mahāyāna spiritual potential (*enki junjuku* 圓機純熟) as demonstrated by the fact that there are no non-Buddhist religions, unlike India where Brahmans slander Buddhism or China where Daoists slander Buddhism.
19 Ouyang Xiu supervised a new compilation of the Tang Dynastic History (*Tangshu*, 1060), which systematically eliminated the references to Buddhism and to supernatural

events found in the earlier Tang Dynastic History (*Jiu Tangshu*) that had been compiled by Liu Xu 劉煦 (887–946).

20 Okada (1985) has shown that the law codes of early Japan describe Ise not as a shrine of the government nor as an ancestral shrine of the royal family as a whole, but rather as being primarily a shrine of royal succession.

21 These figures are based on computer searches of the electronic edition of the *Shakusho* published by the International Research Institute for Zen Buddhism.

22 Shiren reports that the ordination platform that had been established in eastern Japan no longer existed.

23 Normally distinct and universal refer to two different types of ordination ceremonies. Distinct refers to ceremonies involving only one type or class of precepts, while universal refers to ceremonies involving all types or classes of precepts.

24 Bielefeldt 1993–1994: 227.

25 E.g., see Kitabatake's *Meaning of the Inner Realization of True Words* (*Shingon naishōgi* 眞言内證義, 1345).

26 Thus, Kitabatake writes (*Jinnō shōtōki*, p. 114) that abhidharma "exists as an academic subject (*shū*), but not established as a separate lineage (*shū*)" (*egaku no shū nite, betsu ni isshū wo tatsuru koto nashi* 依學の宗にて、別に一宗を立つることなし) and Shiren writes (fasc. 30, K 31.448) in practically identical words that abhidharma is provided for study, but not established as a doctrinal lineage (*gaku ni sonowaru nomi ni shite, shū wo tatezu* 備于學而已、不立宗). Shiren then goes on to use the same logic (and language) to assert that Confucianism and Daoism do not exist in Japan.

27 Shiren refers to Hossō as the Yuishiki 唯識 (Consciousness Only) school.

28 The Sōjiin 総持院 temple in the Eastern Pagoda (Tōtō 東塔) region of Mt. Hiei performs tantric rituals directed to the ruler's birth star (*honmyōshō* 本命星), which consists of one of the seven stars of the Big Dipper (*hokuto shichishō* 北斗七星). Mt. Hiei and Onjōji represent mixed exoteric-esoteric because both function as headquarters for their own branches of Tendai (exoteric) and Shingon (esoteric).

29 Shiren merely says that Genshin 源信 (942–1017) and Hōnen promoted Pure Land practices, but lack a lineage (*mutōkei* 無統系). Nichiren is not mentioned by either author.

30 Shiren seems primarily concerned with showing that Japan's royal sponsorship of Buddhism surpasses that of China. He notes that when a Chinese monk witnessed a Saishō-e held at the court during the Bun'ei 文永 period (1264–1275), the Chinese monk could only sigh and lament that royal court in China had never staged such a grand ceremony for the Buddha.

31 The *Shakusho*'s chronological table (*hyō* 表) mentions several instances of the court appointing a disciplinarian, but Shiren does not explain that title in this section.

6 Vows for the masses

Eison and the popular expansion of precept-conferral ceremonies in premodern Japan[1]

Lori Meeks

Over the course of his roughly fifty-year ministry, the Japanese *Vinaya* (*Ritsu* 律) revivalist priest Eison 叡尊 (also read "Eizon," 1201–1290) is said to have bestowed the bodhisattva precepts upon some 97,710 people. Many of these conferrals were given *en masse*, with tens or hundreds (and, according to some records, even thousands) taking precepts (受戒 *jukai*; Chn. *shoujie*) from Eison together, in single ceremonies. This study places Eison's use of precept-conferral ceremonies in the broader historical context of East Asian, and especially Japanese, Buddhist practice. It then focuses on the particular methods used and innovations introduced by Eison and his vinaya-revival movement, paying close attention to the socio-political roles that precept-conferral ceremonies played in relationships between monks, monasteries, and lay devotees in medieval Japan.

The merits of leaving home

Early Buddhist texts state clearly, and with considerable frequency, that "leaving home" (出家 *shukke*)—abandoning one's secular life, taking the precepts, and joining the saṃgha—creates profound merit.[2] Of the many texts extolling the merits of leaving home, the *Xianyu jing* 賢愚經 (*The Sutra of the Wise and the Foolish*, Jpn. *Gengukyō*; T. 4, no. 202), an apocryphal sūtra compiled by Chinese monks in Central Asia, became particularly influential in East Asian Buddhist circles.[3] In the twenty-third section of the *Xianyu jing*, titled "Sirī-vaddhi Section on the Merit of Leaving Home" 出家功德尸利苾提品, leaving home is praised as an act of supreme merit:

> Thus I have heard. Once, when the Buddha was at Karan . ḍa's Bamboo Grove Monastery (Karan . ḍaven . uvana) in Rājagr . ha, Magadhā, at that time the World Honored One praised the act of leaving home, [saying that,] as a source of merit, its blessings are extremely great. If you release men or women [to leave home], if you release male or female servants [to leave home], if you allow the common people [to leave home], or if you yourself leave home and enter the Way, the merit [created by this act] is immeasurable. As for the rewards of *dāna*, they cause blessings to be received over ten lifetimes, and for beings either in the six heavens or in the [world of] humans, after this being repeated for

ten [lifetimes] one is as before. This is not like releasing people to leave home or leaving home oneself. Why is this? As for the rewards of *dāna,* its blessings have limits. [But] as for the blessings of leaving home, they are immeasurable and boundless. Also, the rewards of upholding the precepts cause the transcendents who have mastered the five supernormal powers to receive the blessings of heaven and to reach the Brahmā world. Within the Buddha-Dharma, the rewards of leaving home cannot be fathomed. Even until one reaches *nirvāṇa,* its blessings are inexhaustible. For example, if there were a person who erected a seven-jeweled stupa [so tall] that reached the Heaven of the Thirty-Three, the merit that would be received would not equal that of leaving home. Why is this? It is because greedy, evil, and ignorant people can destroy a seven-jeweled stupa, [but] the virtue (lit., the "dharma") of leaving home cannot be damaged.[4]

The sutra goes on to relate the story of Sirī-vaddhi, a man who hears about the vast blessings of leaving home and decides, at the age of one hundred, to leave his household and enter the saṃgha. Having so resolved, he bids farewell to his wife, children, and servants and heads to the Bamboo Grove Monastery (Karaṇḍaveṇuvana). When he arrives and asks for the World Honored One, he is told that the Buddha is away. Unable to speak with the Buddha directly, Sirī-vaddhi shares his desire to leave home with Śāriputra. But Śāriputra's response is cold and dismissive: "You go away. You are too old; you cannot leave home."[5] Sirī-vaddhi continues to beg Śāriputra, but Śāriputra will not relent. Within a few lines, we find Sirī-vaddhi crying in frustration and sadness as he is told to leave the monastery. It is at this juncture that the Buddha appears to Sirī-vaddhi in a great light, asks why he is crying, and grants him the privilege of leaving home.[6] Śāriputra, of course, had considered the question only from the perspective of whether or not an old man could contribute to the life of the monastery and had failed to have compassion for the old man and his desire to create merit. But the blessings of leaving home, this story teaches, is something that the Buddha makes available to young and old alike.[7]

An important concept at work in this story is the notion that in the act of leaving home, it is one's personal resolve to abandon the world and take up the Buddhist path—and not one's ability to make quantifiable contributions in the Buddhist community—that produces great merit. Even those unable to assume key roles in the monastic order, then, can access the merit of leaving home. In addition to elderly men like Sirī-vaddhi, whose physical condition would not have allowed him to work in the monastery alongside younger monks, kings and other elites whose social positions prevented them from taking up life in a monastery, were also able to "leave home."

This same theme is picked up in the *Foshuo chujia gongde jing* 佛說出家功德經 (*Sutra on the Merit of Home-Leaving;* Jpn. *Busshō shukke kudoku kyō,* T. no. 707, translator and date unknown), a text that Daoshi 道世 (591–683) cites, alongside the *Xianyu jing,* in his own influential discussion of the merits of leaving home (see chapter 22 of his *Fayuan zhulin* 法苑珠林). The *Foshuo chujia gongde jing* centers on the story of a prince named Beiluoxianna 鞞羅羨那. When the Buddha realizes that this prince, who lives a life of unapologetic hedonism, will pass away in seven days and fall into the hell realms, he sends Ānanda to warn him. Attached to his life of pleasure and luxury, the prince is unwilling to leave home right away, but he says that he will take vows on the seventh—and last—day of his life. As promised, the prince comes to the Buddha seven days later and takes vows. After maintaining the precepts for one day and one night, he dies. The rewards of these twenty-four hours of home-leaving, the reader is told, are immeasurable: the prince avoids hell, is reborn into the upper levels of heaven, does not fall into the three lower paths for twenty kalpas, and eventually becomes a pratyekabuddha. The primary teaching of this sutra overlaps with that of the *Xianyu jing*: leaving home and taking the precepts creates more merit than any other Buddhist activity; its benefits are inexhaustible and are always worth seeking, even during the last moments of one's life.

The attitudes towards taking the precepts presented in these two texts were considerably influential in East Asia. Daoshi cites the primary narratives of both sutras in his encyclopedic *Fayuan zhulin*, which was circulated widely and studied carefully, both in China and Japan. The central terms and themes of the *Xianyu jing* can also be found both in a variety of subsequent texts, ranging from the early sixth-century Chinese scholarly work *Jinglü yixiang* (經律異相 T. no. 2121, by Baochang 寶唱) to the early twelfth-century *Konjaku monogatarishū* 今昔物語集, a collection of popular tales compiled in Japan.[8] Many tales in the *Konjaku* borrow stock phrases such as "it does not equal the merit of leaving home" (不如出家功德) from the Buddhist doctrinal texts mentioned above, usually in the context of explaining why leaving home and taking the precepts is superior to some other form of Buddhist merit-making.

Of particular interest here is the degree to which texts extolling the merit of leaving home came to associate the act of taking the precepts with that of leaving home. In many texts, taking the precepts came to be viewed as synonymous with leaving home. Indeed, the two were often grouped together in the single phrase *chujia shoujie* 出家受戒, "to leave home and take the precepts." This compound can be found in dozens of sutras in the Taishō canon and in Japanese literary sources as well.[9]

The close association between leaving home and taking the precepts meant that the merit associated with leaving home also came to be associated with taking the precepts. Chinese texts advocating the bodhisattva precepts also came to suggest that the act of taking the bodhisattva precepts, even when such precepts were taken alone (rather than as a supplement to the monastic precepts of the vinaya) and did not constitute home-leaving, was one of vast merit. And thus we can find a number of texts that shorten the more traditional notion of the "merit of leaving home and taking the precepts" (*chujia shoujie gongde* 出家受戒功德) to speak instead of the "merit of taking the precepts" (*shoujie gongde* 受戒功德).[10] In formal monastic practice, of course, those *shoujie* (Jpn. *jukai*) taken by novices and monks and those taken by lay devotees—in other words, those that counted as initiation into the priestly order and those that did not—were always clearly distinguished. Still, the close association between the two acts meant that many came to view the precept-conferral ceremony as one that transmitted the merit embodied in the act of leaving home. Even ordinary laypeople could access some of the merit associated with home-leaving by taking precepts in a formal ceremony that simulated the ordination ceremony of those who were, in fact, leaving the lay life. In Japan, the situation was even more complex: from the mid-Heian period, many lay elites took the *endonkai* (perfect and sudden precepts)[11] of the Tendai school and declared themselves *shukke,* even when they did not become official members of the monastic order. In these cases, laypeople clearly believed that *jukai* taken outside the official monastic protocols could still render recipients home-leavers and could still bestow upon them the merits of leaving home.

Conceptual overlap between the *jukai* and the act of leaving home is also evident in the practice of taking the precepts as a means of preparing for death. The logic operative here takes us back to the *Foshuo chujia gongde jing:* it was believed that if one were to take Buddhist vows just before death—as Prince Beiluoxianna did—one could secure a favorable rebirth and avoid suffering in the hell realms. What's more, as noted in the passage from the *Xianyu jing* translated above, the merit of taking precepts was deemed powerful enough to extend beyond the human realm in order to save spirits as well. Thus we find in the *Haedong Kosŭng Chŏn* (*Lives of Eminent Korean Monks*), for example, the story of a protective spirit who asks the monk Wŏn'gwang for the precepts, saying, "My end is drawing near, and I want to receive the Bodhisattva ordination [i.e., precepts of the *Fanwang jing*] so that I can be qualified for eternity."[12]

Precept-conferral ceremonies thus point to the particular ways in which the merit of acts associated with leaving home came to be made available to lay audiences in East Asia. A related phenomenon within Southeast Asian Buddhism is better known: here I refer to Theravādin traditions of temporary home-leaving that allowed laypeople wishing to access the merit of leaving home to do so without making a long-term commitment to monastic life. In Thailand, for example, it became common for young men to receive ordination, to spend a short period of time living as a monk at a temple, and then to disrobe and return to lay life having created a significant store of merit. No similar practice of temporary ordination and monkhood gained currency in East Asia. The practice related to home-leaving that came to be valued as a merit-making activity in East Asia was not time spent living as an ordained member of a monastic community, but rather the act of receiving precepts in a formal ceremony. Precepts taken by laypeople in East Asia did not result in the conferral of either long-term or temporary clerical status; as such, the ceremonies in which they were conferred cannot be described as ordinations. But insofar as these precept conferral ceremonies were modeled upon—and in some cases carried out in conjunction with—the ordination ceremonies of monks and nuns, the merit they were thought to bestow upon their recipients was conceptually related to the merit of leaving home. In this sense, we might view the popularization of precept conferral ceremonies in East Asia as related, in broad terms, to traditions of temporary home-leaving in Southeast Asia. Although the practices made distinct demands of their participants, both allowed laypeople to simulate (albeit to different degrees and in different ways) the process of becoming a monk or a nun and to acquire, in the process, great merit.

Models of precept-conferral

Precept-conferral ceremonies made available to members of the laity in East Asia varied widely, but the following three types appear to have been the most common. First, there were private ceremonies for elites who could afford to invite Buddhist monks to their own homes. These ceremonies usually involved members of the royal family or high aristocracy. Although the practice experienced waves of popularity and decline, many emperors and kings in China, Korea, and Japan received conferrals of the precepts, usually the bodhisattva precepts of the *Fanwang jing* 梵網經 (or, in Japan, the Perfect and Sudden Precepts of Tendai lineages), from eminent Buddhist priests. While it was most often a single, powerful individual who sought the precepts, others in his or her entourage often followed suit, taking the precepts along with the individual who had invited the precepts-granting monk to the elite residence. Depending on the context, these private ceremonies were directed at a variety of outcomes: they sometimes marked one's devotion to a particular Buddhist teacher, for example, but they could also be used as a means of preparing for death. In some contexts, such as that of Koryŏ rule, the conferral of precepts upon imperial figures became an annual rite carried out as a matter of course rather than in response to acute need. According to Peter Lee, Koryŏ kings received the bodhisattva precepts from the National Preceptor every year, between 1032 and 1352, on the fifteenth day of the sixth month.[13]

The remaining two types of lay precept-conferral ceremonies were more public in nature but differed in location and timing. One type of public precepts ceremony was held on fixed days, usually once or twice per year, at large temples. Many temples ordained monks only on certain days annually or every few years. On these days, they would hold large *shoujie-hui* 授戒会 (Jpn. *jukai-e*), or precept-conferral ceremonies, which were often several days in duration. At some temples, laypeople would be incorporated in these ceremonies and would be given the opportunity to take either the bodhisattva precepts or the lay precepts. Finally, both in China and in Japan, certain charismatic Buddhist priests traveled through the countryside and conferred precepts upon commoners *en masse*. These ceremonies, which typically centered on the ten major bodhisattva precepts, could take place on any day of the year, according to the needs of the community being served, and did not require the existence of an established precepts platform.

With these three types of lay precept-conferral ceremonies in mind, we will now turn to the Japanese case. While all three models can be found in Japan, private ceremonies involving the elite appear to have been the most common form in which precepts were formally conferred upon laypeople in early Japan. As we will see below, mass conferrals of the precepts upon non-elites did take place at least as early as the Heian period, but only on a limited scale. The popularity of such ceremonies spread, however, during the mid-Kamakura period, around the time that Eison's vinaya-revival movement began to gain momentum.

Private precept-conferral ceremonies for the lay elite

Priests performed private precept-conferral ceremonies for members of the imperial family and aristocracy with great regularity throughout early Japanese history. This practice, which appears to have first gained currency during the eighth century, grew increasingly fashionable throughout the Heian and Kamakura periods. Chinese vinaya master Jianzhen's 鑒真 (688–763; Jpn. Ganjin) 753 visit to Japan surely played a large role in the spread of such ceremonies within in Japan. Jianzhen, who is recognized as having transmitted authentic vinaya monastic ordinations to Japan, established an ordination platform at Tōdaiji. Atop this platform he is said not only to have ordained monks, but also to have bestowed the major bodhisattva precepts upon Emperor Shōmu and Empress Kōmyō. Japanese narratives of Jianzhen's visit thereby suggest that the conferral of precepts upon members of the royal family in Japan dates at least to the eighth century. When, exactly, laypeople of lower status—courtiers and even commoners—began receiving precepts in formal ceremonies is less clear. We do know, however, that by the ninth century, the Tendai priest Ennin 円仁 (794–864), for one, was bestowing a variety of precepts upon a wide range of court elites. While these ceremonies were private in nature and were limited to those associated with the court, they often involved large numbers of lay participants who would receive precepts together, in single ceremonies.

The *Jikakudaishiden* 慈覚大師伝, a biography of Ennin, includes many passages that describe Ennin's conferrals of the precepts upon large groups of court elites. In the year 848, for example, he is said to have been invited by the high-ranking courtier Tomo no Yoshio (809–868) to bestow the esoteric *sanmaya-kai* 三味耶戒 upon over one thousand courtiers.[14] The next year he was invited to give the bodhisattva precepts to the Emperor Seiwa (850–880), and in 860, he engaged in several large-scale precept-conferral ceremonies at court. In the fifth month he gave bodhisattva precepts to Emperor Junna's consort, her close relatives, and other members of her entourage, totaling over 150 people. He is also said to have administered the *sanmaya-kai* to 270 people on this occasion. Later, in the eighth month of 860, he is said to have given the bodhisattva precepts to Emperor Junna's consort and to members of her entourage yet again, this time granting vows to more than 170 individuals.[15]

By the tenth century, taking formal bodhisattva or other precepts from a prominent *kaishi* 戒師, or precepts priest, was a well-established and highly fashionable practice. These ceremonies often constituted *shukke* 出家, or home-leaving, especially if the recipient chose to take on the appearance of a monk or nun following the ceremony, to intensify his or her daily devotions, and to change his or her lifestyle, perhaps by moving into a small chapel on the grounds a family villa or by taking up the itinerant life of a pilgrim. But precept ceremonies did not always lead to such changes: many took the precepts without the intention of taking on a monkish appearance or of engaging in serious Buddhist study or practice. They sought the precepts instead as a way of forging *kechien* 結縁, or positive karmic ties. Formal conferrals of the precepts were often carried out as merit-making ceremonies believed to bring what the *Xianyu jing* and *Foshuo chujia gongde jing* refer to as merit (功德) and blessings (福). Many sought conferrals of the precepts in times of illness, danger, or imminent death. The aristocratic diaries of the Heian period are replete with records of aristocrats calling upon priests to administer precepts to women whose lives had become threatened by a difficult childbirth, or to individuals believed to facing imminent death.[16] Many elites sought the precepts during times of health and prosperity as well, simply as a means of gaining personal protection and accumulating good merit. Because precept ceremonies were understood as merit-creating events, individuals often took the same sets of precepts on multiple occasions. For laypeople, the religious and social significance of a given precept-conferral ceremony was contextual; its meaning often depended on the particular needs of its recipient or recipients, needs that were often determined by age, health, and marital status. Precepts through the early and middle years of one's life were often regarded as ceremonies that created merit or brought healing, while those taken later in life were often used to mark a transition into retirement, to signal that one was giving up the obligations of the household life in order to prepare for death. When used as a means of preparing for death, precept conferrals were typically understood as *shukke*.

The dominant role played by Tendai priests within the religious world of the Heian court meant that, on the whole, elite courtiers who sought the *jukai* received the Perfect and Sudden Precepts of the Tendai school. Their *jukai* ceremonies were typically held in the privacy of their apartments. In the eleventh and twelfth centuries the Tendai priests Genshin 源信 (942–1017) and Ryōnin 良忍 (1072–1132) composed manuals that set the standards by which the conferrals of precepts upon royalty and courtiers were to proceed. The manuals, Genshin's *Shukke jukai sahō* 出家授戒作法 and Ryōnin's *Shukke sahō* 出家作法, both draw upon what had become, by their time, a well-established rhetoric on the merits of leaving home. Tendai priests continued to confer the perfect and sudden precepts (*endonkai*) on courtiers throughout the Heian period, and as time went on, these ceremonies were performed with increasing frequency. By the thirteenth century, many members of the court took the precepts not just several times over the course of their lifetimes, but several times per year. As Mitsuhashi Tadashi has suggested, Heian aristocrats viewed religious merit as something to be pursued in abundance: since it believed that one's fate in the next life was determined by the merit accrued to one, it made sense to commission as many rituals as possible, and to make each ritual as extravagant as possible.[17] Precept-conferral ceremonies, too, are best understood within the context of this greater emphasis on merit-making.

A somewhat humorous episode from the *Toganoo Myōe Shōnin denki*, one of the biographies of the Kegon priest Myōe 明恵 (1173–1232), illustrates the degree to which ceremonies offering precepts to members of the laity had become an accepted part of court life by the twelfth century. This episode relates Myōe's encounter with the Imperial Lady Shikikenmon'in, who had requested the precepts from him. According to the narrative, Myōe was insulted by Shikikenmon'in's failure to treat him—and the ceremony itself—with proper respect. The passage explains that Shikikenmon'in had grown used to taking the *jukai* from behind a blind as she sat, elevated above the precepts priest, in her own private quarters and without engaging in any real interaction with the priest. When Shikikenmon'in orders Myōe's to perform the ceremony in this same manner, he boldly admonishes her, reminding her that the *jukai* was no frivolous matter and that, as the recipient of the precepts, she is required to show her preceptor proper respect. Having been reprimanded, Shikikenmon'in is full of regret and embarrassment:

> The Imperial Lady, who had [up until then] thought that anyone would do and who had been inviting those [priests] whom she did not truly respect, saying that she needed to receive the precepts but then sending them away afterwards, was aghast. She came out from behind the blind and apologized profusely, expressing her regrets. She [then] went over to the ritual platform in the Gojibutsu Hall, climbed atop it, and received the precepts with ever-truer faith. After that, she said that she especially respected this master [Myōe], and that, until her death, she remained a deeply devoted patron.[18]

The Shikikenmon'in example is instructive insofar as it suggests that by the twelfth century, Japanese courtiers were taking the precepts both with frequency and in accordance with their own personal preferences. This narrative reflects the tendency for elites to receive the precepts multiple times and from multiple *kaishi*, or precepts teachers, all in an effort to build up vast stores of merit. Shikikenmon'in, for one, is described as having commissioned many priests to perform this same ritual on a regular basis. The passage further indicates that elites understood precept-conferral ceremonies as a kind of ritual commodity easily acquired through financial means. Concern with upholding the precepts received, or with cultivating personal morality, appears to have played little, if any, role at all in Shikikenmon'in's commissioning of the ritual.

Public precept-conferral ceremonies for ordinary laypeople

Although the degree to which mass precept-conferral ceremonies for laypeople were held in India and Central Asia is unknown, recent scholarship has suggested that the practice may have spread within China as early as the fifth century. The *Lives of Eminent Monks* tells, for example, of a monk named Daojin 道進 who bestowed the bodhisattva precepts on over 1,000 people in the fifth century. Following the Northern Wei defeat of the Northern Liang in 439, Daojin fled with members of the Northern Wei's Juqu clan to Turfan. As Nobuyoshi Yamabe has suggested, the discovery in Toyok of a copy of the *Youposajie jing* 優婆塞戒經 (*Sutra on the Lay Precepts*, Skt. *Upāsakaśīla sūtra*, T. no. 1488) suggests that Daojin successfully spread within Turfan the practice of conferring precepts upon laypeople.[19] Large-scale bodhisattva precepts ceremonies that included lay masses appear to have gained greater prevalence in China during the seventh and eighth centuries. Daoxuan's 道宣 (596–667) *Guang hongming ji* 廣弘明集 (T. no. 2134) and *Xu gaoseng zhuan* 續高僧傳 (T. no. 2060), in particular, make frequent reference to such events.[20] The tenth-century *Song gaoseng zhuan* 宋高僧傳 (T. no. 2061) also mentions the practice, making note of several seventh- and eighth-century figures said to have bestowed precepts upon hundreds or thousands of laypeople. This text tells us that the master Yinzong 印宗 (627–713), for example, built ordination platforms throughout China, bestowing the precepts on many people. It also tells of a priest named Xuanyan 玄儼 (675–742) who is said to have given the precepts to over 10,000 people in the areas now known as Jiangsu and Zhejiang. And, as John McRae has pointed out, Xuanyan's disciple Dayi 大義 (691–779) is also famed for large-scale conferrals of precepts upon laypeople: the *Song gaoseng zhuan* says that, over the course of his career, Dayi bestowed the precepts on over 30,000 individuals.[21]

Similar practices may have been implemented in Japan as early as the Heian period. Albeit limited, there is some evidence that certain temples included laypeople (both commoners and elites) in public ordinations during the Heian period. One such example can be found in the 984 *Sanbōe kotoba* of Minamoto Tamenori. In the twentieth fascicle of the third volume, Tamenori mentions that bodhisattva precept ceremonies were held annually at the Nara temple Hasedera 長谷寺. He describes the event as a public one open to the local community; on the day that the ceremony is held, he writes, "devout laymen and laywomen gather to participate. There are others who come simply to watch and listen." In explaining the origin of the bodhisattva precepts ceremony, Tamenori says that "the Masters of T'ien-t'ai and Nan-yüeh promoted this ordination [or ceremony]," while "Ganjin [Jianzhen] and Dengyō [Saichō] fostered it" in Japan.[22] Of particular interest is what comes next: Tamenori describes the manner in which monks typically receive the bodhisattva precepts and then adds, "in some places lay[people] may receive them as well."[23]

Unfortunately, the degree to which laypeople participated in Heian-period bodhisattva precept ceremonies outside Hasedera remains largely unknown. Tamenori hints at the possibility of a widespread practice, but few sources address the topic. Nevertheless, it should be noted that the tradition of holding bodhisattva precept ceremonies once per year is quite common; many temples, including those in Korea, Taiwan, and North America, continue to practice the rite as an annual one held within the temple. Ordinations in early Japan appear to have been held in the fourth month of the lunar year (see *Sanbōe kotoba* 3.19); in many places, they are still held during this same time of year.[24]

Large-scale lay bodhisattva precept ceremonies gained greater visibility during the Kamakura period. This increased popularity is undoubtedly linked to two innovations in particular: first, itinerant priests began to hold such rituals at local temples in the countryside, places perhaps more accessible to members of the laity; and, secondly, priests began to offer the rites on a more frequent basis. A passage from Fujiwara no Teika's diary *Meigetsuki* reveals that Myōe, for one, performed precept-conferral ceremonies for the laity in Toganoo twice monthly:

> During the hour of the dog (7–9 pm), the meditation nun and her daughter [my wife and daughter] secretly went to Toganoo. At [his monastery] there, the

priest Myōe confers the precepts on the fifteenth and last days of each month. It is said that all the ordained and lay under Heaven line up at that place, as if the Buddha were alive in this world. As for me, even though I highly value karmic ties, the thought of massive crowds fills me with discomfort, and [thus] I did not follow [my wife and daughter there]. [Because of the crowding], this poor outcaste [meaning "I"; Teika uses "hinin" here to refer to himself in a self-effacing manner] ultimately missed out on Myōe's teachings on the precepts.[25]

This passage, which is said to record events of the year 1229, provides several insights. First of all, it suggests that Myōe's bodhisattva precept ceremonies were understood as possessing some kind of mystical power, and that this power was intimately linked to the perception of Myōe as a charismatic, if not superhuman, figure. Indeed, Teika's use of simile in describing the popularity of Myōe's precept ceremonies ("all the ordained and lay under Heaven line up at that place, as if the Buddha were alive in this world") suggests that Myōe was perceived, at least by some, as a sacred, larger-than-life, figure. Secondly, the passage reveals that even members of the aristocracy—people who regularly commissioned Buddhist monks of Myōe's stature to come to the court and perform services in the comfort of their personal quarters—were interested in participating in these ceremonies.

Teika's comments suggest that he was not terribly interested in battling the crowds in the name of Buddhist merit-making. But his wife and daughter and, as is suggested later in the passage, other members of the elite, were clearly interested in participating in these rites, despite the fact that their participation would require them to come into contact with hordes of commoners. It is possible that Teika's wife and daughter simply delighted in the spectacle promised by such events; after all, as ladies well connected in court circles, these women had both the influence and the financial backing necessary to commission private rites and services directly. But Myōe's willingness to minister to the masses, and his ability to attract large crowds, attracted the fascination of Kamakura courtiers and warrior elites. Indeed, it appears that Myōe's popularity among the common people was largely proportional to his visibility at court. He was simultaneously involved both in outreach targeted at commoners and in the performance of private services for wealthy courtiers. (For patron Imperial Lady Kita-Shirakawa-in, for example, Myōe provided a range of services, from conferring the bodhisattva precepts on her privately to providing her daughter with a talisman meant to protect a romantic relationship.) Perhaps it was Myōe's ability to gain attention from those at both extremes of the socio-economic spectrum that served to reinforce his popularity with both groups. His immense popularity among common folk convinced the courtiers that he was a charismatic figure deserving of devotion and patronage, and his access to the court and its elite, in turn, undoubtedly increased his reputation among commoners, as it identified him as a master capable of transcending even the most rigid of social boundaries, those of class and rank.

Myōe's popularity as a precepts priest among aristocrats is paralleled in the example of Shunjō 俊芿 (1166–1227), a contemporary of Myōe. A Tendai priest,

Shunjō is famed for his twelve-year stay in Song China, where he studied Vinaya, Tiantai, and Chan doctrines. Upon his return he introduced new Chinese Vinaya lineages to Japan and also sought to implement in Japan the monastic lifestyle he had experienced in China. Related, most likely, to this broader commitment to introducing Chinese Buddhist practices to Japan, Shunjō appears to have administered the bodhisattva precepts to laypeople, both commoners and elites, even before Myōe's time. According to the *Sennyūji fukaki hōshiden* 泉涌寺不可 棄法師傳, a 1244 biography of Shunjō (also known as the Master Fukaki), Shunjō conferred the bodhisattva precepts upon large groups of commoners as early as the 1190s.[26] Such large-scale precept-conferral ceremonies do not appear to have been the focus of Shunjō's activities, however, and the degree to which Shunjō's precept-conferral practices overlapped with those of Myōe is not clear. I have not yet found any evidence suggesting that Shunjō held regular precept ceremonies in a fixed location, although it is possible that he may have done so. It was more likely the case, however, that Shunjō, who traveled wide and far through Japan's countryside, sometimes stopped to confer the bodhisattva precepts on locals who believed the ritual to be efficacious.

The *Sennyūji fukaki hōshiden* includes long narratives describing Shunjō's activities in China. These portions of the biography suggest that he did not seclude himself in Chinese monasteries but instead took on the greater social roles of Song-period priests. The biography relates a number of episodes in which Shunjō visits the homes of wealthy elites or officials and offers services for women experiencing difficulty in labor, for the ill, and for the deceased.[27]

Shunjō appears to have sought a similar role upon his return from China in 1211. Once settled in Japan, he attracted the patronage of a powerful Bizen warrior named Nakahara Nobufusa, who bequeathed to Shunjō the Kyoto temple Sennyūji. As the recipient of Nobufusa's patronage, Shunjō performed a number of services on behalf of the Nakahara family. Among these services—of course— was the conferral of the bodhisattva precepts.[28]

Shunjō's popularity and influence spread, and by the year 1218 he was able to launch a widely successful, large-scale revival of Sennyūji. In 1219 the Retired Emperor Go-Toba became a devotee of Shunjō, providing him with funding generous enough to support substantial construction projects at Sennyūji. As Shunjō's relationship with Go-Toba deepened, he was asked to confer the bodhisattva precepts upon a great number of imperial personages, ranging from Go-Toba himself to Juntoku-in (Go-Toba's son), Go-Takakura-in, and the Imperial Lady Higashi Ichijō-in, Juntoku's consort, among others.[29] Shunjō soon came to be regarded as a figure of divine proportions, a bodhisattva living in the human realm. In fact, when Emperor Shijō (1231–1242) passed away, people began to say that he had been an incarnation of the priest Shunjō.

While Myōe administered precepts to commoners on a regular basis, Shunjō's conferrals of the bodhisattva precepts appear to have been targeted primarily at elite patrons, although records do suggest that he ordained ordinary laypeople from time to time. There is little evidence, however, that Shunjō offered large-scale bodhisattva precept conferrals with the same frequency as Myōe and Eison.

Still, Shunjō's example is illustrative for several reasons. First, the patrons of Shunjō, much like those of Myōe, appear to have found the bodhisattva precept ceremony to be of great appeal. Secondly, these cases all illustrate how successful movements on the ground eventually won charismatic priests attention from courtiers, who desired precept conferrals in return for their patronage.

Although there are no comprehensive studies that consider the growth and spread of large-scale lay precept-conferral ceremonies across sectarian and regional boundaries in Kamakura-period Japan, it is clear that the practice was much larger than the individual movements of Myōe, Shunjō, and Eison. Surviving records suggest that Shōkū 証空 (1177–1247), the priest recognized as the founder of the Seizan sect of Jōdo-shū, for example, was popularizing the bodhisattva precepts among common lay folk when Eison was still in the early years of his ministry. On a name register discovered inside a statue of Amida at Dainenji 大念寺, Shōkū urges sentient beings to take the bodhisattva precepts and says that the precepts, once taken, can never be lost. He also writes that the precepts are the foundation or source of all buddhas (諸仏の本源). This concept— that the realization of buddhahood is based in the precepts—is invoked by Eison as well, as we will see below. Using phrases such as "kainen ittō" 戒念一到 and "kainen ichinyo" 戒念一如, Shōkū's Seizan sect understood the precepts and the *nenbutsu* as one and the same: both give rise to *bodhicitta*, leading to rebirth in the Pure Land and, ultimately, to Buddhahood.[30] Following this philosophy, Shōkū appears to have offered the bodhisattva precepts to large groups of lay followers. Like Myōe, Shunjō, and Eison, Shōkū also performed private precept conferrals for the elite. In 1243, for example, he administered precepts at the court of the Emperor Go-Saga. Shōkū's Seizan sect continued to emphasize the efficacy of precept conferrals upon the laity and is known for popularizing the practice during the Muromachi period, when Jōdo sects, Sōtō Zen groups, and Vinaya priests, among others, were also performing the rite.

As we have seen, then, large-scale, lay-oriented precept-conferral ceremonies were not unknown in early Japan but appear to have been quite rare through the late Heian and early Kamakura periods. They began to gain visibility in the historical record from the early-to-mid Kamakura period, but even during these years, we find only limited mention of the practice. The practice gained great momentum, however, in the late 1200s, when Eison's Shingon Ritsu movement reached its peak. By the Muromachi period, large-scale precept-conferrals aimed at laypeople were performed widely: numerous sects throughout Japan had incorporated various versions of such rites into their ritual repertoire.

The causes and conditions generating this sudden rise, in late Kamakura Japan, of lay-oriented, precept-conferral ceremonies were surely numerous and complex. One possible factor was increased interest, on the part of Japanese monastics, in how Buddhism was practiced in China, where large-scale ceremonies in which the precepts were administered to laypeople had become ubiquitous by this time. Shunjō, for example, would have witnessed, and likely participated in, such ceremonies during his time in China. Another possible factor is that, domestically, common lay folk had become the primary consumers of *hōe* 法会, or large-scale

Buddhist ceremonies. As the power of the court waned, Buddhist institutions, increasingly unable to depend on state patronage, were forced to cater to laypeople, the group that came to supply their most reliable source of income. From the late Heian period onwards, Buddhist ceremonies thus came to incorporate the needs and interests of laypeople.[31] Precept-conferral ceremonies for laypeople, which came to be known as *jukaie* 受戒会, or "precept-receiving ceremonies," fit into this broader trend.[32]

In China, too, such ceremonies had been popularized as part of a larger effort to better incorporate laypeople into the economic and social structures of Buddhist monasteries. As Daniel Getz has explained, Chinese masters produced, from the late Tang through the Song, numerous versions of the bodhisattva precept-conferral rite, each new ceremony "address[ing] in a more focused way the needs and concerns of a lay audience."[33] Tiantai priests successfully popularized these new rites, many gaining fame based on the numbers of precept recipients they attracted. The *Jingde chuandeng lu* 景德傳燈録 (T. no. 2076) claims that the master Yanshou, for example, attracted some 10,000 devotees to a precept-conferral ceremony atop Mt. Tiantai in the year 974.[34] Getz's work analyzes the activities of numerous other Tiantai priests, figures like Zhili, Zunshi, Benru, Huicai, and Yuanzhao, who were all actively involved ceremonies in which they administered the precepts to laypeople *en masse*. As Getz remarks, these figures strove to include as many laypeople as possible in their precept-conferral ceremonies and measured their success according the size of the crowds they were able to draw.[35]

Precept-conferral ceremonies in Eison's movement

Now that we have sketched the basic contours of the history of large-scale precept-conferral ceremonies for laypeople in China and Japan, let us return to the case of Eison. As has been well documented elsewhere, Eison launched a large-scale revival of the Ritsu, or Vinaya, School from the Nara temple Saidaiji, which he began to restore in the late 1230s. According to the 1290 Saidaiji document *Shien Shōnin donin gyōhō kechige ki* 思円上人度人行法結夏記, Eison administered the bodhisattva precepts to 97,710 individuals. Of these, 96,016 are said to have been householders.[36] Although these numbers may have been inflated by Eison's disciples, the proportions suggest that his movement, despite its emphasis on the restoration of the monastic order, was primarily focused on the laity: according to Saidaiji's own documents, a striking 98 percent of those who received the precepts from Eison were laypeople.

Many, if not most, of the precept ceremonies Eison performed were sizeable events in which he ordained a large group of people all at once. Such examples abound in Eison's autobiography, *Kongō Busshi Eison kanjin gakushōki* 金剛仏子叡尊感身学正記. Looking just at the year Kōan 8 (1285), for example, we see that Eison, even at the age of 84, is said to have administered the precepts to large groups in rapid succession. According to this text, he gave the bodhisattva precepts to 730 people at the Gochikō-in of the temple Tennōji on the third day of the fourth month of 1285. Eight days later, the diary claims, he gave the bodhisattva precepts to 629 people in the lecture hall at the Kawachi temple Kyōkōji. Then, on the 26th day of the seventh month, he gave the bodhisattva precepts to 139 people, and on the seventh day of the eighth month, to 2,124 people in the Hyōgo countryside. On the 13th day of that same month, he is said to have given the bodhisattva precepts to 972 people at the Hyōgo temple Anyōji. On the same occasion, he is said to have given the (eight) pure precepts to over 1,700 prostitutes (*injo* 淫女). On the 22nd day of the ninth month, he is said to have given the bodhisattva precepts to over 700 people at the Seijōkōin, a temple on a *shōen* (landed estate) in Kawachi. He gave another 24 people the bodhisattva precepts on the 19th day of the tenth month. And on the fourth day of the eleventh month, he went to the Yamato temple Daigorinji and bestowed the bodhisattva precepts on over 400 people. Well over 6,718 people, then, are said to have taken some form of the precepts from Eison in the year 1285 alone.[37]

What was expected of these large groups who took Eison's precepts? Standard readings of Eison have emphasized his concern with the need to observe all of the precepts in detail and with great care. There is a certain tendency, then, to read Eison's vinaya-revival movement not merely as an attempt to revive the morality of the Buddhist order, but also as an initiative to cultivate lay morality.

Certainly Eison's writings and activities do demonstrate an interest in furthering public morality. Entries from his biographical and sermon collections suggest, for example, that one of the major goals of his vinaya-revival movement was to outlaw the killing of all forms of life, including fish, birds, and wild game. A 1290 biography of Eison (*Shien shōnin donin gyōhō kechige ki*) claims that Eison declared a total of 1,356 villages, estates, and other locales as places prohibiting the slaying of living beings (*sesshō kindan* 殺生禁断). Eison is also known to have encouraged those working in livelihoods understood as karmically disadvantageous—prostitutes, hunters, fishermen, and the like—to give up their livelihoods and to begin observing the lay precepts.[38] He also worked towards such goals as prohibiting liquor.

But while Eison may indeed have understood his movement as working towards the moral cultivation of the masses, he was also working within a certain set of popular assumptions regarding the ritual power of precepts conferrals. To begin with, precepts conferrals had, throughout East Asia, already been conceptualized as soteriological rites imbued with the power to liberate beings from their karmic fates. Daoxuan's *Xu gaoseng zhuan* (*Continued Biographies of Eminent Monks*), for example, is replete with stories of priests using precepts-bestowal ceremonies to free various beings, including menacing spirits, local deities, and animals, from their karmic destinies.[39] In these stories, that which is highlighted is not the moral commitments of those receiving the precepts; instead, the stories are reflective of the spiritual power of the priest who administers the precepts, and of the power embodied in, and transmitted through, the ritual itself. By Eison's time, the notion that precept conferral was a mysterious rite of unfathomable merit—an idea that we can trace back to texts like the *Xianyu jing* and the *Foshuo chujia gongde jing*—was a deeply entrenched one.

So while it would be presumptuous to say that precepts-conferrals given to lay groups did not seek to encourage moral cultivation, we cannot assume that the efficacy of the precepts ceremony was understood as dependent upon one's success in (or even concern with) upholding those precepts received. A 1414 copy of the Saidaiji ritual guide *Jubosatsukai yōi monsho* 受菩薩戒用意聞書, which explains the ritual procedures for conferring the bodhisattva precepts, supports this view. The manual states, rather matter-of-factly, that since the laypeople living at the temple (a group to be described in greater depth below) who take the bodhisattva precepts are basically just given a *kaimyō* 戒名, or a Buddhist name, in order to create karmic bonds (結縁 *kechien)*, the precepts priest need not give them a careful explanation of the precepts. Minowa Kenryō has read this remark as evidence that Eison and his disciples did not expect laity receiving the precepts to actually uphold them.[40]

The spiritual efficacy of Eison's precept-conferrals

Before Eison's movement caught the attention of elites, he and his disciples spent much of their time traveling throughout the countryside regions of the Kinai, soliciting people of all backgrounds to contribute to their campaign to restore the precepts and to rebuild temples left devastated through warfare or neglect. They had no strong financial base but instead depended on the accumulation of many small contributions. And although Eison and his disciples would eventually attract the patronage of the wealthy, their primary benefactors, especially in the early years of their movement, were common lay folk who could afford to make only humble donations. While Eison and his disciples offered a great number of services aimed at helping—or attracting (depending on one's view, of course)—common laypeople, two services, in particular, sealed their success in the countryside. The first was the Kōmyō Shingon, or Mantra of Light, ritual, which allowed participants to transfer merit to deceased loved ones. Eison's group used this ritual to perform funerary rites in the countryside. Commoners would contribute funds not only for funerary rites as such, but also for memorial rites, also using the Kōmyō Shingon, that commemorated the dead annually or at other marked intervals. The second service offered by Saidaiji vinaya priests that gained particular popularity among the laity was the precept-conferral ceremony.[41]

One of the great draws of Eison's movement was that he and his disciples regularly gave ordinary laypeople the chance to receive the precepts—the bodhisattva precepts of the *Fanwang jing*, as well as those precepts from the vinaya that targeted lay followers: the eight pure precepts, and the five lay precepts. Receiving the precepts, as we have seen, was understood as an act of immeasurably positive karmic consequence. Indeed, Eison goes so far as to argue that the ritual conferment of the five lay precepts or the ten major bodhisattva precepts essentially guarantees one's salvation. Responding to debates concerning the relative efficacy of various precept conferrals, he says in one of his sermons:

> What people of the world say—that taking the five precepts leads to rebirth as a human being and that taking the ten leads to rebirth in a heavenly realm—is

nonsense.... Whether it be the bodhisattva precepts, the five [lay precepts], the eight [pure precepts], the ten precepts, or the complete precepts, all are causes of Buddhahood....[42]

In addition to the long-term goal of Buddahood, these precept conferrals were also associated with more mundane goals, with what has often been termed *genze riyaku*, or worldly benefits. Throughout the Heian period, as previously mentioned, the *jukai* had been practiced with a variety of practical goals in mind, such as extending one's lifespan, healing an illness, securing safe childbirth, and the like. It is likely that many of those who participated in Eison's mass ceremonies would have considered the ceremonies an opportunity to acquire such worldly benefits. Certainly the fact that Eison administered the precepts to the sick, especially to those afflicted with leprosy, suggests that healing powers were attributed to the precept-conferral ritual.[43]

Another point worth emphasizing is that many people took the precepts—even the same sets of precepts—from Eison on multiple occasions; numerous documents associated with Eison's movement, including the record of his trip to the Kantō region in 1262 (*Kantō ōkanki* 関東往還記) and his autobiography (*Kongō Busshi Eison kanjin gakushōki* 金剛仏子叡尊感身学正記), attest that this was the case. The record of his trip to the Kantō indicates than a number of Bakufu elites (primarily members of the Hōjō) took the precepts from him multiple times within a period of several months.[44] Similarly, his autobiography shows that at least a handful of elite court figures received the precepts from him multiple times. As Ōishi Masaaki has pointed out, Eison often used the bodhisattva precepts simply as a means of giving laypeople the opportunity to create good karma.[45] It appears to have been widely assumed that the precept-conferral ceremony, like other merit-making activities, was most effective when repeated again and again; according to the logic of merit-making, each repetition of a meritorious act would contribute to the karmic reserves of the individual in question.

The rewards of bestowing merit

What did Eison and his movement gain in offering commoners formal conferrals of the precepts? As suggested earlier, these ceremonies must first be understood within the greater context of fundraising. It was likely the opportunity to participate in Eison's bodhisattva precept and other ceremonies that motivated many of his lay donors to contribute small landholdings and other financial resources to Eison's movement. Related to this goal of raising funds was another crucial objective: expansion into the countryside.

Saidaiji's years of rapid expansion into the countryside appear to have begun just a few years before Eison's death. Over the next century, the Saidaiji network expanded far and wide: the 1391 document *Saidaiji shokoku matsuji chō* (*Register of Saidaiji Branch Temples in All Provinces*) claims over 250 temples, stretching from Dewa in the north to Satsuma and Ōsumi in the south, as Saidaiji branch temples.[46] Although many of the temples absorbed into the Saidaiji network appear to have been voluntarily handed over, from their rightful administrators, to Saidaiji priests, other temples, especially those in more remote areas, were likely "converted" to the Saidaiji vinaya movement in a more coercive manner.

In converting local temples, Saidaiji would first install a Saidaiji priest as abbot, then raise funds for temple repairs, and finally perform rituals to gain local support. And one of the most important rituals used to gain local support would have been bodhisattva precept and other precept-conferral ceremonies.[47] To give an example of how local support might be generated, consider the case of the Saidaiji branch temple Sairinji: Although the administration rights (*bettō shiki*) to the Kawachi temple Sairinji appear to have been handed over to Eison's nephew and disciple Sōji (1233–1312) voluntarily, Sōji was likely concerned over the degree to which locals would be supportive of the temple's new association with Saidaiji. Once he arrived at the post, he immediately invited Eison to come and confer the bodhisattva precepts to 256 locals, undoubtedly in an attempt to win local support for the temple's new Saidaiji-led administration.[48]

Saidaiji's precept-conferral ceremonies can also be understood, then, within the larger framework of "conversion" narratives used to explain expansion into regional areas with strong, often non-Buddhist, local traditions of their own. In his studies of fourteenth- and fifteenth-century Sōtō Zen expansion into the countryside, William Bodiford has highlighted the important role that precept ceremonies played in the "conversion" of local spirits and communities. During the fifteenth century, Sōtō Zen priests sponsored various mass precept ceremonies in rural society, offering participants the promise of salvation while simultaneously garnering support for the school's own expansion into the countryside and, more specifically, for its conversion of village temples into Sōtō institutions. Saidaiji's precept-conferral ceremonies represent, it would seem, a kind of precedent for these later Sōtō practices. (Bodiford also speculates that the Sōtō priests who ordained large groups most likely did not expect people to actually uphold the precepts.)[49]

Large-scale precept-conferral ceremonies that garnered both political and financial support for the growing Saidaiji network represent one side of Eison's work with the bodhisattva and other precepts given to the laity. On the other end, and after his Saidaiji network had already begun to establish itself in rural areas throughout the Kinai, Eison began to receive more and more attention from elite groups, from courtiers and from members of the warrior classes who wanted to receive some form of the precepts from him.

Although Eison's autobiography and biographies do not indicate that he visited imperial residences or had any regular contact with high-ranking figures during the first twenty or more years of his career, they describe frequent interaction with elite society from the late 1260s on. For example, Eison's autobiography indicates that he gave the precepts to the daughter of Konoe no Motomichi 近衛基道, a member of the northern branch of the Fujiwara clan, in the year 1269. At the time that this high-born woman took the bodhisattva precepts, nineteen others joined her. Eison says that he received, as his payment, a grain of the Tōshōdaiji relics during this encounter.[50]

A couple of weeks later, Eison was invited to the residence of the Kanpaku Regent Takatsukasa Mototada 鷹司基忠. There he gave the bodhisattva precepts to forty people.[51] Less than a week after this large event, Eison visited the residence of the wife of Bakufu official Rokuhara-den (Hōjō Tokishige; 1241–1270). There, Tokishige's wife, along with twenty-four others, is said to have taken the bodhisattva precepts from Eison.[52]

In the year 1276, at age of 76, Eison was given an imperial order to visit the Daitashōin 大多勝院 in Saga (one of the Retired Emperor's residences), where he gave the bodhisattva precepts to the Retired Emperor Kameyama (1249–1305; r. 1259–1274), his two Imperial Ladies (*nyōin*), and one lady-in-waiting (*nyōbō*). (Eison notes here that the Retired Emperor took only nine of the ten major precepts, having excluded the precept against illicit sexual relations from his vows. This is an interesting detail, in that it suggests there was still some degree of concern over whether or not one could actually observe the vows he/she was taking. Although Eison taught that people should not take the precepts until they had given rise to the mind of enlightenment and intended to observe the precepts, but of course it is impossible to know if he expected people to follow his advice.[53])

In 1278, Eison gave the bodhisattva precepts to the Retired Emperor and some sixty aristocrats. In 1279, he was invited to the residences of the Retired Emperors again. He gave the bodhisattva precepts to Retired Emperor Go-Fukakusa and one of his consorts, and to Kameyama again. In addition, nearly sixty officials of the court took the precepts from him. In return, the Retired Emperor ordered that a complete set of the Buddhist sutras (*issaikyō*) be given to Eison. That same year, Eison also gave the bodhisattva precepts to the Imperial Lady Muromachi (1228–1300), who rewarded him with a number of Buddha Tooth Relic grains. The following year, he gave the bodhisattva precepts to Kameyama's new Imperial Lady, Shinyōmeimon'in (1262–1296), who was 18 years old at the time.[54]

A year later, in 1281, Eison was invited to Daitashōin Residence again, where he gave the *hassaikai* (eight pure precepts) to the Retired Emperor and one Imperial Lady.[55] He is also said to have given the bodhisattva precepts to the Emperor Go-Uda during the same month, and to have given the *saikai* (pure precepts) to the emperor's consort. In 1282, he is said to have given the bodhisattva precepts to an imperial princess.[56] In the third month of 1284, he gave the bodhisattva precepts to five ladies-in-waiting, the Retired Emperor, and seventy people below him. A couple of weeks later, he bestowed the bodhisattva precepts on the Retired Emperor, one of his Imperial Ladies, and seventy others. Soon after, he returned to the inner palace, this time bestowing the bodhisattva precepts on everyone from the emperor to various ladies-in-waiting, including a total of some forty-six court figures.[57] And the ceremonies continued.

Eison, whose movement first focused on common lay folk, spent his final years in diverse company. Though his own writings speak of distaste for fame and fortune, the elite eventually demanded his ritual services, and he obliged. By agreeing to perform rituals for imperial family members, courtiers, and elite warriors, Eison was able to win the support of those in power, those who would, following Eison's death, enable his movement to expand even further.

Saidaiji precept-conferral liturgies

One of the innovations of Eison's precept-conferral ceremonies was their flexibility: these rituals could take place at any time, in any location, and on any scale. Although Tendai priests had long offered elites the chance to undergo precept-conferral ceremonies in the privacy of their own residences and at times convenient for them, it appears that most ceremonies for the masses had taken place at fixed locations and times (as in the case of Hasedera, for example). But Eison and his disciples bestowed the precepts in various places, as they were traveling through the countryside. Precepts could be administered for a single individual (a practice especially common in the case of elite patrons), or they could be bestowed upon a group large or small. As Eison notes in one of his sermons:

> Generally, the precepts for lay believers are comprised of the receiving of the Three Refuges [Refuge in the Buddha, Refuge in the Dharma, and Refuge in the Saṃgha] and the Five Precepts [do not kill, do not steal, do not engage in sexually impure behavior, do not misuse language, and do not drink alcohol] from a precepts master. As for the precepts master, so long as he is a *biku* 比丘 [full-fledged monk], anyone will do. As a rule, there is only a single precepts master [in a given ceremony]. . . .[58]

That precept-conferral ceremonies could be easily adapted to different situations is also suggested in an early section of the *Jubosatsukai yōi monsho* titled "On the Recipients" (受者の事): "As for those who are receiving the precepts for *kechien* 結縁, they may be one or many, receiving all precepts or partial, male or female, high-born or low-born: there are no rules regarding these things."[59]

Though versatile, the precept ceremonies offered by Eison's group were far from simple. Granted, they were not as lengthy as the traditional ordination ceremonies that took place on fixed dates at places like Tōdaiji (these rituals typically lasted for three days). But Vinaya-School precept-conferral ceremonies did employ a detailed liturgy. According to Minowa, who has carefully analyzed surviving Saidaiji precept-conferral manuals, the basic liturgical structure used to confer the ten major bodhisattva precepts upon a layperson or group of laypeople looked something like this:

> First the Recipient(s) (*jusha* 受者) and Witnesses (*shōmei* 證明) all take their seats;
> The Precepts Master (戒師 *kaishi*) enters, performs the Sanrai 三礼 (Three Respects),[60] and takes his seat;
> The Precepts Master performs the *ānāpāna-smṛti* 阿那波那念 (breath-counting meditation);[61]
> The Precepts Master gives the *hyōbyaku* 表白 (Opening);
> Sanki 三帰 (Three Refuges);
> Hosshin 発心 (Arousal of the Aspiration for Enlightenment);
> Invitation to the Masters Before Us 請現前師;[62]

Invitation to the Mysterious Five Masters 請冥五師;[63]
Zange (Repentance) 懺悔;[64]
Explanation of *hosshin* (Arousal of the Aspiration for Enlightenment) 問発心;
Konma 羯磨 (Ritual Procedures);[65]
Second Konma;
Third Konma;
Precepts Master questions the Witnesses;
Precepts Master performs the Sesshō 説相 (Explanation of the Precepts);
Precepts Master burns incense;
Recipients perform Sanrai;
[Recipients] withdraw;
Precepts Master and order of priests perform Sanrai and withdraw;
Exiting of the hall.[66]

Most of these steps represent *shōmyō* 声明 (Chn. *shengming*), or Buddhist liturgical chants, that would have been intoned aloud according to set pitches and rhythms. While the use of chant in Buddhist ritual can be traced back to India and China, the Japanese case was particular insofar as it combined a range of different genres and languages. Some *shōmyō* were based on Sanskrit and Chinese language texts and were chanted with the aid of pronunciation glosses that provided transliterations; others, especially those that had been composed in Japanese, were chanted in a more vernacular form. Most *shōmyō* focused on passages from sutras, but some were comprised of hymns written in Sanskrit, Chinese, or Japanese.[67]

While the content of the *hyōbyaku* would be altered in order to accommodate the particular occasion at hand, the other *shōmyō* listed here most likely employed fixed verses that had been used in Buddhist ceremonies for centuries. The actual conferring of the precepts begins in the Konma section. Saidaiji precept-conferral manuals include the liturgy for this section, which begins with the precepts priest and the witnesses putting their hands in *gasshō* 合掌. The manual then instructs the precepts priest to address the recipients, using their names if the group is small enough, and referring to them as "good sons and good daughters" 善男子, 善女人. From there, the priest was to intone a long text, taken mostly from the *pusadi jiepin* 菩薩地戒品 section of the *Yuqie(shidi)lun* 瑜伽(師地)論 (*Yogācāra-bhūmi,* Jpn. *Yuga(shiji)ron,* T. no. 1579). These lines praise the three pure precepts as that which the bodhisattvas of the past, present, and future are always studying and embodying. The recipients are told that they must resolve to uphold these precepts always and are then asked if they can do so. The entire Konma section is then to be repeated two additional times, thereby enabling the recipients to become familiar with the content of the precepts they are taking.[68]

During the Sesshō, the ten major bodhisattva precepts were to be read aloud, one by one. Minowa has pointed out that the actual phrasing of the ten major bodhisattva precepts employed in Saidaiji manuals follows the terminology found in the Silla master Taehyŏn's 太賢 *Fanwang jing* commentary *Pŏmmanggyŏng gojŏkki* 梵網經古跡記 (T. no. 1815). Having chanted aloud the ten bodhisattva precepts, the precepts priest is to read aloud a few summary remarks, reminding recipients that they are to honor these vows forever.[69]

As Minowa's research has clarified, this Saidaiji liturgy combined terms, ideas, and rites taken from a number of different sources, including Tendai liturgical manuals, Silla commentaries, Xuanzang's 玄奘 translation of the *Apidamo jushe lun* 阿毘達磨俱舍論 (T. no. 1558), the writings of the Nanshan Vinaya School's Yuanzhao, and, of course, the *Brahmā Net Sūtra* and the *Yuqie lun*.[70] Eison's piecing together of diverse interpretations of the precepts and their conferrals meant that his ceremonies combined the familiar with the unfamiliar.

More complex than any single liturgy itself was the relationship between the various forms of precept conferral offered and the divisions within Eison's order. Eison's movement employed a multi-tiered system of administering the precepts. The first division was twofold: followers were to receive both the *tsūju* 通受, or comprehensive conferral, and a *betsuju* 別受, or separate conferral. As a general rule, comprehensive conferrals included both traditional vinaya precepts (largely relying on the *Sifen lü*) and bodhisattva precepts (taken from the *Fanwang jing* and the *Yuqie lun*), while separate conferrals included only the former.[71] The Saidaiji manual *Jubosatsukai sahō* 授菩薩戒作法 explains the system as follows:

> As for the World-Honored One's most cherished wish upon emerging in this world, it is nothing other than these precepts. As it is said, even though sentient beings possess the Buddha-nature, due to false discrimination, they do not manifest it. The first step in manifesting the Buddha-nature, then, is to uphold the precepts. In receiving these precepts, there are two methods. These are the *tsūju* and the *betsuju*. As for the *betsuju*, the procedures for those [precepts] upheld by each of the seven groups (七衆) are different. As for the *tsūju*, [everyone] takes the same three sets of pure precepts (三聚). Then they advance from the coarse to the fine, from the ten major precepts for *kechien* to the great *bhikṣu* precepts 大芯蒭戒 (*dai bishu kai*).

In other words, everyone in Eison's order—from the full-fledged *biku* down to the common lay believer—was to receive the same comprehensive conferral. One's place within the order, then, was determined according to the *betsuju*, or separate conferral, that one received. As suggested above, one could progress through many levels of separate conferral over time.

In the excerpt above, the Eison's Vinaya order is described as having seven *shū* 衆, or groups. But as Minowa has illustrated, close attention to Saidaiji documents reveals that Eison's order was actually divided into nine groups (or eleven, if the last two lay groups are further divided by sex). Each group was distinguished by the *betsuju* its members had received:

1   Full-Fledged Monk (*biku* 比丘, also *daisō* 大僧 and *bishu* 芯蒭)
2   Full-Fledged Nun (*bikuni* 比丘尼, also *daini* 大尼 and *bishuni* 芯蒭尼)
3   Probationary Nuns (*shikishamana* 式叉摩那)
    Novice Monks (*shami* 沙彌)

4 Novice in "Outer Form" (*gyōdō* 形同 type)
5 Novice in Accordance with the Dharma (*hōdō* 法同 type, also *gonsaku* 勤策)
   Novice Nuns (*shamini* 沙彌尼)
6 Novice in "Outer Form" (*gyōdō* 形同 type)
7 Novice in Accordance with the Dharma (*hōdō* 法同 type, also *gonsakunyo* 勤策女)
8 Resident Lay Devotees (*gonjū* 近住, male and female)
9 [Ordinary] Lay Devotees (*gonshi* 近士, also *gonji* 近事, male and female)

The traditional sevenfold division of the *saṃgha* includes full-fledged monks and nuns, probationary nuns, novice monks and nuns, laywomen and laymen. Eison introduced new groups into his order by dividing the rank of novice into the categories of *gyōdō* and *hōdō* and the rank of layperson into *gonshi* and *gonjū*. While these classifications were based on passages from Chinese vinaya texts, especially those of Daoxuan, Yuanzhao, and Xuanzang, Eison appears to have been the first to use these particular classifications to create actual groups within the order.[72] These new groups are of particular interest insofar as they provided a number of intermediary options for those who sought affiliation with Eison's group (and with the merit of home-leaving) but who were unable, for whatever reason, to embark upon the path of full renunciation.

For laypeople, many options were available. First, one could simply take the ten major bodhisattva precepts in order to form *kechien* with Eison's group. This conferral could be accomplished rather easily: one needed only to participate in one of the large-scale bodhisattva precept-conferral ceremonies offered by the Saidaiji order. These ceremonies took place frequently and followed the liturgical format outlined above. For one who simply wished to create some merit and to form a bond with Eison's movement, participation in this one ceremony would suffice.

Laypeople who wanted to create even more merit, and to establish a more lasting bond with Eison's movement, could take, in addition to the bodhisattva precepts, the five traditional lay precepts.[73] This step would mark them as *gonshi*. *Gonshi* were laypeople; they did not shave their heads, nor did they live on the grounds of the temple. Although surviving sources do not allow us to determine the situation with any certainty, it seems that, in taking an extra set of precepts from Eison's group, *gonshi* established a bond with Eison's group that exceeded that created by those who simply participated in mass bodhisattva precept-conferral ceremonies. That *gonshi* created a more enduring bond with Eison's group is suggested by the existence of *kōmyō* 交名, or name registers, listing the names of *gonshi* who had taken the bodhisattva precepts from Eison.[74] This evidence suggests that *gonshi* were given *kaimyō*, or Buddhist names, and that they were given the opportunity to sign name registers that sealed their affiliation with the Saidaiji movement. Although we cannot be sure that ordinary participants in large-scale bodhisattva precept ceremonies were not bestowed with *kaimyō* or given the opportunity to have their name recorded in *kōmyō*, Minowa suggests that, given the sheer volume of people who participated in the large ceremonies, it is unlikely that Saidaiji priests would have had the time to record so many names. Moreover, he adds, paper was extremely valuable during this period, and most of the common folk participating in mass precept ceremonies would not have been able to read, anyway.[75]

Above the *gonshi,* the rank of *gonjū* represents a higher level of lay commitment. *Gonjū* took the five traditional vinaya precepts for the laity and the eight pure precepts (*hassai kai* 八斎戒).[76] Although local lay groups had only been expected to observe the eight pure precepts six days per month in India, the *gonjū* in Eison's order were told to uphold these precepts for life. Those who observed these eight pure precepts indefinitely constituted a group known as the *saikaishu* 斎戒衆.[77] While the *gonjū*, or members of the *saikaishū*, did not shave their heads, they did leave their secular lives behind insofar as they took up residence on the grounds of Saidaiji-branch Vinaya temples.[78] Particularly telling here is the fact that Saidaiji liturgical manuals often refer to members of the *saikaishū* as *shukke no gonjū* 出家の近住, indicating that these recipients, though they had not received the precepts of a novice, monk, or nun, were still deemed *shukke*, or home-leavers.[79]

Yet another option for laypeople was monastic novice-hood. Eison divided novices into the categories of *gyōdō shamini* (novice in outer form only) and *hōdō shamini* (novice in accordance with proper method). *Gyōdō shami* and *shamini* looked like *shukke* insofar as they shaved their heads, but they received only the ten major bodhisattva precepts (*jūjūkai* 十重戒). A *gyōdō shami* or *shamini* could choose to stop at this rank or could chose to progress to full novice-hood, a path that could eventually lead to ordination as a fully-fledged monk or nun. To advance as full fledged novices, or *hōdō shami/shamini*, *gyōdō shami/shamini* were required to take the ten precepts for novices (*jūkai* 十戒).[80] Once this step was complete, the recipients would be considered *shukke* rather than lay believers.[81]

Attention to surviving Saidaiji liturgical manuals has enabled us both to gain a sense of what the basic liturgical content of Eison's bodhisattva precept-conferral ceremonies was like and to understand how the different precepts Eison offered corresponded to ranks within his order. From the liturgical structure of Eison's precept-conferral ceremonies, we can see that his large-scale ceremonies allowed devotees to participate in an elaborate ritual performance. Devotees must have found the performance of the bodhisattva precept ceremony stimulating both visually and aurally. In rural areas where common folk had had little exposure to Buddhist ceremony on such a grand level, these rituals surely must have provided a delightful spectacle. While the opportunity to create karmic merit surely attracted many to Eison's precept conferrals, one can imagine that, in particularly remote rural areas, anyway, the mere pageantry associated with such a ceremony would have drawn large crowds.

For those who wanted further association with Eison's vinaya-revival movement, participation in additional precept-conferral ceremonies enabled locals to join various groups within the order. In particular, Eison introduced several new categories that blended the basic characteristics of lay status with those of monastic status. The *gyōdō shamini*, for example, shaved their heads like full novices but were considered laypeople until they took the ten novice precepts, and the *gonjū* kept their hair but took up residence within the temple complex, meaning that they had, in many ways, given up their secular lives. In adding these new categories of belonging, Eison expanded the scope of his order. Not only did these new categories blur the line between the laity and the monastic order, creating a spectrum of possible positionalities between layperson and monastic, but it also enabled the movement to absorb new members both quickly and from a range of backgrounds.

Divisions within the order

That Eison bestowed precepts upon such a large and varied group of people might lead one to assume that his movement had a grassroots flavor. In the sense that he and his disciples interacted with common folk, with women, and with the diseased, this assumption might not be altogether incorrect. But it would be wrong to assume that his movement was nonhierarchical; as Hosokawa Ryōichi has demonstrated, the Saidaiji-branch Vinaya order was organized according to a complex hierarchy that tended to reify distinctions such as social class and gender. Against the notion that the *saikaishū* was a benign designation for committed laypeople, for example, Hosokawa reveals that this group was an underclass consisting of laypeople interested in full world renunciation but prohibited, likely on the base of class, from pursuing that goal. These men, he argues, faced numerous forms of discrimination. Unlike full Saidaiji priests, for example, *saikaishū* members were not allowed to bathe at the local Hokkeji bath. Moreover, members of the *saikaishū* assembly were given the task of handling corpses when the Saidaiji movement began to perform great numbers of funerals on behalf of its supporters and patrons. Unlike full *biku*, who handled *kuyō* 供養 commemorative services, as well as the other aspects of funerary procedures considered to be non-defiling, the *saikaishū* was responsible for "polluting" duties such as guarding the graves (*hakamori*).[82]

Hosokawa's argument in the case of the *saikaishū* is illuminating because it illustrates the degree to which one's access to certain precepts was bound up with one's social status. Hosokawa shows that in the case of Tōshōdaiji, many members of the *saikaishū* were local villagers (*muranin*). While these men were granted a place in the temple community, they were not given the opportunity to advance through the same hierarchies. In the case of Saidaiji, the *saikaishū* likely consisted of farmers.[83] This group was responsible for carrying out much of the "dirty work" that higher-ranking Saidaiji priests presumably wanted to avoid.[84] In fact, some scholars have suggested that one's access to various conferral rites was largely determined by one's social class.[85] Ordination as a full monastic may have been limited to the elite; namely, to those who were educated and who had ties to the capital or to Kamakura. People who had grown up in the countryside but who had had access to education and who had some connection to the capital likely would have had the opportunity to advance from *gyōdō shami/shamini* to *hōdō shami/shamini* and perhaps even to full monk or nun-hood. But locals without impressive ties—farmers, low-level warriors, and local landholders—appear to have been barred, though unofficially, from attaining high ranks within the order. Farmers, who represented the lowest level of social class and education, were most likely restricted to the *saikaishū*. Those of a slightly higher status may have been given the opportunity to become *gyōdō shami/shamini* but were restricted from advancing to the status of *hōdō shami/shamini.*

Nevertheless, prospective members of Eison's movement appear not to have been discouraged by the fact that their social class would largely determine their opportunities within the order. Rigid social distinctions were, after all, such an entrenched part of medieval Japanese society that we can hardly expect would-be Vinaya-School precept recipients to have doubted the validity of class-based discrimination. Farmers who joined the vinaya-revival movement as members of the *saikaishū* must have found the position appealing on several fronts, despite the fact that it involved work with the dead. Membership in the group would have enabled them to build great stores of karmic merit, to live on temple grounds as a part of a learned community with ties to the capital, to have access to powerful ritual performances on a regular basis, and to interact with men and women deemed holy. The opportunity to participate in this rich culture, in however limited a way, surely outweighed any disadvantages associated with handling corpses.

The big picture: precept conferral, merit, and Eison's new model of lay–monastic relations

Precept-conferral ceremonies in China and Japan, and especially the bodhisattva precepts ceremony, built on the notion that the conferral of the precepts produced mystical and immeasurable merit similar to that created by those who made the decision to leave home. Texts such as the *Xianyu jing* and the *Foshuo chujia gongde jing* explicitly state that the merit of leaving home far exceeds the merit of all other Buddhist activities. Mass bodhisattva precept ceremonies enabled great numbers of laypeople both to access vast merit and to allay fears associated with death without leaving home.

As we have seen, mass precept-conferral ceremonies did not become common in Japan until the late Heian and early Kamakura periods, when priests like Shunjō, Myōe, and Shōkū began to administer precepts to large groups of laypeople. Eison's use of the precept-conferral ceremony introduced many innovations, innovations that undoubtedly played key roles in the overwhelming growth of his movement. First of all, as mentioned before, Eison and his disciples performed precept-conferral ceremonies constantly and in a wide variety of locations. Unlike earlier Japanese priests, who tended to administer the precepts on a less frequent basis, typically at fixed locations and times, Eison and his disciples made the bestowal of precepts upon laypeople a central focus of their movement, performing conferrals unceasingly and in often in remote or unorthodox locations. Second, Eison used the precept-conferral ceremonies in a more complex fashion. While earlier priests had administered the precepts to laypeople primarily as a means of granting devotees the opportunity to create some merit for themselves, Eison's ordinations added to this long-accepted view of the conferral upon laypeople a second meaning: his conferrals could also be used to bestow specific ranks and roles upon those receiving the precepts. While some of Eison's recipients did opt to take only the bodhisattva precepts so they could store up merit for themselves, others wanted to go a step further, to place themselves even closer to the ideal of leaving home. Eison's group made *betsuju* conferrals available to those who wanted to take this extra step. These devotees thus had the opportunity to establish a more enduring bond with the monastic community and, of course, to create even greater merit.

In a sense, Eison's decision to expand the order by creating new categories of membership is suggestive of inclusiveness found in the *Xianyu jing*. When the 100-year-old Sirī-vaddhi travels to the Bamboo Grove and announces his desire to leave home, he is first dismissed as an inappropriate candidate for tonsure. But when the Buddha appears, he immediately grants Sirī-vaddhi's wish. No one, however unsuitable for monastic life he or she may appear to be, is to be denied the merit of leaving home.

Surely most Buddhist priests living in Japan would have considered unlettered farmers to be the most unlikely candidates for ordination. In finding a way to include uneducated laypeople into his order, Eison made the merit of receiving the precepts—which was conceptually related to the merit of leaving home—available to a diverse group. An optimistic reading might suggest that Eison was attempting to approximate the spirit of inclusiveness conveyed in the Buddha's response to Sirī-vaddhi. An important distinction puts all comparison to rest, however. If one were to consider the situation crudely, as Śāriputra did, the Buddha's order had little to gain from the inclusion of a 100-year-old man who would likely become ill, require medical treatment, pass away, and then require memorial services all before he had made any contribution to the order. Eison's group, by contrast, had everything to gain from the inclusion of local farmers. In creating the *saikaishū*, Eison created a devoted workforce that enabled his movement to grow. Yes, local farmers and other commoners who would have otherwise had few opportunities to participate in the practice of home-leaving were given a chance to join the Saidaiji community and to access the merit of monastic life. But in return they provided a service crucial to the success of Saidaiji's expansion into the countryside: they handled the dead, enabling the higher echelons of Vinaya priests to offer great numbers of funerals throughout the countryside, an activity that helped the movement gain an even stronger hold in the countryside.

The successful expansion of Eison's Saidaiji Vinaya movement is surely attributable to his innovative uses of the precepts. Eison used the precepts not only to bestow merit upon laypeople, but also as a way of integrating a diverse range of people—elite and non-elite, educated and uneducated, cosmopolitan and provincial—into the membership of his order. At the top, the popularity of his precept-conferral ceremonies enabled him to win the political and economic support of court and warrior elites who simply wanted to partake in the merit of receiving the precepts. On the ground, however, the ceremonies enabled his group to incorporate ordinary laypeople in the countryside. Through the rites of precept conferral, Eison established powerful links between local lay communities and his Saidaiji-based monastic order. The most obvious illustration of this coming together, of course, lies in the fact that the conferrals brought the two groups together for ritual performances. But on a more profound level, Eison's use of various levels of precept conferral expanded the scope of the monastic order and created a spectrum of possible roles within it. Since many of these roles could not be unambiguously labeled as monastic or lay, their very existence obscured the distinction between monks and the laity. In this sense, Eison's system of precept conferral offered a new model of lay–monastic interaction and interdependence. Although Eison's group was clearly hierarchical, the fact that it created so many positions and opportunities for laypeople (even if some of these methods of inclusion might today be viewed as exploitative) must have greatly contributed to its success in the countryside. If the precept-conferral ritual can be understood as a form of cultural or spiritual capital, then Eison's skillful use of that capital was surely unprecedented.

Notes

1 This chapter was previously published in *Numen* 56.1 (January 2009). I would like to thank the editorial staff of *Numen,* as well as Brill, *Numen*'s publisher, for generously allowing me to reprint the article in this volume. Thanks are also due to John R. McRae, Jacqueline Stone, Jinhua Chen, Paul Groner, Ryūichi Abé, Minowa Kenryō, and Katsuura Noriko.

2 What, exactly, constituted *shukke* status often remained ambiguous, especially in Japan. In China, government control over the ordination process allowed for standardization, and only those who had received ordination certificates were recognized as *shukke*. In Japan, however, many laypeople declared themselves *shukke* simply by shaving their hair (or, in the case of women, cropping their hair) and donning monastic robes. Although the Japanese state also made attempts to control the *shukke* process by implementing an ordination certificate system based on Chinese models, its control of the process had grown lax by the middle years of the Heian period, when many aristocrats began to style themselves as *shukke*, often without official ordination certificates. From at least the mid-Heian-period forward, then, *shukke* as practiced among those in courtly social circles did not necessarily involve the abandoning of secular life, the joining of a monastic community, or even participation in a formal ceremony.

3 Mair (Forthcoming) demonstrates that *The Sūtra of the Wise and the Foolish* was compiled by Chinese monks who had been studying Buddhism in Khotan. He further shows that the basic content of the sutra is based on Indic materials disseminated in Khotan. In particular, *The Sutra of the Wise and the Foolish* shows substantial overlap with the *Jātakamālā* of the poet Haribhaṭṭa; with variants of the *Daśa-karmapatha-avadānamālā* found in Central Asian languages; and with the Khotanese *Jātaka-stava*.

4 T. 4.376b3–16.

5 T. 4.376c27.

6 T. 4.77a16–b1.

7 T. 4.76c13.

8 Kashiwahara 1998: 58c.

9 See, for example, *Genpei jōsuiki* chapters 9 and 43.

10 See, for example, *Pusazang jing* 菩薩藏經, T. 24.1089a1, and Guanding's *Pusajie yishu* 菩薩戒義疏, T. 40.569a2.

11 According to the Tendai school, its *endonkai*, or "perfect and sudden precepts," embodied the essence of all forms of the precepts, including the traditional vinaya precepts, the Mahāyāna bodhisattva precepts, and the esoteric *sanmaya* precepts. The Tendai school used its *endonkai* both to ordain monks and for precept conferrals upon laypeople. For a fuller explanation of the *endonkai*, see Bodiford 2005b: 12–13, and Stone 1999: 18–19, 126–128.

12 Lee 1969: 77.

13 Lee 1969: 77, n. 379.

14 The *sanmaya* precepts refer to four vows to be taken by those preparing for esoteric initiation (*kanjō* 灌頂, Skt. *abhiṣeka*). Candidates are to promise that they will not do any of the following: (1) abandon the True Dharma; (2) abandon their *bodhicitta*, or aspiration to attain enlightenment; (3) treat the True Dharma with stinginess or petty-mindedness; (4) commit any action that harms sentient beings. Fukuda 2001: 93a.

15 *Jikakudaishiden*, vol. 8b: 691b, 693b–694a, 696b.

16 Okano 1998: 81.

17 Mitsuhashi 2000: 394–400, 437, 497–499, 511, 531, 771.

18 *Toganoo Myōe Shōnin denki*, 354–355. In some other versions of the story, Myōe gives the precepts to Kenreimon'in (d. 1213) rather than Shikikenmon'in (d. 1251).

19 Yamabe 2005: 21.

20 Cf. Shinohara 1994: 81–90.

21 McRae 2005: 87–88.

22 *Sanbōe kotoba* 3:20. Translation from Edward Kamens 1988: 321.

23 Translation from Kamens 1988: 321.

24 For a more detailed explanation of annual ordination ceremonies at major temples, see Matsuo 1995, esp. pp. 196–214.

25 *Meigetsuki*, 28–29. I follow Richard Bowring's interpretation of "hinin" here. See Bowring 2005: 256.

26 *Sennyūji fukaki hōshiden*, 45–58. See, for example, p. 46b.

27 See, for example, *Sennyūji fukaki hōshiden*, pp. 46b, 48-49, 53, 56.

28 *Sennyūji fukaki hōshiden*, 53.

29 Shunjō's disciples further exploited the priest's close ties to the imperial house. His disciple Tankai, in particular, followed in his master's footsteps, spending time in Song China and then returning to Japan with a variety of Buddhist treasures. Among that which he brought back to Japan was a relic of the Buddha's tooth, which he used to attract court patronage. Tankai took the relic to court for a *degaichō* 出開帳. Various imperial personages, including the Retired Emperor and Imperial Ladies, worshiped the relic, and once the relic was installed at Sennyūji, it attracted the pilgrimage of numerous court aristocrats. *Sennyūji fukaki hōshiden*, 53.

30 Tanabe 2000: 99–100.

31 For recent work on Buddhist ceremonies in medieval Japan, see Satō 1994; Nagamura 2001; and Uejima 2004.

32 *Jukaie* can also be written 授戒会, in which case it means "precepts-bestowing ceremony." Different characters are used depending on the perspective of the subject.

33 Getz 2005: 161–162.

34 Getz 2005: 167.

35 Getz 2005: 179.

36 *Shien Shōnin donin gyōhō kechige ki*, 212–215.

37 *Kongō Busshi Eison kanjin gakushōki* [Hereafter *KJGSK*]. The first two (of the three) sections also appear in a volume edited by Hosokawa (1999).

38 Inoue 1971: 14.

39 Shinohara 1994: 81–90.

40 Scholars believe that this manual was first written in 1290, right around the time of Eison's death. According to Minowa (1999: 65–66), the manual appears to reflect the procedures used by Eison himself in conferrals of the bodhisattva precepts. Cf. Minowa 1996a: 66.

41 Ōishi 2001: 44.

42 Quoted and trans. in Watt 1999: 96 (translation altered slightly).

43 Minowa 1999: 450.

44 *Kantō ōkanki*, 67–91.

45 Ōishi 2001: 44.

46 Ōishi 2001: 42.
47 Sawa 1990.
48 Hosokawa 1987: 85–86.
49 Bodiford 1993: 163–184.
50 *KJGSK*, Bun'ei 6. The text refers to the "shōdai" relics, most likely referring to relics that had been installed at the temple Tōshōdaiji. Ruppert (2000) mentions some of the relics linked to Tōshōdaiji (pp. 61, 180, 194, 216).
51 *KJGSK*, Bun'ei 6.
52 *KJGSK*, Bun'ei 6.
53 *KJGSK*, 43.
54 See *KJGSK*, 45–48; and the *Saidai chokushi kōshōbosatsu gyōjitsu nenpu*, 169–172.
55 *KJGSK*, 51.
56 *Saidai chokushi kōshō bosatsu gyōjitsu nenpu*, 177, 179.
57 *KJGSK*, 56.
58 Minowa 1996a: 71.
59 Minowa 1996b: 61b.
60 A chant in which three beings or concepts are recognized and honored.
61 According to Minowa (1996a: 62b), the *ānāpāna-smṛti*, or breath-counting meditation, was not included in Tendai precept-conferral manuals. This unusual element likely points to the influence of Zen thought and practice within medieval Nara circles.
62 i.e., to those masters participating in the present ceremony.
63 In this instance the Five Mysterious Masters refer to Śākyamuni (as the *wajō* 和尚); the Bodhisattva Mañjuśrī (as the bodhisattva precepts *ajari*); the Buddha Maitreya (as the instructional preceptor, *jiaoshou shi* 教授師); the Buddhas of the Ten Directions (as the Witnesses 証戒尊師); and all bodhisattvas (as Dharma Companions 同法侶). This step was based on the Tendai bodhisattva ordination manual 授菩薩戒法 (See Minowa 1996a: 83b).
64 In Japanese Buddhist liturgies, "Zange," typically refers to the chanting of the "zange verse" (*zange mon* 懺悔文), a line found in the *Huayan jing* 華嚴經 (T. no. 293, Skt. *Avataṃsaka-sūtra*) Chapter on the Vows of Samantabhadra 普賢行願品:

我昔所造諸惡業
皆由無始貪瞋痴
從身語意之所生
一切我今皆懺悔 (T. 10.847a16–17).
The evil karma I created in the past
All came from desire, hatred, and ignorance, which are without beginning,
And were born of [my] body, speech, and mind.
For all [my evil deeds] I now repent.

65 "Konma" is a transliteration of *karma*; as such, it means "deed" or "action." In this particular usage it refers to ritual procedures standardized within vinaya lineages (Entry for "羯磨," *Digital Dictionary of Buddhism*).
66 Minowa 1996a: 71.
67 For a more comprehensive introduction to Japanese Buddhist chant, see Hill 1982.
68 Minowa 1996a: 71–72.
69 Minowa 1996a: 72.
70 Minowa 1996b.
71 Minowa 1999: xiv–xv, 316–330, 372–381. These texts are mentioned in the first note of the Introduction.
72 Minowa 1996b, esp. pp. 78–81. Daoxuan's *Jiemoshu* 羯磨疏, for example, uses much of the language that Eison invokes (*gyōdō shami, hōdō shami*). See Minowa 1999: 321.
73 The five precepts for the laity are the first five of the ten novice precepts: no killing, no stealing, no inappropriate sexual behavior, no lying, and no drinking of alcohol.

74 See *Jubosatsukai deshi kōmyō*, 372–379; *Gonjū nannyo kōmyō*, 379–383; and Matsuo 1996.
75 Personal e-mail communication with Minowa, December 15, 2006.
76 Minowa 1999: 316–330. The *hassaikai* include the five lay precepts, plus (6) no adorning the body, listening to music, or dancing; (7) no sleeping on a high, wide bed; and (8) no eating at forbidden times.
77 Minowa 1999: 316–330; xiv–xv.
78 Minowa 1996b: 90.
79 Minowa 1996a: 65.
80 The five layperson's precepts, plus (6) not eating during forbidden times; (7) not adorning the body; (8) not partaking in song and dance; (9) not sleeping on a high, wide bed; and (10) not possessing valuables.
81 Minowa 1999: 316–330; xiv–xv.
82 Hosokawa 1987: 11–24.
83 Minowa 1999: 338.
84 Hosokawa 1987: 11–24.
85 See, for example, Ōishi 1997: 187.

7 Kōen and the "consecrated ordination" within Japanese Tendai

Paul Groner

Introduction

The Japanese Tendai School of the late Heian and Kamakura periods is often stereotyped as a monolithic institution that persecuted the newly emerging schools of Kamakura Buddhism. Terms such as "secularization" are used to characterize its interest in political, economic, and military power. Doctrinal traditions such as "original enlightenment" (*hongaku* 本覚) and a complex of Exoteric and Esoteric Buddhism (*kenmitsu taisei* 顕密体制) are said to have provided the intellectual foundations for these developments. In this chapter, I focus on one monk, Kōen 興円 (1262 or 1263–1317), who serves as a counter-example to many of these stereotypes. Sources that are similar to those employed by William Bodiford elsewhere in this volume to discuss first-hand accounts of monasticism are used; however, many of the documents considered in this essay are more prescriptive than descriptive. Because Kōen's movement was a small one, the distinction made by James Robson and others between larger monasteries and smaller institutions such as hermitages is instructive. However, Kōen certainly had aspirations of making his reforms to Tendai broader based and perhaps applying them to large monasteries.

Kōen was an important member of the Kurodani lineage of the Tendai School, a group that traced its lineage back to Hōnen 法然 (1133–1212), the founder of the Jōdo School. By Kōen's time, the lineage was clearly strengthening its ties with the Tendai School, rather than the Jōdo School.

Kōen and the Kurodani lineage present a significant counterexample to stereotypes to the usual image of medieval Tendai for several reasons. First, the Kurodani lineage was an example of a Tendai group that stressed adherence to the precepts, and thus differed from Tendai groups that interpreted the precepts in such an abstract fashion that they ceased to be relevant to the everyday lives of monks. Other monks within the Tendai tradition also stressed the importance of monastic discipline; among them were Eisai 栄西 (1141–1215), Shunjō 俊芿 (1166–1227) and Jitsudō Ninkū 実導仁空 (1307–1388).

Second, the arguments on the precepts within the Kurodani lineage are based on teachings of original enlightenment (*hongaku* 本覚), a tradition that is often thought of as contributing to the laxness in monastic discipline. Because this lineage stressed the importance of monastic discipline, it serves as an example of the complexity and multi-faceted nature of medieval Tendai thought. Kōen's biography illustrates some of the mechanisms used by Tendai monks to arrive at a variety of interpretations of the precepts. The documents from the Kurodani lineage can often be dated and are usually attributed to their actual authors, thus providing scholars with benchmarks in their efforts to date other texts that have been attributed to past figures. The emphasis on dreams and revelations from major figures of the past that is found in Kōen's biography stands in stark contrast with the approach used by other Tendai monks emphasizing monastic discipline who stressed a careful analysis of authentic documents by major Tendai thinkers. Among the latter type are Hōchibō Shōshin 法地房証真 (1131?–1215?) and Jitsudō Ninkū. Kōen's dreams provide us with a different dimension than those mentioned by Robson in the Introduction to this volume. Instead of using dreams to found or locate monasteries, Kōen used them to justify the revival of traditions that he traced back to Saichō.

Third, the Kurodani lineage of the Tendai School differed from other precepts revival movements because the monks of the Kurodani lineage looked back to Saichō 最澄 (767–822), the founder of the Tendai School, instead of at Indian and Chinese models.[1] In addition, the monks of the Kurodani lineage are noteworthy for another reason; Tendai *hongaku* thought is often explained as providing a rationale that enabled Tendai monks to abandon monastic discipline because it suggested that people were enlightened just as they are and had little or no need for practice. In fact, *hongaku* thought included a variety of positions on religious practice.

The Kurodani lineage represents one of the most conservative positions in the *hongaku* tradition because of its emphasis on the importance of the precepts, a position that is clearly pointed out in a discussion of the "precepts in principle" (*rikai* 理戒) in the medieval text cited below. The concept of precepts in principle can be thought of as an extension to ideas that have been present in Buddhism since its earliest times. The Buddha was said to embody the precepts even before they had been specified. In other words, realizations of enlightenment or the attainment of certain meditative states indicated that the practitioner might naturally embody the precepts. In medieval Tendai, similar ideas were found, but with the difference that such natural embodiments of the precepts were believed to occur in people with low levels of religious attainment by virtue of their inherent nature. Such ideas are exemplified in an Eshin 恵心 lineage text dated 1501, Sonshun's 尊舜 (1451–1514) *Nichōshō kenmon* 二帖抄見聞. Sonshun begins by describing his own lineage's position, one that subordinated any adherence to the precepts to realization of certain teachings.

> According to this (Eshin) lineage, there should be no ordination ceremony of the Perfect precepts other than the three views in a single instant (*isshin sankan* 一心三観). This lineage maintains the position that the vehicle and the precepts are identical and that the three trainings are non-dual. . . . What is it that we refer to as the true essence of the Perfect precepts? It is simply to adhere to the *Lotus Sūtra*. The three views in a single instant are found in the term "wondrous Dharma" (*myōhō* 妙法, the first two characters of the *sūtra's* title).[2]

A member of the Eshin lineage need only follow the *Lotus Sūtra*. The Kurodani lineage's position was based on *hongaku* positions similar to those of the Eshin lineage. For example both groups argued that the three learnings (*sangaku* 三学) were non-dual—in other words, that any one of the elements of morality, meditation, and wisdom could be identified with the other two. However, they differed about which of the three learnings should be emphasized. The Kurodani lineage stressed the importance of decorum and the precepts. Sonshun continued on to describe the Kurodani position:

> The precepts and meditation are not confused. The three views in an instant is a discernment of realization of one's nature (*naishō no kanmon* 内証観門). The precepts are identical with the decorum found in their details and their maintenance. Even if one's meditation and wisdom of inherent nature is clear, without the decorum that arises from the precepts, then the principles of Buddhism will not be manifested.[3]

Thus the Kurodani lineage also argued that the precepts arose from one's inherent nature, but the Kurodani differed from the Eshin lineage in stressing the importance of adhering to the precepts so that the principles of Buddhism might be manifested. Moreover, Kurodani monks argued that Saichō included separate lineages for these transmissions in his *Naishō buppō kechimyakufu* in order to indicate that the precepts should not be subordinated to an abstract principle.[4]

Fourth, the Kurodani lineage offers important insights into how *hongaku* ideas were used ritually. The "consecrated ordination" (*kaikanjō* 戒灌頂) ritual for which the lineage is famous is informed by *hongaku* ideas. Because many *hongaku* texts are attributed to earlier figures in Tendai history, modern scholars frequently do not have a clear idea of the social and ritual context in which these views were circulated. Although the Kurodani lineage's use of *hongaku* views is not typical of most Tendai groups because it emphasizes the importance of adherence to the precepts, it enables us to investigate the ritual context for some of these medieval views, thereby providing us with a more complex and nuanced view of medieval Tendai.

The Kurodani lineage can be traced back through a number of Tendai figures including Hōnen, the monk who is often said to be the de facto founder of the Jōdo School. This chapter focuses on Kōen, a monk who represents the Kurodani lineage when it had begun to define itself as a Tendai movement through the "consecrated ordination" ritual. The chapter is divided into three parts. The first is a biography of Kōen. Next, the rules for monasteries controlled by Kōen and the Kurodani lineage are considered. Finally, the "consecrated ordination," the ritual that gave the Kurodani lineage its unique place in Tendai, is examined.

Kōen's biography

The Kurodani lineage is based on a Tendai ordination that runs from Saichō through various monks up to Hōnen. Because Hōnen was the founder of the Jōdo School, the sectarian affiliations of several generations following him have been ambiguous. Two generations before Kōen, Gudōbō Ejin 求道房恵尋 (d. 1289) had combined Pure Land and monastic discipline early in his life. When the Tendai establishment on Mount Hiei pressed him to clarify his sectarian affiliation, he had chosen to demonstrate his loyalty to Tendai by re-establishing Saichō's plan for a twelve-year retreat on Mount Hiei. Although he only remained in the retreat for six years, his attempt and attitude were an important inspiration for Kōen. The Kurodani lineage continued with Ejin's student, Egai 恵顗 (d. 1301), Kōen's teacher.

Kōen, also known as Denshin kashō 伝信和尚, was born in Ōshū 奥州 and was a descendant of the Taira 平 clan.[5] In 1276 Kōen entered a temple, and in 1278 he was initiated as novice.[6] Kōen's initial interest in the precepts is recorded as occurring in a meeting with his teacher Enson Shōnin[7] 円存上人 in the summer of 1287. When Kōen received the teaching of the wondrous tenet of the three views in a single instant, he asked,

> According to Saichō's explanation, "The three views in a single instant are transmitted with a single word; the Perfect bodhisattva precepts are transmitted with the ultimate mind *shishin* 至心."[8] I have already heard about the three views in a single instant and have attained their original sudden import, but why have I never heard of the interpretation (*ketsu* 決) concerning the phrase "the Perfect bodhisattva precepts are conferred with ultimate faith 至信?"

His teacher replied,

> The profundities of the three views are transmitted by our lineage, but I have not heard Saichō's original intention concerning the Perfect precepts. I have heard that in Kurodani there is an illustrious teacher named the Saint Who Seeks the Way (Gudō shōnin 求道上人).[9] He is a master of the Perfect precepts who understands the *Vinaya* and preaches its teachings. You should go ask him.[10]

Around 1287 at the Konkaiin 金戒院 in Shin-kurodani, Kōen studied both Esoteric and Exoteric Buddhism as well as the precepts under Egai. Kōen then went to Kyoto and traveled to Kiyomizudera 清水寺, where he turned (*tendoku* 転読) the *Guanyinjing* 観音經 333 times each day for one thousand days. Eventually he had a dream on the day when he completed the practices (*ketsugan* 結願). In the dream the three thousand realms appeared before his eyes and the ten thousand realms were understood in a single instant.[11] The passage, of course, indicates that Kōen had realized enlightenment.

Kōen spent the next eighteen years in Shin-kurodani 新黒谷.[12] During this time, Kōen asked Egai what the basis of the precepts should be; Egai said the *Lotus Sūtra*. Further questioning revealed that it all came down to the "Chapter on the Lifespan of the Buddha" ("Juryōbon" 寿量品) of the *Lotus Sūtra*.[13] Kōen's differences with Egai are clearly revealed in the following dream recorded in Kōen's biography:

Around the same time, Kōen had a dream. In the Guest's Quarters of the old lodgings, there was a mat with a small pattern; on it sat Egai, an unidentified elder, and himself (Kōen). The three of them sat in a triangle facing each other. The [older] monk asked, "What is the essence of the precepts?'

Egai answered, "As for the precepts, they are primordial and innate (*rigu honbun* 理具本分); make no mistake about this. Your very body is the observance of the precepts (*jikai* 持戒)."

The monk said, "This view is not the same as my original view."

Next, he asked Kōen who replied, "The significance of the precepts lies in using the phenomenal to master the principle; it is the observance of the prohibitions on no killing and not stealing. If one focuses on the letter of the rules and their observance, then one will master the origins of the principle and will return to the direct path (*jikidō* 直道) to enlightenment.[14] Thus the Buddha compiled the ten major and forty-eight minor rules." The old monk agreed with Kōen.

This dream marked the beginning of Kōen's efforts to follow the precepts. Following it, he went to Saichō's mausoleum (*gobyō* 御廟) and made vows to follow the precepts.[15]

In this passage, Kōen revealed his penchant for emphasizing the literal meaning of the precepts instead of subordinating the precepts to an abstract teaching or principle. His understanding, different from that of Egai, is confirmed by the old monk who is identified in a note following the passage as none other than Saichō. The importance of dreams in Kōen's spiritual life is noteworthy. In fact, his decision to differ with his teacher was based on a dream, which made him confident that his view was in accord with Saichō.

In his writings on the "Consecrated Ordination" (*kaikanjō* 戒灌頂), Kōen discussed the significance of each item that a monk received in the ordination, a very concrete example of moving from the concrete aspects of monastic discipline to principle. Kōen's decision to go to Saichō's mausoleum to make his vow is typical of the tendency of Kamakura Buddhist traditions to emphasize the founders. In the case of the Kurodani lineage, that emphasis extended to the production of apocryphal traditions and texts concerning Saichō.[16]

On 11-22-1288, Kōen received the Perfect precepts at the Konkaikōmyōji (Light of the adamantine precepts temple) in Shin-kurodani from Egai, who said he had conferred the precepts often, but had never seen the type of faith exhibited by Kōen. Kōen would surely spread the precepts in the future. Egai said that Kōen reminded him of Saichō's disciple Enchō 円澄 (771–836).[17]

On 10-20-1305, Kōen embarked on the twelve-year confinement (*rōzan* 籠山) at the Non-retrogression Quarters (Futaibō 不退房) in Kurodani 黒谷 with Enkan 円観. Less than one month later, on 11-15-1305, Kōen vowed not to eat after the hour of noon for eons to come (*chōsai* 長斎). During this time, when Egai was about to confer the lineage of the three views in an instant of the precepts lineage (*kaike sōjō* 戒家相承) on Kōen, Kōen, without waiting for the oral instructions, began to expound his view of the three views. The teacher scolded him for not waiting for the lineage's views, but then came around to thinking that it was due to the excellence of Kōen's innate knowledge (*shōchi shūzai* 生知秀才).[18]

The three views in an instant was the subject of many of the lineages of medieval Tendai, partly because its importance had been indicated by the statement that Saichō had received a teaching concerning the three views in a single word from Daosui. In this story, Kōen seems to know the teaching from the outset and Egai only confirms his understanding. The story does more than glorify Kōen's understanding, however; it also reflects Tendai debates over whether such teachings (which are tantamount to enlightenment) must be conferred by a teacher or whether they come from one's own mind with a teacher serving only to confirm the understanding.[19]

In the fifth month of 1307, Egai dreamt about Ejin who appeared just as he had in life, but then Ejin appeared angry and scolded Egai for not conferring the *kaikanjō* on Kōen sooner.[20] The dream may well reflect the tension that seems to have been present in the relationship between the two men. Finally, on 6-11-1307, at the age of 44, Kōen received the *kaikanjō* from Egai in the Non-retrogression Lodgings at Kurodani.[21] Kōen received a number of items that had been used by Ejin that authenticated his succession to the lineage: one mirror, one box for incense; and a robe used by Zhanran 湛然 (711–782) that had been brought to Japan by Saichō.[22]

On 2-17-1308, Kōen directed his disciple Enkan 円観 (1281–1356) to move to Jinzōji 神蔵寺, a dilapidated temple in the Eastern Pagoda (Tōdō 東塔) area of Mount Hiei to continue the twelve-year seclusion alone.[23] The move back to Mount Hiei may have signaled a desire to establish his tradition as being firmly in the Tendai tradition, rather than the emerging Jōdoshū.[24] With members of his group based in the heart of Mount Hiei, the actions of Kōen and his disciples led to criticisms from Tendai monks. Ejin, Egai, and Kōen had worn robes prescribed by the monastic rules (*ritsue* 律衣). In contrast, the Tendai monks from much of the rest of Mount Hiei wore robes that might be made of raw silk, be dyed with primary colors, and have elaborate patterns. Although the *Vinaya* had not prohibited silk, Chinese monks beginning with Daoxuan 道宣 (596–667) had argued that silk should not be worn because sericulture resulted in the death of so many silkworms.[25] Monks' robes were to be dyed bland colors and have some discoloration so that they had no value. Silk robes (*soken no koromo* 素絹衣) are said to have been used by Tendai monks since the time of Ryōgen 良源 (912–985), but their origins may be as late as the middle of the thirteenth century.[26] If this is the case, then the new style of robes would have appeared around the same time that the Kurodani monks went back to an earlier and simpler style. Mainstream Tendai monks used primary (or pure) colors because the monks performed rituals for the emperor and for *kami* in which purity was required. As a result Kōen's group was criticized by other Tendai monks, but on 3-15-1309 an elder of the Chroniclers (Kike 記家), the Master of Esoteric Buddhism Gigen[27] 義源 (fl. 1289–1351) sent a letter supporting Kōen's efforts to revive the precepts. Later, on 10-25-1309, archbishop (*daisōjō*) Chōjin 澄尋, a Master of Esoteric Buddhism in the Sanmai 三昧 lineage also sent a letter sympathizing with Kōen's efforts to revive the precepts.[28] The types of robes and the decorum with which they were worn was one of the hallmarks of Buddhist monasticism.

From the first to the twelfth day of the seventh month of 1308, Kōen wrote a short text, the "Commentary concerning the the observance of the ten major and forty-eight [lesser] rules of the Perfect-Sudden bodhisattva precepts" (*Endon bosatsukai jūjū shijūhachi gyōgi shō* 円頓菩薩戒十重四十八行儀鈔). The text is a straight-forward discussion of the *Fanwang* 梵網 precepts, going through the details of how each was to be practiced. Rather than being a scholarly treatise discussing the differences in interpretations of the precepts, Kōen wrote a text as a guide for practice, relying primarily on Zhiyi's 智顗 (538–597) commentary on the *Fanwang jing* 梵網經, with occasional references to Mingguang's 明曠 (fl. 777) commentary.[29] Kōen did not call for absolute adherence to the letter of the precepts, but asked that his followers observe them to the extent that they were able to. As long as they were motivated by compassion, the inability to completely observe each precept did not constitute a violation. Although Kōen's attitude may seem lax, in the context of his times (believed by him to be the Final Dharma age), he was asking for serious and careful adherence to the precepts. Possibly because Kōen's flexibility might open his students to criticism, he cautioned that the text was to be kept secret from those who had not received the precepts, a prohibition not unlike those found in the *Vinaya* prohibiting laymen from participating or witnessing monastic rituals or the fortnightly assembly.[30] A number of Kōen's texts contain additions by his student Enkan, but serious research analyzing the similarities and differences between the thought of the two men has still not been conducted.[31]

One indication of the seriousness of Kōen's practice can be gained by a comparison with another text on the precepts compiled around the same time, Enrin's 円琳 "Subcommentary on the bodhisattva precepts" (*Bosatsu kaigi shoshō* 菩薩戒義疏鈔), completed in 1237. Enrin's text is a subcommentary based on Zhiyi's commentary on the *Fanwang jing*. It devotes considerable space to a learned discussion of the essence of the precepts (*kaitai* 戒体), taking a serious attitude towards monastic discipline. Although it is a more academic text than Kōen's work, it lacks the practical immediacy of Kōen's commentary.[32]

On 10-25-1309, Kōshū 光宗 (1276–1350) went to Jinzōji to join Enkan's twelve-year retreat. Kōen then invited Kōshū to Kurodani and on 11-6 bestowed the precepts on him.[33] Jinzōji was designated a place for the practice of the precepts. Finally, on 4-5-1310, two years after he sent Enkan to Jinzōji, Kōen moved to Jinzōji, joining Enkan, to complete the twelve years of seclusion. The move to Jinzōji may have reflected the difficulties that Kōen experienced with his teacher Egai and other monks. As was noted above, Egai seems to have been hesitant to confer the *kaikanjō* on Kōen. Perhaps Egai resented Kōen's assiduous attitude towards the precepts, an attitude that seemed more serious than that of Egai who had spent much of his time at the Konkaikōmyōji in Shin-kurodani completing the monastic complex and did not seem particularly enthusiastic about strict adherence to the precepts. Egai may also have resented Kōen's determination to complete the twelve-year retreat, a task that Egai's teacher Ejin had abandoned during his own retreat. In addition, Kōen's single-minded emphasis on the precepts may have bothered monks who were more comfortable with Shin-kurodani's traditional stance combining Pure Land and the precepts. Finally, in a vow made at the beginning of the establishment of the rainy season retreat, Kōen seems to be defending himself against possible charges that he was not loyal to Egai in his vow concerning his twelve-year retreat. Egai left Kurodani to one of his other students, Ninkū 任空 (d. 1336), rather than to Kōen; Kōen only took over Kurodani in 1314.[34]

On 4-16-1310, several days after Kōen arrived at Jinzōji, an order of five monks[35] was formed and the observance of the rainy season retreat, long ignored, began. A vow by Kōen from this time, the *Kōen kishōmon* 興円起請文 survives.[36] The vow contains a passage suggesting that some sort of dispute had occurred between Kōen and his teacher Egai, leading to the move to Jinzōji. Among those participating in the summer retreat were: Kōshū, Enkan, Junkan 順観, Tsūen 通円, and Kōen. On the 30th, they revived the fortnightly assembly with the above-named five monks. Later four other monks, Rikan 理観, Gyōen 尭円, Dōkū 道空, and Zen'a 禅阿, participated in a latter rainy season retreat, a retreat that began and ended one month after dates of the former retreat.[37]

As he progressed through the twelve-year retreat, Kōen's practices seem to have become more intense. He did not go through the carefully measured practices of monks in traditional monasteries regulated by the *Vinaya*, but rather followed the intensity of monks on a long uninterrupted period of religious austerities. The pilgrimages that he undertook near the end of his life, the conch shell that was conferred in the *kaikanjō*, and the emphasis on dreams and visions all seem more reminiscent of the search for visions of a mountain ascetic than a person committed to the administration of monastic discipline. The descriptions of the locations on Mount Hiei found in his biography reflect a sacred geography that is interpreted both in terms of the *Lotus Sūtra* and Esoteric Buddhism; these are narratives reminiscent of those found in Robson's essay on sacred mountains. The significance of mountain practices for Śākyamuni, Huisi 慧思 (515–577), Zhiyi, Saichō, Ennin 円仁 (794–864), and Ryōgen are mentioned.[38] From 10-10-1311 to 7-5-1314, Kōen performed a 1,000-day uninterrupted practice of the *goma* 護摩 with a group of twelve monks, taking turns so that someone would always be performing the ritual. Other practices conducted during this time included two periods of sitting meditation and three periods of chanting (*nenju* 念誦) each day. Kōen carved various images at this time, probably for use in some of the rituals he performed. During the eleventh month of 1312, an image of Daikokuten 大黒天 (Mahākāla), the deity for whom Kurodani was named, was carved and dedicated. In the fourth month of 1313, he refurbished the Nyohōdō 如法堂, the chapel where Ennin's 円仁 (794–864) copy of the *Lotus Sūtra* that served as the spiritual center of Yokawa was kept. Later that year, he carved and dedicated images of Mañjuśrī and the Medicine Buddha (Yakushi nyorai 薬師如来). Near the end of this period of intensive activity, in 1316, Kōen composed the *Jūroku jō kuketsu* 十六帖口訣 (Sixteen articles of oral transmission), a text that serves as an authoritative source for the early *kaikanjō*.[39]

On 1-8-1316, Kōen completed his twelve-year retreat. For the following seven days, he sequestered himself in the Kōnpon chūdō 根本中堂, the central building on Mount Hiei. From 1-16, he went to the Seiryūji 青龍寺 at Kurodani and sequestered himself there for three days. From 1-19, he made a pilgrimage to the three main areas of Mount Hiei (Santō 三塔). On 1-21, he descended Mount Hiei to the Hiyoshi 日吉 Shrine. He sequestered himself in the Nenbutsudō (Hall for the recitation of the Buddha's name) with ten monks who spent seven days chanting every line (*shindoku* 信読) of the 600-fascicle *Greater Perfection of Wisdom Sūtra* (*Da banruo jing* 大般若經).[40]

In the tenth month of 1316, Kōen went to the former palace of the Imperial Lady (Nyōin gosho 女院御所) Kita-shirakawa 北白川 (Fujiwara no Nobuko 藤原陳子, d. 1238), where he lectured on the *Mohe zhiguan*. The building was later turned into the Gennōji 元応寺. During this time, he also strove to rebuild a variety of buildings on Mount Hiei.

During the first month of 1317, he announced that he was 55 and would not live much longer, noting that Saichō had died at about the same age;[41] the years of intense practice had clearly taken their toll. Shortly thereafter he conferred the "consecrated ordination" on Enkan. During the third month of 1317, he prepared the platforms for the transmissions of the three advanced consecrations in Taimitsu (*sanbu kanjō kyōkadan* 三部潅頂許可壇) for Shōzu 承頭 and others. In the fourth month of 1317, he performed the Yugi 瑜祇 consecration, an advanced conse-cration initiating his students into the teaching that womb and diamond realms were non-dual. He then went on a pilgrimage during which he lectured at Taishakuji 帝釈寺 on 4-25 and died the following day.[42]

Kōen's biography included a consideration of his activities concerning the precepts in the light of other efforts to revive the precepts:

> In 753, Jianzhen 鑑真 (699–763, Jpn. Ganjin) came to Japan; he established an ordination platform in 754. In 822, Saichō's ordination platform was built. Sixty-nine years had elapsed between the two events. In 1236, Eison revived the Nara precepts (*kaihō* 戒法). In 1304, Kōen revived the Tendai precepts. In each case seventy years had elapsed between the two events; this can certainly be called "inexplicable." In addition, Saichō's lifespan was fifty-six years; Kōen's was fifty-five years. In this time of the decline of the Dharma, it has declined by one year; this seems natural. Who wouldn't call this wondrous?[43]

Jianzhen had brought the first Tendai texts to Japan and had interpreted the pre-cepts with teachings from the *Lotus Sūtra*. Even though Saichō rejected the ordina-tion system that Jianzhen had brought to Japan, Jianzhen had been respected by the Tendai tradition. The comparison of Jianzhen and Eison reveals a certain respect for Eison, even though Kōen and his followers did not accept his interpretation of the precepts. In particular, Eison's self-ordination and the emphasis on dreams and spe-cial signs from the Buddha must have impressed Kōen and his followers. Eison's autobiography reveals a number of dreams and experiences that contributed to his self-confidence; similar experiences are found in Kōen's biography. Moreover, the earnestness of Eison's practice and proselytizing must also have impressed Kōen and his followers.

Kōen's plan for the twelve-year confinement

In 1309, during the fourth year of his retreat on Mount Hiei, Kōen wrote the "Collection of rules concerning the rise of solely Mahāyāna temples" (*Ikkō daijōji kōryū henmoku shū* 一向大乘寺興隆篇目集) in one fascicle. In the text, Kōen discussed monastic life for the students under his supervision, clearly relying on the rules Saichō had propounded several centuries earlier. Because few detailed collections of rules for Tendai monasteries survive from this period, the text provides insight into how some Tendai monasteries might have been structured at that time; however, little evidence exists demonstrating that the plans were actually carried out. The text is divided into the following seven sections:

1   Because solely Mahāyāna temples are appropriate for the latter period of the Dharma, they should be established in Japan and propagate the Mahāyāna precepts.
2   An image of Mañjuśrī as a monk should replace Pindola as the head (*jōza* 上座) of a solely Mahāyāna monastery.
3   The reasons why the bodhisattva precepts are superior to the Hīnayāna precepts and details concerning their practice.
4   The full bodhisattva precepts should be conferred at the beginning of the twelve-year confinement.
5   A description of the daily life and practices of those studying Tendai and Esoteric Buddhism.
6   A description of the officials and their duties at the temple.
7   A chart of the layout of the monastery and a list of the images to be installed at the various halls.

The text is primarily based on Kōen's teachings with additions by his disciple Enkan. The first four sections of the text take the form of comments on Saichō's "Rules in four articles" (*Shijōshiki* 四条式). At times, it also refers to Saichō's "Rules in six articles" (*Rokujōshiki* 六条式) and "Treatise revealing the precepts" (*Kenkairon* 顕戒論). However, while Saichō's works focused on defending his proposals for a purely Mahāyāna ordination against the attacks of his Nara critics, Kōen's text has a very different emphasis, reviving and adapting Saichō's plan to have his monks sequestered on Mount Hiei for twelve years. Thus the last three articles concern the ritual life and administrative structure that Kōen wished to establish on Mount Hiei; these were issues that Saichō had not considered in sufficient detail because of his early death.

The text represents one of the first attempts to revive Saichō's plans for Mount Hiei. It fits in with Matsuo Kenji's statement that one of the characteristics of "new Kamakura Buddhism" was the veneration of the founders of the schools and a renewed interest in their teachings.[44] In this sense, Kōen's movement differs from many other medieval monks who compiled new texts that they attributed to Saichō or who ignored much of what Saichō wrote even though they might honor him in the abstract as a patriarch of the school.

Kōen's text differs from Saichō's position even as it claims to return to his system in several noteworthy ways. Kōen, like many of his contemporaries, believed that he was living during the Final Dharma age (*mappō* 末法). Saichō, in contrast, had believed that he lived during the last part of the Semblance of the Dharma age (*zōmatsu* 像末). For Kōen, *mappō* was a time when only the teaching of Tendai meditation remained; no one practiced or realized enlightenment. Although ordinations might be conducted, no one actually observed the precepts themselves. People were lazy in their religious observances. As a result, both Buddhism and the state declined.[45] Like Saichō and numerous Tendai monks after him, Kōen linked Buddhism to the protection of the state. Kōen's solution to the religious and secular problems of *mappō* lay in the revival of the three trainings: morality, meditation, and wisdom. Because morality was the foundation of the three trainings, the precepts were to be emphasized above the other two. As Kōen wrote,

> Because we have entered the Final Dharma age, the three trainings (*san-gaku* 三学) of the Perfect School should flourish. They are the direct path to Buddhahood for sentient beings and teachings by which the times and the faculties of sentient beings can be brought into accord. Without the resplendent power of the purely Perfect three trainings, how will sentient beings during this period of the five pollutions be able to avoid endless eons (of suffering and practice) and realize Buddhahood with this very body?[46]

Saichō had made a provision in his "Rules in four articles" that Tendai monks might take a Hīnayāna ordination as an expedient (*keju shōkai* 仮受小戒) to benefit sentient beings after they had completed their training on Mount Hiei. Kōen goes to considerable length to explain why this should not be the case. Moreover, Tendai monks should not live in "mixed" temples; in other words, they should not stay in monasteries together with those who followed the Hīnayāna precepts. The result was a thorough and complete repudiation of the Hīnayāna precepts that went beyond that proposed by Saichō.[47] With few exceptions, the Tendai School had not adopted Saichō's proposal to allow "Hīnayāna" ordinations and the issue had ceased to be an issue for most Tendai monks in the Heian period. The effort Kōen expends in criticizing them was probably a response to the Tendai monk Shunjō's adoption of the Hīnayāna ordinations at Sennyūji 泉涌寺 in Kyoto.[48]

The longest section of the text concerned the bodhisattva precepts for the fully ordained monk (*bosatsu daisōkai* 菩薩大僧戒). The section begins with a consideration of the precepts used to initiate novices. Saichō had simply stated that the Perfect ten good precepts (*en jūzenkai* 円十善戒) should be used. However, this ambiguous term had allowed various interpretations during subsequent centuries, notably the ten good precepts (*jūzenkai* 十善戒), the ten precepts in the *Vinaya* traditionally used to initiate novices (*jū shamikai* 十沙弥戒), and the ten major precepts of the *Fanwang jing* (*jūjūkai* 十重戒). Kōen noted that other precepts were also used such as the five lay precepts and partial sets of the ten major precepts. He concluded that the ten good precepts were the set that should be used. However, a note (*uragaki* 裏書き), possibly by Enkan, argued that a follower of the Perfect

Teaching need not even pass through the stage of being a novice and should simply become a monk.[49]

The precepts for a full-fledged monk consisted of the serene and pleasant activities (*anrakugyō* 安楽行) from the *Lotus Sūtra*, three collections of pure precepts (*sanju jōkai* 三聚浄戒), and the *Fanwang* precepts.[50] Kōen thus followed the tradition that combined the *Lotus Sūtra* and *Fanwang jing*, but emphasized the importance of actually following the provisions of the *Fanwang* precepts rather than subordinating the specific requirements of the precepts to abstract principles, the approach that was used when the *Lotus Sūtra* was given prominence in the interpretation of the precepts. This emphasis is developed in Kōen's discussion of fasting after the hour of noon (*chōsai* 長斎). After reviewing the various practices followed by both lay and monastic believers, options that required fasting on certain days or certain months, Kōen concluded that the monks should always fast after noon. He notes that because some pious lay believers do so, monks should not refuse to follow this practice. Moreover, he noted that because both the lay donor and the monk would incur a karmic penalty if the monk ate after noon, the monk should take pains to protect his lay patron by following this rule.

Kōen followed the *Fanwang jing* in requiring his followers to possess the following eighteen items, a list found only in the *Fanwang jing*: a stick to clean their teeth, cleansing powder, three robes, pot, bowl, cloth for sitting or lying down, staff, censer, net for filtering water, cloth for wiping hands, razor, implements for lighting fires, tweezer for removing nose hair, stool for sitting, sūtras, rules, Buddha images, and bodhisattva images.[51]

The schedule of events at the monastery was divided into three lists: daily, monthly, and yearly. The daily schedule at the monastery was as follows:

One should ceaselessly (*fudan* 不断) perform the three extensive lectures[52] and recite the secret mantras in the inner sanctum (*naijin* 内陣) of the main hall (*hondō* 本堂) in order to protect the nation.

5–7 a.m. sitting meditation in the refectory (*jikidō* 食堂);

When light appears in the east, gruel is eaten;

After the gruel has been eaten, confession and vows are recited;

11 a.m.–1 p.m. rice is eaten;

1–3 p.m. the great discussion of doctrine (*daidangi* 大談義) is held in the Lecture Hall;

5–6 p.m. Concluding service (*shūreiji* 終例時), [usually consisting of the recitation of the *Amituo jing* 阿弥陀經 and the *nenbutsu*];

7–9 p.m. sitting meditation in the refectory.

After sitting meditation, those who seriously practice should enter study halls to ponder Exoteric and Esoteric doctrines. Practitioners should remain in the refectory for (additional) sitting meditation. The amount of time for rest is left to the needs of the individual.[53]

The monthly calendar specified that fortnightly assemblies be held. In addition, each month was divided into three periods. During the first, lectures dedicated to the main image (*honzon* 本尊) were held, with three questions being asked for each lecture. The second period included lectures and questions dedicated to the guardian deities of Mount Hiei (Sannō 山王), and the third period had sets of lectures and questions dedicated to the founders of the school. Face-to-face debates (*tsugai rongi* 番論議) were scheduled during these three periods.[54] Debate thus played a major role in the training of the monks and was frequently conducted throughout the year. In addition, other debates were scheduled on certain days throughout the year, such as the anniversaries of the deaths of Ennin and Saichō.[55]

The annual calendar included a number of lectures and debates dedicated to figures that had played major roles in Tendai history. They are listed below with the dates on which they were held.

1–8: Assembly for the benevolent king (Ninnōe 仁王会), consisting of one hundred monks[56]

1–14: Offerings to the *maṇḍala* in honor of Ennin; examinations

2–15: Nirvāṇa assembly

4–8: Buddha's birthday

4–16: beginning of summer retreat

6–4: assembly in honor of Saichō, consisting of lectures with five questions for each lecture (*ichiza gomon* 一坐五問), two one-on-one debates, and offerings to the *maṇḍala* at night

7–8: week-long observance of the assembly of the primordial vows (Hongan-e 本願会), consisting of lectures with five questions for each lecture (*ichiza gomon* 一坐五問), two one-on-one debates, and offerings to hungry ghosts (*segaki* 施餓鬼) at night

7–15: dissolution of summer retreat, accompanied by elementary Esoteric consecrations (*kechien kanjō* 結縁灌頂) and a "summer fortnightly assembly" (*kefusatsu* 夏布薩).[57]

10–16: beginning of winter retreat (*fuyu ango* 冬安居; ends on 1–15)[58]

11th month: four days (eight lectures) in honor of Zhiyi 智顗[59]

In the sixth section of the text, Kōen outlined a detailed administrative structure consisting of seventeen men. The abbot (*chōrō* 長老) was the head of the monastery in both secular and religious affairs; two attendants assisted him: one who aided him in secular affairs and one who helped him with religious issues.

Seven men were classified as directors (*shijin* 司人):

1 Vice-abbot (*gon-chōrō* 権長老), received orders from the abbot and carried out Buddhist services at the monastery; aided the abbot in carrying out duties and encouraged the monks in their religious practices and studies.

2 Principal (*daigakutō* 大学頭), administered the annual religious observances and the monthly lectures; recorded the results of the examinations and the debates and deposited those records in the library (*hōzō* 法蔵).

3 Vice-principal (*shōgakutō* 小学頭), administered the daily lectures (*dangi* 談義).

4 Librarian (*zōsu* 蔵司).
5 Precentor (*ina* 維那), in charge of the fortnightly assembly and other religious ceremonies (*tsutome* 勤).
6 Guest prefect (*shika* 知客) in charge of arrivals and departures of guests and the travels of resident monks.
7 Verger (*densu* 殿主), oversaw the adornments in front of the images at such major halls as the Golden Hall and Lecture Hall; coordinated the offerings of incense and flowers.

The following seven administrators (*chiji* 知事) are listed:

1–2 Functionaries in charge of collecting rents from temple lands and receiving offerings from lay believers. These monks would then distribute these in accordance with need.
3 Head cook (*tenzo* 典坐).
4 Administrator in charge of construction and clearing land (*eizōshi* 営造司).
5 Bath house administrator (*yokushu* 浴主).
6 Water steward (*chisui* 知水) in charge of filtering water and ascertaining that no insects are found in it.
7 Sanitation steward (*jōtō* 浄頭), oversees the latrines.[60]

Debate played a major role in promotion to the various offices. For example, the vice-principal (*shōgakutō* 小学頭), the fourth-ranking official in the monastery, was in charge of the daily lectures on doctrine. He was required to have held the post of lecturer at the Lecture Hall one time. After that, he was to hold positions as lecturer in several of the major events on Mount Hiei (*suigō* 遂業).[61] After serving as vice-principal, he could be appointed principal, and finally after serving one term as principal, he could be appointed as vice-abbot (*gon-chōrō* 権長老). During his service as vice-abbot, he was in charge of the affairs (*sata* 沙汰) of the monastery. He was to ascertain that Tendai and Shingon (Esoteric) texts were copied and transmitted without omission. No one who was not a master of both Exoteric and Esoteric Buddhism was to be appointed abbot or principal of the monastery.[62]

The seriousness with which the monks were to observe the rules of propriety is reflected in a text with the title "Digest on the realization of Buddhahood with this very body" (*Sokushin jōbutsu shō* 即身成仏抄).[63] The text has the subtitle "The daily procedures" (*Ichinichi ichiya gyōji shidai* 一日一夜行事次第). Kōen's disciple, Enkan, compiled the text in 1337 on the basis of Kōen's instructions. As the title indicates, the text associates the daily activities of the monk with the realization of Buddhahood during one's current existence. Rather than focusing on the *Fanwang* precepts, the text concentrates on the daily rules of propriety that monks were to follow when they performed such daily activities as taking meals, using the toilet, and entering the halls to participate in religious assemblies. The import of the text is captured in the following statement:

> The rules for each day and night are generally like this. . . . They are precisely the rules for the realization of Buddhahood with this very body. Sentient beings

all fully embody the three uncreated bodies (of the Buddha); furthermore, they are not worldlings who transmigrate in ignorance. However, during a day, they are constantly attacked by the three poisons and five desires so that they forget that their minds are innately pure. But now they fortunately have encountered a single issue [of doctrine] or a single precept. Each precept can be the central aspect of the Dharma-realm. They are at once actions that prevent evil and promote good on a daily basis. They are the practices that result in non-retrogression during a lifetime. How could they not be the causes for the mastery of the meditative concentrations? Moreover, whether it is a single action or all actions, the four meditations are constantly cultivated. Whether it is a single form or all forms, the three collections of precepts are constantly encouraged. These are the wondrous actions of both the three bodies (of the Buddha) and the single body (of the practitioner). They are the keys to the three thousand realms realized in an instant. In other words, one must strive for accomplishment in the duties and rituals of the realm of phenomena and should not make light of (these rules).[64]

This passage is based on *hongaku* views that sentient beings are already Buddhas, but still insists on the value of assiduous practice. In fact, Kōen found ultimate value in the correct performance of the simplest and most basic of everyday actions, from eating to excretory functions.

Kōen's rules were influenced by the traditional practices outlined in the so-called "Hīnayāna *Vinaya*s," such as the *Sifenlü,* to some extent. Monks were required to have three robes, a cloth to sit upon, begging bowl, cleanser, hand towel, a pot for water, and even a water strainer.[65] Although many of these items were specified in the *Fanwang jing*, Kōen frequently cited such sources as the Chinese master of precepts Daoxuan in his analysis of them.[66] Although he was willing to relax some of the rules, requiring these traditional accoutrements in a Japanese monastery was unusual and an indication of how serious the monks were.

Consecrated ordinations

The hallmark of the Kurodani lineage was its usage of a ritual called the "consecrated ordination," a ceremony that is still performed today. This ritual differs radically from traditional ordinations. It serves to confirm comments in the chapters by William Bodiford and Lori Meeks about how Japanese ordinations differed from traditional descriptions or were sometimes not even performed.

Some Kurodani sources trace the ritual back to a text called the *Kaidan'in chūdai shōgonki* (Record of the adornment of the central altar of the ordination platform) that was attributed to Saichō.[67] The earliest date suggested by modern scholars for the origins of the *kaikanjō* relies on a text on the precepts that are attributed to Ryōgen's disciple Jinzen 尋禅 (943–990).[68] However, this attribution is clearly a later attempt by Tendai monks to make the ritual more authoritative by attributing it to earlier Tendai masters. Although a text attributed to Jinzen, the *Ju ichijō bosatsu kanjō jukaihō* 授一乗菩薩潅頂受戒法 (Consecrated Ordination for the

One Vehicle bodhisattva) is included in the *Zoku Tendaishū zensho*,[69] no corroborating evidence exists for such an early date for the *kaikanjō*.

Many modern scholars believe that the *kaikanjō* began with Ejin. However, clear evidence for the appearance of the ritual does not appear until Kōen in a text called "Sixteen chapters on the Perfect Precepts" (*Enkai jūrokuchō* 円戒十六帖). This text refers to the transmission of a ritual from Egai, but no textual evidence for the ritual survives in any document written by Egai. Moreover, as has been noted above, Egai occupies an ambiguous place in the ordination lineage; thus scholars such as Shikii Shūjō 色井秀讓 have argued that the actual origins lie not with Egai, but with his teacher Ejin.[70] Much of the argument has been based on the colophon for the text on *kaikanjō* attributed to Jinzen that was copied by Egai; the colophon refers to Egai's teacher, presumably Ejin.[71] In 1980, Ōkubo Ryōjun 大久保良順 argued that direct evidence for Ejin's involvement with the *kaikanjō* ritual could be seen in his concern with the *gasshō* (the joining of the hands flat together), a key element in the *kaikanjō* ritual.[72] In a comment in the *Isshin myōkai shō* 一心妙戒鈔 (Compilation on the wondrous precepts of the One-mind), Ejin likens the ten fingers to the ten realms; because the fingers touch in a standard *gasshō*, each realm contains the other nine.[73] Thus the *gasshō* becomes a metaphor to help explain the three thousand realms. However, Ejin's discussion is not nearly as complex and developed as the typology of four *gasshō* that appear in the later *kaikanjō*, which is discussed below. Ejin's participation in several lineages from the Eshin and Danna lineages of Tendai suggests that he may have used elements from these traditions in developing the *kaikanjō*. Nomoto Kakujō 野本覚淨 has clarified how elements of the *kaikanjō* probably depended on medieval Tendai rites from the Danna lineage of the Tendai School, specifically the consecration of the profound tenet (*genshi kanjō* 玄旨潅頂), a ritual used to confer oral teachings about the three views in an instant.[74] Thus even though the *kaikanjō* has elements based on traditional Tendai ordinations, it also is based on *hongaku* teachings.

Ishida Mizumaro has suggested that the origins of the *kaikanjō* could be pushed back further to Ejin's teacher, Tankū 湛空 (1156–1253). While he acknowledged the force of arguments that Ejin had performed the ceremony, he noted that none of the documents indicate that Ejin originated the *kaikanjō*. On the basis of admittedly slender evidence, Ishida argued that Tankū might have begun the *kaikanjō*. At the same time he noted that the *kaikanjō* could not be earlier because Eisai, a Tendai monk vitally concerned with the precepts, was unaware of the *kaikanjō*.[75]

Although the origins of the *kaikanjō* may lie with Ejin, the ritual assumes a form close to its modern configuration in the writings of Kōen, indicating that Kōen played a key role in the development of the ritual. Such elements as the three types of *gasshō*, two interpretations of the mirror and its images, and the use of the Onmyōdō (Yin-yang 陰陽) techniques of shutting out misfortune and inviting fortune (*hanpei* 反閇) in establishing the ritual boundaries (*kekkai* 結界) for the ceremony are found first in Kōen's writings.[76]

Because the *kaikanjō* developed over time, the various ritual texts describing it are difficult to date and often have been emended. Moreover, the ritual undoubtedly depended on oral instruction, resulting in incomplete descriptions of the ritual. Instead of attempting to isolate an early version of the ritual, I have relied on a highly developed version of the ritual in the following description. According to Shikii Shūjō, the *Kaikan denju shidai* 戒潅伝授次第 is the most clearly organized of the approximately ten ritual manuals that have survived; the text was compiled by Ganchō 元超 around 1693 when he was appointed abbot of Hosshōji.[77] However, various parts of the ritual appear in early works by Kōen and Yuiken 維賢 (1289–1378), suggesting that most of the ritual as described would have been recognizable to Kōen and his disciples. I refer to the high points of the ritual below rather than describing the entire ceremony in detail.

The term *kanjō*, translated as "consecration" or "initiation," is usually considered to be an Esoteric Buddhist term. In fact, because the origins of the practice lie in ceremonies to install a new ruler, the term need not be limited to Esoteric Buddhist rituals. In medieval Tendai, the term was used in both Esoteric and Exoteric rituals. For example, a *kanjō* might be used to suggest that a monk had mastered material used in debates, a usage that is primarily Exoteric. The distinction between Esoteric and Exoteric uses of the ritual was blurred when *kanjō* are utilized to mark the transmission of oral teachings (*kuden* 口伝) that are only to be given to a single person. The *kaikanjō* evolves out of this type of ceremony.[78]

Both medieval and modern scholars have differed on the importance of Esoteric influence in the *kaikanjō*. Although the term *kanjō* was used to describe the ritual, some Kurodani writers argued that the *kaikanjō* was not based on Esoteric Buddhist teachings even though the structure and name of the ritual reflected Esoteric influence.[79] One possible explanation of this position is that it may have been a response to Nichiren School's criticisms of the Esoteric influence on Tendai. In contrast, Nomoto Kakujō argues that the Kurodani lineage may have been defending themselves against criticisms from within the Tendai School that they had simply "stolen" elements of Esoteric Buddhist ritual.[80]

The revival of the twelve-year period of seclusion (*rōzan*) spent on Mount Hiei played a significant role in the formation of the *kaikanjō* tradition. No evidence exists of the direct association of *rōzan* and *kaikanjō* during Kōen's seclusion, but Kōen did receive the *kaikanjō* as a mark of his advanced practice. According to Shikii Shūjō, the *kaikanjō* took place twelve years after the practitioner's ordination qualifying him to be a monk. During that twelve-year period, he was to perform *shido kegyō* 四度加行, the four-part set of practices required for an advanced Esoteric consecration. Although such an Esoteric course did not require the recipient to spend twelve years on Mount Hiei, the twelve-year period reflects the *rōzan* tradition. Thus, in the early Kurodani tradition two ordinations differing in function can be distinguished, with the first being an ordination conferring the status of monkhood on a person and the second, the *kaikanjō*, marking the attainment of a particular level of spiritual advancement resulting from twelve years of seclusion.

The *kaikanjō* is an impressive ceremony, filled with fascinating symbolism. After Kōen's time, it gradually came to reflect a decline in rigor of monastic discipline from the ascetic ideal of Kōen and his followers. The twelve-year seclusion was too stringent a requirement to last for more than a few generations at most. Moreover, as the ritual became more elaborate, it was easy to place less emphasis on rigorous adherence to the precepts and more on the details of the rituals.[81] In other words, the ritual could be interpreted both as requiring adherence to monastic discipline as a prerequisite for conferral but also as an expression of the recipient's innate precepts that required minimal ascetic practice. However, the exact balance between these two tendencies has not been traced.

Three types of ordinations are enumerated in Kōen's "Sixteen Chapters on the Perfect Precepts."[82] The first is the ordination used to confer the status of monks. The second and third are performed after twelve years of practice on the outer and inner platforms, also known as the platforms for conferral (*denjudan* 伝受壇) and realization (*shōkakudan* 正覚壇); these last two correspond to the *kaikanjō*.

Scholars have not determined whether the rituals on the two platforms developed simultaneously.[83] The ritual on the platform for conferral is similar to the conferral of the precepts from teacher to student that occurs in a traditional ordination making one a monk, but on the platform for conferral, the precepts are not bestowed from an outside source but called forth from within the student. The teacher sits in a superior position and the student in an inferior position. The process of realization is seen from the perspective of following the causes to the effect or "acquired enlightenment" (*shikaku* 始覚).

In the third type of ordination, the ordination on the platform of realization is seen from the perspective of innate enlightenment (*hongaku* 本覚); it expresses the manner in which the precepts are innately found in the very fabric of phenomena (*jissō* 実相). Consequently, the teacher and student sit next to each other and are equal in rank in this ordination.[84]

A variety of participants are involved in the ritual, including a number of monks who chant and play three types of drums to mark the sections of the ceremony. However, they do not actually enter the inner and outer platforms. That role is reserved for the teacher who transmits the precepts (*denkaishi* 伝戒師), the student, and those who assist them. The teacher is assisted by a master of ceremonies (*katsuma ajari* 羯磨阿闍梨); the student is instructed by an instructor (*kyōju ajari* 教授阿闍梨). The teacher transmitting the precepts was expected to have gone through performing various roles in the ceremony before he assumed the central office in the ritual. Today he is also expected to be the abbot of Saikyōji.[85] Below the rituals conducted on the two platforms are examined in more detail.

The platform of conferral

The sense of conferral is conveyed in the building through the presence of pictures of the various Tendai patriarchs in the lineage of the bodhisattva precepts, beginning with Zhiyi.[86] In the center of the platform is a representation of a golden mountain (*konzan* 金山); on its peak is a pagoda with a relic of the Buddha. In addition, several key texts for the ordination are also placed on the platform: the *Lotus Sūtra*, *Fanwangjing*, Zhiyi's commentary (*Pusajie yishu* 菩薩戒義疏) on the

Fanwang jing, and a text with the title *Guanxin shi'erbu jingyi* 観心十二部経義.[87] In front of them, five medicines, five jewels, and five types of grain are placed for use in the consecration. The platform itself represents the three thousand realms that are realized in an instant in enlightenment; in some texts, it is said to be Vulture's Peak (Ryōzen 霊山), the site where Śākyamuni eternally preaches the *Lotus Sūtra.*

The ritual on the platform for conferral focuses on the consecration (*kanjō* 潅頂), which uses five vases. *Kanjō* were used to enthrone kings, with four of the five vases used for the waters of four major Indian rivers. These waters were then combined in the fifth vase and the water used to anoint the new king. In a similar manner, when the student is anointed, he is told that he is about to become a Buddha, a status equal to that of a king; the correlation between kingship and Buddhahood was found in a number of traditional descriptions of paths leading to Buddhahood. In addition, the five vases can be interpreted as representing five aggregates with the central vase symbolizing consciousness, the aggregate upon which the other four depended.[88] This interpretation thus emphasized the origins of the precepts in the student's own consciousness. When the *kaikanjō* is considered in terms of the twelve-part ordination ceremony outlined by Zhanran, it corresponds to the seventh section, the "conferral of the precepts."[89]

Later ritual texts in the Kurodani lineage discussed the ritual in terms of two sites: an outer (*gedōjō* 外道場) and an inner (*naidōjō* 内道場). In some texts, the outer site is the ordination platform on which the traditional ordination takes place. The inner consisted of the platform of realization. Thus the two sites help the recipient of the precepts understand that more than the conferral of the precepts by an outside source was being discussed, that in fact, the precepts were called forth from within the practitioner himself. Through the ordination the practitioner realized his own inherent Buddhahood.[90] A key aspect of this interpretation was the statement that the true ordination platform was not an external site, but the practitioner himself.[91]

The *gasshō* played a key role in ordination rituals, with the practitioner using *gasshō* when he performed such actions as kneeling and asking for the precepts. In the *kaikanjō,* the type of *gasshō* used becomes more complex and the explanations more detailed. In some of the ceremonies, only three *gasshō* are used,[92] but in the following more complex ceremony, two sets of four *gasshō* are used. In the outer ceremony, conferred on the platform for conferral, the four *gasshō* are equated with the following four phrases from the *Fanwang jing* that are cited repeatedly in medieval Tendai literature on the precepts:

1 Sentient beings receive the precepts of the Buddhas,
2 And enter the ranks of the Buddhas.
3 Their rank is the same as that of the great enlightened.
4 Truly they are sons of the Buddha.[93]

The conferral of the precepts and the realization of Buddhahood (the essential identity of the student and teacher) are symbolized by the type of *gasshō* done as each phrase is uttered. As the first phrase is recited, the ordination master (*kaishi* 戒師) and the student each make a standard *gasshō.* With the recitation of the second phrase, the master's left hand and the student's right hand are joined to make a *gasshō*. When the third phrase is recited, a similar *gasshō* is performed with each using the opposite hand. Finally, when the fourth phrase is uttered, the previous two *gasshō* are combined. Thus both of the master's hands are joined with both of the student's hands, symbolizing the conferral of the precepts. The master concludes this part of the ceremony by tracing a reverse swastika, an auspicious symbol denoting his divinity or Buddhahood, on the chest of the student.[94]

Little explanation of the meaning of the four *gasshō* transmitted on the outer platform is included in the ordination manuals. However, because the four passages recited are all included in the second *gasshō* of the ritual conducted on the inner platform, the meaning of the outer platform can be deduced. The entire ritual on the outer platform corresponds with "verbal identity" (*myōji soku* 名字即) in the path known as the six degrees of identity.[95] In other words, the outer platform rituals are designed to verbally inform the practitioner that he has the inherent nature that is Buddhahood. A deeper realization of what this means must await the ceremony on the inner platform, the platform of realization.[96]

The platform of realization

The ceremony then moves to the inner area where a platform of realization (*shōkakudan* 正覚壇) has been established. In the outer area, several students are allowed to enter the platform at the same time. However, in the inner area, only one may enter at a time. This is referred to as "conferral on only a single person" (*yuiju ichinin* 唯授一人), a phrase that traditionally refers to the rule allowing only one transmission of a teaching in a lifetime. In this case, it has been radically reinterpreted to refer to mean only one candidate for ordination may enter the platform at a time.[97] The master and the student sit facing each other with an ornamental canopy (*tengai* 天蓋) hung above the platform. Because such canopies are normally placed above the heads of images of the Buddha, the use of the canopy clearly indicates that the ordination master and the student are Buddhas. For a Tendai monk, two Buddhas sitting side by side is a clear reference to the Tahōtō 多宝塔 (Prabhūtaratna) stūpa that appears in the *Lotus Sūtra*, and this is clearly indicated in the text. This scenario might have led monks to recall how Saichō traced his bodhisattva precepts ordination back to a transmission in the Tahōtō when Huisi and Zhiyi listened to the Buddha preach in their past lives.[98]

The master of ceremonies sits beneath the platform on the ordination master's side. The teacher (*kyōju* 教授) sits beneath the platform on the student's side. The consecration with the five vases performed on the platform of conferral is not repeated on the inner platform; rather the ceremony focuses on the transmission of the four *gasshō,* symbolic of the transmission of enlightenment. Various interpretations of the four *gasshō* are found in the Gennōji and Hosshōji transmissions; the Gennōji tradition has remained stable, but Hosshōji documents reveal changes in the *gasshō* over the centuries.[99] I follow the later Hosshōji traditions here because they are the most developed tradition and include more explanation enabling the outside scholar to interpret some of the symbolism in the ritual.

The four *gasshō* are preceded in some ordination manuals by a statement that the precepts are the correct way to enter the true, the essential way to leave delusion behind.[100] The four *gasshō* are interpreted in an even more profound manner than in the outer platform rituals by describing them as corresponding to the six degrees of identity (*rokusoku* 六即). The first *gasshō* consists of the ordination master and student each making an ordinary *gasshō* as they recited a phrase from the *Fanwang jing*, "You shall realize Buddhahood."[101] This represents the first of the six degrees of identity, identity in principle (*risoku* 理即), in other words, the principle that each sentient being is inherently the Buddha even though he or she is not aware of it. The ordinary *gasshō* is interpreted with the five fingers of the left hand representing the inherent nature (*shōtoku* 性徳) of the five elements while the five fingers of the right hand represent the five elements acquired through cultivation (*shutoku* 修得). When the two hands are joined, it represents the eternal coincidence of the inherent and cultivated. In other words, the *gasshō* represents the essence of the precepts (*kaitai* 戒体) that is both called forth from the practitioner himself and which is conferred. At the same time, the interpretation of the *gasshō* suggests that the practitioners of this tradition were aware of the importance of maintaining a balance between practice and beliefs about their innate nature. The ordination master confers the essence of the precepts with a *gasshō* and the student receives it with a *gasshō*. In addition, the five fingers on each hand are interpreted as representing the five elements (*godai* 五大), and the ten fingers of the two hands signify the ten realms (*jikkai* 十界) ranging from denizens of hell to Buddhas. The *gasshō* used at this point is thus called the sign or *mūdra* of the true characteristic of phenomena (*jissōin* 実相印), a title that reinforces the sense that everyone and everything is inherently a Buddha.

The second *gasshō* is performed while all four of the *Fanwang jing* phrases used in the ritual for the outer platform are recited. This corresponds to verbal identity (*myōji soku* 名字即), the stage when one hears about the teaching that one is the Buddha, or in this case when a person hears about the Buddha-nature precepts and states that he accepts them. The *gasshō* consists of horizontal and vertical hand positions. The terms "horizontal" and "vertical" refer to the orientation of the hands while the fingers point in other directions. Thus when the palms are horizontal, the fingers cross and point up and down. The *gasshō* are interpreted in Ganchō's text as referring to the five elements. However, in other texts, the vertical *gasshō* represents the three times (past, present, and future) in a single instant, while the horizontal *gasshō* represents the ten directions in a single instant.[102] These *gasshō* are called "the *mūdra* of responding to the faculties of sentient beings" (*fukiin* 赴機印), emphasizing the ways in which the Buddha responds to the needs of beings by preaching in various ways.

The third *gasshō* corresponds to the third through the fifth degrees of identity, those of practical (*kangyō soku* 観行即), seeming (*sōji soku* 相似即), and partial (*bunshō soku* 分証即) identity. These are the stages in which practice would normally occur. The ordination master's right hand is placed over the student's left arm with student and master's palms joined; and the master's left hand is placed over the student's right arm with the student and master's palms joined. Figure 7.1 shows

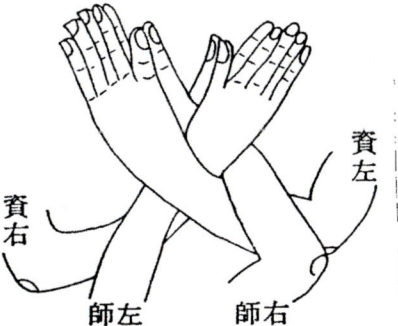

貧右　貧左　師左　師右

Figure 7.1 Kaikanjō gasshō

an illustration of the positions of the hands from an ordination manual.[103] The fore-heads of the two monks then touch, and the soles of their feet are placed together; this *mudrā* is called "the mark of the essential and mysterious unity of Buddha-nature and delusion" (*honpō kijō myōgōin* 本法機情冥合印) and embodies the perfect fusion of subjective and objective aspects of both the master and student. The name of the *mudrā* is not found in any dictionaries of Buddhism or Esoteric Buddhism and may be unique to the Kurodani tradition.

The third *gasshō* is also interpreted as representing a further identity of teacher and student based on the union of the subjective and objective aspects affirmed in the second *gasshō* in which the teacher and student are in union as is indicated by the five points of their bodies that touch. Doctrinally, this is called "the unity of the three bodies of the Buddha." The teacher represents Tahō Buddha (Prabhūtaratna, the Dharmakāya). The student represents Śākyamuni Buddha, the *sambhogakāya*. When they are unified, together they produce the *nirmanakāya* Buddha. In addi-tion, the teacher is said to represent the Buddha of the past while the student repre-sents the Buddha of the present.

The fourth *gasshō* represents the degree of ultimate identity (*kukyō soku* 究竟即) and consists of the master's right palm and the student's left palm both being raised, but not touching each other.[104] This represents the essential identity of worldlings and sages. While the earlier *gasshō* emphasized the non-dual nature of the relation-ship between such categories as worldlings and sages or principle and phenomena, this stage teaches that duality is established on the basis of that non-duality. Thus although the practitioner is inherently a Buddha, he still is a worldling who must realize Buddhahood in this stage. One text emphasizes the affirmation of things as they are with the quotation, "Willows are green and flowers are red."[105]

The teacher then admonishes the student to observe the precepts, but his words clearly subsume the actual provisions of the precepts to the abstract principle that the student has realized. Good and evil vanish into non-substantiality and the practitioner is given permission to reformulate the teachings, precepts, and rituals as needed. As a result, the student is not asked whether he will observe the pre-cepts as he was in the previous ordinations. The admonition gives the practitioner permission to develop the ritual in new ways. Although Kōen's emphasis on trying to observe the precepts as closely as possible has probably been weakened, for the serious student, the ritual enabled him to realize the true significance of the *Fanwangjing* statement that the recipient of the precepts has entered the ranks of the Buddhas. According to the manual:

> The water of the mind of the Buddha has been used to consecrate your mind .... Buddhas of the past stated, "Refrain from doing evil, perform good. The mind will be naturally purified. This is the teaching of the Buddhas." You should follow this. If you can purify your mind, then all good will be uncreated (*musa* 無作). How much more so evil? One is freed without depending on others. Thus it is called "natural." There are no phenomena that are defiled, thus it is called "pure." . . . You have appeared in the world only for the great purpose [of saving sentient beings]. Various paths are preached for the One Buddha vehicle. Teachings are established in accord with people's religious faculties. When one knows the illness, one can administer the medicine. If a precept that has not been formulated by a previous Buddha is needed, then one should formulate it. If a practice [is needed] that has not been used by previous Buddhas, then one should enact it. . . .[106]

Because only a Buddha changes and formulates new precepts, the newly ordained person is clearly seen as essentially a Buddha. At the same time, the power to change and formulate precepts endows him with a defense against any charge that he was weakening the precepts.

The ritual proceeds with the ordination master and student exchanging robes. A number of ritual objects used in ordinations are then given to the student and the special meaning of each is explained. These objects are not treated simply as the implements the new Buddha will need, but as the ornaments of Mahāvairocana himself. The objects are given to the new Buddha in the following order with explanations. The three robes are worn by those who have realized salvation; they are the skin and flesh of the three bodies of the Buddha with each robe representing one of the bodies of the Buddha. In addition, each robe is identified with a specific virtue of the Buddha: the five-part robe with compassion and the abandonment of selfishness, the seven-part robe with wisdom and the abandonment of wrong views, and the nine-part robe with forbearance and the abandonment of hatred.

The begging bowl is conferred next. Traditional explanations treating the bowl as an indication that the practitioner should be satisfied with whatever he receives are cited. However, other interpretations are also advanced. Its shape is round, revealing the Perfect (literally "round") and replete characteristics of principle and wisdom. It is empty within expressing the absence of any characteristics of the land of quiescence and light. A cloth to sit on (*zagu* 座具 or *nishidan* 尼師壇), mirrors (*myōkyō* 明鏡), a conch shell (*hora* 法螺), and a water pot (*hōbyō* 法瓶) are then bestowed on the student. The explanation of the mirrors is particularly detailed because they were used in rituals conferring teachings about the three views realized in an instant. When the various implements have been conferred, the teacher and student again exchange robes returning them to their original owners.

Conclusion

Medieval Tendai monks are often stereotyped as ignoring the precepts and lacking in monastic discipline. Although such a view is accurate when applied to certain monks, it certainly could not be applied to all monks. Because ordinations served as initiation rituals into the Tendai order and because the precepts were traditionally seen as being the basis of practice, Tendai monks could not ignore these topics. If they chose to subordinate them to an abstract principle or to the *Lotus Sūtra*, they had to explain their position. In fact, a variety of theories explaining the relation between the *Lotus Sūtra* and the precepts circulated among Tendai monks; some of these fostered lax adherence to monastic discipline and others supported strict adherence to monastic ideals. This chapter concerned one monk's efforts to revive the precepts. In the conclusion, I discuss several aspects of Kōen's significance for medieval Tendai monasticism by placing him in a wider context.

First, the Tendai School was not as monolithic as scholars have sometime thought after reading about Tendai power and Tendai persecutions of some of the new traditions of Buddhism during the Kamakura period. Although the term "Exoteric-Esoteric establishment" (*kenmitsu taisei* 顕密体制) might seem to imply a monolithic organization, Mount Hiei tolerated a number of different interpretations of the precepts. Although the laxer interpretations favored by groups such as the Eshin-ryū 恵心流 seem to have dominated the central establishment on Mount Hiei, some of the Tendai temples on the peripheries of the central establishment were occupied at least temporarily by monks who favored stricter interpretations. Kōen's Kurodani lineage was one of these. Others were Ninkū, abbot of Sangoji 三鈷寺 in the western hills outside of Kyoto and Rosanji 盧山寺 in Kyoto, also known as the Mount Hiei in the capital, and Shunjō at Sennyūji 泉涌寺 in Kyoto. Although Hōchibō Shōshin lived on Mount Hiei, his scholarly demeanor placed him on the periphery of Tendai power. Although these monks offered interpretations of the precepts that could have been interpreted as criticisms of the establishment on Mount Hiei, they remained within the Tendai fold. The one exception was Shunjō, who advocated a return to the "Hīnayāna" *Sifenlü*, a proposal that seemed to directly criticize the founder of the Tendai School, Saichō, and affirm the views of the Nara schools. An understanding of these varied positions yields a portrait of a vital tradition. This differs markedly from the view that the medieval Tendai School lacked vitality and was easily displaced by the new Kamakura schools.

Second, Kōen's biography provides insight into how new interpretations arose in lineages that utilized so-called "original enlightenment thought." The frequent references to dreams in Kōen's biography and the manner in which some of them were taken to be authoritative suggest a mechanism for introducing new interpretations of doctrine and the precepts. As Kōen's biography shows, these new interpretations did not all lead to a decline in the rigor of monastic discipline and scholarship. Instead, they may have to a renewed commitment to strict adherence to the precepts. Kōen's mode of argumentation can be contrasted to that of other Tendai scholars such as Ninkū and Hōchibō Shōshin. These two scholars relied on sources that are generally regarded as authentic by modern scholars. Dreams did not play a significant role in their arguments. Their presence suggests that Tendai monks were well aware of the different possibilities of interpretation.

Third, Kōen's biography helps explain the importance of lineage for monks interested in the precepts. Everyone had to trace their tradition back to some author-ity and argue that they were part of an unbroken lineage. Kōen relied on Saichō the founder of the Tendai School, as his authority. Saichō appeared in Kōen's dreams, and Kōen commented on Saichō's writings. In addition, Kōen emulated Saichō's practices by reviving the sequestration on Mount Hiei. Other Tendai monks relied on other sources; Eshin-ryū monks used fabricated texts attributed to Tendai patri-archs; Shunjō relied on the traditions used by Chinese Tiantai monks during the Song dynasty. Ninkū relied on Zhiyi's commentary on the *Fanwang jing*, the *Pusajie yiji* 菩薩戒義記, and a secret transmission that he traced through Hōnen.

Fourth, Kōen's role in developing the *kaikanjō* is indicative of the importance of ritual in identifying positions on the precepts. The *kaikanjo* differentiated the Kurodani lineage from other groups. Holding fortnightly assemblies to recite the precepts, observing rainy season retreats, and the confession ceremony marking the conclusion of the retreats suggested a strict attitude toward the precepts. Monks interested in the precepts sometimes relied on traditions and rituals found in the *vinaya*, indicating that some Tendai monks had a complex relationship with the *vinaya*.[107] In contrast, some of the Eshin-ryū advocates so de-emphasized the ordi-nation ritual, replacing it with adherence to the *Lotus Sūtra*, that the ordination virtually disappeared.[108] Another perspective can be found in Ninkū's writings that differentiated between the various levels of ordination by specifying different pre-cepts for different levels, while striving to reflect Saichō's position. A completely different approach is found in Shunjō, who returned to the *Sifenlü* full ordination, thereby rejecting Saichō's approach.

Fifth, the detailed descriptions of administrative structure and ritual calendars found in Kōen's writings can be seen as an attempt to rationalize and reform the monastic establishment on Mount Hiei. How much they reflect actual practice remains to be seen. Ample evidence for certain practices such as the lectures and debates held on the death anniversaries of Zhiyi and Saichō can be found in a vari-ety of sources. Other issues, such as the administrative structure and structures available for advancing in rank on Mount Hiei, still need research. With the grow-ing importance of the sons of nobles on Mount Hiei, monastic organization clearly changed over time.[109]

Finally, the Kurodani lineage's use of the *kaikanjō* suggests the difficulty that Tendai lineages had in maintaining strict monastic discipline for very long. The *kaikanjō* gave leaders added prestige, virtually turning them into Buddhas. A per-son was given the authority to alter or create new precepts when he underwent the *kaikanjō*. As a result the twelve-year sequestration soon ceased to be a requirement for receipt of the *kaikanjō*. The *kaikanjō* thus became a hallmark of one Tendai lin-eage rather than an indication of adherence to monastic discipline. Although most

Tendai lineages returned to the lax adherence of monastic discipline that had been prevalent throughout its history, other reform movements, such as the movement by the monks of the Anrakuritsu in 安楽律院 subsequently arose.

Notes

1 For a study of Saichō and the precepts, see Groner 2000. However, the Kurodani lineage did not regard Saichō in the manner I have described in this study because they believed that Saichō was the author of several texts that have proven to be apocryphal, most notably the *Tendai Hokkeshū gakushōshiki mondō* 天台法華宗学生式問答, a text that argues for the primacy of the *Lotus Sūtra* over the *Fanwangjing* in the interpretation of the precepts. The *Mondō* is cited in Ejin's *Endonkai kikigaki*, in *Zoku Tendaishū zensho (ZTZ) Enkai* 1: 205. For a study of the *Mondō*, see Tamayama 1973.

2 *Tendaishū zensho* 9: 225.

3 *Tendaishū zensho* 9: 224.

4 For Saichō's lineages, see Groner 2000: 257–259.

5 *Denshin kashōden, ZTZ Shiden* 2: 410a; The *Denshin kashōden* was compiled by the disciple of Kōen's student Enkan, a monk named Kōshū (Shikii 1989: 9).

6 *Denshin kashōden, ZTZ Shiden* 2: 410a.

7 Nothing is known of Enson's biography.

8 *Kenkairon*, 1: 35. The *Kenkairon* has the term "ultimate faith" (*shishin* 至信) which is a homonym with "ultimate mind" (*shishin* 至心) that appears here; however, the passage later includes the term "ultimate faith." The switch gives the passage a more metaphysical sense. The *Kenkairon* passage refers to the teachings that Daosui 道邃 conferred on Saichō in China. The claim that Saichō received a teaching about the three views in a single word became a major topic in medieval Tendai.

9 The reference is to Ejin.

10 *Denshin kashōden, ZTZ Shiden* 2: 410a–b. Some scholars have questioned whether Kōen actually met Ejin. Shikii (1989: 8) has convincingly demonstrated that they did meet.

11 *Denshin kashōden, ZTZ Shiden* 2: 410b.

12 Shikii 1989: 10.

13 *Denshin kashōden, ZTZ Shiden* 2: 411b.

14 The term "direct path" is found in the beginning of Zhiyi's commentary on the *Fanwang jing*; it became one of Saichō's favorite terms (T. 40.563a10; Groner 2000: 185–189).

15 *Denshin kashōden, ZTZ Shiden* 2: 412a.

16 Nomoto Kakujō 1988: 686–690.

17 *Denshin kashōden, ZTZ Shiden* 2: 414b. Enchō may have been mentioned in such a positive light because he was one of Saichō's closest disciples and the victor in the dispute with Enshu 円修 (n.d.), Gishin's 義真 (781–833) disciple, over who should be head (*zasu* 座主) of the Tendai School; in addition, he played a major role in the establishment of the Western Pagoda (Saitō 西塔) section of Mount Hiei, where Kurodani was located (*Denshin kashōden, ZTZ Shiden* 2: 420b). Finally, he was originally a disciple of Dōchū, who had studied the precepts under Ganjin. Enchō was one of the first Tendai monks to receive the bodhisattva precepts from Saichō.

18 *Denshin kashōden, ZTZ Shiden* 2: 414b–415a.

19 Nomoto (1994: 683–710) demonstrates that many of these issues are found around the time when the *kaikanjō* movement flourished; they are particularly evident in Kōshū's *Keiran jūyōshū*.

20 *Denshin kashōden, ZTZ Shiden* 2: 412b.

21 *Denshin kashōden, ZTZ Shiden* 2: 415a.

22 *Denshin kashōden, ZTZ Shiden* 2: 417b–418a.
23 *Denshin kashōden, ZTZ Shiden* 2: 422b–424a. Jinzōji was somewhat removed from the center of the Tōdō 東塔 area, being located near the junction of the Ōmiyadani 大宮溪 and Hidendani 悲田谷 roads; only ruins survive today (Take 1993: 100–101; for a map, see p. 245).
24 Terai 2000: 285.
25 Shunjō had rejected silken robes for cotton ones as soon as he decided to carefully follow the precepts. In contrast, Ninkū, following Yijing's travel diary, allowed silk robes (Kieschnick 2003: 98–100).
26 Toriimoto 1984: 293. The *soken no koromo* also had changes in style from earlier robes; for a picture, see Nihon daijiten kankōkai 1973–1976: 12:366a.
27 *Denshin kashōden ZTZ Shiden* 2: 418b; Nomoto 1985. Gigen received and conferred initiations concerning Esoteric Buddhism and the teachings of the "chroniclers" on a number of members of the Kaike lineage.
28 *Denshin kashōden ZTZ Shiden* 2: 418a.
29 The *Pusajie yiji* 菩薩戒義記 is a commentary attributed to Zhiyi; its authenticity has been questioned because some of its positions differ from those found in other works by Zhiyi (Satō 1960: 412–415). For a discussion of Mingguang's commentary and its importance for Saichō, see Groner 2000: 229–236. The use of the commentary by Kōen and his disciples indicates that the commentary continued to be an important source for Tendai monks. For a summary of the scant information available concerning Mingguang's life, see Penkower 1993, chapter 5.
30 Because the *Endon bosatsukai jūjū shijūhachi gyōgi shō* 円頓菩薩戒十重四十八行儀鈔 remains in the Saikyōji 西教寺 library and has not been published, I rely on the analysis by Kubota 1984: 203–206. Kubota has been kind enough to give me a copy of the text. In addition, a subcommentary on Zhiyi's commentary on the *Fanwangjing* is extant at the Hōmyōin at Miidera, but no one has published any research on the text. For the *vinaya* restrictions on lay believers, see Upasak 1975: 51.
31 Terai 2000: 282–283.
32 For information on Enrin, see Nakao 1979a and Nakao 1979b.
33 *ZTZ Shiden* 2: 424a.
34 Kubota 1984: 206; Shikii 1989: 10.
35 Five monks was the minimum required to hold the *pravāraṇa*, a ceremony in which each monk asks whether he has incurred any faults during the rainy retreat. Because the successful completion of the rainy season retreat as a full order required that this ceremony be held, Kōen managed to assemble the bare minimum required to hold the retreat (Upasak 1975: 147–149).
36 *ZTZ Enkai* 1: 202–203.
37 *Denshin kashōden, ZTZ Shiden* 2: 418b.
38 *Denshin kashōden, ZTZ Shiden* 2: 420a–421a.
39 *Denshin kashōden, ZTZ Shiden* 2: 424a–b. Several versions of the text exist with major differences in the order of the sixteen chapters; see the chart in Tendai shūten hensanjo 2000: 216–218; Shikii 1983.
40 *Denshin kashōden, ZTZ Shiden* 2: 425a. Xuanzang's massive translation of Perfection of Wisdom literature had traditionally been chanted to bring such benefits as protecting the state.
41 *Denshin kashōden, ZTZ Shiden* 2: 425b.
42 *Denshin kashōden, ZTZ Shiden* 2: 425–427. Taishakuji was probably located in Imurodani in Yokawa (Take 1993: 177).
43 *Denshin kashōden, ZTZ Shiden* 2: 415a–b.
44 Matsuo 1988: 252–256.
45 *ZTZ Enkai* 1: 167a; 168a.
46 *ZTZ Enkai* 1: 167b–168a.
47 *ZTZ Enkai* 1: 168–171; for an analysis of Saichō's proposal for provisional Hīnayāna

ordinations and the Tendai School's immediate rejection of them, see Groner 2000: 195–205.

48 For Ninkū's rejection of Shunjō's position, see Groner 2003: 66–68.

49 *ZTZ Enkai* 1: 173–174. For study of the term "Perfect ten good precepts," see Kodera 1987: 188–202. Kodera notes that eminent Tendai monks held a variety of views on the issue. Kōjō argued that the ten major precepts of the *Fanwang jing* should be used to initiate novices. Ennin and Enchin both used the ten good precepts. Ninkū argued that when novices were initiated in a comprehensive ordination (*tsūju* 通受), they received the three collections of pure precepts, but when they underwent distinct ordinations (*betsuju* 別受), they received the ten good precepts (Groner 2003: 56). Keikō 敬光 (1740–1795) argued that the traditional precepts for novices should be used.

50 The serene and pleasant activities are discussed in Groner 2000: 207–210; the three collections of pure precepts are described on pp. 219–220. For a description of the *Fanwang* precepts, see Groner 1990: 255–256.

51 The list of eighteen items is based on the *Fanwang jing* (T. 24.1008a).

52 The contents of the three lectures are not clearly defined. Two possibilities exist: the three *sūtras* associated with the *Lotus Sūtra* or the three *sūtras* associated with protecting the nation (*Lotus Sūtra, Sūtra of the Benevolent King*, and the *Sūtra of Golden Light*). Because the passage is a commentary on a passage in Saichō's *Rokujōshiki*, the latter seems more likely.

53 *ZTZ Enkai* 1: 183a–b.

54 *ZTZ Enkai* 1: 183b.

55 *ZTZ Enkai* 1: 183b–184a. For more information on the Tendai examination system, see Groner 2002, chapter 8.

56 This assembly was begun by Amoghavajra and introduced to the Tendai School by Saichō; see Groner 2000: 177, n. 26.

57 The term "summer fortnightly assembly" is unusual. A survey of dictionaries, indices and encyclopedias turned up virtually no other instances of the term. However, a note in the text indicates that the *pravāraṇa* ritual is indicated in which all monks ask their compatriots whether they committed any infractions of the rules during the rainy season retreat (*ZTZ Enkai* 1: 184a). The retreat is officially over when this procedure has been concluded.

58 The winter retreat is mentioned in the *Fanwang jing* (T. 24.1008b). Winter retreats are not mentioned in Indian literature, but such a practice was mentioned by Xuanzang in his travel diary as being held in Tukhāra in modern Afghanistan (*Daitō saiiki ki*, 32); however, in most cases, monasteries seem to have practiced either a summer or a winter retreat. The system of two retreats came to Japan with Zen practices. Eisai mentions that Chinese monks practiced both retreats (Ichikawa *et al.* 1972: 83).

59 *ZTZ Enkai* 1: 182b–184b; such occasions as the assemblies for Saichō and Zhiyi were used to hold examinations and debates.

60 *ZTZ Enkai* 1: 184b–185b. In determining the pronunciation of the titles of the various offices, I have relied on Zen sources. Medieval Tendai monks may have used other pronunciations.

61 The term suigō 遂業 is not defined in Kōen's text, but may refer to serving as lecturer at a series of thirty lectures in Tōdō and twenty-eight in Saitō areas of Mount Hiei (Ishida 1997: 641a).

62 *ZTZ Enkai* 1: 185a.

63 *ZTZ Enkai* 1: 191–98.

64 *Ichinichi ichiya gyōji shidai, ZTZ Enkai* 1: 197a–b; also see Terai 1999: 84–85.

65 *ZTZ Enkai* 1: 178–82.

66 For an example, see *ZTZ Enkai* 1: 178b–179a.

67 Included in the *Kaidan'inki, ZTZ Enkai* 1: 126–127.

68 Ninomiya and Asukai 1933: 56.

69 *ZTZ Enkai* 1: 29–37.

70 Shikii 1961: 188–193.
71 *Ju ichijō bosatsukai kanjō jukaihō shiki, ZTZ Enkai* 1: 38b; for other evidence, see Ishida 1963: 479–481.
72 Ōkubo 1980.
73 *Isshin myōkai shō, ZTZ Enkai* 1: 260–261.
74 Nomoto 1991: 718–722.
75 Ishida 1963: 483–487.
76 Nomoto 1991: 719.
77 "Kaidai," *ZTZ Enkai* 1: 1; the text is found on pp. 12–28. My descriptions have been aided by Shikii's description of the ritual in *Kaikanjō*, which are particularly valuable because he has presided over the ritual. Until very recently the secrecy surrounding the *kaikanjō* was maintained. An important break in the tradition came with the publication of several documents by Uesugi (1935: 897–912). In recent years, Shikii has published several articles and a book about the tradition; he was also instrumental in the publication of a number of manuscripts in the *Zoku Tendaishū zensho*.
78 Nomoto 1991.
79 For an example of a statement that the ritual is not esoteric and yet is the ultimate of secret rituals, see *Chingoku kanjō shiki, ZTZ Enkai* 1: 1a.
80 Nomoto 1988: 687–688. Such criticisms were made by Ninkū; see Groner 2003: 66–68.
81 Ishida 1963: 475.
82 *Enkai jūrokuchō, ZTZ Enkai* 1: 88b–89a.
83 Shikii 1968: 278.
84 The three aspects of the precepts mentioned here are mentioned in Annen's *Futsū jubosatsukai kōshaku* (T. 74.773c–74a) as the precepts transmitted through a lineage of teachers (*denjukai* 伝受戒), the precepts called forth from within the candidate through the ordination ceremony (*hottokukai* 発得戒), and the precepts that are innate and based on one's unchanging nature (*shōtokukai* 性徳戒). Shikii (1968: 276) identifies them with the three types of ordinations in Kurodani literature.
85 Shikii 1981: 27.
86 For a diagram of the platform, see Shikii 1989: 80. A description of the platform is found on pp. 84–85, 140.
87 For a list of the texts installed on the platform according to various texts, see Nomoto 1988: 690. The actual texts installed on the altar varied over the years. In some versions of the ritual, only the *Lotus Sūtra* or parts of it were installed. The *Fanwang jing* and Zhiyi's commentary appear in six of the nine texts surveyed.

The *Guanxin shiribu jingyi* is attributed to either Zhiyi or his disciple Guanding 潅頂 (561–632). The 41 page manuscript that exists today begins with one and one-half pages that were composed in China. Although the authorship is not clear, it did exist during the Tang dynasty. The following 40 pages were probably composed in Japan by the late Heian period to elucidate the first page and a half. The text was used by the Kurodani lineage as an outline of Tendai doctrine, which chose it for several reasons. The study of twelve divisions of the canon was mentioned in a variant text of the *Fanwangjing* (Ishida 1971: 177). The text's focus on discernment of the mind (*kanjin* 観心), the three truths, and the single essence of the three refuges played roles in the *kaikanjō*. See Nomoto 1986: 113–118; and Satō 1960: 280–284. The text has been published in *ZTZ Enkai* 1: 334–364.
88 This interpretation is found in the Gennōji version of the ritual (*Kaikan juhō, ZTZ Enkai* 1: 7b), but is not found in many of the other ritual manuals. However, because many of the ritual manuals refer to other texts for the details of the ritual, this issue requires further investigation.
89 For a list of the twelve parts of Zhanran's ritual manual, see Groner 1990: 261. For a discussion of Annen's views on conferred and innate precepts, see pp. 269–270. For

statements regarding the relation of the consecration of the five vases to the conferral of the precepts, see *Chingoku kanjō shiki*, *ZTZ Enkai* 1: 2a; *Kaikan juhō*, ibid., p. 7b.

90 Shikii 1968.
91 This theme is found in Annen's *Futsū jubosatsukai kōshaku* (T. 74:761a) and many subsequent texts on Tendai precepts.
92 For an example of a ceremony using a simple set of three *gasshō*, see *Chingoku kanjō shiki*, *ZTZ Enkai* 1: 2b. The basic structure in this ceremony is not very different from the more complex arrangement of two groups of four, described below in the main text. The three *gasshō* are: (a) the teacher and student each perform his own *gasshō*; (b) the teacher and student perform a *gasshō* in which the palms of the hands, soles of the feet and forehead of the teacher touch those of the student; (c) the teacher and student each performs his own *gasshō*. In the last phase, the two participants return to their original posture, representing the re-establishment of duality, but this time on the basis of non-duality and the interpenetration of the ten realms. Only three *gasshō* are specified in Kōen's *Enkai jūrokujō kuketsu*, *ZTZ Enkai* 1: 102b–105a.
93 *Fanwang jing*, T. 24.1004a; *Kaikan denju shidai*, *ZTZ Enkai* 1: 20a. The numbers of the phrases are added.
94 *Kaikan denju shidai*, *ZTZ Enkai* 1: 20a.
95 For the classic Chinese exposition of the six degrees of identity, see Donner and Stevenson 1993: 206–218.
96 Shikii 1989: 237.
97 Shikii 1968: 278, n. 4. Other Tendai teachers such as Ninkū 仁空 (1309–1388), who noted that Tendai ordinations had traditionally been conferred on several people at one time, criticized this aspect of the ceremony; see Groner 2003: 68.
98 Groner 2000: 259.
99 Shikii 1989: 221–238.
100 Shikii 1989: 228; *ZTZ Enkai* 1: 21a.
101 T. 24.1004a.
102 *Kaikan denju shidai*, *ZTZ Enkai* 1: 22; Shikii, *Kaikanjō no nyūmon*, pp. 229–230.
103 For an other illustration of this *gasshō*, see Shikii 1982: 12.
104 *Kaikan denju shidai*, *ZTZ Enkai* 1: 23; Shikii 1968: 277.
105 Shikii 1989: 227, 236. The explanation about duality established on the basis of non-duality comes from the *Kaikan denju shidai* 戒灌伝授次第 by Shinshū 真秀, a version of the manual not included in the *Zoku Tendaishū zensho*. The *ZTZ* version has a statement about affirming duality in the third *gasshō* (p. 21b).
106 *Kaikan denju shidai*, *ZTZ Enkai* 1: 24a.
107 For an example, see Groner 2001.
108 Groner 2007.
109 See Groner 2002 for discussions of the increasing power of nobility, the evolution of such posts as *zasu* (head of the school), *jūzenji* (ten meditation masters), the debate system and other topics.

Bibliography

Abbreviations

CKSSS= Chūgoku kodai shahon shikigo shūroku 中國古代寫本識語集錄, ed. Ikeda On 池田溫. *Tōyō bunka kenkyūjo sōkan* 東洋文化研究所叢刊, no. 11. Tokyo: Tōkyō daigaku tōyō bunka kenkyūjo, 1990.

DDC= Dunhuangxue dacidian 敦煌學大辭典, ed. Ji Xianlin 季羨林. Shanghai: Shanghai cishu chubanshe, 1998.

DSQ= Dunhuang shiku quanji 敦煌石窟全集, ed. Duan Wenjie 段文傑. Hong Kong: The Commercial Press, 2000.

DZ= Daozang 道藏. Beijing: Wenwu chubanshe; Shanghai: Shanghai shudian; Tianjin: Tianjin guji chubanshe, 1987.

GBSS= Gozan bungaku shinshū 五山文學新集, ed. Tamamura Takeji 玉村竹二. Tokyo: Tokyo Daigaku Shuppankai, 1977.

GBZS= Gozan Bungaku Zenshū 五山文學全集 by Kamimura Kankō 上村観光. Tokyo: Gozan Bungaku Zenshū kankōkai, 1936.

*JTS= Jiu Tang shu*舊唐書. Beijing: Zhonghua, 1975.

K= Shintei zōho kokushi taikei. 新訂増補国 史大系, ed. Kuroita Katsumi 黒板勝美. Tokyo: Yoshikawa kōbunkan, 1976.

KJGSK= Kongō Busshi Eison kanjin gakushōki 金剛仏子叡尊感身学正記, in *SEDS*, 1–76.

LS= The Lotus Sūtra. Translated by Burton Watson. New York: Columbia University Press, 1999.

P= Pelliot Dunhuang Manuscripts.

S= Stein Dunhuang Manuscripts.

SEDS= Saidaiji Eison denki shūsei 西大寺叡尊伝記集成, ed. Nara Kokuritsu Bunkazai Kenkyūjo 奈良国立文化財研究所. Kyoto: Hōzōkan, 1977.

T= *Taishō shinshū daizōkyō* 大正新修大藏經 (100 vols., eds. Takakusu Junjirō 高楠順次郎 and Watanabe Kaigyoku 渡邊海旭, *et al.*). Tokyo: Taishō issaikyō kankōkai, 1924–1932.

THY= *Tang huiyao* 唐會要. Beijing: Zhonghua, 1954.

TWBXD= Tang Wudai biji xiaoshuo daguan 唐五代筆記小說大觀. Shanghai: Shanghai guji, 2000.

*XTS= Xin Tang shu*新唐書. Beijing: Zhonghua, 1975.

XZJ=*Xuzangjing* 續藏經. Taipei: Xinwenfeng, 1968–1978. Reprint of *Dai Nihon Zokuzōkyō* 大日本續藏經. Kyōto: Zōkyō Shoin, 1905–1912.

YJQQ= Yunji qiqian 雲笈七籤. Annot. Jiang Lisheng 蔣力生, *et al.* Beijing: Huaxia chubanshe, 1996.

ZBQD= Zhongguo bihua quanji Dunhuang 中國壁畫全集敦煌, ed. Zhongguo bihua quanji bianji weiyuanhui 中國壁畫全集編輯委員會. Tianjin: Tianjin renmin meishu chubanshe, 1989–.

ZSDM= Zhongguo shiku Dunhuang Mogaoku 中國石窟敦煌莫高窟, ed. Dunhuang wenwu yanjiusuo 敦煌文物研究所. Beijing: Wenwu chubanshe, 1982.

ZTZ– Zoku Tendaishū zensho 続天台宗全, cd. Tendai shūten hensanjo 天台宗典編纂所. Tokyo: Shunjūsha, 1987–1999.

ZZTJ= Zizhi tongjian 資治通鑑. Beijing: Guji chubanshe, 1956.

Pre-modern works

Chutan ji 初潭集 by Li Zhi李贄 (1527–1602). Beijing: Zhonghua, 1974.

Daitō saiiki ki 大唐西域記 by Genjō 玄奘 [Xuanzang], translated by Mizutani Shinjō 水谷真成, *Chūgoku koten bungaku taikei*中国古典文学大系, vol. 22. Tokyo: Heibonsha, 1971.

Dengyō daishi zenshū 傳教大師全集, ed. Hieizan senshuin fuzoku Eizan gakuin 比叡山專修院附属叡山学院. Tokyo: Sekai seiten kankō kyōkai, 1975.

Dunhuang yuanwen ji 敦煌願文集, Huang Zhen 黃徵 and Wu Wei 吳偉 (comp.). Changsha: Yuelu shushe, 1995.

Electronic Text of the Genkoo Shakusho by Kokan Shiren, ed. Michel Mohr. Kyoto: International Research Institute for Zen Buddhism, 2001.

Genpei jōsuiki 源平盛衰記, edited and annotated by Ichiko Teiji市古貞次 *et al.* Tokyo: Miyai Shoten, 1991–1994.

Han Wei Liuchao biji xiaoshuo daguan 漢魏六朝筆記小說大觀. Shanghai: Shanghai guji chubanshe, 1999.

Jikakudaishiden 慈覺大師傳. In *Zoku gunsho ruijū* 續群書類従, ed. Hanawa Hokiichi 塙保己一, revised, Ōta Tōshirō 太田藤四郎, vol. 8b. Tokyo: Zoku Gunsho Ruijū Kanseikai, 1923–1928.

Jinshi cuibian 金石萃編. rept. in *Shike shiliao xinbian* 石刻史料新編. Taibei: Xinwenfeng, 1977–.

Jinshi lu 金石錄. rept. in *Shike shiliao xinbian* 石刻史料新編. Taibei: Xinwenfeng, 1977–.

Kenkairon, in *Dengyō daishi zenshū*, ed. Hieizan senshuin fuzoku Eizan gakuin. Tokyo: Sekai seiten kankō kyōkai, 1975.

Lidai minghua ji 歷代名畫記, by Zhang Yanyuan 張彥遠, annot. Yu Jianhua 俞劍華. Shanghai: Shanghai renmin meishu chubanshe, 1964.

Meigetsuki 明月記 in *Kundoku Meigetsuki* 訓読明月記, ed. Imagawa Fumio 今川文雄, vol. 5. Tokyo: Kawade Shōbo Shinsha, 1977–1979.

Quan Tang shi 全唐詩. Beijing: Zhonghua, 1990.

Quan Tang wen 全唐文. Kyoto: Chūbun, 1976.

Sanbōe 三寶繪 (984), by Minamoto Tamenori 源爲憲 (d. 1011), ed. Mabuchi Kazuo 馬淵和夫, Koizumi Hiroshi 小泉弘, Konno Tōru 今野達, *Sanbōe Chūkōsen* 三寶繪 注好選, *Shin Nihon Koten Bungaku Taikei* 新日本古典文学大系, vol. 31. Tokyo: Iwanami Shoten, 1997.

Taiping guangji 太平廣記. Beijing: Renmin wenxue chubanshe, 1959.

Tendaishū zensho 天台宗全書, ed. Tendai shūten kankōkai 天台宗典刊行会. Tokyo; Daiichi shobō, 1972–1973.

Toganoo Myōe Shōnin denki 栂尾明惠上人伝記, in *Myōe shōnin shiryō* 明惠上人資料. Tokyo Daigaku Shuppankai, 1971–1987.

Wenxuan 文選. Chengdu: Zhonghua shuju, 1981 reprint of Hu edition.

Youyang zazu 酉陽雜組, by Duan Chengshi 段成式 [d. 863]. Beijing: Zhonghua, 1981.

Zhongzhou jinshi kao 中州金石考 rept. in *Shike shiliao xinbian* 石刻史料新編. Taibei: Xinwenfeng, 1977–.

Modern works

Acker, William Reynolds Beal. (1954) *Some T'ang and Pre-T'ang Texts on Chinese Painting*. Leiden: E.J. Brill.

Adamik, T. (1996) "The Baptised Lion in the Acts of Paul." In *The Apocryphal Acts of Paul and Thecla*, edited by J.N. Bremmer, 60–73. Kampen: Kok Pharos Publishing House.

Adolphson, Mikael S. (2000) *The Gates of Power: Monks, Courtiers, and Warriors in Premodern Japan*. Honolulu: University of Hawai'i Press.

Alec-Tweedie, Mrs. (1936) *My Legacy Cruise*. London: Hutchinson & Co.

App, Urs. (1994) *Concordance to the Wumenguan*. Kyoto: International Research Institute for Zen Buddhism.

——. (1996) *Concordance to the Lidai Fabao Ji*. Kyoto: International Research Institute for Zen Buddhism.

——. (1997) *Concordance to the Record of Xuansha*. Kyoto: International Research Institute for Zen Buddhism.

Arai, Paula Kane Robinson. (1999) *Women Living Zen: Japanese Sōtō Buddhist Nuns*. Oxford: Oxford University Press.

Arnold, Philip C. (1988) *The British Discovery of Buddhism*. Cambridge: Cambridge University Press.

Ayusawa Shintaro. (1953) "The Types of World Map Made in Japan's Age of Isolation." *Imago Mundi* 10: 123–127.

Barnard, Leslie W. (1990) "Two Eighteenth Century Views of Monasticism: Joseph Bingham and Edward Gibbon." In *Monastic Studies: The Continuity of Tradition*, edited by Judith Loades, 283–291. Bangor: Headstart History.

Barrett, T.H. (1996) *Taoism Under the T'ang: Religion and Empire During the Golden Age of Chinese History*. London: Wellsweep.

——. (1998) "The Religious Affiliations of the Chinese Cat." *Louis Jordan Occasional Papers in Comparative Religion*, 2. London: SOAS.

——. (2003) "Hanshan's Place in History." In Peter Hobson, *Poems of Hanshan*, 115–147. Walnut Creek, CA: AltaMira Press.

Batchelor, Martine, trans. (2004) *The Path of Compassion: The Bodhisattva Precepts*. Walnut Creek, CA: AltaMira Press.

——, and Son'gyong Sunim. 2006. *Women in Korean Zen: Lives And Practices*. Syracuse, NY: Syracuse University Press.

Bendix, Reinhard. (1977) *Max Weber: An Intellectual Portrait*. Berkeley: University of California Press.

Bhikkhu Nānamoli, trans. (1979) *The Path of Purification: Visuddhi Magga*. Kandy: The Buddhist Publication Society.

Bielefeldt, Carl. (1993–1994) "Filling the Zen-shū: Notes on the 'Jisshū yōdō ki.'" *Cahiers d'Extrême-Asie* 7: 221–248.

——. (1997) "Kokan Shiren and the Sectarian Uses of History." In *The Origins of Japan's Medieval World: Courtiers, Clerics, Warriors, and Peasants in the Fourteenth Century*, edited by Jeffrey P. Mass, 295–317. Stanford, CA: Stanford University Press.

Birnbaum, Raoul. (1983) *Studies on the Mysteries of Mañjuśrī*. Boulder, CO: Society for the Study of Chinese Religions.

——. (1984) "Thoughts on T'ang Buddhist Mountain Traditions and Their Context." *T'ang Studies* 2: 5–23.

——. (1986) "The Manifestation of a Monastery: Shen-ying's Experiences on Mount Wu-t'ai in T'ang Context." *Journal of the American Oriental Society* 106, no. 1: 119–137.

——. (1989–1990) "Secret Halls of the Mountain Lords: The Caves of Wu-t'ai Shan." *Cahiers d'Extrême-Asie* 5: 115–140.

Blackburn, Anne M. (1998) "Magic in the Monastery: Textual Practice and Monastic Identity in Sri Lanka." *History of Religions* 38, no. 4: 354–373.

——. (2001) *Buddhist Learning and Textual Practice*. Princeton, NJ: Princeton University Press.

Blier, Susan Preston. (1987) *The Anatomy of Architecture: Ontology and Metaphor in Batammaliba Architectural Expression*. Chicago, IL: University of Chicago Press.

Bodiford, William M. (1993) *Sōtō Zen in Medieval Japan*. Honolulu: University of Hawai'i Press.

——. (1999) "Keizan's Dream History: Yōkōji's Origins." In *Religions of Japan in Practice*, edited by George J. Tanabe, Jr., 501–522. Princeton, NJ: Princeton University Press.

——. (ed) (2005a) *Going Forth: Visions of Buddhist Vinaya*. Honolulu: University of Hawai'i Press.

——. (2005b) "Introduction." In *Going Forth: Visions of Buddhist Vinaya*, edited by William M. Bodiford, 1–16. Honolulu: University of Hawai'i Press.

——. (2006) "The Medieval Period: Eleventh to Sixteenth Centuries." In *The Nanzan Guide to Japanese Religions*, edited by Paul L. Swanson and Clark Chilson, 163–183. Honolulu: University of Hawai'i Press.

Boisvert, Matheiu. (2000) "Origins: Comparative Perspectives." In *Encyclopedia of Monasticism*, edited by William M. Johnston, 645–664. Chicago, IL: Fitzroy Dearborn Publishers.

Bokenkamp, Stephen R. (1990) "Stages of Transcendence: the Bhūmi Concept in Taoist Scriptures." In *Chinese Buddhist Apocrypha*, edited by Robert E. Buswell, Jr., 119–147. Honolulu: University of Hawai'i Press.

——. (1997) *Early Daoist Scriptures*. Berkeley: University of California Press.

Bowring, Richard. (2005) *The Religious Traditions of Japan, 500–1600*. Cambridge: Cambridge University Press.

Brinker, Helmut. (1987) *Zen in the Art of Painting*. London: Routledge and Kegan Paul.

Brook, Timothy. (1993) *Praying For Power: Buddhism and the Formation of Gentry Society in Late-Ming China*. Cambridge, MA: Harvard University Press.

——. (2005) "Institution." In *Critical Terms for the Study of Buddhism*, edited by Donald S. Lopez, Jr., 143–161. Chicago, IL: University of Chicago Press.

Bumbacher, Stephan Peter. (2000) *The Fragments of the Daoxue zhuan: Critical edition, Translation, and Analysis of a Medieval Collection of Daoist Biographies*. Frankfurt am Main: Peter Lang.

Burton, Janet. (1994) *Monastic and Religious Orders in Britain 1000–1300*. Cambridge: Cambridge University Press.

Buswell, Robert E., Jr. (1992) *The Zen Monastic Experience*. Princeton, NJ: Princeton University Press.

Cabezón, José Ignacio, ed. (1998) *Scholasticism: Cross-Cultural Perspectives*. Albany: State University of New York Press.

Cahill, James. (1980) *An Index of Early Chinese Painters and Paintings*. Berkeley: University of California Press.

Campany, Robert Ford. (1995) "To Hell and Back: Death, Near-Death, and Other Worldly Journeys in Early Medieval China." In *Death, Ecstasy, and Other Worldly Journeys*, edited by John J. Collins and Michael Fishbane, 343–360. Albany: State University of New York Press.

——. (2002) *To Live as Long as Heaven and Earth: A Translation and Study of Ge Hong's Traditions of Divine Transcendents*. Berkeley: University of California Press.

Camporesi, Piero (1994 [1984]). *The Anatomy of the Senses: Natural Symbols in Medieval and Early Modern Italy*. Cambridge: Polity Press.

Carrette, Jeremy R., (ed) (1999) *Religion and Culture: Michel Foucault*. New York: Routledge.

Casey, Edward. (1993) *Getting Back Into Place: Toward a Renewed Understanding of the Place-World*. Bloomington: Indiana University Press.

Cassidy-Welch, Megan. (2001) *Monastic Spaces and Their Meanings: Thirteenth-Century English Cistercian Monasteries*. Belgium: Brepols.

Chen Jinhua. (2002) *Monks and Monarchs, Kinship and Kingship: Tanqian in Sui Buddhism and Politics*. Kyoto: Italian School of East Asian Studies.

——. (2007) *Philosopher, Practitioner, Politician: The Many Lives of Fazang*. Leiden: E.J. Brill.

Cheng Zai 承載. (1999) *Lidai minghua ji quanyi* 歷代名畫記全譯. Guiyang: Guizhou renmin chubanshe.

Chikusa Masaaki 竺沙雅章. (1982) *Chūgoku bukkyō shakaishi no kenkyū* 中国仏教社会史の研究. Kyoto: Dōhōsha.

——. (1987) "Sō Gen Bukkyō ni okeru an dō" 宋元佛教における庵堂. *Tōyōshi kenkyū* 東洋史研究 46, no. 1: 1–28.

Chittick, Andrew Barclay. (1997) "Pride of Place: The Advent of Local History in Early Medieval China." Ph.D. diss., University of Michigan.

Collcutt, Martin. (1981) *Five Mountains: The Rinzai Zen Monastic Institution in Medieval Japan*. Cambridge, MA: Harvard University Press.

Collins, Steven. (1988) "Monasticism, Utopias and Comparative Social Theory." *Religion* 18: 101–135.

Covell, Stephen G. (2005) *Japanese Temple Buddhism: Worldliness in a Religion of Renunciation*. Honolulu: University of Hawai'i Press.

Dai kanwa jiten 大漢和辭典. (1955–1960) Edited by Morohashi Tetsuji 諸橋轍次. Tokyo: Taishūkan Shoten.

DeBlasi, Anthony. (1998) "A Parallel World: A Case of Monastic Society, Northern Song to Ming." *Journal of Song-Yuan Studies* 28: 155–175.

de Certeau, Michel. (1985) "Practices of Space." In *On Signs*, edited by Marshall Blonsky, 122–145. Baltimore, MD: The Johns Hopkins University Press.

Demiéville, Paul and Jacques May, *et al.* (eds) (1929–1999) *Hôbôgirin: Dictionnaire encyclopédique du bouddhisme d'après les sources chinoises et japonaises*. Fascicules I–VIII (to date). Tokyo: Maison Franco-Japonaise.

Dobbins, James. (2004) *Letters of the Nun Eshinni: Images of Pure Land Buddhism in Medieval Japan*. Honolulu: University of Hawai'i Press.

Donner, Neil, and Daniel Stevenson. (1993) *The Great Calming and Contemplation: A Study and Annotated Translation of the First Chapter of Chih-i's Mo-ho-chih-kuan*. Honolulu: University of Hawai'i Press.

Dreyfus, Georges B.J. (2003) *The Sound of Two Hands Clapping: The Education of a Tibetan Buddhist Monk*. Berkeley: University of California Press.

Dumont, Louis. (1980 [1970]) *Homo Hierarchicus: The Caste System and Its Implications.* Revised ed. Chicago, IL: University of Chicago Press.

Dunhuang Yanjiuyuan 敦煌研究院. (ed) (1986) *Dunhuang Mogaoku gongyangren tiji* 敦煌莫高窟供養人題記. Beijing: Wenwu chubanshe.

Dutt, Sukumar. (1962) *Buddhist Monks and Monasteries of India.* London: George Allen and Unwin Ltd.

Eitel, Ernest John. (1976) *Hand-book of Chinese Buddhism, being a Sanskrit-Chinese Dictionary: With Vocabularies of Buddhist Terms in Pali, Singhalese, Siamese, Burmese, Tibetan, Mongolian and Japanese.* San Francisco, CA: Chinese Materials Center.

Elvin, Mark. (2004) *The Retreat of the Elephants: An Environmental History of China.* New Haven, CT: Yale University Press.

Engels, Donald. (1999) *Classical Cats: The Rise and Fall of the Sacred Cat.* London and New York: Routledge.

Fang Guangchang 方廣錩. (1997) *Dunhuang fojiao jinglu jijiao* 敦煌佛教經錄集校. Nanjing: Jiangsu guji chubanshe.

Faure, Bernard. (1992) "Relics and Flesh Bodies: The Creation of Ch'an Pilgrimage Sites." In *Pilgrims and Sacred Sites in China*, edited by Susan Naquin and Chün-fang Yü, 150–189. Berkeley: University of California Press.

——. (1993) *Chan Insights and Oversights: An Epistemological Critique of the Chan Tradition.* Princeton, NJ: Princeton University Press.

——. (1996) *Visions of Power.* Princeton, NJ: Princeton University Press.

Feuchtwang, Stephan D.R. (1974) *An Anthropological Analysis of Chinese Geomancy.* Laos: Vithagna.

Forte, Antonino. (1983) "Daiji 大寺 (Chine)." In *Hôbôgirin: Dictionnaire encyclopédique du bouddhisme d'après les sources chinoises et japonaises*, vol. 6, 682–704.

——. (1988) *Mingtang and Buddhist Utopias in the History of the Astronomical Clock: The Tower, Statue and Armillary Sphere Constructed by Empress Wu.* Rome and Paris: Istituto italiano per il Medio ed Estremo Oriente and Ecole française d'Extrême-Orient.

——. (1992) "Chinese State Monasteries in the Seventh and Eighth Centuries." In *Echō ō Go-Tenchikukyū den kenkyū* 慧超往五天竺国伝研究, edited by Kuwayama Shōshin 桑山正進, 213–258. Kyoto: Jinbun kagaku kenkyūjo.

Foucault, Michel. (1979) *Discipline and Punish: The Birth of the Prison.* New York: Vintage Books.

Foulk, T. Griffith. (1987) "The Ch'an School and its Place in the Buddhist Monastic Tradition." Ph.D diss., University of Michigan.

——. (1993) "Myth, Ritual, and Monastic Practice in Sung Ch'an Buddhism." In *Religion and Society in T'ang and Song China*, edited by Patricia Buckley Ebrey and Peter N. Gregory, 147–208. Honolulu: University of Hawai'i Press.

——. (1995) "Daily Life in the Assembly." In *Buddhism in Practice*, edited by Donald S. Lopez Jr., 455–472. New Jersey: Princeton University Press.

——, and Robert H. Sharf. (1993–1994) "On the Ritual Use of Ch'an Portraiture in Medieval China." *Cahiers d'Extrême-Asie* 7: 149–219.

Fukuda Ryōsei 福田亮成. (2001) *Shingonshū shojiten* 真言宗小事典. Kyoto: Hōzōkan.

Funayama Tōru 船山徹. (1995) "Rokuchō jidai ni okeru bōsatsugai no juyō katei, 六朝時代における菩薩戒の受容過程." *Tōhō gakuhō* 67: 1–135.

Furumatsu Takashi 古松崇志. (2006) "Fajun to Yanjing Maashan no bosatsukaidan—Qidan (Liao) ni okeru bosatsukai no ryūkō" 法均と燕京馬鞍山の菩薩戒壇—契丹（遼）における大乗菩薩戒の流行. *Tōyōshi kenkyū* 65, no. 3: 407–444.

Gadamer, Hans-Georg. (1995) *Truth and Method.* New York: Continuum.

Gellner, David N. (2001) *The Anthropology of Buddhism and Hinduism: Weberian Themes.* Oxford: Oxford University Press.

Gernet, Jacques. (1995) *Buddhism in Chinese Society: An Economic History from the Fifth to the Tenth Centuries.* Translated by Franciscus Verellen. New York: Columbia University Press.

Getz, Daniel. (2005) "Popular Religion and Pure Land in Song-Dynasty Tiantai Bodhisattva Precept Ordination Ceremonies." In *Going Forth, Visions of Buddhist Vinaya*, edited by William Bodiford, 161–184. Honolulu: University of Hawai'i Press.

Gimello, Robert M. (1992) "Chang Shang-ying on Wu-t'ai Shan." In *Pilgrims and Sacred Sites in China*, edited by Susan Naquin and Chün-fang Yü, 89–149. Berkeley: University of California Press.

Gjertson, Donald E. (1989) *Miraculous Retribution: A Study and Translation of T'ang Lin's Ming-pao chi.* Berkeley: University of California Press.

Goodwin, Janet R. (1994) *Alms and Vagabonds: Buddhist Temples and Popular Patronage in Medieval Japan.* Honolulu: University of Hawai'i Press.

Goossaert, Vincent. (2000) *Dans les temples de la Chine. Histoire des cultes, Vie des communautés.* Paris: Albin Michel.

——. (2007) *The Taoists of Peking, 1800–1949: A Social History of Urban Clerics.* Cambridge, MA: Harvard University Press.

Graham, A.C. (1960) *The Book of Lieh-tzu.* London: John Murray.

——. (1981) *Chuang Tzu: The Inner Chapters.* London: George Allen & Unwin.

Grapard, Allan G. (1994) "Geosophia, Geognosis, Geopiety: Orders of Significance in Japanese Representations of Space." In *NowHere: Space, Time, and Modernity*, edited by Roger Friedland and Deirdre Boden, 372–401. Berkeley: University of California Press.

——. (2000) "The Economics of Ritual Power." In *Shinto in History: Ways of the Kami*, edited by John Breen and Mark Teeuwen, 68–94. Surrey: Curzon Press.

——. (2003) "The Source of Oracular Speech: Absence? Presence? Or Plain Treachery?: The Case of Hachiman Usa-gū gotakusenshū." In *Buddhas and Kami in Japan: Honji Suijaku as a Combinatory Paradigm*, edited by Mark Teeuwen and Fabio Rambelli, 77–94. London: RoutledgeCurzon.

Grey, Leslie. (2000) *A Concordance to Buddhist Birth Stories.* 3rd ed. Oxford: Pali Text Society.

Groner, Paul. (1990) "The Fan-wang ching and Monastic Discipline in Japanese Tendai: A Study of Annen's *Futsū jubosatsukai kōshaku*." In *Chinese Buddhist Apocrypha*, edited by Robert E. Buswell, Jr., 251–290. Honolulu: University of Hawai'i Press.

——. (2000) *Saichō: The Establishment of the Japanese Tendai School.* Honolulu: University of Hawai'i Press.

——. (2001) "Ninkū Jitsudō's View of the Hīnayāna Precepts." *Indogaku Bukkyōgaku kenkyū*, 50, no. 1: 6–10 (left).

——. (2002) *Ryōgen and Mount Hiei: Japanese Tendai in the Tenth Century.* Honolulu: University of Hawai'i Press.

——. (2003) "Jitsudō Ninkū on Ordinations." *Japan Review* 15: 51–75.

——. (2007) "Rationales for the Lax Adherence to the Precepts: Some Tendai 天台 Interpretations of the Precepts Based on the *Lotus Sūtra*." In *Contribution of Buddhism to World Culture*, edited by Ichijō Ogawa, Kalpakam Sankarnarayan, and Ravindra Panth, vol. 2: 310–330. Mumbai: Somaiya Publication Pvt. Ltd.

Hagiwara Tatsuo 萩原龍夫. (1962) *Chūsei saishi soshiki no kenkyū* 中世祭祀組織の研究. Tokyo: Yoshikawa Kōbunkan.

Halperin, Mark. (1997) "Pieties and Responsibilities: Buddhism and the Chinese Literati: 780–1280." Ph.D. diss., University of California Berkeley.

——. (2006) *Out of the Cloister: Buddhism in Elite Lay Discourse in Sung China, 960–1279*. Cambridge, MA: Harvard East Asia Monograph Series.

Hammond, Charles E. (1992–1993) "Sacred Metamorphosis: The Weretiger and the Shaman," *Acta Orientalia* (Hungary) 46, nos. 2–3: 235–255.

Hansen, Valerie. (1990) *Changing Gods in Medieval China 1127–1276*. Princeton, NJ: Princeton University Press.

Hao Chunwen 郝春文. (1996) "Guanyu Dunhuang xieben zhaiwen de jige wenti" 關於敦煌寫本齋文的幾個問題. *Shoudu shifan daxue xuebao* 首都師範大學學報 109, no. 2: 68.

——. (1998) *Tang houqi Wudai Song chu Dunhuang sengni de shehui shenghuo*唐后期五代宋初敦煌僧尼的社会生活. Beijing: Zhongguo shehui kexue chubanshe.

Harley, J.B., and David Woodward. (eds) (1994) *The History of Cartography, Volume Two, Book Two: Cartography in the Traditional East Asian and Southeast Asian Societies*. Chicago, IL: University of Chicago Press.

Harrison, Paul. (2003) "Relying on the Dharma and not the Person: Reflection on Authority and Transmission in Buddhism and Buddhist Studies." *Journal of the International Association of Buddhist Studies* 26, no. 1: 9–24.

Hatta Yukio 八田幸雄. (1991) *Kamigami to hotoke no sekai* 神々と仏の世界. Tokyo: Hirakawa Shuppan.

He Shizhe 賀世哲. (1986) "Cong gongyangren tiji kan Mogaoku bufen dongku de yinjian niandai" 從供養人題記看莫高窟部分洞窟的營建年代. In *Dunhuang Mogaoku gongyangren tiji* 敦煌莫高窟供養人題記, edited by Dunhuang Yanjiuyuan 敦煌研究院, 194–236. Beijing: Wenwu chubanshe.

Heilbron, J.L. (1999) *The Sun in the Church: Cathedrals as Solar Observatories*. Cambridge, MA: Harvard University Press.

Henricks, Robert G. (1990) *The Poetry of Han-shan*. Albany: SUNY Press.

Henry, Patrick G., and Donald K. Swearer. (1989) *For the Sake of the World: The Spirit of Buddhist and Christian Monasticism*. Minneapolis, MN: Fortress Press.

Herrou, Adeline. (2005) *La Vie entre soi. Les moines taoïstes aujourd'hui en Chine*. Nanterre: Société d'ethnologie.

Hertz, Robert. (1983) "St. Besse: A Study of an Alpine Cult." In *Saints and Their Cults: Studies in Religious Sociology, Folklore and History*, edited by Stephen Wilson, 55–100. Cambridge: Cambridge University Press.

Hill, Jackson. (1982) "Ritual Music in Japanese Esoteric Buddhism: Shingon *Shōmyō*." *Ethnomusicology* 26, no. 1: 27–39.

Ho Peng Yoke. (2000) *Li, Qi and Shu: An Introduction to Science and Civilization in China*. New York: Dover.

Ho, Puay-peng. (1995) "The Ideal Monastery: Daoxuan's Description of the Central Indian Jetavana Vihâra." *East Asian History* 10: 1–18.

Hori, Victor Sōgen. (1996) "The Study of Buddhist Monastic Practice: Reflections on Robert Buswell's *The Zen Monastic Experience*." *The Eastern Buddhist* (new series) 29, no. 2: 239–261.

Horner, I.B. (trans.) (1949–1966) *The Book of the Discipline* (Vinaya-Pitaka). London: Luzac.

Hosokawa Ryōichi 細川凉一. (1987) *Chūsei no Risshū jiin to minshū* 中世の律宗寺院と民衆. Tokyo: Yoshikawa Kōbunkan.

——. (1999) *Kanjin gakushōki: Saidaiji Eison no jiden* 感身学正記・西大寺叡尊の自伝. Tokyo: Heibonsha.

Huang, H.T. (2000) *Science and Civilisation in China*, Volume VI.5. Cambridge: Cambridge University Press.

Hur, Nam-lin. (2000) *Prayer and Play in Late Tokugawa Japan: Asakusa Sensōji and Edo Society*. Cambridge, MA: Harvard University Press.

Hurst, Cameron G., III. (1997) "The Warrior as Ideal for a New Age." In *The Origins of Japan's Medieval World: Courtiers, Clerics, Warriors, and Peasants in the Fourteenth Century*, edited by Jeffrey P. Mass, 209–233. Stanford, CA: Stanford University Press.

Ichikawa Hakugen市川白弦, Iriya Yoshitaka 入矢義高, and Yanagida Seizan 柳田聖山. (eds.) (1972) *Chūsei zenke no shisō* 中世禅家の思想. *Nihon shisō taikei* 日本思想大系, vol. 16. Tokyo: Iwanami shoten.

Ichimura Shohei. (trans.) (1993) *Zen Master Eihei Dōgen's Monastic Regulations*. Woodinville, WA: North American Institute of Zen Studies.

Imamura Yoshio 今村与志雄. (1986) *Neko dangi: ima to mukashi* 猫談義:今と昔. Tokyo: Tōhō shoten.

Inoue Mitsusada. (1971) "Eizon, Ninshō, and the Saidai-ji Order." *Acta Asiatica* 20: 77–103.

Ishida Mizumaro 石田瑞麿. (1963) *Nihon Bukkyō ni okeru karitsu no kenkyū* 日本佛教における戒律の研究. Tokyo: Zaike Bukkyō kyōkai.

——. (1971) *Bonmōkyo* 梵網経. Tokyo: Daizō shuppan kabushiki kaisha.

——. (1997) *Reibun Bukkyōgo daijiten* 例文仏教語大辞典. Tokyo: Shōgakkan.

Jacobi, Hermann. (trans.) (1884) *Jaina Sutras*, Part 2, *Sacred Books of the East* Vol. 45. Oxford: The Clarendon Press.

Jedrej, Tony. (1994) *Cambridge Cats*. London: Gerald Duckworth & Co.

Jensen, Lionel M. (1997) *Manufacturing Confucianism: Chinese Traditions and Universal Civilization*. Durham, NC: Duke University Press.

Ji Xianlin 李羨林. (1990 [1985]) *Da Tang xiyu ji jiaozhu* 大唐西域記校注. Beijing: Zhonghua shuju.

Jiang Liangfu 姜亮夫. (1985) *Mogaoku nianbiao* 莫高窟年表. Shanghai: Shanghai guji chubanshe.

Johnston, R.J., Derek Gregory, Geraldine Pratt, and Michael Watts. (eds.) (2000) *The Dictionary of Human Geography*. 4th edition. Oxford: Blackwell.

Johnston, William M. (2000a) "Introduction." In *Encyclopedia of Monasticism*, edited by William M. Johnston, ix–xiii. Chicago, IL: Fitzroy Dearborn Publishers.

——. (ed.) (2000b) *Encyclopedia of Monasticism*. Chicago, IL: Fitzroy Dearborn Publishers.

Jorgensen, John. (2000) "China" in *Encyclopedia of Monasticism*, edited by William M. Johnston, 280–284. Chicago: Fitzroy Dearborn Publishers.

Jullien, François. (1999) *The Propensity of Things: Toward a History of Efficacy in China*. New York: Zone Books.

Kamens, Edward. (1988) *The Three Jewels: A Study and Translation of Minamoto Tamemori's Sanbōe*. Ann Arbor, MI: Center for Japanese Studies, University of Michigan.

Kashiwahara Nobuyuki 柏原信行. (1998) "Gengukyō 賢愚経." In *Daizōkyō zenkaisetsu daijiten* 大蔵経全解説大事典, edited by Kamata Shigeo 鎌田茂雄, *et al.* Tokyo: Yūzankaku Shuppan.

Kedar, Benjamin Z. and R.J. Zwi Werblowsky. (eds.) (1998) *Sacred Space: Shrine, City, Land*. New York: New York University Press.

Kemper, Steven. (1990) "Wealth and Reformation in Sinhalese Buddhist Monasticism." In *Ethics, Wealth, and Salvation: A Study in Buddhist Social Ethics*, edited by Russell F. Sizemore and Donald Swearer, 152–169. Columbia, SC: University of South Carolina Press.

Kiekhefer, Richard, and George D. Bond. (eds) (1988) *Sainthood: Its Manifestations in World Religions*. Berkeley: The University of California Press.

Kieschnick, John. (2003) *The Impact of Buddhism on Chinese Material Culture*. Princeton, NJ: Princeton University Press.

Knechtges, David. (1982) *Wen Xuan or Selections of Refined Literature vol.1: Rhapsodies on Metropolises and Capitals*. Princeton, NJ: Princeton University Press.

Kodera Bun'ei小寺文頴. (1987) *Tendai enkai gaisetsu*天台丹戒概說. Ōtsu: Eizan gakuin.

Kodera, James Takashi. (1980) *Dōgen's Formative years in Sung China*. London: Routledge and Kegan Paul.

Kohn, Livia. (1995) *Laughing at the Tao: Debates among Buddhists and Taoists in Medieval China*. Princeton, NJ: Princeton University Press.

——. (2003) *Monastic Life in Medieval Daoism: A Cross-Cultural Perspective*. Honolulu: University of Hawai'i Press.

Kornicki, Peter. (1998) *The Book in Japan: A Cultural History from the Beginnings to the Nineteenth Century*. Leiden: E.J. Brill.

Kubota Tetsumasa 窪田哲正. (1984) "Kōen no *Endon bosatsukai jūjū shijūhachi gyōgi shō* ni tsuite" 興円の 『円頓菩薩戒十重四十八行儀鈔』 について. *Indogaku Bukkyōgaku kenkyū* 33, no. 1: 203–206.

Lauer, Ute. (2002) *A Master of his Own—The Calligraphy of the Chan Abbot Zhongfeng Mingben (1261–1323)*. Stuttgart: Steiner.

Lawrence, C.H. (1984) *Medieval Monasticism: Forms of Religious Life in Western Europe in the Middle Ages*. London: Longman.

Lee, Peter H. (1969) *Lives of Eminent Korean Monks: Haedong Kosŭng Chŏn*. Cambridge, MA: Harvard University Press.

Lewis, Mark Edward. (1990) "The Suppression of the Three Stages Sect: Apocrypha as a Political Issue." In *Chinese Buddhist Apocrypha*, edited by Robert E. Buswell Jr., 207–238. Honolulu: University of Hawai'i Press.

Li Fengmao 李豐楙. (1996) *Wuru yu zhejiang: Liuchao Sui Tang Daojiao wenxue lunji* 誤入與謫降: 六朝隋唐道教文學論集. Taibei: Taiwan xuesheng shuju.

Li Jianchao 李健超. (1996) *Zengding Tang liangjing chengfang kao* 增订唐两京城坊考. Xi'an: Sanqin chubanshe.

Liebenthal, Walter. (1952) "The Immortality of the Soul in Chinese Thought," *Monumenta Nipponica* 8, no. 1–2: 327–397.

Loewe, Michael. (ed.) (1993) *Early Chinese Texts: A Bibliographic Guide*. Berkeley: Society for the Study of Early China and Institute for East Asian Studies, University of California, Berkeley.

Lopez, Donald S., Jr. (1998) *Prisoners of Shangri-La: Tibetan Buddhism and the West*. Chicago, IL: The University of Chicago Press.

Lu Xun 鲁迅. (ed.) (1967) *Gu xiaoshuo gouchen* 古小說鉤沈. Hong Kong: Xinye chubanshe.

Ma Dezhi 馬得志. (1987) "Tang Chang'ancheng fajue xinshouyou" 唐長安城發掘新收穫. *Kaogu* 考古, no. 4: 329–336.

Mair, Victor. (1986) The Origins of an Iconographical Form of the Pilgrim Hsüan-tsang." *T'ang Studies* 4: 29–42.

——. Forthcoming. "The Khotanese Antecedents of *The Sutra of the Wise and the Foolish (Xianyu jing)*." In *Buddhism Across Boundaries*, edited by John McRae. Honolulu: Hawai'i University Press.

Marks, R.B. (1998) *Tigers, Rice, Silk and Silt: The Ecology of Lingnan*. Cambridge: Cambridge University Press.

218　*Bibliography*

Markus, R.A. (1998 [1990]) *The End of Ancient Christianity*. Cambridge: Cambridge University Press.

Matsuo Kenji. 松尾剛次. (1988) *Kamakura Shin-Bukkyō no seiritsu: Nyūmon girei to soshi shinwa* 鎌倉新仏教の成立: 入門儀礼と祖師神話. Tokyo: Yoshikawa kōbunkan.

——. (1995) *Kanjin to hakai no chūseishi:chūsei Bukkyō no jisshō* 勧進と破戒の中世史: 中世仏教の実相. Tokyo: Yoshikawa Kōbunkan.

——. (1996) "Saidaiji Eisonzō ni nōnyū sareta 'jyūbosatsukai deshi kōmyō' to 'gonjū nannyo kōmyō'" 西大寺叡尊像に納入された「重菩薩戒弟子交名」と「近住男女交名」. *Nanto bukkyō* 73: 87–107.

McCormick, Michael. (2003) "Rats, Communications, and Plague: Towards an Ecological History." *Journal of Interdisciplinary History* 34, no. 1: 1–25.

McMullen, James. (1999) *Idealism, Protest, and The Tale of Genji*. Oxford: Oxford University Press.

McMullin, Neil. (1984) *Buddhism and the State in Sixteenth-Century Japan*. Princeton, NJ: Princeton University Press.

McRae, John R. (2005) "Daoxuan's Vision of Jetavana: The Ordination Platform Movement in Medieval Chinese Buddhism." In *Going Forth, Visions of Buddhist Vinaya*, edited by William Bodiford, 68–100. Honolulu: University of Hawai'i Press.

Michihata Ryōshū 道端良秀. (1983) *Chūgoku bukkyō shakai keizaishi no kenkyū* 中国仏教社会経済史の研究. Kyoto: Heirakuji shoten.

Mills, D.E. (1970) *A Collection of Tales from Uji*. Cambridge: Cambridge University Press.

Minakata Kumagusu 南方熊楠. (1971 [1912]) "Neko ippiki no chikara ni yotte daifuku to narishi hito no hanashi 貓一疋の力に憑て大富と成し人の話." *Minakata Kumagusu Zenshū* 南方熊楠全集, vol. 3, 97–109. Tokyo: Heibonsha.

——. (1994) *Jūnishi kō* 十二支考. Tokyo: Iwanami bunko.

Minowa Kenryō 蓑輪顕量. (1996a) "Eison kyōdan ni okeru bosatsukai no juju : Saidaijizō 'Jubosatsukai yōi monsho' to 'Jubosatsukai sahō' o chūshin ni'" 叡尊教団に於ける菩薩戒の授受―西大寺蔵『授菩薩戒用意聞書』と『授菩薩戒作法』を中心に. *Nanto Bukkyō* 73: 60–86.

——. (1996b) "Eison kyōdan ni okeru kōseiin no kaisō―gonji, gonjū to gyōdō, hōdō shami," 叡尊教団における構成員の階層: 近事・近住と形同・法同沙弥. *Shūkyō kenkyū* 309: 75–98.

——. (1999) *Chūsei shoki Nanto kairitsu fukkō no kenkyū* 中世初期南都戒律復興の研究. Kyoto: Hōzōkan.

Mitsuhashi Tadashi 三橋正. (2000) *Heianjidai no shinkō to shūkyō no girei* 平安時代の信仰と宗教の儀礼. Tokyo: Zoku Gunsho Ruijū Kanseikai.

Miura, Isshū and Ruth Fuller Sasaki. (1966) *Zen Dust*. New York: Harcourt, Brace & World.

Miyakawa Hisayuki 宮川尚志. (1983) *Chūgoku shūkyōshi kenkyū* 中国宗教史研究. Kyōto: Dōhōsha.

Mochizuki Shinkō 望月信亨. (ed.) (1958–1963) *Bukkyō daijiten* 仏教大辞典. Tokyo: Sekai Seiten Kankō Kyōkai.

Moroto Tatsuo 諸戸立雄. (1990) *Chūgoku bukkyō seidoshi no kenkyū* 中国仏教制度史の研究. Tokyo: Hirakawa shuppansha.

Naba Toshisada 那波利貞. (1962) "Tōdai ni okeru Dōkyō to minshū to no kankei ni tsuite" 唐代に於ける道教と民衆との關係に就いて. *Konan Daigaku Bungakukai ronshū* 甲南大學文學會論集17: 1–42.

Nagamura Makoto 永村真. (2001) "Jiin shakaishi no kanten kara miru chūsei no hōe" 寺院社会史の観点からみる中世の法会. In *Girei ni miru Nihon no Bukkyō* 儀礼にみる日

本の仏教, edited by Nara Joshi Daigaku Kodaigaku Gakujutsu Kenkyū Sentā Setsuritsu Junbishitsu, 53–91. Kyoto: Hōzōkan.

Nakamura Kōji 中村興二. (1979–1981) "Saihō jōdohen no kenkyū" 西方浄土変の研究. *Nihon bijutsu kogei* 日本美術工藝, no. 491 (1979): 84–90, through no. 519 (1981): 31–35.

Nakao Ryōshin 中尾良信. (1979a) "Enrin no *Bosatsukaisho shō* ni tsuite" 円琳の『菩薩義疏鈔』について. *Indogaku Bukkyōgaku kenkyū* 27, no. 2: 618–619.

——. (1979b) "Enrinshō ni okeru Shōshin no in'yō" 『円琳鈔』に於ける証真の引用について. *Komazawa Daigakuin Bukkyō kenkyūkai nenpō* 駒沢大学大学院仏教学研究会年報 13: 66–73.

Naquin, Susan. (1998) "Sites, Saints, and Sights at the Tanzhe Monastery." *Cahiers d'Extrême-Asie* 10: 183–211.

——. (2000) *Peking: Temples and City Life 1400–1900*. Berkeley: University of California Press.

Ng, Wai-ming. (2000) *The I Ching in Tokugawa Thought and Culture*. Honolulu: University of Hawai'i Press.

Nickerson, Peter. (1994) "Shamans, Demons, Diviners, and Taoists: Conflict and Assimilation in Medieval Chinese Ritual Practice (c. A.D. 100–1000)." *Taoist Resources* 5, no. 1: 41–66.

Nienhauser, William H., Jr. (ed.) (1986) *Indiana Companion to Traditional Chinese Literature*. Bloomington: Indiana University Press.

Nihon daijiten kankōkai 日本大辞典刊行会. (ed.) (1973–76) *Nihon kokugo daijiten* 日本国語大辞典. Tokyo: Shōgakkan.

Niida Noboru 二井田陞. (1961) "Tō no sōdō jikan kankei no denryō no ibun" 唐の僧道寺観関係の田令の遺文, *Bukkyō shigaku ronshū* 仏教史学論集. Kyoto: Tsukamoto hakushi shōju kinenkai.

Ninomiya Morito 二宮守人 and Asukai Shuntatsu 飛鳥井舜達. (1933) "Nihon Tendai ni okeru Enkai gisoku no hattatsu" 日本天台における円戒義足の発達. *Eizan gakuhō* 7: 56.

Nishiwaki Tsuneki 西脇常記. (2000) *Tōdai no shisō to bunka* 唐代思想と文化. Tokyo: Sōbunsha.

Nomoto Kakujō 野本覚成. (1985) "Jōjōbō Gigen no gyōseki: Kamakura-matsu Hieizan no gakushō" 成乗坊義源の行跡:鎌倉末比叡山の学匠. *Tendai gakuhō* 27: 99–102.

——. (1986) "Kaikanjō ni okeru *Kanjin jūnibu kyōgi* no imi" 戒潅頂における「観心十二部経義」の意味. *Tendai gakuhō* 28: 113–118.

——. (1988) "Saichō no kaikanjō ni mirareru Daijōkai rinen" 最澄の戒潅頂に見られる大乗戒理念. *Indogaku Bukkyōgaku kenkyū* 35, no. 2: 686–690.

——. (1991) "Genshi kanjō yori kaikanjō e," 玄旨潅頂より戒潅頂へ. In *Shioiri Ryōdō Sensei tsuitō ronbunshū: Tendai shisō to Higashi Ajia bunka no kenkyū* 塩入良道先生追悼論文集：天台思想と東アジア文化の研究, 703–724. Tokyo: 山喜房仏書林.

——. (1994) "Hongaku shikaku funi no shisō: Isshin sankan denju no shōmeisho" 本覚始覚不二の思想:一心三観伝授の証明書. In *Ōkubo Ryōjun sensei sanju kinen ronbunshū: Bukkyō bunka no tenkai* 大久保良順先生傘寿記念論文集：仏教文化の展開, 683–710. Tokyo: Sankibō Busshorin.

Norman, K.R. (1997) *A Philological Approach to Buddhism*. London: SOAS.

Obeyesekere, Gananath. (2002) *Imagining Karma: Ethical Transformation in Amerindian, Buddhist and Greek Rebirth*. Berkeley: University of California Press.

Ōishi Masaaki 大石雅章. (1997) "Ama no Hokkeji to Sō no Hokkeji" 尼の法華寺と僧の法華寺. In *Hotoke to onna* 仏と女, edited by Nishiguchi Junko 大石雅章, 181–217. Tokyo: Yoshikawa Kōbunkan.

——. (2001) "Chūsei Risshū kyōdan no tokushitsu to sono katsudō: Saidaijiryū Risshū no katsudō wo chūshin ni" 中世律宗教団の特質とその活動・西大寺流律宗の活動を中心に. In *Chūsei setouchi no tera to shakai* 中世瀬戸内の寺と社会. Vol. 12 of *Asahi hyakka: Kokuhō to rekishi no tabi*. Tokyo: Asahi Shinbun shuppan.

Okada Seishi 岡田精詞. (1985) "Kodai Ise jingū no shinkō to seikaku" 古代伊勢神宮の信仰と性格. In *Ise shinkō i* 伊勢信仰 I, edited by Hagiwara Tatsuo 萩原龍夫, 59–70. Minshū Shūkyōshi Sōsho 民衆宗教史草書, vol. 1. Tokyo: Yūzankaku.

Okano Kōji 岡野浩二. (1998) "Mudoen senji, isshin ajari, sōzu chokunin" 無度縁 宣旨・一身阿闍梨・僧都直任. In *Inseiki no bukkyō* 院政期の仏教, edited by Hayami Tasuku 速水侑, 80–117. Yoshikawa Kōbunkan.

Okimoto Katsumi 沖本克己. (1997) "Zen shisō keiseishi no kenkyū 禪思想形成史の研究." *Hanazono Daigaku Kokusai Zen Kenkyūjo Kenkyū Hōkoku* 花園大学国際禅学研究所研究報告 5: 1–453.

Ōkubo Ryōjun 大久保良順. (1980) "Jūju kaikanjō no kigen" 重授戒潅頂の興起. *Tendai gakuhō* 22: 1–9.

Ono Genmyō 小野玄妙. (ed.) (1932–1936) *Bussho kaisetsu daijiten* 佛書解説大辭典. 12 vols. Tokyo: Daitō shuppansha.

Ono Katsutoshi 小野勝年 and Hibino Takeo 日比野丈夫. (1942) *Godaizan* 五台山 [Wutaishan]. Tokyo: Zayūhō.

Ono Katsutoshi 小野勝年. (1989) Chūgoku Zui TōChōan jiin shiryōshūsei 中国隋唐長安寺院史料集成. Kyōto: Hōzōkan.

Ōtani daigaku toshokan 大谷大學圖書館. (comp.) (1961) *Ōtani daigaku toshokan zempon shūei* 大谷大學圖書館善本聚英. Kyoto: Ōtani daigaku toshokan.

Owen, Stephen. (1996) *An Anthology of Chinese Literature: Beginnings to 1911*. New York: W.W. Norton & Company.

Parker, Joseph D. (1999) *Zen Buddhist Landscape Arts of Early Muromachi Japan (1336–1573)*. Albany: State University of New York Press.

Pelliot, Paul. (1923) "Notes sur quelques artistes des six dynasties et des T'ang." *T'oung Pao* 22, no. 4: 268–282.

Penkower, Linda L. (1993) "T'ien-t'ai during the T'ang Dynasty: Zhanran and the Sinification of Buddhism." Ph.D. diss., Columbia University.

Pichard, Pierre and François Lagirarde. (eds.) (2003) *The Buddhist Monastery: A Cross-Cultural Survey*. Paris: École Française d'Extrême-Orient.

Pollack, David. (1985) *Zen Poems of the Five Mountains*. New York and Decatur, GA: Crossroads Publishing Company and Scholars Press.

——. (1986) *The Fracture of Meaning: Japan's Synthesis of China from the Eighth through the Eighteenth Centuries*. Princeton, NJ: Princeton University Press.

Prince, A.J. (2002) "Everyday Miracles." In *Religion and Biography in China and Tibet*, edited by Benjamin Penny, 49–73. Richmond, Surrey: Curzon.

Pripp-Møller, Johannes. (1982 [1937]). *Chinese Buddhist Monasteries: Their Plan and Its Function as a Setting for Buddhist Monastic Life*. Hong Kong: Hong Kong University Press.

Rambelli, Fabio. (2003) "Honji suijaku at Work: Religion, Economics, and Ideology in Pre-modern Japan." In *Buddhas and Kami in Japan: Honji Suijaku as a Combinatory Paradigm*, edited by Mark Teeuwen and Fabio Rambelli, 268–273. London: RoutledgeCurzon.

Rao Zongyi 饒宗頤 [Jao Tsung-i]. (1993) "Cong shike lun Wuhou zhi zongjiao xinyang" 從石刻論武后之宗教信仰. Reprinted in *Rao Zongyi shixue lunzhu xuan* 饒宗頤史學論著選. Shanghai: Shanghai guji chubanshe.

Reed, Carrie E. (2001) *Chinese Chronicles of the Strange: The "Nuogao ji."* New York: Peter Lang.

Remensnyder, Amy. (1995) *Remembering Kings Past: Monastic Foundation Legends in Medieval Southern France*. Ithaca, NY: Cornell University Press.

Rhie, Marylin M. (1977) *The Fo-kuang ssu: Literary Evidence and Buddhist Images*. New York: Garland Publishing.

Rhys Davids, T.W. (1899) *Dialogues of the Buddha (The Dîgha-Nikâya)*. London: Oxford University Press.

Robinet, Isabelle. (1979) "Metamorphosis and Deliverance from the Corpse in Taoism." *History of Religions* 19, no. 1: 37–70.

——. 1993. *Taoist Meditation: The Mao-shan Tradition of Great Purity*. Trans. Julian F. Pas and Norman J. Girardot. Albany: State University of New York Press.

Robson, James. (1995a) "Polymorphous Space: The Contested Space of Mt. Nanyue." In *The Sacred Mountains of Asia*, edited by John Einarsen, 121–124. Boston: Shambala.

——. (1995b) "The Polymorphous Space of the Southern Marchmount [Nanyue 南嶽]: An Introduction to Nanyue's Religious History and Preliminary Notes on Buddhist-Daoist Interaction." *Cahiers d'Extrême-Asie* 8: 221–264.

——. (2002) "Imagining Nanyue: A Religious History of the Southern Marchmount through the Tang Dynasty [618–907]." Ph.D. diss., Stanford University.

——. (2004) "Buddhism and the Chinese Marchmount System [Wuyue]: Excavating the Strata of Mt. Nanyue's Religious History." In *Religion and Chinese Society*, edited by John Lagerwey, 341–383. Hong Kong: The Chinese University Press.

——. (2009) *Power of Place: The Religious Landscape of the Southern Sacred Peak [Nanyue 南嶽] in Medieval China*. Cambridge: Harvard University Press, East Asian Monograph Series.

——. (Forthcoming) "Local History, Lost Monks: The *Biographies of the Eighteen Eminent Monks of Nanyue [Nanyue shiba gaoseng zhuan 南嶽十八高僧傳]*." In *Études d'apocryphes bouddhiques: Mélanges en l'honneur de Monsieur Makita Tairyō*, edited by Kuo Li-ying. Paris: École Française d'Extrême-Orient.

Ruppert, Brian. (2000) *Jewel in the Ashes: Buddha Relics and Power in Early Medieval Japan*. Cambridge, MA: Harvard University Asia Center.

Salomon, Richard. (1999) *Ancient Buddhist Scrolls from Ghandhāra: The British Library Kharosthi Fragments*. Seattle: University of Washington Press.

Sasaki, Ruth Fuller, Yoshitaka Iriya, and Dana R. Fraser (trans.) (1971) *A Man of Zen: The Recorded Sayings of Layman P'ang*. New York: Weatherhill.

Satō Michiko 佐藤道子. (ed.) (1994) *Chūsei jiin to hōe* 中世寺院と法会. Kyoto: Hōzōkan.

Satō Tatsugen 佐藤達玄. (1986) *Chūgoku bukkyō ni okeru kairitsu no kenkyū* 中国仏教における戒律の研究. Tokyo: Mokujisha.

Satō Tetsuei 佐藤哲英. (1960) *Tendai daishi no kenkyū* 天台大師の研究. Kyoto: Hyakkaen.

Sawa Hirokatsu 沢博勝. (1990) "Saidaijiryū ni yoru dōmyōji no 'fukkō' ni tsuite" 西大寺による道明寺の「復興」について. *Historia* (ヒストリア) 127: 88–101.

Schafer, Edward H. (1962) *The Golden Peaches of Samarkand: A Study of T'ang Exotics*. Berkeley: University of California Press.

Schapiro, Meyer. (1945) "*Muscipula diaboli*: The Symbolism of the Mérode Altarpiece." *Art Bulletin* 27: 183–187.

Schmithausen, Lambert. (1986) "Critical Response." In *Karma and Rebirth: Post Classical Developments*, edited by Ronald Neufeldt, 210–216. Albany: State University of New York Press.

Schopen, Gregory. (2004a) *Buddhist Monks and Business Matters: Still More Papers on Monastic Buddhism*. Honolulu: University of Hawai'i Press.

———. (2004b) "The Good Monk and His Money in a Buddhist Monasticism of the 'Mahāyāna Period.'" In *Buddhist Monks and Business Matters: Still More Papers on Monastic Buddhism*, 1–18. Honolulu: University of Hawai'i Press.

———. (2004c) "The Suppression of Nuns and Ritual Murder of Their Special Dead." In *Buddhist Monks and Business Matters: Still More Papers on Monastic Buddhism*, 329–359.

———. (2004d) "Art, Beauty, and the Business of Running a Buddhist Monastery in Early Northwest India." In *Buddhist Monks and Business Matters: Still More Papers on Monastic Buddhism*, 19–44.

Seidensticker, Edward G. (trans.) (1981) *The Tale of Genji*. Harmondsworth: Penguin Books.

Serpell, James. (1996) *In the Company of Animals: a Study of Human-animal relationships*. Cambridge: Cambridge University Press.

Shahar, Meir. (2000) "Epigraphy, Buddhist Historiography, and Fighting Monks: The Case of the Shaolin Monastery." *Asia Major*, 3rd series, 13, no. 2: 15–36.

Sharf, Robert H. (1995) "Buddhist Modernism and the Rhetoric of Meditative Experience." *Numen* 42, no. 3: 228–283.

———. (2001) "Prolegomenon to the Study of Japanese Buddhist Icons." In *Living Images: Japanese Buddhist Icons in Context*, edited by Robert H. Sharf and Elizabeth Horton Sharf, 1–18. Stanford, CA: Stanford University Press.

———. (2002) *Coming to Terms with Chinese Buddhism: A Reading of the Treasure Store Treatise*. Honolulu: University of Hawai'i Press.

Shih Heng-ching. (1994) *The Sutra on Upāsaka Precepts*. Berkeley: Numata Center for Buddhist Translation and Research.

Shikii Shūjō 色井秀讓. (1961) *Tendai Shinzeishū shūgaku hanron* 天台真盛宗宗学汎論. Kyoto: Hyakkaen.

———. (1968) "Kurodani Hosshōji-ryū kaikanjō ni tsuite" 黒谷法勝寺流戒灌頂について. *Indogaku Bukkyōgaku kenkyū* 17, no. 1: 278: 275–278.

———. (1981) "Jūju kaikanjō: Sokuji nishin on shōchōteki gyōgi" 重授戒灌頂:即事而真の象徴的行儀. *Tendai* 4: 27–37.

———. (1982) "Kaikanjō to *gasshō*" 戒灌頂と合掌. *Tendai gakuhō* 24: 18–23.

———. (1983) "Kaikanjō hisho *Jūrokujō kuketsu* ni tsuite" 戒灌頂秘書『十六帖口決』について. *Tendai gakuhō* 25: 1–10.

———. (1989) *Kaikanjō no nyūmonteki kenkyū* 戒灌頂の入門的研究. Osaka: Tōhō shuppan.

Shinohara, Koichi. (1991a) "Ji shenzhou sanbao gantong lu: Some Explanatory Notes." In *Kalyana Mitta: Professor Hajime Nakamura Felicitation Volume*, edited by V.N. Jha, 203–224. Delhi: Indian Book Center.

———. (1991b) "A Source Analysis of the *Ruijing lu* ("Records of Miraculous Scriptures")." *The Journal of the International Association of Buddhist Studies* 14, no. 1: 73–154.

———. (1992) "Guanding's Biography of Zhiyi, the Fourth Chinese Patriarch of the Tiantai Tradition." In *Speaking of Monks: Religious Biography in India and China*, edited by Phyllis Granoff and Koichi Shinohara, 98–218. New York: Mosaic Press.

———. (1994) "Buddhist Precepts in Medieval Chinese Biographies of Monks." In *Buddhist Behavioral Codes and the Modern World*, edited by Charles Wei-hsun Fu and Sandra A. Wawrytko, 81–90. Westport, CT: Greenwood Press.

———. (1998) "Changing Roles for Miraculous Images in Medieval Chinese Buddhism: A Study of the Miracle Image Section in Daoxuan's 'Collected Records.'" In *Images, Miracles, and Authority in Asian Religious Traditions*, edited by Richard H. Davis, 141–188. Oxford: Westview Press.

———. (1999) "Literary Construction of Buddhist Sacred Places: The Record of Mt. Lu by Chen Shunyu." *Asiatische Studien/Etudes Asiatiques* LIII, no. 4: 937–964.

Silber, Ilana Friedrich. (1995) *Virtuosity, Charisma, and Social Order: A Comparative Sociological Study of Monasticism in Theravada Buddhism and Medieval Catholicism.* Cambridge: Cambridge University Press.

Smith, Jonathan Z. (1982) "In Comparison A Magic Dwells." In *Imagining Religion: From Babylon to Jonestown,* 19–35. Chicago, IL: University of Chicago Press.

Soothill, William Edward and Lewis Hodous. (1977) *A Dictionary of Chinese Buddhist Terms: With Sanskrit and English Equivalents and a Sanskrit-Pali Index.* Delhi: Motilal Banarsidass.

Soper, Alexander C. (1948) "Hsiang-Juo-Ssu: An Imperial Temple of Northern Sung." *Journal of the American Oriental Society* vol. 68, no. 1: 19–45.

———. (1959) *Literary Evidence for Early Buddhist Art in China.* Ascona: Artibus Asiae Publishers.

———. (1960) "A Vacation Glimpse of the T'ang Temples of Ch'ang-an: The *Ssu-T'a Chi* by Tuan Ch'eng-Shih." *Artibus Asiae* 23: 15–40.

Sowerby, Arthur de C. (1933) "The Chinese Tiger." *China Journal of Science and Art* 18: 94–101.

Spring, Madeleine. (1993) *Animal Allegories in T'ang China.* New Haven, CT: American Oriental Society.

Steinhardt, Nancy Shatzman. (1998) "Early Chinese Buddhist Architecture and Its Indian Origins." In *The Flowering of a Foreign Faith: New Studies in Chinese Buddhist Art,* edited by Janet Baker, 38–53. Mumbai: Marg Publications.

Sterckx, Roel. (2002) *The Animal and the Daemon in Early China.* Albany: State University of New York Press.

Stevenson, Daniel. (1995) "Tales of the Lotus Sūtra." In *Buddhism in Practice,* edited by Donald S. Lopez, Jr., 427–451. Princeton, NJ: Princeton University Press.

———. (1996) "Visions of Mañjuśrī on Mount Wutai." In *Religions of China in Practice,* edited by Donald S. Jr. Lopez, 203–222. Princeton, NJ: Princeton University Press.

Stone, Jacqueline. (1999) *Original Enlightenment and the Transformation of Medieval Japanese Buddhism.* Honolulu: University of Hawai'i Press.

Strassberg, Richard E. (1994) *Inscribed Landscapes: Travel Writing from Imperial China.* Berkeley: University of California Press.

Strong, John. (1977) "Gandhakuti: The Perfumed Chamber of the Buddha." *History of Religions* 16, no. 4: 390–406.

———. (1992) *The Legend and Cult of Upagupta: Sanskrit Buddhism in North India and Southeast Asia.* Princeton, NJ: Princeton University Press.

———. (2000) *The Experience of Buddhism: Sources and Interpretations.* Belmont, CA: Wadsworth.

Su Bai 宿白. (1996) *Zhongguo shikusi yanjiu* 中国石窟寺研究. Beijing: Wenwu chubanshe.

Sun Xiushen 孫修身. (1990) "Dunhuang shiku zhong de guan wuliangshou jing bianxiang" 敦煌石窟中的觀無量壽經變相. In *1987 nian Dunhuang shiku yanjiu guoji taolunhui wenji shiku kaogu bian* 1987 年敦煌石窟研究國際討論會文集石窟考古編, 215–246. Shenyang: Liaoning meishu chubanshe.

———. (1994) "Tangchao jiechu waijiao huodongjia Wang Xuance shiji yanjiu" 唐朝杰出外交活動家王玄策事蹟研究. *Dunhuang yanjiu* 敦煌研究 3: 17–32

Takakusu, J. (1896) *A Record of the Buddhist Religion as Practiced in India and the Malay Archipelago.* London: Clarendon Press.

Take Kakuchō 武覚超. (1993) *Hieizan santō shodō enkakushi* 比叡山三塔請堂巡拝記. Ōtsu: Eizan gakuin.

Tamayama Jōgen 玉山成元. (1973) "'Tendai Hokkeshū gakushōshiki mondō' (Tōji-hon) no shiteki kachi" 『天台法華宗学生式問答』(東寺本)の史的価値. In *Dengyō Daishi kenkyū* 伝教大師研究, 739–763. Tokyo: Waseda daigaku shuppanbu.

Tambiah, Stanley J. (1970) *Buddhism and the Spirit Cults in North-East Thailand.* Cambridge: Cambridge University Press.

Tanabe Hideo 田辺英夫. (2000) "Chūsei Seizanha-shi ni okeru Ao no Kōmyōji ni tsuite" 中世西山派史における粟生光明寺について. *Seizan Gakuhō* 48: 95–105.

Tang Yongtong湯用彤. (1982) *Sui Tang fojiao shigao* 隋唐佛教史稿. Beijing: Zhonghua.

Teiser, Stephen F. (1988) "'Having once died and returned to life': Representations of Hell in Medieval China." *Harvard Journal of Asiatic Studies* 48, no. 2: 433–464.

Tendai shūten hensanjo天台宗典編纂所. (ed.) (2000) *Shōzoku Tendaishū zensho mokuroku kaidai* 正続天台宗全書目録解題. Tokyo: Shunjūsha.

Terai Ryōsen 寺井良宣. (1999) "Chūko Tendaiki no Eizan (Kurodani) ni okeru rōzan shugyō," 中世天台期の叡山(黒谷)における籠山修行. *Eizan gakuin kenkyū kiyo* 20: 71–86.

——. (2000) "Hieizan Kurodani ni okeru kairitsu fukkō to sono shisō" 比叡山黒谷における戒律復興とその思想. *Indogaku Bukkyōgaku kenkyū* 96: 282–285.

te Velde, H. (1982) "The Cat as Sacred Animal of the Goddess Mut." In *Studies in Egyptian Religion Dedicated to Professor Jan Zandee*, edited by M. Heerma van Voss, D.J. Hoens, G. Mussies, D. van der Plas and H. te Velde, 127–137. Leiden: E.J. Brill.

Thurman, Robert A.F. (1993) "Monasticism and Civilization." In *Buddhist Spirituality: Indian, Southeast Asian, Tibetan and Early Chinese*, edited by Takeuchi Yoshinori, 120–134. London: Crossroads Publishing Company.

Tonami Mamoru. (1990) *The Shaolin Monastery Stele on Mount Song*. Translated by Pamela Herbert. Kyoto: Italian School of East Asian Studies.

Toriimoto Yukiyo 検索結果. (1984) "Jie Daishi no hōe: Soken ranshōsetsu wo megutte" 慈恵大師の法衣：素絹濫觴説をめぐって. In *Issen-nen onki kinen Ganzan Jie Daishi no kenkyū* 一千年遠忌記念元三慈恵大師の研究, edited by Eizan gakuin. Kyoto: Dōhōsha.

Trombert, Éric. (1995) *Le Crédit à Dunhuang: Vie Matérielle et Société en Chine Médiévale.* Paris: IHEC.

Tsai, Kathryn. (1994) *Lives of the Nuns: Biographies of Chinese Nuns*. Honolulu: University of Hawai'i Press.

Tsukamoto Zenryū 塚本善隆. (1974) "Kokubunji to zui tō no bukkyō seisaku narabini kanji" 国分寺と隋唐の仏教政策並びに官寺. In *Tsukamoto Zenryū chosakushū* 塚本善隆著作集, vol. 6, 1–50. Tokyo: Daitō shuppansha.

Twitchett, Denis C. (1956) "Monastic Estates in T'ang China." *Asia Major* n.s. 5: 123–146.

——. 1970. *Financial Administration under the T'ang Dynasty*. Cambridge: Cambridge University Press.

Uejima Susumu 上島享. (2004) "Chūsei kokka to jisha" 中世国家と寺社. In *Nihonshi kōza 3: Chūsei no keisei* 日本史講座 3 : 中世の形成. Tokyo: Tokyo University Press.

Uesugi Bunshū 上杉文秀. (1935) *Nihon Tendaishi* 日本天台史. Nagoya: Hajinkaku shobō.

Upasak, C.S. (1975) *Dictionary of Early Buddhist Monastic Terms (Based on Pāli Literature)*. Varanasi: Bharati Prakashan.

Ury, Marian B. (1970) "'Genko Shakusho,' Japan's First Comprehensive History of Buddhism: A Partial Translation, With Introduction and Notes." Ph.D. dissertation. Berkeley: University of California.

——. (1992) *Poems of the Five Mountains: An Introduction to the Literature of the Zen Monasteries*. Ann Arbor: Center for Japanese Studies, University of Michigan.

Verellen, Franciscus. (1988) "Shu as a Hallowed Land: Du Guang-ting's *Record of Marvels.*" *Cahiers d'Extrême-Asie* 10: 213–254.

Waley, Arthur. (1931) *A Catalogue of Paintings Recovered from Tun-huang by Sir Aurel Stein*. London: The British Museum.

Wan Gengyu 萬庚育. (1986) "Zhengui de lishi ziliao—Mogaoku gongyangren huaxiang tiji" 珍貴的歷史資料—莫高窟供養人畫像題記. In *Dunhuang Mogaoku gongyangren tiji* 敦煌莫高窟供養人題記, 179–193. Beijing: Wenwu chubanshe.

Wang, Eugene Y. (2005) *Shaping the Lotus Sutra: Buddhist Visual Culture in Medieval China*. Seattle: University of Washington Press.

Wang, Yi-t'ung. (trans.) (1984) *A Record of Buddhist Monasteries in Lo-yang*. Princeton, NJ: Princeton University Press.

——. (trans.) (2000) "The Establishment of the White Horse Temple from The Record of the Monasteries of Loyang." In *The Shorter Columbia Anthology of Traditional Chinese Literature*, edited by Victor H. Mair, 395–396. New York: Columbia University Press.

Ware, James R. (trans.) (1967) *Alchemy, Medicine, Religion in the China of A.D. 320: The Nei P'ien of Ko Hung*. Cambridge, MA: MIT Press.

Warner, Langdon. (1938) *Buddhist Wall-Paintings: A Study of a Ninth-Century Grotto at Wan Fo Hsia*. Cambridge, MA: Harvard University Press.

Watson, W. (ed.) (1981) *The Great Japan Exhibition: Art of the Edo Period*. London: Royal Academy of Arts.

Watt, Paul. 1999. "Eison and the Shingon Vinaya Sect." In *Religions of Japan in Practice*, edited by George J. Tanabe, Jr., 89–97. Princeton, NJ: Princeton University Press.

Weber, Max. (1958) *The Religion of India*. New York: The Free Press.

——. (1993a [1922]) *The Sociology of Religion*. Boston: Beacon Press.

——. (1993b [1930]) *The Protestant Ethic and the Spirit of Capitalism*. London: Routledge.

Weckman, George. (2005) "Monasticism: An Overview." In *The Encyclopedia of Religion*, 2nd edition, edited by Lindsay Jones, vol. 9, 6121–6126. Detroit, MI: Macmillan Press.

Weidner, Marsha. (2001) "Imperial Engagements with Buddhist Art and Architecture: Ming Variations on an Old Theme." In *Cultural Intersections in Later Chinese Buddhism*, edited by Marsha Weidner, 117–144. Honolulu: University of Hawai'i Press.

Weinstein, Stanley. (1987) *Buddhism Under the T'ang*. Cambridge: Cambridge University Press.

Welch, Holmes. (1967) *The Practice of Chinese Buddhism 1900–1950*. Cambridge, MA: Harvard University Press.

——. (1968) *The Buddhist Revival in China*. Cambridge, MA: Harvard University Press.

Wen Duanzheng 温端政, *et al.* (comp.) (1989) *Zhongguo suyu dacidian* 中國俗語大辞典. Shanghai: Shanghai cishu chubanshe.

Wheatley, Paul. (1971) *The Pivot of the Four Quarters*. Edinburgh: Edinburgh University Press.

Wixted, John Timothy. (1998) "*Kanbun*, Histories of Japanese Literature, and Japanologists." *Sino-Japanese Studies* 10, no. 2: 23–31.

Wijayaratna, Mohan. (1990) *Buddhist Monastic Life: According to the Texts of the Theravāda Tradition*. Cambridge: Cambridge University Press.

Woodward, F.L., Caroline A.F. Rhys Davids, and E.M. Hare. (1932) *The Book of the Gradual Sayings (Anguttara-nikaya) or More-numbered Suttas*. London: Published for the Pali Text Society by Oxford University Press.

Wright, Arthur F. (1990 [1954]) "Biography and Hagiography: Hui-chiao's 'Lives of Eminent Monks.'" In *Studies in Chinese Buddhism*, edited by Robert M. Somers, 73–111. New Haven, CT: Yale University Press.

Wu Chi-yu. (1957) "A Study of Han-shan." *T'oung Pao* 45, nos. 4–5: 392–450.

Wu Hung. (1992) "Reborn in Paradise: A Case Study of Dunhuang Sūtra Painting and its Religious, Ritual and Artistic Context." *Orientations* 23, no. 5: 52–60.

Wu, Nelson. (1963) *Chinese and Indian Architecture: The City of Man, the Mountain of God, and the Realm of Immortals*. New York: George Braziller.

Xiao Dengfu 蕭登福. (1989) *Han Wei Liuchao Fo Dao liangjiao zhi tiantang diyu shuo* 漢魏六朝佛道兩教之天堂地獄說. Taibei: Taiwan xuesheng shuju.

Xiehouyu cidian 歇後語詞典. (1984) Beijing: Beijing chubanshe.

Xu Song 徐松. (1985) *Tang liangjing chengfang kao* 唐兩京城坊考. Beijing: Zhonghua, 1985.

Yamabe, Nobuyoshi. (2005) "Visionary Repentance and Visionary Ordination in the *Brahmā Net Sūtra*." In *Going Forth: Visions of Buddhist Vinaya*, edited by William M. Bodiford, 17–39. Honolulu: University of Hawai'i Press.

Yan Gengwang 嚴耕望. (1992) "Tangren xiye shanlin siyuan zhi fengshang 唐人習業山林寺院之風尚." In *Yan Gengwang shixue lunwen ji* 嚴耕望史學論文集, 271–316. Taibei: Lianjing.

Yanagida Seizan 柳田聖山. (1972) "Eisai to 'Kōzen gokokuron' no kadai" 栄西と「興禅護国論」の課題. In *Chūsei Zenke no shisō* 中世禪家の思想, edited by Ichikawa Hakugen 市川白弦, Iriya Yoshitaka 入矢義高, and Yanagida Seizan, 439–486. Nihon Shisō Taikei 日本思想大系, vol. 16. Tokyo: Iwanami Shoten.

Yang Hongnian 楊鴻年. (1999) *Sui Tang liangjing fangli pu* 隋唐兩京坊里譜. Shanghai: Shanghai guji.

Yang, Lien-sheng. (1950) "Buddhist Monasteries and Four Money-Raising Institutions in Chinese History." *Harvard Journal of Asiatic Studies* 13: 174–191.

Yifa. (2002) *The Origins of Buddhist Monastic Codes in China: An Annotated Translation and Study of the* Chanyuan qinggui. Honolulu: University of Hawai'i Press.

Yoshioka Yoshitoyo. (1979) "Taoist Monastic Life." In *Facets of Taoism*, edited by Holmes Welch and Anna Seidel, 220–252. New Haven, CT: Yale University Press.

Zengaku daijiten 禅学大辞典. (1978) Tokyo: Taishūkan shoten.

Zhang Gong 張弓. (1997) *Han Tang Fosi wenhua shi* 漢唐佛寺文化史. Beijing: Zhongguo shehui kexue chubanshe.

Zheng Binglin 郑炳林. (1989) *Dunhuang dili wenshu huiji jiaozhu* 敦煌地理文書匯輯校注. Lanzhou: Gansu jiaoyu chubanshe.

Zürcher, Erik. (1989) "Buddhism and Education in T'ang Times." In *Neo-Confucian Education: The Formative Stage*, edited by Wm. Theodore de Bary and John W. Chaffee, 19–56. Berkeley: University of California Press.

——. (2007) *The Buddhist Conquest of China: The Spread and Adaptation of Buddhism in Early Medieval China*. 3rd ed. Leiden: Brill.

Index

Acker, William 69–70, 94
Acts of Paul and Thecla 117
Adams, Sir Thomas 107
Adams, William 107
āgama 19, 28, 29, 35, 38
Ajātaśatru, King 39, 77, 78, 87, 88, 89, 92
Ambapālī 19–39 *passim*
Amitābha 69, 70, 77, 82, 88, 143
Ānanda 27, 141, 150
Ānanda Rites of Repentance (*Anan senbō* 阿難懺法) 127
Anāthapiṇḍata 39
Anāthapindika 3, 8
animals 91, 108–119 *passim* 123
Anle 安樂, Princess 68, 78, 94
ārāma 13
arhat 35, 41, 54, 116
Āṭavaka 31
āvāsa 13
Avataṃsaka Sūtra 67, 176

Banri Shūkyū 萬里集九 (1428–1502) 114
Baochang 寶唱 150
Baoyu jing 寶雨經 (Treasure Rain Sūtra) 67, 75, 93
Beiluoxianna 鞞羅羨那 149, 151
Bielefeldt, Carl 131, 139
Bieyi za ahan jing 別譯雜阿含經 24, 39
Bimbisāra, King 34, 39, 77, 80
Biographies of Eminent Monks of Our Kingdom (*Honchō kōsōden* 本朝高僧傳) 131
Blossom Red (Hualiu 驊駵) 114, 123
Bodhidharma 131
Bodhiruci 67
Book of Kells 110
Brahmanical sacrifice 25, 40
Brahmans 25, 67, 140
Bremmer, Jan N. 122, 123

Brook, Timothy 15, 49, 60
Buddhabhadra 56
Buddhaghosa 4, 10
Buswell, Robert 10

Caligula 117
Cambridge 107–108, 119, 121
Camporesi, Piero 53
Chang ahan jing 長阿含經 19, 20, 21, 38
Chengyuan 承遠 (713–803) 57
Chen Tianfu 陳田夫 50–51
Chittick, Andrew 48
Chronicle of Gods and Sovereigns (*Jinnō shōtōki* 神皇正統記) 136
Collins, Steven 8
Cullavagga 3

dakṣiṇā (gifts) 18, 24, 25, 30, 34, 36–37, 40–1
Dao'an 道安 (312–385) 25, 29, 30, 41
Daojin 道進 155
Daolin 道琳 (447–519) 33
Daomeng 道猛 33–34
Daoshi 道世 (596?–683) 19–42 *passim* 149, 150
Daoxuan 道宣 (596–667) 14, 19, 25–42 *passim* 121, 144, 169, 183, 192
Dayunjing shenghuang shouji yishu 大雲經神皇授記義疏 67
de Certeau, Michel 54
denggong 等供 25, 39
Dhammapada 34
Dharmaguptaka vinaya 26–27, 30, 40, 41; see also Sifenlü
Dharmaruci 67
dhūta 26, 135
Diamond Sūtra 75, 81, 82, 94, 95
Dōgen 道元 (1200–1253) 12, 111, 119
Duan Chengshi 段成式 (803?–863) 61, 66

Dumont, Louis 8
Dunhuang 14, 38, 65–92 *passim*, 116, 120
Dutt, Sukumar 8

Egai 惠顗 (d. 1301) 181–185, 193
Eisai 榮西 (1141–1215) 127, 132, 178, 193, 205
Eison 叡尊 (1201–1290) 13, 136, 148–177, 186
Encyclopedia Britannica 5
Encyclopedia of Religion 46
Endon bosatsukai jūjū shijūhachi gyōgi shō 円頓菩薩戒十重四十八行儀鈔 184, 204
Enkan 円観 (1281–1356) 182–188, 191, 203
Enni Ben'en 圓爾辯圓 (1202–1280) 132
Ennin 円仁 (794–864) 142, 153, 185, 190, 205
"Exoteric-Esoteric Establishment" 11, 125, 201

Fachang 法場 30
Fachao 法超 33–34
Fanwang jing 梵網經 151, 162, 167, 168, 184–207 *passim*
Faure, Bernard 57, 62, 64
Fayuan zhulin 法苑珠林 31–3, 40–42, 50, 62, 93, 96–97, 149–150
Fazang 法藏 (643–712) 67, 94
Fazhao 法照 (fl. eighth century) 57
Fazong 法宗 33–34
Fenggan 豐干 116
fengshui 風水 43, 48, 50
fengsu 風俗 48
Fengsu tongyi 風俗通義 48
Forte, Antonino 46, 93, 94, 96
Foshuo chujia gongde jing 佛說出家功德經 149, 151, 154, 161, 172
Foucault, Michel 16
Foulk, T. Griffith 46
Fuhu 伏虎 ("tiger tamer") 116
Fuli 復禮 (fl. 681–703) 67
Funayama Tōru 38

Gadamer, Hans-Georg 6
Ganjin (Jianzhen 鑑眞, 688–763) 135, 137, 153, 156, 186, 203
Gaoseng zhuan 高僧傳 29, 30, 33, 41, 50, 132, 144
Gautama 22
Ge Hong 葛洪 (283–363) 83
Genkō Era Account of Buddhism (*Genkō shakusho* 元亨釋書) 131–134, 137,

138, 139, 144–147
Genshin 源信 (942–1017) 140, 154
"geopiety" 48, 61
Gernet, Jacques 13, 16, 46
Getz, Daniel 160
ghosts 23, 28, 31, 33, 34, 41, 54, 63, 79, 87, 143, 190
Gibbon, Edward 1, 7, 107
Gidō Shūshin 義堂周信 (1325–1388) 114
Godaigo 後醍醐 (1288–1339) 136
gods (local) 11, 28, 31, 58, 64, 92, 126, 128–138 *passim*, 144, 147; *see also* names of individual gods
gods (celestial) 20, 22, 23, 37, 91
Gozan 五山 111–121, 124, 131
Grapard, Allan 61, 126
Gray, Thomas (1716–1771) 107
Greek Anthology 110
grotto-heavens 51, 83
Guang hongming ji 廣弘明集 58, 155
Guang qingliang zhuan 廣清涼傳 50
Guanyin 80, 81, 89, 105; *see also* Kannon
Guanyin Sūtra 80, 81
Gudōbō Ejin 求道房惠尋 (d. 1289) 181, 183, 184, 193
Gyōnen 凝然 (1240–1321) 126

Hachiman 八幡 134, 137, 143
Hakusan *myōjin* 白山明神 134
Halperin, Mark 60
Hammond, Charles E. 116
Hanshan 寒山 110–112, 114, 116
Han Yu 韓愈 (768–824) 52
Harrison, Paul 10
hassai kai 八齋戒 127, 141, 170
He Chong 何充 (296–346) 32, 42
Hengyue shiba gaoseng xu 衡嶽十八高僧傳序 55
Herbert, Penelope 52
Hobson, Peter 110
Hōnen 法然 (1133–1212) 126, 136, 140, 178, 180, 202
hongaku ("original enlightenment") 11, 178, 179, 180, 192, 193, 195, 201
Hori, Victor Sōgen 9
Hosokawa Ryōichi 171
Hossō 法相 129, 136, 140, 142
Huang, H.T. 109
Huangfu Shi 皇甫湜 (777–830) 52
Huihai 慧海 51, 62–63
Huijian 慧簡 29
Huijiao 慧皎 (497–554) 33, 144
Huili 慧立 (615–?) 66
Huishao 慧韶 33

Huisi 慧思 (515–577) 55, 63, 185, 197

incense 25, 30, 40, 65, 90, 141, 167, 183, 191
Ise 134, 140
Izanagi 伊奘諾 134

Jerome 117
Jesuits 5
Jetavana 4, 17, 27 39, 57
Jikakudaishiden 慈覚大師伝 153
Jinglü yixiang 經律異相 150
Ji shenzhou sanbao gantong lu 集神州三寶感通錄 42, 50, 62
Jitsudō Ninkū 実導仁空 (1307–1388) 178, 179, 207
Jīvaka 39
Jōdo hōmon genrushō 浄土法門源流章 126
Jorgensen, John 46
Jotika 29, 32
Jubosatsukai sahō 授菩薩戒作法 168
Jubosatsukai yōi monsho 受菩薩戒用意聞書 162, 166
Jyoṣṭika 39

"Kamakura New Buddhism" 11, 125, 187
Kampō Shidon 乾峰士曇 (1285–1361) 113
Kannon 觀音 138
kechien 結緣 153, 162, 166, 168, 169, 190
Kegon 華嚴 129, 136, 154
Kemper, Steven 7
kenmitsu taisei 顕密体制 125, 178, 201; *see also* "Exoteric-Esoteric Establishment"
Kieschnick, John 14, 60
Kitabatake Chikafusa 北畠親房 (1293–1354) 36, 140
Kitano *tenjin* 北野天神 134
Kōen 興円 (1262 or 1263–1317) 11, 12, 178–207
Kokan Shiren 虎関師錬 (1278–1345) 117, 124, 131, 139
Kongō Busshi Eison kanjin gakushōki 金剛仏子叡尊感身学正記 160, 163, 175
Korea 1, 16, 111, 112, 134, 151, 152, 156
Kōshū 光宗 (1276–1350) 128–130, 140, 184, 185
Kumazawa Banzan 熊沢蕃山 (1619–1691) 124
Kuroda Toshio 黒田俊雄 (1926–1993) 125

Layman Pang 2
Leaves Gathered from Stormy Streams (*Keiran shūyōshū* 溪嵐拾葉集) 128
le Compte, Louis 5
lena 13
Liang Wudi 梁武帝 (r. 502–49) 32, 41
Li Chongjun 李重俊 (d. 707) 77
Lidai fabao ji 曆代法寶記 12, 109
Li Hong 李弘 66, 94
Li Shaowei 李少微 83–84
Liu Yuxi 劉禹錫 (772–842) 116, 123
Lopez, Donald 5
Lotus sūtra 33, 53, 72–105 *passim* 142, 143, 179–189 *passim* 195–206 *passim*
Lu Cangyong 盧藏用 (656–713) 55, 63
Lu Deyan 路德延 (*jinshi* 進士 898) 109
Luoyang qielan ji 洛陽伽藍記 52–53

Mahākāśyapa 41
Mahāsaṃghika Vinaya 27, 37–38
Mahīśāsaka Vinaya 30, 40
Mair, Victor 116, 174
Maitreya 14, 56, 68, 69, 71, 78, 80, 89, 91, 95, 138, 142, 176
Mangen Shiban 卍元師蛮 (1625–1710) 131
Merit 7, 8, 13, 19–42 *passim* 49, 60, 88, 90, 127, 144, 148–173 *passim*
Minakata Kumagusu 南方熊楠 (1867–1941) 12, 108, 122
Minamoto Tamenori 源爲憲 (d. 1011) 127, 141, 156
Mingguang 明曠 184, 204
Mingxiang ji 冥詳記 32, 42
Mingzan 明瓚 (fl. eighth century) 51
Miscellaneous Discussions (*Zōdanshū* 雑談集) 128
Monasteries, architecture of 1, 13–14, 15, 46, 57, 63, 64, 65; individual monasteries: Bamboo Grove Monastery (Zhulin si 竹林寺) 57–58; Chōhōji 頂法寺 137; Daianji 大安寺 127, 137, 142, 146; Daigoji 醍醐寺 137, 139, 146; Dajue Monastery 大覺寺 53; Dapiankong Monastery 大遍空寺 67; Enkyōji 圓教寺 138; Fangguang chongshou chansi 方廣嵩壽禪寺 53–54, 62, 63; Foshoujisi 佛授記寺 66–67; Gangōji 元興寺 137, 146; Great White Horse Monastery (Dabaimasi 大白馬寺) 67; Hasedera 長谷寺 138; 142, 156, 166; Hengyue Monastery (Hengyue chansi 衡嶽禪寺) 51–52, 62; Inudera 犬寺 137; Ishiyamadera 石山寺 138;

Monasteries, architecture of (*cont.*):
Jing'ai monastery 敬愛寺 14, 66–93
passim; Jinganji 神願寺 137; Jingoji 神
護寺 137, 142; Jingyansi 浄嚴寺 58;
Jinzōji 神蔵寺 183, 184, 185, 204;
Kachiodera 勝尾寺 138; Kaimanji
蟹満寺 137; Kannōji 感應寺 138;
Kanzeonji 觀世音寺 135; Karaṇḍa's
Bamboo Grove Monastery (Karaṇḍaveṇ
uvana) 148, 149, 173; Kiyomizudera
清水寺 128, 138, 139, 181; Kōfukuji
興福寺 (Yamashinadera 山階寺) 127,
135, 136, 137, 139, 141, 143, 146;
Kokawadera 粉河寺 138; Konkaiin
金戒院 181; Kuramadera 鞍馬
寺 138; Longhua 龍華 monastery 33;
Mukuharadera 向原寺 137; Nanzenji
南禪寺 131; Ninnaji 仁和寺 137, 146;
Onjōji 園城寺 (a.k.a. Miidera 三井
寺) 128, 132–140 *passim*; Quanlin
monastery (Quanlinsi 泉林寺) 33;
Saidaiji 西大寺 136, 137, 160–173
passim; Sannōin 山王院 138; Seisuiji
(a.k.a. Kiyomizudera) 清水寺 138;
Sennyūji 泉涌寺 136, 158, 175, 188,
201; Shaolin 少林 monastery 52, 56,
62, 63; Shengshansi 聖善寺 76, 80;
Shitennōji 四天王寺 137; Sufukuji 崇
福寺 137, 142; Tanzhe monastery 潭柘
寺 56; Teidenji 鵜田寺 138; Tōdaiji 東
大寺 127, 134–143 *passim* 146, 153,
166; Tōfukuji 東福寺 131, 136, 137,
139, 146; Tōshōdaiji 唐招提寺 137,
164, 171, 176; Xiangguo si 相國寺 57;
Ximing monastery (Ximingsi 西明
寺) 31, 66; Yakushiji 藥師寺 127, 135,
137, 139, 142, 146; Yaoguang Nunnery
瑤光寺 52–53; Yongning si 永寧
寺 52–53; Zenrinji 禪林寺 (Taimadera
當麻寺) 137, 146;
"Monastery," as term 2–3, 12–13, 45–46
Monasticism, Buddhist, origins of 3;
Christian 2–5, 7; contemporary 1;
Indian 6; Korean 1; Tibetan 1.
Mount Hiei 比叡山 127–141 *passim*
181–203 *passim*
Mount Katsuragi 葛木山 138
Mount Kinpusen 金峰山 134
Mount Kōya 高野山 128, 134, 137, 139,
146
Mount Wutai *see* Wutai shan
Mugan Soō 夢巌祖應 (?—1374) 112, 119
Mujū Dōgyō 無住道暁 (Ichien 一圓;
1226–1312) 128

Mūlasarvāstivāda vinaya 41, 109
Myōe 明恵 (1173–1232) 154–159, 162,
165

Nagasawa Rosetsu 長澤蘆雪
(1754–1799) 117
Nanquan Puyuan 南泉普願 (748–835) 12,
109
Nanyue da chanshi lishi yuanwen 南嶽大
禪師立誓願文 55–56
Nanyue shiba gaoseng zhuan 南嶽十八高
僧傳 55
Nanyue zhi 南嶽誌 54–55
Nanyue zongsheng ji 南嶽総勝集
(NYZSJ) 50–58, 62
Naquin, Susan 56, 62, 64
Nichiren 日蓮 (1223–1283) 136, 140
Nichiren School 125, 194
Nirgrantha Jñātaputra 22, 24, 39
Niu *myōjin* 丹生明神 134
Nomoto Kakujō 193, 194, 203

Okimoto Katsumi 沖本克己 110, 122
Ōkubo Ryōjun 193
original enlightenment, see *hongaku*
ordination 12, 13, 46, 127, 133–135, 138,
140, 142, 145, 148–207
Ōsen Keisan 横川景三 (1429–1493) 117
Ouyang Xiu 歐陽脩 (1007–1072) 134,
140
Overview of Monastic Life (*Shukke taikō*
出家大綱) 127
Oxford 107

parivrājaka 3
Pengzu 彭祖 116
Piṇḍola Bhāradvāja 25, 28–35 *passim*
Pini taoyao 毗尼討要 26
Pliny 117
Pollack, David 113, 119
pravrajyā 3
precepts: eight precepts 127, 141, 161,
163, 165, 170; five precepts 18, 20,
24, 162, 163, 166, 169, 170, 188; ten
major bodhisattva precepts 152, 162,
165–170 *passim* 188, 205; ten novice
precepts 170, 176
Pripp-Møller, Johannes 61
Pulleyblank, E.G. 110
Purāṇa 39
Pure Land 57, 69, 80, 82, 88, 89, 145,
159,
Pure Land School 125, 126, 129, 136, 140,
181, 185

Qing bintoulu fa 請賓頭盧法 (Scripture on Inviting Piṇḍola) 29, 31, 32

Rājagṛha 22, 23, 148
relics 44, 47, 50, 51, 54, 56, 58, 59, 62, 64, 142, 164, 176
repentance 23, 32, 127, 141, 167
Rhinoceros Horn Sūtra 7
Rinzai 臨濟 111, 136
Rujing 如淨 (1163–1228) 111, 116, 119, 121
Ryōnin 良忍 (1072–1132) 154
Ryūsen Ryōzei 龍泉令澤 113

Saichō 最澄 (767–822) 12, 135, 156, 178–207 *passim*
St. Benedict 4
St. Bernard 4
Saint Paul 117
Śākyamuni 26, 39, 69, 73–7 *passim* 85, 86, 89, 92, 95, 106, 132, 176, 185, 196, 199
Salvation Scripture (*Durenjing* 度人經) 82–88, 96
saṃgha 3, 20, 24, 37, 44, 50, 120, 135, 141, 148, 149, 166, 169
Saṃgha of Four Directions 20, 29
Samprāgata 25, 27, 36, 38, 39
Sand and Pebbles (Shasekishū 砂石集) 128
Sannō 山王 130, 134, 137, 190
Sanron 三論 129, 136
Śāriputra 149, 173
Sarvāstivāda Vinaya 29, 39, 40, 41
Satyaka Nirgranthaputra 24, 39
Sāvatthī 3
Schopen, Gregory 6, 13, 14, 50
Seiin Shunshō 西胤俊承 (1358–1422) 113
sengba 僧跋 25
Sengmiao 僧妙 33–34
Sennyūji fukaki hōshiden 泉涌寺不可棄法師傳 158
Shahar, Meir 61, 62
Shandao 善導 (613–681) 77
Shangguan Wan'er 上官婉兒 (d. 713) 77–78
Sheli ganying ji 舍利感應 58
Shide 拾得 111, 116
Shien Shōnin donin gyōhō kechige ki 思円上人度人行法結夏記 160, 161
Shikii Shūjō 193, 194, 203, 206
Shimen zijing lu 釋門自鏡錄 42
Shingon 128, 129, 132, 138, 140, 146, 159, 191

Shinra *myōjin* 新羅明神 134
Shinran 親鸞 (1173–1263) 126
Shintō 129, 130, 133
shishangfa 食上法 26, 27
Shitou Xiqian 2
Shōkū 証空 (1177–1247) 159, 172
Shōtoku *taishi* 聖徳太子 (574–622) 137
Shūbun inryaku 聚文韻略 131
Shukke jukai sahō 出家授戒作法 154
Shukke sahō 出家作法 154
Shunjō 俊芿 (1166–1227) 136, 157–159, 172, 175, 178, 188, 201–205
Sifenlü 四分律 20, 26 30, 192, 201, 202
Śikṣānanda 實叉難陀 (652–710) 67, 94
Sirī-vaddhi 148–149, 173
smell 62, 72
Smith, J. Z. 4
Song gaoseng zhuan 宋高僧傳 40, 57, 64, 94, 156
Sonshun 尊舜 (1451–1514) 179, 180
Sōtō 曹洞 111, 136, 159, 164
Sowerby, Arthur de C. (1885–1954) 115
Spiro, Melford 9
Spring, Madeleine 109
Śrīgupta 22–41
Stevenson, Dan 57–58
Strong, John S. 34, 63, 122
Sugawara Michizane 管原道眞 (845–903) 134

Tale of Genji 108
Tambiah, Stanley 9
Tankū 湛空 (1156–1253) 193
tanuki 狸 114
Tendai 11, 12, 127–140 *passim* 143, 146, 151–174 *passim* 176, 178–207
Tenshō *daijin* 天照大神 134
Thailand 151
Thales (c. 624–546 BCE) 54
Three Jewels with Illustrations (*Sanbōe* 三寶繪) 127
Tigers 12, 109–123 *passim*
Twitchett, Denis 46

Ugrataśarīra 24, 39, 40
Unified Record of the Buddha and Ancestors (*Fozu tongji* 佛祖統紀) 132, 145
Upāsakaśīla sūtra 79, 155
upāsaka 23
upāsikā 20, 23
Ury, Marian 131

Vaidehī, Queen 77, 80, 89

Vairocana 68, 69, 76, 102, 134, 143

Vaiśālī 19, 20, 39

vihāra 13

Vimalakīrti 68, 69, 76, 95

vinaya 3, 8, 18, 19, 25–38, 135, 144, 148, 153, 162, 168–174 *passim*, 181–88 *passim* 202, 204

vinaya exegetes 123, 144

vinaya master 12, 90, 109, 153

Vinaya School 135–136, 148, 158, 159, 162, 164, 166, 168–173 *passim*

Visuddhimagga 4, 10

Visualization Sūtra 69, 77, 79, 80, 88, 96, 103, 104

Vulture Peak 73, 76, 92

Wang Shao 王邵 (fl. sixth century) 58

Wang Xuance 王玄策 (fl. 640–670) 66, 68, 93

Wang Yan 王琰 (b. ca. 454, fl. late fifth to early sixth century) 32

Weber, Max 1, 7, 8

Wei 韋, Empress 67, 68, 76

Welch, Homes 43, 46, 49

William of Wykeham (1324–1404) 118

Wright, J. K. 48

Wu Chengsi 武承嗣 75

Wu Daozi 吳道子 83

Wumenguan 無門關 109, 122

Wu Sansi 武三思 67, 75, 77

Wutai shan 50, 57, 62, 64, 65

Wu Zhao (Empress Wu, Wu Zetian) 14, 66–92 *passim*

Xianyu jing 賢愚經 148–151, 154, 161, 172, 173

Xiaowen 孝文 (r. 471–499) 52, 56

xingshi 形勢 49

Xuansha Shibei 玄沙師備 (835–908) 109

Xuanzang 玄奘 (602–664) 39, 66, 168, 169, 204, 205

Xue Huaiyi 薛懷義 (d. 693) 67, 75

Xu gaoseng zhuan 續高僧傳 42, 155, 161

Xutang Zhiyu 虛堂智遇 (1185–1269) 112–115

Xu Xiake 徐霞客 (1586–1641) 115

Yama 14, 69, 78, 82, 88, 91, 92, 94

Yamabe, Nobuyoshi 155

Yan Gengwang 12

Yang Chan 羊闡 34

Yang Lien-sheng 46

Yijing 義淨 (635–713) 39, 56, 67, 204

Ying Shao 應劭 (ca. 140–ca. 206) 48

Yin Chou 陰稠 70

Yin Sijian 陰嗣監 71

Yin Siyu 陰嗣玉 70–71

Yin Siyuan 陰嗣瑗 70–71, 81–82, 94, 96

Yin Sizhang 陰嗣彰 71

Yinzong 印宗 (627–713) 156

Yin Zu 陰祖 71

Yuanzhao 元照 (1048–1111) 41, 160, 168, 169

Yuiken 維賢 (1289–1378) 194

Za ahan jing 雜阿含經 25, 39

Zao 藏王 134

Zen 2, 12, 16, 107–24 *passim*; 125, 128–132, 135, 136, 139, 140, 159, 164, 176, 205

Zengi gemon shū 禪儀外文集 131

Zengyi ahan jing 增一阿含經 20, 22, 23, 24, 38, 39

Zhang Daoling 張道陵 116

Zhang Yanyuan 張彥遠 (ca. 815–?) 14, 66, 68, 69, 76, 92

Zhanran 湛然 (711–782) 183, 196

Zhaozhou Congshen 趙州從諗 (778–897) 109–110

Zhipan 志盤 132–133

Zhiyi 智顗 (538–597) 64, 143, 184, 185, 190, 195, 197, 202–206

Zhongfeng Mingben 中峰明本 (1262–1323) 112

Zhongzong 中宗 (r. 705–710) 67, 68, 76, 80, 94

zhouyuan 咒願 (spell, or blessing) 18, 20, 25, 30, 39, 41

Zhuangzi 113, 114, 123

Zhu Jingxuan 朱景玄 (fl. ninth century) 66

Zong Bing 宗炳 (375–443) 54

Zürcher, Erik 60, 64